WHERE
THE LIGHTNING
STRIKES

WHERE THE LIGHTNING STRIKES

The Lives of

American Indian

Sacred Places

PETER NABOKOV

VIKING

VIKING
Published by the Penguin Group
Penguin Group (USA) Inc., 375 Hudson Street,
New York, New York 10014, U.S.A.
Penguin Group (Canada), 90 Eglinton Avenue East, Suite 700, Toronto,
Ontario, Canada M4P 2Y3 (a division of Pearson Penguin Canada Inc.)
Penguin Books Ltd, 80 Strand, London WCR2 0RL, England
Penguin Ireland, 25 St. Stephen's Green, Dublin 2, Ireland
(a division of Penguin Books Ltd)
Penguin Books Australia Ltd, 250 Camberwell Road, Camberwell,
Victoria 3124, Australia (a division of Pearson Australia Group Pty Ltd)
Penguin Books India Pvt Ltd, 11 Community Centre,
Panchsheel Park, New Delhi – 110 017, India
Penguin Group (NZ), Cnr Airborne and Rosedale Roads, Albany,
Auckland 1310, New Zealand (a division of Pearson New Zealand Ltd)
Penguin Books (South Africa) (Pty) Ltd, 24 Sturdee Avenue,
Rosebank, Johannesburg 2196, South Africa

Penguin Books Ltd, Registered Offices: 80 Strand, London WC2R 0RL, England

First published in 2006 by Viking Penguin, a member of Penguin Group (USA) Inc.

1   3   5   7   9   10   8   6   4   2

Copyright © Peter Nabokov, 2006
All rights reserved

ISBN 0-670-03432-0

Printed in the United States of America
Set in Minion
Designed by Francesca Belanger

For Vine Deloria Jr.

Contents

PART IV: WEST

Introduction

My first encounter with the merging of physical and spiritual habitats described in this book came on a hot South Dakota afternoon in 1958. A Lakota Indian friend named Ed Clown from the Cheyenne River Sioux Reservation had a place he wanted me to see. For an hour we followed dirt roads west of the town of Dupree until we parked on a road shoulder and began to walk across ranks of plowed furrows. A quarter mile off stood a solitary butte with unmowed ground cover, rounded boulders and stunted pines. Up top looked like a good place to catch a breeze. Later I learned we were not far from the geographical center of North America.

Encircling the butte were busted strands of rusty wire that drooped between rotting posts. We stepped over them and didn't look back. Unlike those regimental lines of naked, sliced dirt behind us, here the grass blew and peaked like waves. Big rocks, crusted with patches of gray and ocher lichen, sank into the earth. We used a single-file path that lay so deep the grass tunneled over it. The smell was of sage and manure. Our movements flushed insects; a dirty-yellow meadowlark skipped ahead.

Ed turned with a sharp glance; I stepped up the pace. On the summit I followed him to a rock with charred spots. He dribbled tobacco from a Bull Durham pouch, cracked a match, burned the mixture and said some words. My eyes strayed past some U-shaped rock enclosures at the rim, across the fields to a hazy line of cottonwoods along a river. Under the sky the horizon was wide and curved and spread, as a Lakota phrase goes, with *awanka toyala*, "the greenness of the world."

I think the butte belonged to a white rancher who looked the other way about Indians' coming up. But Ed wasn't behaving as if anybody owned the place. It seemed more the opposite, as if the real authorities hovered in the air around us.

When I was six, my mother told me that American Indians "were here first," and I've spent much of my life investigating what that all means. Certainly one of the results of such a long residence is a range of deep and complex ties to the environment, including those that prompted an Australian Aborigine to ask a *National Geographic* writer if America had people who had lived there as long as his had in Australia. "Only the American Indians," the visitor replied, "[are] as old in that land as your people are in this one." The Aborigine nodded thoughtfully. "That's very old. Perhaps as old as the Dreamtime," he said. "They must have sacred places in the land as we have."

My awareness of this older Indian presence in America deepened when I was twelve and our school class stumbled upon the remains of a Pautuxant Indian village near my hometown. There was something raw about the way that evidence rose from the dirt. The sense of responsibility we felt toward those arrowheads, beads and trade pipes was serious and new to us. Ten more years of reading and thinking about Indians led me to this butte in South Dakota.

A gentle man of few words, Ed Clown didn't explain the place. Now I know that once upon a time a solitary vision seeker had experienced an important revelation here, which launched its reputation as a promising location to encounter spirits and beg for luck and power. At that time it seemed enough that Ed had brought me to a place he cared about, that I knew it was a sacred spot, and that I'd behaved accordingly. Today I wonder whether he also wanted me to understand that there was more to some American places than met the eye and to appreciate that his people had known that for a long time.

We didn't unwrap our lunches until we were back at the road shoulder and sitting on Ed's tailgate. By the time we were driving away and I had twisted around, the butte was a bump on the skyline. The whole trip took little more than six hours. Yet in that time I'd discovered something new about the possible lives of places in this country of mine. In ways that I had years and years ahead to learn more about, that butte was alive.

After that experience I found other environments all across North America with similar powers and biographies. The anthropologist Robert Heizer used to say that California Indians lived in two worlds at the same time. There was the practical world where they hunted, traveled, loved, fought and died. And there was the equally real world of the spirits. Trees, animals, springs, caves, streams and mountains might each contain a life force, spirit or soul and must be treated with caution and respect.

Since that summer in 1958, I have put a lot of time into investigating how different American Indian societies positioned their people between those two worlds, how they believed the spirits of place responded and how transactions and relationships between them conferred various senses of the "sacred" upon those places.

This book is not about Indian systems of land tenure or indigenous techniques for management of land and natural resources or environmental laws affecting Indians. I wrote it to establish the pre-Christian origins of religion in North America, to give readers a sense of the diversity of American Indian spiritual practices by focusing on beliefs related to different American environments, to remind them of the profound affection and affiliation that many Indians felt and still feel toward this American earth and to illustrate the persistence of those beliefs, practices and feelings against great odds.

Especially revered were the locations where their creators, or spirit beings, had formed the cosmos: the planets, the earth's topography and plants and fellow creatures. Indians often named places to commemorate where the earliest mythic figures had played out their great adventures. In story and song they memorialized the landscapes which supernatural heroes or trickster spirits had transformed into their present shapes, or special places where they left traces behind them. They noted how odd-looking rocks or other landscape features bore resemblance to characters in their stories, and they considered this more than coincidence.

They cherished the places where a First People had emerged from the earth or landed from the sky or been created in situ, and they remembered the lakes, caves, bluffs and mountains where they settled, even before human beings as we know them ever arrived on the scene. Some of these locations stood out as freaks of nature; others were remarkably monumental or beautiful while some would not draw a second glance.

Their spirits of place dwelled among, could be identified with, or were embodied by stars, planets, clouds, mountains, caves, trees, lakes, rivers, springs, rocks and plants. The linkages between these spirits, their habitats and early Indian communities determined everyone's health and success or failure in life.

On isolated overlooks and at cave mouths and other sites considered to be portals or thresholds between human and spirit worlds, individual Indians suffered, prayed and sought visions and transacted with the shy, evasive entities who lived there.

But they also undertook collective pilgrimages to contact their mythological beings on their own grounds and noted places where moral or religious teachings were first given to them.

They painted on rocks and carved into trees so that future generations would know the powers of these special locations and give them wide berth or use them with care.

Indians avoided ominous, frightening spots known to be associated with dangerous spirits, or sometimes they deliberately headed for them to acquire the powers to do harm.

Around grounds set aside for group ceremonies, tribal councils and lawmaking, they behaved with circumspection and respect. During visits to them, they refrained from speaking loudly, displaying weapons or quarreling.

Indians credited their myths and tales with explaining why the natural world behaved and looked the way it did and with identifying their sacred places. They wore masks to merge with the spirits during rites that tied their societies to particular landscapes.

They revered and revisited routes where their ancestors had migrated across the land, especially those spots where they had stopped, died, rested, split off or resumed their travels.

They piled rocks into cairns to remember fallen heroes and places of victory in battle.

They honored locations associated with great prophets, teachers and leaders.

They consecrated areas for the peaceful rest of their dead.

They marked the best traveling routes and mountain passes and short-cuts to locations where they gathered natural resources or traded for them.

Through place-names, they staked user claims to these foraging areas, hunting grounds, fishing stations and historical and sacred locations.

They cherished the places where they gathered ritual materials, the meadows where they collected plants, the rapids and riverbanks where they fished and the woods, seas and plains where they hunted. They reciprocated with offerings to the plants they harvested and the animals they killed.

All over North America the landscape is saturated with Indian memories and stories that describe such beliefs. Of course, these practices differed greatly from habitat to habitat, but it is fair to say that Indians played a part in the inner life of the land, and it responded as an influential participant in theirs.

One need not romanticize Indian attitudes toward nature in order to acknowledge that attitudes and ethics about beings and forces that reside in the natural environment and the wider universe were and remain a bedrock of American Indian belief systems.

This book focuses on relationships between Indians, environments and religions. Along the way I also challenge three stereotypes.

First is the mistaken idea that before the arrival of Europeans, the religious attitudes of Indians toward the natural environment were frozen in time. Before 1500, Indian peoples responded to changing environmental and historical circumstances; after that their cultural lives continued to evolve down to the present day. This process of adaptation, and the tensions between doing things the old way and trying (or being forced to try) something new—what we might call conservatism versus innovation—had been going on long before Euro-Americans arrived. Rarely did it mean the disappearance of earlier religious beliefs. Some transformed, others withered, but many became more complex through the winnowing, blending and layering processes over time. Like societies everywhere, American Indian cultures and their religious systems are the products of this tug-of-war between historical change and inherited traditions.

A second error is thinking that Indian attitudes toward the environment were simple and similar. In the past, when Indian rituals and beliefs were more dependent upon and interwoven with highly localized ways of living off the land, their differences may have been more pronounced. But even today, we have no monolithic Indian culture, no single web of relationships to nature. Shared themes and common principles may resurface throughout this book. But these sixteen biographies of place dramatize a tribal diversity that is the result of different ecologies, histories, languages, economies, worldviews and values.

A third problem with understanding American Indian sacred places is the expectation that they will please the eye. It may be misleading to conjure up a picturesque mountain or lake, or some promontory where local lore describes Indian lovers leaping to their deaths. Coffee-table books or calendars with color photos may not be the best way to appreciate the time-depth, spatial variety and cultural complexities of Indian ties to their religious landscapes.

This book also tries to counterbalance writings on American Indians and ecology that are driven by romantic ideas about "harmony with nature" or are turned to the service of environmental advocacy. I profile landscapes that are often unlike those enjoyed by outdoor tourists, photographers and sports buffs. I focus on habitats permeated with beliefs about what lies *within* or *beneath* what the eye can see. The environments whose "lives" I narrate should also be distinguished from phrases like "spirit of place" or "geography of hope" by which nature writers or conservationists evoke the psychological benefits and moral and political responsibilities of immersion in one's own neck of the woods.

Nor should Indian attitudes about the environment be hijacked in order to confer the blessings of aboriginal authenticity or spiritual supremacy upon a contemporary agenda. And one also distorts Indian religious beliefs by reducing them to universal principles or archetypes, whether they are environmental, psychological or religious. Before we surrender to our own concerns, with their relevance to our ecological emergencies, it may be more respectful and interesting to learn about these aboriginal American thought worlds on their terms. One would be a fool not to applaud and explore whatever tips or inspirations they might offer for living more equitably and sustainably with the environment. But the less anyone pontificates how that should be done, the less readers will look for prepackaged self-help or cultural conversion programs and the more they will take their environmental futures into their own hands.

The prompt for this book was my dismay at what happened following the passage of the American Indian Religious Freedom Act. When President Jimmy Carter signed that legislation on August 28, 1978, for a fleeting moment the topic of American Indian sacred places commanded the nation's attention. It felt like a great success on behalf of more than fifteen thousand years of Indian presence, prayer and practice in this land. But it was not.

The act was the climax of two decades of mounting complaints about the abuse of Indian religious and cultural rights. Iroquois from New York State demanded the repatriation of wampum belts that were locked up in their state museum. Taos Pueblo fought for return of its Blue Lake watershed in northern New Mexico, taken from them by the U.S. government in 1906. Lakota tribes sought the return of lands in the Black Hills of South Dakota, appropriated from them in the 1870s. Indians from California to Illinois to Minnesota were outraged by museum displays of Indian skulls and skeletons. Alaskan native whalers and hunters resisted environmental laws that restricted their hunting practices. Native parents fought school codes that forbade their children from wearing long hair. Native prison inmates petitioned for the right to pray in traditional sweat baths. Oklahoma craftsmen protested arrests for using feathers from protected birds on their ritual fans and rattles. Members of the Native American Church were fed up with harassment by lawmen for using a controlled substance (peyote cactus) as their sacramental food. For the first time in more than half a century, Indian concerns were not only political and economic. They were cultural once again.

Most challenging to America's values of inviolable private property and the government's mandate to keep its public lands available to boaters, campers, extreme sportsmen, hunters, tourists, miners and lumbermen were Indian claims to special places that their oldest stories talked about and where their oldest spirits still lived.

Land developers, road builders and park rangers learned that whenever bulldozers unearthed old Indian bones in inconvenient places, a ceremonial reburial could be negotiated without too much delay. More stubborn conflicts arose when Indians claimed that the government's multiple-use policies or private development threatened their sacred rivers, mountains or forests. The beliefs and practices related to these "cultural resources" were rooted in the American earth and could not be relocated.

At long last, in late 1977, the U.S. Senate's Select Committee on Indian Affairs responded. It drafted Senate Joint Resolution 102, which had two goals: first, it reaffirmed the First Amendment's freedom-of-religion privileges for native practices, "including but not limited to sites, use and possession of sacred objects, and the freedom to worship through ceremonials and traditional rites." Second, it made doubly sure that federal agencies extended all First Amendment rights to Indians. After a year of public hearings, the American Indian Religious Freedom Act was passed by the Senate and the House and signed by President Carter.

Then came the backlash. In defiance of every guiding principle in the 1978 Religious Freedom Act, each following year saw Indians losing more and more control over their rights to sacred places on public lands. Indeed, the major court decisions that compose this book's four sections seemed almost calculated to send a symbolic message by securing the government's claims to the four sacred directions and reminding Indians who was still in charge.

To the east, in eastern Tennessee in 1979, members of the Cherokee Nation proved no match for powerful interests that were bent on constructing the Tellico Dam across the Little Tennessee River.

To the south, in northern Arizona in 1977 and 1983, complaints by the Navajo that their Rainbow Canyon was being destroyed by Glen Canyon Dam fell on deaf ears, as did Hopi and Navajo arguments that expanded ski-lift facilities threatened the sanctity of the San Francisco Peaks.

To the north, in western South Dakota in 1982, law suits by Lakota and Cheyenne religious leaders to halt the expansion of parking lots on the slope of Bear Butte in the Black Hills were dismissed.

To the west, in northern California in 1988, a campaign by Yurok, Karuk and Tolowa tribes to halt a U.S. Forest Service road in their sacred high country went all the way to the U.S. Supreme Court, where it ended with a devastating legal precedent for Indians everywhere.

Subsequent orders and directives restored some bite to the 1978 legislation. In 1992, amendments to the National Historic Preservation Act passed by the U.S. Congress preserved Indian rights of privacy about sacred places. President Clinton's 1996 Executive Order asked federal land managers to "accommodate access to and ceremonial use of Indian sacred sites."

But more recent court losses, such as the Devil's Tower Case of 1998, reminded one and all that on the legal level, native terrain was as vulnerable as ever. Indian places were still drowned by dams, drained by wells, stripped by chainsaws, peeled by mines, penetrated by oil rigs and overcome by land developers, tourists, spiritual seekers, skiers, hikers and rock climbers.

I have organized this book around those four major court cases in the east, south, north and west. Within these four sections I reconstruct sixteen stories of American Indian habitats and associated belief systems that introduce a range of different tribal relationships to the natural world. Each chapter sketches the conditions that established those relationships and the creeds and rituals that sustained them. Included also are stories about scholars—Indian and non-Indian—who helped us understand them and some personal experiences that helped me make sense of them.

My hope is that these narratives will make readers more aware of the diversity of native heritages and the complexities of Indian-white relations that still echo in their own backyards.

May they become more respectful of the thousands of years of human thought, prayer and ritual that have saturated the places where they live. And may they be more willing to support Indian peoples in their struggles to maintain these sorts of connections to the American earth.

PART I

EAST

In 1979, a year after passage of the American Indian Religious Freedom Act, a group of Cherokee Indians sued in a Tennessee court to stop construction on the Tellico Dam on the Little Tennessee River in the eastern part of the state. Although none of these Indians lived in the river valley anymore, it was the heartland of the old Overhill Cherokee Nation. Along its banks were once politically powerful towns, extensive cornfields, hunting grounds and cemeteries. Surrounding the valley was a landscape unequaled in America for the density of medicinal plants, Indian foot trails and the homes of spirit beings. For thousands of years earlier Indians had occupied this environment, long before the first Cherokee moved in. The Indians said the proposed dam would obliterate their historic villages, ancestral burial grounds and sacred sites. Without this access, even as occasional visitors, the umbilical cord between their spiritual and physical worlds would be cut for good.

CHAPTER ONE

WORLDS IN AN ISLAND

Penobscot

T he sacred places of American Indians may include cliffs spilling with waterfalls, caves splattered with bat excrement, rock bridges arching across pastel canyons and desert sinks rimmed with algae. Many are now under suburban housing tracts, dam reservoirs or asphalt roads. Some survive as officially sacred, like the graveyards, ceremonial buildings and powwow arenas still used by Indian communities, or the battlegrounds that wars have hallowed with Indian blood. All may retain potency, a tug on Indian affections and values, or a reason for steering clear of them, or some claim in Indian hearts and minds because of their reflection of the animated world that still breathes within the landscape.

Their meanings are preserved in the narratives and memories Indians share among themselves. Anecdotes and place-names remind them that *here* an emissary from the world of myth or dream or legend made its presence known; over *there* something wondrous or unexplainable or terrifying happened; right *there* some spark was struck between the everyday and the extraordinary, creating a memory so bright that some still go there to pay respects or conduct rituals or contact the spirits.

Rarely are outsiders privy to these stories or the extent of an Indian community's precious places. For Indian residents who have lived there for generations, the secrets stay at home. And even when the locations are altered beyond recognition, or newcomers can't find out what happened there and nobody seems willing to recall their meanings, Indians say that the places themselves remember. But it takes awhile to hear them.

When I first arrived at Indian Island in southern Maine about thirty years ago, the image of a sacred place did not spring to mind. Centuries of clear-cutting virgin forests, quarrying granite mountains and diverting rivers to run textile and leather mills had turned the local ecology into a disaster zone. Discharge from the Diamond International pulpwood plant permeated the air with the stench of rotten vegetables. Spindly second- and third-growth woods clogged the shorelines of the Penobscot River; they resembled thickets for hobo camps. Wherever they pooled, the waters had a greasy surface, with unnatural foam bobbing in the shallows. The land seemed beat up and worn out. The few residents I saw through the window of my rental car on the sidewalks of Old Town looked hunched over and depressed.

At one time, this stretch of the Penobscot River was a prime fishing spot because of the topography of its bedrock, which is evoked in one translation of the Penobscot Indian name for themselves: *People of the River of White Rocky Slopes*. But those terraces were dynamited a hundred years ago to channel the water for wool factories and sawmills. Vine-covered brick walls of abandoned plants rose from the riverbanks like ramparts of a deserted prison. "A number of travelers are disappointed in the reservation on an island in the Penobscot River," said the Fodor's travel guide I'd consulted before my trip, "possibly partially because it just doesn't resemble their romantic notions of what an Indian village should look like."

For three months I lived on Indian Island, working as a consultant for the adult education program. The inhabitants were descendants of the northeastern branch of the Algonquian-speaking tribes who knew themselves collectively as Abenaki, or *Dawn Land People*. Islands like this one are large nervous systems: gossip travels fast, and everyone knows everything about everyone. Residents may backbite, but they close ranks against outside threats to the collective body. Pride of membership in one known patch of ground is counterbalanced by a suspicion of know-it-all outsiders; a protectiveness toward shared habits, family histories and community secrets; and a defensiveness about their slower pace of life, special habits of speech and idiosyncratic customs.

At Indian Island these sensitivities were accentuated by another contrast between themselves and everyone else: the community across the river was white; they were Indians.

Many stories held dear by Indian Island residents related to places within and beyond their hideaway. In their reluctance to share this information, they were not alone. Across North America, native peoples with ties to old spirits and sites are still angry about past suppression and scorn and are wary about exposure and exploitation. It is also common knowledge that the spirits share their shyness and need for privacy, for their existence is tied up with "their" people, not with tourists and strangers. Talk about spirits behind their backs and they might retaliate. What made Indian Island a good introduction to American Indian cultural and spiritual geography was the range of its storied locations, which exposed themselves to me month by month and place by place.

My day job was testing innovative methods for teaching basic language and math skills to underemployed adults. But outside of class I also kept my eyes and ears open.

Indian Island is shaped like a human heart turned upside down. Its artery is the Penobscot River, which points downstream toward the Atlantic Ocean, about forty miles away. For more than three centuries, the narrower southern portion of its 315 acres has supported the principal Penobscot village, their "capital." But former generations of Indians coveted these white-water ledges for at least seven thousand years or more before that. While shoveling out root cellars, my neighbors occasionally turned up their tools: slender slate spear points, exquisitely rounded ax heads made of granite, and lovely stone weights for fishing nets, all clotted in reddish deposits of puttylike hematite, as if socked away for the ages.

Of the 146 tribally owned islands that dot the upper reaches of the Penobscot, only this one remains inhabited. During my sojourn, fewer than 700 Indians were living there. Linking them to the white community of Old Town, famed for its handmade wooden canoes, was a single-lane bridge. Before the bridge's trusses were riveted together in 1951, island visitors boarded a small ferry in summer or trudged on a sawdust path that was spread across the ice in winter. After the bridge went up, some Indians boycotted the white man's intrusion and insisted on canoeing back and forth.

From the first time I crawled up to it, honked my horn and craned my neck to see if the coast was clear, the bridge struck me as a barrier as much as a conduit—a New England counterpart to the border checkpoints of the West Bank or Baghdad. It discouraged two-way commerce or communication between Indians and whites. And I was never sure which side of the river wanted me to think twice about traveling between cultural realms, or wanted me to know that I was being watched and that I'd best be off—or on—the island by sundown. The sort of psychological apartheid that open range maintained between white towns and Indian reservations out west was accomplished here by a narrow metal passage that ran for 630 feet. No wonder that the only Old Town resident I saw on the island was the furtive Indian agent who darted in and out of his car to the low-shingled house that served as his office. And no surprise that Old Town's Elks lodge still refused to admit Indians.

The island's two-story saltbox homes, with no porches and clapboard siding that badly needed paint, clustered on the populated southern end, under the shade of thick old maples and hemlocks that seemed to have escaped the axes of earlier days. Their yards held upside-down canoes, toolsheds and the occasional engine block swinging from a log tripod. The hundred-year-old house in which I rented a garret stood on Oak Hill, a few blocks from the old residence of Joseph Polis, a Penobscot hunter who guided for Henry David Thoreau during the writer's time here in the 1850s. The narrow lanes were potholed. My low-silled window looked north, over a clearing for softball games and unbroken tree cover beyond.

My landlord was in his early thirties; the island's only cop, he was married to a white woman, and they had an infant son. Insistent in his pride of ancestry, he put books or articles about his people beside my bacon and eggs, and squired me around the island in his outboard as if he had something to prove. Through his lectures, that reading list (by white and Penobscot writers alike) and tribal elders I met through work, I was drawn into this little cosmos.

Like most American Indian homelands, Penobscot country is a land of myth and magic. In the late sixteenth century, when first encountered by the Italian explorer Giovanni da Verrazano, the Penobscot attributed their river valley to the work of a sacred being named Glooskap, the culture hero known as "the man from nothing." With the world's shape already roughed out, it was his task to refashion it and render it safe for human habitation. Of Glooskap my landlord spoke fondly, as if referring to some larger than life neighbor he'd once known.

A giant and a bachelor, in tribal folklore Glooskap also comes across as a brooder, with a lot on his hands. Among the twenty or so tribes of the extended Abenaki brotherhood, he is regarded as teacher and friend. Glooskap arrived from "over east," they say, and lived with his grandmother. In Nova Scotia, tales from the Micmac Indians have him teaching his Indian children the names of the constellations, showing them how to hunt and fish, helping them organize their society.

Glooskap had an affinity for stone. He paddled a granite canoe, chipped the first arrowheads and molded the islands and conspicuous landmarks of Maine's and Canada's maritime provinces from the calcified body parts of the dangerous monsters and mastodons he had slain. He reduced the size of threatening bears and lynx, forced moose to mind their manners and taught loyalty to dogs. For his Indian people he created the white birch and brown ash trees, then taught them how to debark, carve, split and weave their fibers. He instructed the trees and medicinal plants to look after his people.

The Penobscot River was his doing. When a monster frog swallowed up the world's water, Glooskap promptly snapped his back and squashed him under a yellow birch tree. Then hundreds of rivulets trickled along its branches and swelled into this 240-mile-long waterway. Almost dead from thirst, those original Indians threw themselves into the river and transformed into the water creatures that originated the first Penobscot clans—the family lines that would be known as Crab, Eel, Frog, Neptune, Sculpins and the like. But Glooskap saw that another set of Penobscot clans would be linked to the wooded landscape. My landlord hailed from the Lobster "family," through this process of inheriting clan membership down the female line, which also bound people to other creatures in their environment in a web of kinship.

Glooskap taught Indians how to live off the river. For their canoes, they peeled off panels of paper-birch bark, sewed them over bentwood frames with spruce root lacing, waterproofed them with pine sap, and paddled and portaged through countless waterways. Every spring Glooskap sent a veritable fish market upstream—stocks of spawning sturgeon, salmon, shad, alewives, striped bass and eels, all thrashing against the current to lay their eggs. Old Town Falls was his design—a perfect stretch of rocky shoals for slowing down those schools and leading them toward hooks, nets and weirs.

And when wild fowl, sailing in on northerly and southerly flyways, took breathers on pools below the falls, Glooskap made them easy targets for Penobscot arrows. For villages, he fashioned the low bluffs along the river, which also provided clay for shaping pots and cobbles for grinding into stone tools. He positioned the nearby stands of sugar maple to sweeten the villagers' meals and the birch trees for turning into the bark vessels that collected and stored the sap.

Glooskap was his people's benefactor, my landlord said, and he added somewhat defiantly, *he still was*. When the Jesuits brought Christianity in the mid-seventeenth century, the Penobscot believed that Glooskap retreated to an island up north. There he still bides his time making bows and arrows and waiting for the day to kill the white people and restore the Penobscot to their former prominence.

This mythic landscape also featured its holy mountain. Although he'd never been there, my landlord claimed to know his culture hero's current address. Glooskap could be found on the eastern slopes of Maine's highest peak, the windswept saddle in Baxter State Park that whites call Mount Katahdin. From there he dispensed the deer and moose so Penobscot hunters and their families could make it through the winter. For especially brave Indians the mountain also promised sources of red paint, the gifts of good hunting and other powers from the "spirit" beavers and rabbits that lived there, and in the old days it supplied a burial ground when they passed on.

Spirits of ocean, river and forest populated the old Penobscot territory, but mountains were in control. Known to the Penobscot as Pemola, or Spirit of Night Air, this mountain was a singular personality, especially intimidating and notoriously unpredictable. When asked to draw him on paper, Indians showed Pemola as an overgrown, misshapen thing, all head, legs and arms. Look up into a tree, they said, and he would be leering at you like some berserk Humpty Dumpty while Christianized Indians drew him as a spike-tailed devil. Pemola shared his domain with other extraordinary beings: men made of stone, terrifying cannibals, Thunder creatures, Little People and huge snakes that caused the slide marks on Katahdin's's south slopes and smashed man-made dams.

All this peril and power made the atmosphere of Maine's northern highlands an optimal setting for Penobscot medicine men to work their wonders. Between the summits of high mountains they suspended cradle-like swings for swaying back and forth above the forest canopy. And in the dead of winter once, a nineteenth-century magic maker named Old John Neptune, an infamous womanizer, camped near Mount Katahdin. Though the temperature was well below zero, he hung his clothes on columns of smoke and produced oranges and tobacco out of thin air. Ordinary men also sought Pemola's favor, getting his attention with smoke from signal fires and then begging for his aid as his spirit flew screaming like a comet across the sky. Catching the mountain's reflection in the lake told a hunter that Pemola's spirit might guide him to a more profitable stand. But mountain climbers got a cooler reception; the Penobscot always warned whites about venturing beyond Katahdin's tree line.

Whether these stories emphasize the mountain's benevolent or fear-some sides, they inevitably turn on its relations with humans, which opens the broader question of whether, in the Penobscot view, *the landscape might be lonely without human beings.* Relationships between these Indians and the outdoors could even reach the intimacy of sexual relations. But there is a critical difference between these couplings and the erotic epiphanies with nature in non-Indian fiction, such as the ecstatic union with an oak that climaxes John Steinbeck's *To a God Unknown,* or Robinson Crusoe's mystical immersion in a moist cave in Michel Tournier's *Friday, or The Other Island.* For in Penobscot stories it is usually the environment that flirts with them.

One hears of an Indian wedding that took place on Katahdin's lower slopes. In the sky the happy party noticed a little cloud that shortly built into a blinding curtain of hail, rain and thunder. The spirit of Pemola was claiming the bride who, the Penobscot say, was already secretly stepping out with him. Then the clouds reversed direction, streaming back toward the peak, leaving the sky blue, cloudless and calm. Only the girl was gone, having joined her mountain lover for good.

Women of the historical period were also open to such dalliances. Clara Neptune told Maine historian Fannie Eckstorm about one of her Indian Island neighbors, a respectable lady who was married to a white man. Every Sunday she washed up, fixed her hair, put on her best and walked into a nearby pond until her head disappeared beneath the water. By nightfall she was safely back home, cooking for her husband. Every mountain had an Indian man in it, Clara explained, who could cast a *glamour,* as people used to say, over human beings. That woman was actually enjoying her weekly fling with Mount Waldo, a peak about forty miles southwest of Indian Island.

One celebrity trespasser of Pemola's stronghold was Henry David Thoreau. In early September 1846, he joined one of the earliest climbing excursions up Katahdin. By this time Thoreau's fame derived from meditations written in semisolitude and material simplicity in a homemade cabin beside a pond two miles outside of the town of Concord, Massachusetts. Around his retreat lay unthreatening, sylvan surroundings, which were conducive to the sorts of transcendental meditations that Ralph Waldo Emerson and his generation considered their replacement for the region's old-fashioned Puritanism. Walking amid these mowed meadows and orchards, friendly cows and local characters, Thoreau felt free to imagine living "consciously" and coexisting with the natural environment.

But on Katahdin, Thoreau came face-to-face with what he called "primeval, untamed and forever untameable Nature." Surrounded by its forests, mountains, fast rapids, ice-cold lakes and bogs, the environmental guru who left us the slogan "In wildness is the preservation of the world" lost his bearings. Against Indian warnings, his party pushed above the four-thousand-foot tree line. Amid its swirling mists, slashing winds and icy granite, Thoreau suffered what one admirer termed "a virulent attack of metaphysical dread." Trying to describe the experience later, his fluid prose shattered into pieces. Here was "a place for heathenism and superstitious rites—to be inhabited by men nearer of kin to the rocks and wild animals than we." As if testifying to some unspeakable horror, Thoreau yanked his readers uncomfortably close: "What is this Titan that has possession of me . . . Think of our life in nature—daily to be shown matter, to come in contact with it—rocks, trees, wind on our cheeks! The *solid* earth. The *actual* world. The *common sense! Contact! Contact!* Who are we? *Where* are we?"

To Thoreau's credit, the experience only tied his curiosity tighter to the Penobscot way. With these same Penobscot guides, he returned to the Maine woods in 1853 and 1857. Until tuberculosis cut short his life, he compiled eleven volumes of notes for a projected Indian book. Spellbound by how Indian culture evoked the "eternity behind me as well as the eternity before," Thoreau kept his eye open for arrowheads, what he called "fossilized thoughts," and which he had an uncanny knack for finding. On May 6, 1862, reported a friend, in a delirium he whispered his last word, "Indian."

Another charged place for the Penobscot was a ten-minute walk from my house. The wooden doors of St. Anne's Church were unlocked only on Sundays for mostly elderly devotees. One of New England's oldest churches, it was established in 1668 by the Sisters of Mercy. It was a modest white chapel whose cross-topped steeple spiked through the maples. Its interior once preserved the relic of a second cross that stood on the site of Norridgewock, where the legendary Jesuit missionary Sebastian Rales was tortured and dismembered by the British after he fought alongside his Abenaki converts in 1724.

This austere sanctuary was the most visible reminder of the island's invasion by Europeans in the early seventeenth century. While Glooskap was driven into the mountains, the Penobscot began trapping beaver for their pelts in great and consequently diminishing quantities. And as French and English traders competed for control of their furs, Protestant and Catholic missionaries fought for their souls. Throughout the eight colonial wars, which buffeted Indian Island with hardly a break between 1675 and 1873, Penobscot sympathies leaned toward the French. Living as solitary missionaries in their villages, at least the Gallic "Black Robes" learned something of their language and traditions and, like Father Rales, joined their ranks. But in 1723 this allegiance cost the Penobscot dearly as British troops torched their wigwams and cornfields and razed the island.

Converting New England's natives from their own beliefs was never entirely successful. French Catholicism prevailed in the north because it was less dogmatic and intrusive than the English Protestantism that fell upon the Algonquian-speaking peoples farther south. To the stricter Puritans of central New England, Indian allegiance to spirits of the outdoors, and to creator beings like Glooskap, condemned them to eternal damnation. Their influential minister, Cotton Mather, viewed the American countryside much like the Old Testament landscape that God promised to the Israelites: its raw environment and native inhabitants were equally evil. "The wilderness through which we are passing to the Promised Land is over fill'd with fiery flying serpents," he preached. Indians were "devils in our way. . . ." Before Mather's chosen people could claim their promised land, these obstacles had to be eliminated. Nor was this the only ideology working against New England's Indians and their landscapes. Brushing aside native notions of land ownership and customs for its use, English common law redefined Indian homelands as *vacuum domicilum,* an unpopulated expanse of weeds and wild beasts over which nobody held dominion and which cried out for farming and civilization.

To exterminate Indian religion, Protestant clerics sought to "root out" the "powwows," as Massachusetts minister John Eliot put it. This was an Algonquian term for the medicine men and women who worked with the magical force known as *manitou,* an invisible power that could animate trees, rocks, animals, things and humans. Today the Siberian term *shaman* characterizes these specialists who went into trances and employed hunting magic and various healing techniques on behalf of their people.

In isolated, Catholicized enclaves like Indian Island, shamanism persisted longer than anywhere else in New England. Their own name for these specialists, whom historian of religions Mircea Eliade once called "technicians of ecstasy," was *m'teoulin.* It didn't take long for me to hear more stories about that cunning practitioner Old John Neptune. Especially famous was his duel with a Passamaquoddy Indian shaman at Boyden's Lake in northern Maine.

Rather than fight hand to hand, their spirit helpers were their proxies. The onlookers crowding the lakeshore watched the waters boil and turn brown. Neptune's gigantic eel and his opponent's mammoth horned snail tumbled over and over until finally Neptune's surrogate killed the snail. But since he was a spirit creature, naturally he sprang back to life. Although Neptune had six other mysterious helpers, all Indian Islanders knew the eel was his pet familiar—some had spied him calling the muddy thing out of the depths and stroking it as it slithered to his side. For everyone linked by kinship to such "helpers," the price paid for their alliance was never to eat their delectable flesh.

Over coffee with my new acquaintances I heard about bygone Penobscot shamans who grabbed sunbeams, stretched and folded them like taffy, hung them between chairs, and suspended heavy objects, like metal axes, in these hammocks of pure light. The daughter of Old John Neptune could kindle a fire on a silk handkerchief without burning it. Once she was seen pushing her twins in a swing that she had tied to a rainbow in the sky. Another Indian Island shaman was said to have been in the act of jumping across a stream when he suddenly remembered he'd left his ax at home. In midair he spun around, flew back to snatch the tool and completed his jump without touching the ground.

Eventually I became friends with the only man on Indian Island who bore any resemblance to those wonder workers of old. He was Senabeh Francis, or "Little Man," and his home was a single-room, tar-paper shack known as a beaver hut, which peered out of tree cover near the bridge. Fifty-eight years old, diminutive of stature, with wispy braids and pouched, sad eyes, Senabeh knew the mysteries of the place. He was a World War II veteran, a master carver and herbalist, and one of the last Penobscot speakers—a good storyteller with a weakness for the bottle.

"Almost born in a canoe," Senabeh would say of his upbringing. For more than two decades he had lived as a hermit on Hemlock Island, a narrow, wooded and uninhabited place about twelve miles to the north. By gardening and hunting, he'd survived on rabbits, partridges, deer, fish, dandelions, cucumbers and fiddlehead ferns. But he also foraged for ginseng, mandrake and sweet flag root, which he carted by canoe, together with his birch-root carvings, to peddle on Indian Island and the sidewalks of Old Town. His reputation had spread through the moccasin grapevine—visiting Iroquois from New York State paid their respects, and Senabeh reciprocated with gifts of flag root and sweetgrass. I'd sit on his narrow cot enthralled by stories of the Revolutionary War that sounded like recent history. Senabeh showed me how to write, burn and crumble the ashes of "wind letters" to a sweetheart, communications which then traveled with the speed of light to wherever she was. He told me about the birds and animals that talked back to him.

From conversations with Senabeh and others, I learned of the island's spookier side. Troubled history and strange beings stirred the ground beneath our houses, backyard paths and shorelines. As Thoreau once wrote, these Indians were a winter rather than a summer people, a moon rather than sun people, night folk rather than day, as if withholding their portion of diurnal time as a way to resist total domination by the surrounding whites.

Even in more contemporary times, the Penobscot shared their Island with other beings. "Yes, one lives under my house," Clara Neptune told historian Eckstorm in October 1919 about the sea beast Nodumkanwet, from which the family surname derived. "Stamp on ground and maybe he come out. If you died, he fills your mouth, nose, eyes full of mud." Other residents claimed to have seen him splashing around. And when they did, Eckstorm was told, it usually meant bad times ahead, the way one sighting presaged the white-introduced cholera epidemic that wiped out a third of Indian Island in the 1860s.

New England is notorious for the ghosts of old residences and the restless spirits that continue to haunt its crossroads and clearings. "The land! Don't you feel it," once asked poet William Carlos Williams, closing his evocation of Samuel de Champlain, the first European to visit Penobscot country in 1604. "Doesn't it make you want to go out and lift dead Indians tenderly from their graves, to steal from them—as if it must be clinging to their corpses—some authenticity. . . ." The unredeemed history of Euro-American greed, which evicted most of New England's Indians from their homes and lands and tried to "disappear" them from historical memory, still saturates Indian folk tales and popular fiction.

You find bewitched locations peopled by unsettled native spirits in Washington Irving's "The Legend of Sleep Hollow," with its old Indian powwow grounds where the unwary are "given to all kinds of marvelous beliefs; are subject to trances and visions; and frequently see strange sights, and hear music and voices in the air." It is evoked in the "ancient spirit" that still sleeps beneath the smelly Massachusetts neighborhood of H. P. Lovecraft's short story "The Street," in which he reminds us that "there be those who say that things and places have souls. . . ." The uneasy souls of desecrated Indian grounds come alive in Stephen King's *Pet Sematary* through disturbance of a graveyard belonging to the Penobscot neighbors and linguistic cousins the Micmac. Environmental destruction, symbolically equated with Indian land loss, is suggested by ominous oil trucks rumbling down midnight roads and the "souring" of their burial plot, which drives the Indians away. Then King lends the land the power to turn these native dead into zombielike killers. Eyes glowing in dark woods, eerie full moons and the curse of an "old Indian burial ground" return in his 1992 sequel, *The Tommyknockers,* where malevolence throbs in the "Big Indian Woods," which, we learn from a dying indian chief, are cursed with a uraniumlike greenish glow.

Indian Island had its poltergeists and dead zones, too. With its tipped-over crosses in high grass and creaky wooden gazebo, the most recent of its three cemeteries looked ancient to me. Barely noticeable alongside St. Anne's stood the region's earliest burial ground, with mossy stones bearing seventeenth-century names. But plow a road and take home an unearthed ax head, and long-dead Indian Islanders showed up in one's dreams and demanded their tool back.

If one stayed alert and laid aside aesthetic expectations, many glances around Indian Island brought another kind of "sacred" into focus. It did not stand on pedestals or shout forth from beautiful buildings or idyllic ponds; instead, it evoked the understated and the everyday. "I don't know that I like the idea of distinguishing between the sacred and the non-sacred," writes poet Gary Snyder, articulating the perspective that is as grateful for life's cracks and neglected spaces as it is for what's front and center. "It certainly isn't a word I use . . . an act of attention and appreciation towards any phenomenon will make that phenomenon sacred."

This species of "sacred" was noticeable once I crossed that slender bridge and Indian Time enveloped me. "A country, a landscape, can be sacred in an infinite number of ways," reiterates Rick Bass, and one of them can result, unselfconsciously, from a mix of economic necessity, self-taught inventiveness and a vernacular sense of place. At Indian Island I learned to keep my eyes out for compositions of accidental harmony and ordinary beauty. These sightings included an organic composition in a neighbor's backyard: a nineteenth-century clamp "horse" for splitting white ash into basketry splints, which was moldering in the rain on top of the caved-in roof of a rusting, wheelless 1965 Chevrolet that rested on shaky concrete blocks and sheltered a litter of kittens. This kind of eccentric assemblage also winked at one from the oversized, wood-shingled tipi where a displaced Kiowa Indian named Poolaw, who had married into the island, sold his curios. To the purist and the romantic, Indian Island could be as disappointing as my Fodor's guide had warned. To those with an eye for the offhand and down-home, the place was a treat, even a relief.

Within some homes were storerooms from earlier days, when skilled hands left an earthy sort of sanctity behind them. I'd discovered one during an afternoon when my landlord had left me alone in the house. A room across the stairwell from mine had been declared off-limits. But I leaned on its door and the swollen frame gave way. Window light caught fine dust that stirred from the draft; it smelled cool and woody. The floor was padded with curled shavings.

What clay is to the Pueblo, hide to the Plains, soapstone to the Inuit, ash and birch were to these Algonquians. This scatter of detritus and implements came from my landlord's grandmother, a master basket maker. There were clamps for holding the ash withes prior to further splitting and the makings of an ash splint pack basket, its belled-out interior capable of holding gear for days in the woods. I noticed balls of basswood inner bark; rolls of white birch bark that only needed warming to regain suppleness; strips of the lightweight brown ash for the body of baskets; sections of the stronger white ash for the rigid hoops at the mouths of baskets and for snowshoe frames; and a set of hand gauges that, once an ax had pounded loose these lengthy "grains" from ash logs, sliced the pliable strips to a uniform width for basket making.

This woman knew how to make hand bails for canoes, flat trays, storage baskets and all forms of woven knicknacks to be sold as souvenirs in Old Town's streets or on the island's front porches. Dark corners held dried roots and berries for coloring the baskets, wood pieces for their handles and the makings for the island's older artisan work: moose hair embroideries, sewing and needlework, beadwork and ribbon applique, wood for cradle boards and carving tools. But I didn't enter to handle them. I retraced my steps and set the door back as I'd found it.

Then I discovered that the spirits of Indian Island lived closer than I'd realized. Toward the end of my stay, I got home one afternoon to have my landlord advise me to stay in my room. For my own good, he said. Outside my window the light entered that hour when bug hatches rise and deer cross roads at their peril. I stretched out and dozed off. Yells of alarm from the ball field below brought me to. Night had fallen. There was silence, then voices burst out again, then drumming. More startled cries kept me nervous long after automobiles started up and their lights strobed across my ceiling.

Early the next morning I left the sleeping household and joined a respected teacher from the island's Bear Clan on his coffee rounds. We visited the older generation of confirmed Catholics, who seemed shaken. From her stove, a devout parishioner at St. Anne's cast us side glances. She sat down, her hands cushioning a mug as if to steady them. "They came out from them trees," she said. "Near the ball field, you know. Just there, at the edge, and just covered in those twinkling lights. Yes, Little People, those lights around them, just almost coming out, about this high." She tipped her head to one side, stuck out her flat hand about two and a half feet from the floor, then looked at us with wide eyes, nodding up and down.

So-and-so saw them, so-and-so heard them say something, so-and-so tried to get near but then got scared. Versions of the same story passed over other tablecloths in other kitchens about the Little People of Penobscot legend who had emerged from the shadows. Geographers call this boundary between ecological zones an ecotone, the forest fringe whose "edge effects" produce juicy blackberries, safe places for deer to taste grass and return to safety, and for human and spirit beings to interact. Beckoned from their leafy bower by tobacco offerings, the Little People had paid the Penobscot a visit. People described them to us as behaving like long-lost friends.

Shortly thereafter I left Indian Island and have never returned. But my last week there I hired a helicopter and described a low circuit over the place, shooting slides for future teaching. From aloft it was easier to imagine it as many worlds. "A sacred spot never presents itself to the mind in isolation," wrote French anthropologist Lucien Lévy-Bruhl. "It is always part of a complex of things which include the plant or animal species which flourish there at various seasons, as well as the mythical heroes who lived, roamed or created something there and who are often embodied in the very soil, the ceremonies which take place there from time to time, and all the emotions aroused by the whole."

Below me revolved an island within an island within an island within an island.

Mythically Indian Island was a microcosm of the timeless Turtle Island that predated white invaders and, if the trickster Glooskap had his way, would see them depart one day. Bureaucratically it was a state Indian reserve, removed from the federal apparatus that regulates most American Indian reservations. Politically and culturally it was the last refuge of the Penobscot Nation, while ethnically it was the local pocket of a vernacular "Indian country" lifestyle that persists *outside yet within* the modern United States surrounding it.

And finally it was a separate psychological zone whose residents had inherited the prickly pride of insular peoples the world over—of whom John Fowles has written, "some vision of Utopian belonging, of social blessedness, of an independence based on cooperation, haunts them all." At Indian Island I learned how insecurity about one's sense of self and acceptance on the mainland was offset by the weathered, homely solace and sense of security afforded to the children of an entirely knowable piece of ground.

Looking down I was also reminded how small that ground really was—three and a half miles long and a half mile wide. Within a few years it would become known as the little island that could. Linking forces with their native neighbors, the Passamaquoddies, and basing their joint lawsuit on violations of an eighteenth-century trade act, the Penobscot would demand revocation of subsequent treaties and recovery of a huge piece of the state of Maine. Reaching the highest judicial levels, the case won by the two tribes would call for arbitration at the White House, with President Jimmy Carter himself signing the $81.5 million settlement in 1980, in addition to a $27 million trust fund and $54.5 million for purchasing additional lands—150,000 acres for the Penobscot. Only a gleam in the eye of Indian Island governor Frances Ranco during the summer I was there, the verdict would also bring to the island new homes, freshly paved roads, a casino and tribal museum and a place in history as the tribal David who had whipped the American Goliath.

For now, however, that turn of fortune lay in the future. The little island spun in slow motion—uncertain about progress, suspicious of outsiders, licking historical wounds that went back to the French and Indian wars and clinging to its down-home values.

"Land means Penobscot reverence for the land," wrote an anonymous Penobscot to the island's mimeographed newsletter shortly before I arrived. Then without ever using the word, he tacked on a definition of the "sacred" that would not be found in any dictionary:

"And land means fiddleheads, deer, corn, muskrat, beaver, ermine, fox, bear, bobcat, eel, salmon, the pond, the ledges, the mountains, Sara's springs, birch, ash, sweet grass, poison ivy, Fort Dawson, Sandy Beach, lower village, upper villages, Oak Hill, the swamp, the burial grounds, laughter on a warm summer night, tears at an Indian wedding, coos of a little baby, dogs, cars, oil trucks, Indian drums, old people hiding all the secrets of wisdom, young people finding wisdom through acrid smoke and finding that is not the essence of all things, and that when you come to the land you can't burn it, you can't smoke it, you can't ignore it. Land is forever, and we can't sell it, we can use it, for the benefit of ourselves and our children, and our grandchildren, and even those generations that are not born."

CHAPTER TWO

NAMING THE SPIRITS

Ojibwa

How to talk about Indian spirits of place—what English words can possibly convey their otherworldly power and purpose? Somehow the Latin term *numen,* which means the spiritual force that can infuse objects or places, feels like an interloper in this continent's woods and rivers. A designation by an Arctic scholar, "nonempirical phenomena," may be more accurate but sticks in the throat. I confess a liking for how an old-fashioned Latin phrase, *genius loci,* combines the idea of a "genie," a magic spirit that materializes if one invites it properly, and the notion of "genius" or "charisma," those special gifts whose origins cannot be explained, with the rootedness of "loci," which anchors those qualities to a piece of ground. *Genius loci*—the inward-dwelling and presiding power of a particular place.

But labels coined by outsiders still tell us little about how Indians see and interact with their spirits of place. If translations of Indian beliefs about the natural world are to illuminate, if we are to move past clichéd notions that all tribes possessed "land-based religions" premised upon "harmony with nature," we should get down to cases. What's the best way to learn about Indians? asked poet Ed Dorn of his mentor Charles Olson, the Black Mountain College legend. "*Indians* is criminal," Olson shot back. "Study one tribal tradition for twenty years."

A scholar who followed that advice and explored how one group of Indians experienced their environment was A. Irving Hallowell. But "sacred" was probably the adjective furthest from Hallowell's mind as he crossed Lake Winnepeg on a steamboat in the summer of 1930 and a dark, forested shoreline broke through the morning fog. This inhospitable wall of dense fir bore little resemblance to the sacred groves of ancient Greece that Hallowell had read about in seminars on myth and religion at the University of Pennsylvania. Nor would the Berens River Ojibwa Indians have used it either. In an intimate tone of voice, they might have said, "manitou," and they would have meant a force that contained superhuman possibilities.

A latecomer to anthropology, "Pete" Hallowell was thirty-seven years old and undergoing his discipline's initiation: the ethnographic field trip. As the U.S.S. *Kenora* docked for a few hours near the mouth of the Pigeon River, the eyes of visiting Indians watched him walk off the gangplank and kill time stumbling over the rock-strewn shoreline. This was tough ground: an underlying shield of granite held a thin veneer of soil supporting an expanse of spruce, jack pine and poplar that spread eastward into boot-sucking muskeg veined by fast-moving rivers that tied together hundreds of icy lakes.

Hallowell exchanged looks with one distinguished-looking old-timer. In his threadbare broadcloth suit and shirt buttoned to the neck, the man stood out. Under a shock of white hair, his dark eyebrows and scraggly mustache gave him the look of a Chinese sage. Chief Willie Berens was sixty-five years old and for twenty-three years already he had served as headman of the Berens River Ojibwa, whose traditional hunting grounds lay some fifty miles upstream in western Manitoba. The son of an Indian father and a white mother, Berens had an Indian name—*Sailing Low in the Air After Thunder.*

They struck up a conversation and Hallowell was sufficiently impressed to note in his diary, "very intelligent—excellent English." Before the steam whistle hastened him back on board, the two men had agreed to reconnect in six weeks.

Hallowell was in Canada that summer to resolve a research question that had nothing to do with Indian attitudes about nature. Did Ojibwa men prefer to marry their uncles' or their aunts' daughters, whom anthropology classifies as their cross-cousins? Shortly into their second visit, Chief Berens answered that in a hurry: "Who the hell else would they marry?" Then he mentioned an Ojibwa Indian village that lay even deeper in the Manitoba outback. Its inhabitants still survived off the land and still practiced old ways. He'd been born there, but he hadn't been back for forty years. Was Hallowell interested?

Their trip took a few years to materialize, but in early summer 1932, Berens and his entourage stashed provisions, trade goods and Hallowell in four canoes that were powered by four-to-five-horsepower "kickers." Pushing off from the mouth of the Pigeon, they chugged against the current on a two-week journey that would cover about 260 miles and lead them to Lake Pikangikum and Berens's ancestral home.

Between 1930 and 1940, Hallowell chalked up seven field trips to south-central Canada. Even on this first journey, however, he was smart enough to let the Indians take charge. As the fish-processing plants, trading posts and Christian missions of Lake Winnipeg faded out of sight, they entered a vastness of waterways and forests that for them was full of life.

Hallowell noticed that they rarely referred to the environment in general terms; their vocabulary called for a high degree of specificity. The more than thirty separate ways of describing a lake, for instance, fell into two categories. Some stressed sensory attributes, such as degrees of silt or even flavor, features that evoked lakes as receptacles of external influences. But a second group of descriptors drew upon more innate properties, such as their shape, orientation and inner clarity. Here they seemed to be describing beings whose personal nature emerged from within.

When the Indians spoke among themselves in low voices, this sort of verbal precision helped them navigate a network of unpredictable waterways under a sky that brought uncertain weather. It wasn't maps or compasses, but descriptive phrases, place-names, oft-told stories and personal experiences that provided their bearings. In the first hundred miles between the lake port and Willie Berens's main camp at Little Grand Rapids, Hallowell counted upward of fifty rapids, hairpin turns, intersecting lakes and hull-scraping shallows around which they had to portage supplies and canoes.

Each had its proper name, and the Indians recalled them in unvariable sequences, as if they were stepping-stones on habitual journeys. Some place-names, or toponyms, provided word pictures for features of landscape that led hunters to promising beaver or deer areas. Taken altogether, they amounted to "mental maps" that came to life only, as the Indians put it to Hallowell, "place by place."

Stories anchored these place-names in memory. One told of a string of old women who were stationed at a series of way stations, each one dispensing advice about how best to travel to the next leg of the journey, which would end with another old woman who provided tips for how to reach the next, and so forth, until the trip was done. Similar life lessons were embedded in stories of the Ojibwa trickster Wisakachek. One described him with his head wedged inside a bear's skull. As he blindly staggered through the forest, banging into a succession of different trees, he asked each for its proper name, thus offering an entertaining way for teaching botany to Ojibwa youngsters.

The farther Hallowell got upstream, the more he noticed how the white man's ways of marking time melted away. "As we ascended the river," he wrote later, "the hours soon disappeared, since I was the only person who carried a watch and it soon stopped." The old importance of named weekdays, a free weekend or a solemn Sunday was left behind. One man had brought an alarm clock from the trading post, but on the trip it became a plaything, almost like a pet; once you wound it up, who knew when it might go off?

Instead of using mechanical aids and non-Indian designations for tracking time, Hallowell's companions observed the sun, moon and stars. A "day" was counted when there was light, a "night" when it was dark— although "sleeps" was the more common expression. For gradations of illumination in between, Algonquian vocabulary offered the same specificity that it delivered for "lake." Among the seven intervals that fell before noon, for instance, there was "first sunlight," and then "before [the sun] coming out from the trees," when your eyes began making things out. Next was "red shining [reflected light]," when tree branches were first backlit, and so on.

Longer spans were cued to risings and fallings of the moon, each pegged to named seasons that were linked to the behaviors of natural phenomena, such as the "arriving" of birds, "falling" of snow, "melting" of ice, the "appearing" or "falling" of leaves. And announcing those lunar durations were expressive behaviors to which the Indians stayed alert—the "first"rumblings of thunder during spring moon, the "first" snow of autumn moon.

An outsider like Hallowell took awhile to acclimatize to this way of "seeing" what might otherwise present itself as a repetitive, impersonal wilderness. And that was only the beginning. Next he had to meet the larger forces who were truly in charge.

They were traveling upriver during a season when, without warning, storms swept down upon the lakes. A clap of thunder snapped Hallowell's friends to readiness; they looked around and asked each other: What was just said? In their interpretation of reality, these were conversations among the great thunderbirds, messengers of the Four Winds, generally referred to as the Thunders. It helped to eavesdrop on them—they might be intending to turn placid waters into dangerous chop, drown your boat or tear your campsite to pieces.

These men were always sniffing for signs of the landscape's state of mind, assessing the motivations of forces beyond and behind the merely observable. They practiced what is called "scrying," for instance, scrutinizing the clean waters for readings on the whereabouts of lost items, the location of game, the dangers of hidden enemies or evil spirits. Checkered riffles on a lake's surface indicated dangerous crosscurrents, but also conveyed something else. High-pitched whining in the treetops suggested a storm in the offing, but another message might be coming across as well. They monitored these abrupt shifts the way Hallowell had read the changing expressions on his professors' faces back in Philadelphia. What did this portend; how should one prepare?

Up in Canada, Chief Willie Berens was his professor. He taught Hallowell that the winds were four brothers, each with a distinctive personality and sense of purpose. East Wind was the eldest. After his birth he swore, "I shall be fairly kind to human beings." Second to arrive was South Wind, who blew in from where the migrating souls of deceased Ojibwa ended up. He, too, had a promise. "I'll be very good and treat human beings well," he said. West Wind was not so genial. "I'll be a little rough," he warned, but reassuringly added, "I'll never be wicked." As for the last born,

North Wind, "I'll have no mercy," he declared outright. Rather than fatal-istically accepting these warnings, the Ojibwa learned how to soften them. During ferocious windstorms, when the lakes kicked up, they tossed pinches of tobacco to the North Wind to temper his roaring.

Cardinal directions were not regarded as fixed, abstract points. Instead, the Indians talked about the "homes" of those Wind Brothers, general lo-cations you spoke about only during specific situations. Safe passage up the river's twists and turns was dictated by the mood swings of these living, sentient beings. Traveling this way was less like instrumental navigation and more like picking your way through a rough town on Saturday night.

When Hallowell later recalled their boats pulling at last into the iso-lated Ojibwa community of Willie Berens's birth, he could not resist set-ting the memory within one of the oldest scenarios in anthropological literature, the "trope of arrival." The scholar pulls into a South Pacific beach or a New Guinea valley to discover an isolated, "un-Christianized" native culture (inevitably described as "Stone Age") going about its business as if untouched by the wider world. Later on, Hallowell regretted underplaying how this Lake Pikangikum community had already been influenced by broader economic and cultural forces; his writings would deliberately add the impact of fur traders, Christian missionaries and Canadian govern-ment agents. And he would also remind readers how their different sense of time did not prevent Ojibwa from marking what non-Indians desig-nated as "historical events"—changes in control of inherited hunting tracts, arrivals of white traders or missionaries, or devastating diseases they had suffered over the previous century.

For now, however, he was entranced. The romance of an explorer coming upon a native enclave that seemed to be caught in a time capsule took over:

> The inland Indians were still living in birchbark-covered dwellings and except for their clothing, utensils, and canvas canoes, one could easily imagine oneself in an encampment of a century or more be-fore. Women were mending nets, chopping and hauling wood, and stitching the birchbark covers for their dwellings with spruce

roots . . . scraping and tanning skins for making moccasins, for this article of clothing was used by everyone, although rubbers, purchased at the trading post, might be worn over them. Babies were still snugly strapped to their cradleboards on their mothers' backs. . . . Sphagnum moss, so intimately associated with them because the Indians had discovered its highly absorbent and deodorant properties, could be seen drying in the sun in almost every camp. Evidence of the importance of fish at this season was everywhere. . . . One net I saw lifted in the middle of July at Lake Pikangikum comprised 30 whitefish, a dozen tullibees, several suckers, and a half dozen other fish of different varieties. Fish caught in the morning and scaled, gutted, and split lengthwise, could be seen being cured in the sun before being prepared for eating in the evening. Other fish were being lightly smoked on a rack for longer preservation. Berries were picked by the women and children. As for the men, they were relatively idle but some, at Island lake, were to be seen making snowshoe frames or canoe paddles. There was frequent dancing on specially prepared ground, sometimes within a cagelike superstructure such as that used for the *Wabanowiwin*. . . . At night the beat of a water-drum often reverberated in one's ears. . . .

A measure of this community's "traditional" status was that they still hunted and fished for their food. This hunting and gathering way of life possibly harkened back to the Pleistocene, along with the native worldview that supported it. Once subarctic Indians grew dependent on trading posts and hunting animals for furs, an irreversible line was crossed, and few tribes ever looked back.

Central to Ojibwa metaphysics, as Hallowell learned at Lake Pikangikum, was maintenance of relationships with those invisible authorities whom he could not see. The practical skills of learning to stalk, to make and maintain gear, to skin and process wild foods, were de rigueur; but that was only half their education, and his. Into Hallowell's head was already planted a phrase that Professor Frank G. Speck, his mentor at the University of Pennsylvania, had formulated out of his studies of Indians in Maine and Labrador. This business of hunting, Speck insisted, was a "holy occupation." Here in the Manitoba outback Hallowell learned what that meant.

When referring to their belief that one animal or spirit enjoyed authority over their kind, the Ojibwa themselves used the word "boss," meaning "owners of nature." These "bosses" held sway over parcels of hunting or trapping land; if one wanted to eat, one dealt with them. Within each Ojibwa family's or kin-group's hunting territory, which might cover ninety square miles, lived a similar animal family. Much as Willie Berens functioned as his band's leader, each animal group had its boss. To respectful Indians they handed over their moose, beaver, fox and rabbit. Even birch trees had their boss, who gave of his kind to the axman who treated them properly.

The effective hunter or trapper was not only adept at keeping quiet and covering his prints and scent, but he also should avoid cruelty, kill cleanly and not insult the animal's remains. The bones of aquatic mammals were returned to the water. The noses of bears were hung on peeled spruce, tobacco was offered to their carcasses and then their skulls were hooked on tree limbs, their bones elevated above reach of dogs. During the fall trapping that ended with the first freeze, throughout the winter season that closed with the spring cawing of crows and over the moons of summer fishing and socializing, the successful Ojibwa hunter transacted with every boss beyond the campfire. Hallowell soon realized that these were actually social relationships, which were conducted over the generations under an ethic of reciprocity. Of course, humans were fallible and broke rules and behaved selfishly, but that probably explained why they got sick, or why muskrat or porcupines became scarce in a given year.

Some residents of Lake Pikangikum also practiced a kind of communication with what Hallowell's own culture considered the toughest nuggets of nonconsciousness—*rocks*. Whereas the German philosopher Edmund Husserl argued that "when we perceive a rock what we perceive are really our own perceptions; the rock remains forever beyond our ken in its own inwardness," the Ojibwa saw some rocks as reaching out *to them*. In her book of essays *Teaching a Stone to Talk*, the American environmental writer Annie Dillard described a hermit named Larry trying to coax a stone to speak; the Ojibwa turned it the other way around: rocks showed *them* how to communicate.

Tramping over naked patches where forest fires had cleared the brush, Hallowell noticed the stony understory, and during heavy lifting over portages the "huge, sloping, glacier-smoothed boulders." Tumbled over aeons to globular form, the rocks of Manitoba are among the geologically oldest in North America. Like the Thunders, the Ojibwa recognized a few of them as "grandfathers." Potential containers of life and power, they were inhabited by small humanoids for whom their surfaces opened and closed like doors. The medium through which one learned which rocks contained such personalities and powers was the dream. What the Ojibwa saw in their sleep reigned supreme. Whether one's "dream visitors" (*pawaganak*) were animal, vegetable or mineral, what they did or said carried personal meaning.

While asleep Willie Berens's great-grandfather, a famous shaman named Yellow Legs, learned of his powerful rock. It was the size of a watermelon and lay on Egg Island in the middle of Lake Winnipeg. After his dream he told two men to check it out. From the shoreline, as Yellow Legs quoted his dream, they should follow bear tracks leading to the rock which lay under some broken branches. When his scouts canoed to the island, it was just as he had described, and they returned with the rock. Thereafter he used it in Medicine Lodge rituals. Upon tapping its "mouth" with a new knife, the rock opened wide enough for him to insert his fingers and pull out medicine. During one portage between Popular Narrows and Pikangikum, Hallowell inspected such a "living" rock. An oblong boulder known as "our grandfather's rock," it had been revealed to a medicine man years before, who carried it to this spot. Thereafter the location became a shrine where travelers left tobacco and other offerings.

Also at Lake Pikangikum, Hallowell met Alec Keeper, a man especially wise where such rocks were concerned. Giving Hallowell one stone belonging to his father, he warned the anthropologist to trap it in a tin box lest it flee of its own volition. And Keeper's son told about a dream of a deep lake where he had found another rock shaped like a turtle. "This made me believe I had been really blessed," the young man said. "You may not think this stone is alive, but it is." Whenever he lent it to the sick so they might cure themselves, by the next morning it was back in its leather case in his pocket. One exchange with Keeper seemed particularly revealing. Were *all* rocks alive? Hallowell asked. "No," the old medicine man answered, but then added, *"some were."*

Those that were alive might shoot through the air of their own accord, intending bodily harm. In Keeper's view, shooting stars were simply the spirits hurling bigger rocks at each other. "One time when we were traveling at night," he remembered, "we saw one of these great sparks falling towards the earth. We were approaching a big ridge and it seemed that the great spark was aimed directly at us. When it hit the ground we saw sparks fly upwards and we felt the earth shake much harder than when it thunders. No one ever finds such stones nowadays." Such an event might mark a man's life. Willie Berens's own father was named *Something Going Across the Sky,* after Halley's Comet, which made an appearance the year he was born.

And Hallowell heard of other superhuman forces in the neighborhood. Two other Brothers of the Four Winds lived nearby, the Great Hare, and Flint, a mean child who sliced his mother to pieces when he burst from her womb. Avenging her death, the Great Hare smashed his brother to bits, thereby scattering for the oldtime Ojibwa the first minerals they would chip into arrow and lance points. The river currents through which his Ojibwa ran their canoes were said to be the dwelling places of his shattered body.

Then there were the underwater manitou—beings who looked part snake, part fish and part lynx—and featured buffalolike horns of copper on their heads. Just as offerings were made to the Thunders for success at hunting geese or ducks, when one went fishing, one gave something to these submarine beings. The Ojibwa also told Hallowell of their Little People, the rock-dwelling folk whom hunters sometimes encountered in the bush; the frightening *windigo,* who possessed fellow tribesmen and turned them into skeletons made of ice that were ravenous for human flesh; and Mikinak, a turtle helper of Lake Pikangikum shamans, whose ability to transcend the normal bounds of time and space were witnessed by everyone during their Shaking Tent rituals.

Between his trips, Hallowell tried to put what he was learning into English words and scholarly explanations. His classes at the University of Pennsylvania had exposed him to nineteenth-century "armchair scholars," men like Sir Edward Tylor and Sir James Frazier, the grandfather figures of early folklore and anthropology. In their private libraries they had cross-referenced available writings by early explorers, missionaries and colonial administrators, creating what one author has described as "a motley assemblage of reports by a motley assemblage of authors." Far from the sites and scenes this material described, they compared "exotic" beliefs and pondered what they shared and how they had developed. To evaluate which were more or less "civilized," they created sequences from the simple to the complex, drew up criteria for grand schemes of cultural evolution and coined new terms for behavior such as respecting animal bones and leaving offerings to trees and talking about cardinal directions as if they were alive.

The oldest term for belief in more than one god, Polytheism, proved the least helpful. Once you plastered it onto a given community in order to differentiate it from a monotheistic religion like Judaism, Christianity or Islam, what did you really know? Somewhat of an improvement was Henotheism, which referred to belief systems in which multiple spiritual beings were arrayed in a hierarchy, with higher gods presiding over lesser ones, and reflected more accurately the divisions observed by the Ojibwa between animal bosses and their kind. But where to go from there? Neither label linked those spirit beings, and the invisible worlds in which they operated, to the tangible landscape of sea, earth and sky, as was at least suggested by another old term, Pantheism. Closer to the attitudes of Hallowell's Ojibwa friends, however, was Naturalism, which reflected the widespread tendency of societies throughout history to appeal to cosmic forces like the sun, moon, winds, sky, rivers and stars, and to the earth's natural denizens—rocks, trees, animals and so forth. It also had the virtue of avoiding the problem with Supernaturalism, a term that divorced spirits from rocks, trees and animals as well as from the land's human coinhabitants.

What ultimately won out was Animism. It was invented in 1871 by a tailor's son named Edward B. Tylor, who attained knighthood. From boyhood, Tylor was fascinated by what he saw as a universal belief in spirits. Like many of his generation, he was intrigued by traces of pagan Europe

that peeked out of Christian art and ritual, frequently evoking earth spirits, which often were female.

To explain our waking memories of traveling long distances when
asleep, Tylor hypothesized, early humans came up with the idea of a spirit
"double." Upon the long sleep of death, this "soul" detached from the body
and became a wandering "spirit." Such was the origin of ancestor cults, he
argued, in which offerings, prayers and sacrifices transformed the dead
into new forms of eternal existence. Tylor thought that this evolved into a
general belief in spirits, so that "a cult of nature was established beside the
ancestor cult." Signs of inner life in nature, the movement of waters and
stars, the growth of plants and animals implied the presence of these "an-
imae," or indwelling spirits.

Then Tylor's colleague Richard R. Marett argued that it was less particular spirits and more a diffuse spiritual force, something like electricity,
which primitive peoples believed pervaded all of nature. In 1899 he advanced Animatism as a religious attitude, which predated Tylor's concept.
Yet animism won the day. Open a world atlas from forty years ago, and you
can find color-coded maps for the spread of religion: Hinduism predom-
inating in India; Buddhism in Japan; Christianity in Europe and South
America; Islam in North Africa; with animism covering great blotches of
sub-Saharan Africa, Southeast Asia, Australia and subarctic America.

Calling animism a "religion" and its peoples "followers" implied a
shared set of rituals and beliefs, but there was no universal creed, no set
congregations, no sacred history. The academic word distorted the count-
lessly different ways that villagers, herdsmen and hunters around the
globe articulated and coordinated their moral, aesthetic, spiritual and
practical concerns. Better to speak of religious "ways of life" and their ad-
herents as "members" of social groups whose beliefs were less optional
than those of any denomination or creed. You did not convert to them;
they were *who you were.*

For advice on how to talk more precisely about the nature of American Indian spirits, Hallowell sought out colleagues who had known Indians. From Philadelphia he took a weekly train to New York to attend
seminars with Columbia University's aging lion of anthropology, Franz
Boas. Boas distrusted Tylor's animism, Marett's animatism and most

other "isms" as the useless generalizations of overintellectualizing out-siders. Instead, he believed scholars should conduct on-site fieldwork and become "participant observers" of Indian life while they still had the chance. Then Hallowell was introduced to Gestalt psychology's concept of a "behavioral environment," which stressed how people were indoctri-nated into cultural ways of thinking that they themselves then projected into the wider world around them and which were henceforth considered as "natural" as rain or death.

Hallowell's closest adviser remained the University of Pennsylvania's eccentric "Indian man," Professor Speck. No sooner had Hallowell knocked on Speck's door on College Hall's fourth floor than he smelled it: pipe to-bacco, sweet grass, smoked hides. Everything inside the office whispered "Indian"—woven baskets on top shelves, fish traps on the floor, snow-shoes propped up against the corner, leather-bound books and tattered monographs about Indians strewn about, even a native secretary by the door. A squat, impatient fellow, Speck worked throughout the 1920s with Algonquian speakers and produced classic studies on a half dozen tribes. Hallowell soaked up Speck's stories and remembered him as "always ex-tolling the sovereign virtues of the Indian, and proclaiming the intrinsic virtues of their culture." Like Boas, Speck urged Hallowell to try to de-scribe the world as the Ojibwa themselves made sense of it.

After shuttling between Philadelphia and Manitoba for a decade, it was time for Hallowell to publish his material. Of Ojibwa beliefs about the universe, he wrote in 1934, "This animistic conception is the fundamental dogma in their philosophy." But a few years later he confessed frustration. Ojibwa thinking processes might be animistic, but "it would caricature the beliefs of these people to assert that a spirit lurks in every rock, or that they believed that every stone has a soul." By 1942, he was ready to jettison such notions altogether: "Neither animism in its classical formulation nor ani-matism is the unequivocal foundation of [American Indian] belief."

In a series of pithy essays, produced between the 1940s and 1960, he drew upon his memories of Willie Berens's people. To explain how the Ojibwa imagination "constructed" their natural environment, he dusted off a nineteenth-century German term, *Weltanschauung,* which translated as "worldview." Hallowell redefined it as "the cluster of assumptions and images that a given society shared about the nature of reality."

A worldview worked in two ways: first, it provided members with a more or less static picture of how the whole cosmos was ordered. For Christians, for example, this meant a three-tiered cosmos: hell, earth and heaven; for the Delaware Indians whom Speck had studied it meant a twelve-layered cosmos. But a worldview also told human beings how best and properly to behave within that cosmos, so as to enhance one's possibility of success. It activated their "intimacy with the universe" and outlined the responsibilities that went with it. Within and around the land, rivers, sky and cosmic directions that constituted their "behavioral environment," the Ojibwa envisioned a host of living entities whose actions they might decipher, predict and even influence. Animals, stones, trees, shells and other aspects of environment and climate could be self-aware, autonomous and willful beings (*manitou*) who possessed their own traits and predispositions.

Old Keeper's comment that *some* stones might be alive suggested that to the Ojibwa reality was fluid and circumstantial. The successful hunter and power seeker kept his options open. An aspect of one's environment could shift form at any moment, act unusually, reach out for one's attention and reveal its hidden identity. Stones might speak, lightning could strike from a cloudless sky and the winds might kick up from a weird direction. Through this force field of subjective actions, one maneuvered with caution.

To evoke how these beings were understood by the Ojibwa, Hallowell came up with a replacement for animism. His phrase was "other-than-human person."

It wasn't a cure for cancer, but it was more than a trick of hyphens and reversals of logic. Unlike scientific terms, the ordinary words of Hallowell's phrase lured you in. You thought you understood the "other-than-human" part before that word "person" burst open, exposing you to new possibilities of existence. The phrase clarified and dignified Ojibwa thought. Thunders were "other-than-human persons." So might be beavers, muskrats, porcupines, trees, rocks, clouds and lakes. With such beings one must coexist and transact, much as one did with human "persons." Their feelings were easily hurt, so one must keep on one's toes. By means of soft speech and sweet smoke, one sought their aid and goodwill. When Hallowell stopped projecting his culture's classifications, he came closer to communicating what the Ojibwa meant when they asked, "What did the thunder say?"

Theirs was a world in which sympathy, dependency and reciprocity bound human beings to plants, animals, rocks and stars. And thus they became beings rather than objects, fellows rather than things, and members of a circle of social relations. In some areas the idea of this broader society persists, as suggested in 1990 by a Cree to the east of Lake Winnipeg named Chief Robbie Dick. He was explaining Cree resistance to eviction from their northern Quebec village by the James Bay Hydro-Quebec dam. "It's very hard to explain to white people what we mean by 'Land is part of our life,'" Dick said, facing the certain loss of the wetlands where Indians had hunted and trapped for more than five thousand years. "We're like rocks and trees."

HILLS OF HIDDEN MEANING

Choctaw

One Saturday about a dozen years ago, some of my students at the University of Wisconsin walked up and down the wings of a large bird; they looked like barnstormers inching along the wings of old-fashioned biplanes at a county fair. We had to obtain special permission for this exercise, since the bird was frozen in flight within the sequestered compound of the Mendota Mental Health Institute across the lake from our Madison campus.

They were measuring the earthen sculpture of a flying creature that had been shaped from basketfuls of dirt about a thousand years ago by unknown Indians. Now slumped with age and softened by grass, its wingspan, the students finally determined, extended for about 640 feet. Driving about an equal distance to the north would have let them trace a man crafted from mounded earth who, from his feet to his horned headdress, stood more than 200 feet tall. And on a plowed field some fifty-five miles to the west, they could have measured the wings of an even bigger bird that spread for a quarter mile.

The meanings behind the American Indian creations known variously as mounds, *tumuli* or earthworks remain elusive, but their locations are not. Across the eastern half of the United States one can visit the largest collection of sacred constructions produced by any societies in the world. From the Canadian border to the mouth of the Mississippi, from the eastern Plains to the spine of the Appalachians, thousands of American earthworks keep their secrets in our fields, woods and backyards. And they represent a fraction of the many more that have been obliterated by farming, industrial development and urbanization. These American Indian "figured landscapes" represent another kind of symbolized geography, one that reshaped nature in order to express cosmological beliefs and to choreograph community rituals.

The mounds our students recorded that afternoon belonged to a particular midwestern tradition that has been labeled "effigy mounds." For hundreds of miles all around Madison, across southern Wisconsin, eastern Iowa, eastern Minnesota and northern Illinois, other members of this menagerie still prowl the woods and bluffs: panthers, turtles, bears, wolves, deer and beaver (along with other less decipherable shapes). By constructing these effigy mounds between A.D. 600 and 1100, natives of the American Midwest shaped their environments to reflect their beliefs. Exactly what beliefs remains the big question.

Effigy mounds are best appreciated from a small airplane. Looking down at the bird, panther and bear forms that our students outlined with degradable lime made it easier to understand how the unusual topography of the Madison isthmus, formed by two lakes (Mendota and Menona), almost joined at the waist with fresh streams gushing in from all sides, provided a desirable congregating site for both Late Woodland period Indians and their spirits.

Circling over that big bird, I noticed something else. Under the shelter of its right wing flew a smaller bird, too small for a mate, perhaps an offspring. And alongside it stood a residential treatment unit for the state's most brutalized children—a safe house our students were told to avoid. My imagination conjured up that big flier still meeting some ancient responsibility, protecting its young and ours at the same time.

In Wisconsin alone, claim the state's premier earthwork scholars, Robert Birmingham and Leslie Eisenberg, two to three thousand of these oversized effigies were raised on the land. Often they were just elements within the state's nine hundred mound clusters, in which one might also find older types of conical (often enclosing ritualized burials) and linear (possibly for delineating ceremonial space) earthworks—amounting to more than fifteen thousand mounds all told. And almost invariably they were positioned on prime real estate: river or lake overlooks or hills with great views over the tree canopy of the lakes beyond and approaching storms.

Rather like the method for scarifying the flesh of initiates into secret societies, it is conjectured that the Indians began these mounds with an incision. Possibly their makers trenched out a "reverse cameo" of the effigy, which for a spell was left naked to the sky, allowing for the rituals that readied its body for new growth. By filling in this outline with excavated or even imported substances—a ceremonial hearth of rocks, perhaps a burial or two, ash and charcoal, and soils that may have been chosen for their color value—what was negative space became positive. Dirt from the immediate surroundings was heaped up and shaped. And as scar tissue heals over and lumps up if ash is rubbed into the cut, so did the mound's form grow into an organic part of the landscape.

Effigy mounds that enclose human burials usually don't contain the sorts of exotic grave offerings associated with high-status individuals. This observation causes some scholars to look elsewhere to explain their significance. Did they represent protective "dream animals" for individuals, as Winnebago Indians suggested to ethnomusicologist Frances Densmore? Were they the insignia or "property marks" of particular totemic clans, as others told anthropologist Paul Radin? Or did they project upon the earth a cosmic social system of which human beings were only a part, or were they "corporate monuments of, for, and to clanship"? Following this line of thought, others propose that the creatures reflect a moiety system of social organization in which all creatures are assigned to either an Earth or Sky division of the universe or imagine them as members of a tripartite cosmos associated with the most appropriate Water, Earth or Sky levels of the world.

Yet another interpretation views mound complexes as spectacular ritual grounds where mortuary ceremonies honored the dead and ensured their continued existence in the hereafter. But they also could have served as immense arenas for resisting the demise of whole societies, especially during those uneasy moments, such as equinoxes or eclipses, when celestial bodies seemed to stand perilously still or even to disappear.

When anthropologist Edmund Carpenter made the case to me that earthworks were indeed ceremonial grounds, he harkened to one of America's most artistically compelling mounds. Located four hundred miles southeast of Madison, just outside Locust Grove, Ohio, the Great Serpent Mound writhes across a velvety green park. Its body is twelve hundred feet long; in its open jaws rests an egglike oval. Traces of two smaller elevations sticking from the head portion may represent horns, possibly identifying it as the "horned serpent" that figures in stories from a range of tribes. Conceivably, the great snake represented a clan or group ancestor; perhaps renewal ceremonies took place on or around it. Carpenter suggested that social groups might have moved in solemn procession from the serpent's tail until arriving at the head. There the celebrants "reversed" direction—perhaps during a solstice or equinox, when the seasons likewise turned around—and headed downward again, to be symbolically reborn and renewed for another annual cycle.

Proposing mound arrangements as prosceniums for what theater scholar Richard Schechner calls "performances of great magnitude" is reinforced by recent speculations about a second Indian tradition for molding sacred landscapes from the ground. To the southeast of Wisconsin, across five thousand square miles of central Ohio, one finds the remnants of earthen berms, some of them uncommonly large, which are shaped into circles, octagons, squares and long straight lines.

They were constructed between about 200 B.C. and A.D. 400 by an early Indian society we have named after a farmer, Mordecai Cloud Hopewell, whose property first yielded this culture's distinctive burial goods. Most spectacular of the ten thousand mounds produced by Hopewell people are sites that pair circles and squares, a configuration which is repeated in some dozen locations. Of massive size and geometrical precision, a number are still discernible in the midst of contemporary golf courses, county fairgrounds and cemeteries.

Ever since their discovery in the late eighteenth century, these earthworks have sparked outlandish theories. Indians lacked the skills to make them, it was said; they were built by early settlers, lost Phoenicians or Welshmen, wandering Jews or space aliens. More plausible were nineteenth-century speculations that the miles of Hopewellian dirt walls and accompanying moats, especially those that enclosed "citadels" on hilltop sites, served as defensive fortifications. But the case for forts was weakened when the moats proved to lie *inside* the walls, and when archaeologists found little evidence of weaponry, hacked bones or hasty burials.

More likely, according to former National Park Service director Roger

G. Kennedy, to older ceremonial enclosures were added, over time, stone walls and pavements, timber stockades with interwoven branches that helped to heighten the sanctity of what the Greeks called a *temenos,* or ritual enclosure. Expansions of sacred space and zones for ritual practice on an oversized scale are increasingly the interpretative frameworks we hear applied to Hopewell earthworks.

Although scholars have agreed for years that American Indians designed these landscapes, only recently have they realized that their construction was governed by at least two regularities. At sites like Newark, Circleville, High Banks and Seal, Ohio Valley architects, whom Kennedy characterizes as "geomancers," created uniform diameters for their perfect circles at around 1,050 feet. About the same dimensions went for their giant squares, to which the circles were usually attached.

The second regularity came to light when physicists tested the presumed solar alignments of a number of Hopewell sites. The mathematicians learned, instead, that the circles and squares revealed fairly precise lunar observations. Moreover, the Newark site's eight alignments were made throughout the 18.6-year moon cycle, which suggested a well-planned observation program over time.

Further interpretation of the Hopewell circle-and-square configurations remains open. Were they built to metaphorically represent "houses" for different social populations during group rituals, with the circular spaces assigned to locals and their kin and the square shapes allotted to outsiders and potential enemies, with whom, however, one might form marriage alliances? Or were the rites that took place within these paired geometrical precincts complementary and conducted by different social halves, or moieties, *within* the community? And is it possible that these forms are grandiose precursors of the more modest, summer-use "square grounds" and winter-use circular "town houses," which stood side by side in southeastern Indian villages during the later historic period, and for which we have rich documentation?

More grounded, however, is another thesis regarding Hopewell sacred geography. About ten years ago, Dr. Bradley Lepper, an archaeologist with the Ohio Historical Society, began to speculate, from clues on neglected nineteenth-century maps, that the ceremonies of the Hopewell people took place not only in and around specific circle-and-square sites, but also *between* them.

Looking for likely arteries between these constructions, Lepper focused on one that he called the Great Hopewell Road. It ran for about sixty miles, roughly paralleled the Scioto River, and linked the prominent monuments of Newark in the north and Chillicothe to the south. Lepper's research into early cartography that depicted the Hopewell mounds also revealed "alleys" or "avenues" created by earthen walls. At the Portsmouth site, for instance, near the mound of the Scioto River, parallel embankments extended from a series of crescents and circles across the Ohio River and into Kentucky for about twenty miles. Might these have been part of a well-organized Hopewellian "public works" project? But the extensions that particularly caught Lepper's eye were a six-mile stretch that ran south of the Newark site, and early mention of an additional twenty-four-mile segment.

But a third regularity that Lepper now identified was the fairly constant two-hundred-foot interval between the borders of this "road"— about the width of a six-lane freeway, which he now called the Hopewellian Sacred Way. At intervals along this arrow-straight route he discovered other earth-made features, which conceivably could have served as wayside shrines, much like the *heraduras* known to religious pilgrims in Spain, where pilgrims rest or perform rites along their symbolic journeys.

Confirmation of this sixty-mile *via sacra* awaits further investigation. But scholars have postulated that these earthworks and the possible roads connecting them orchestrated formal ways for entire communities or social groups to transport supplies and tribute. Or they served as thoroughfares for exchanges between sacred centers of nonmaterial goods: symbols, ritual communications or wives. And perhaps they were also pathways for those "performances of great magnitude" in which entire communities celebrated the demise of leaders, or the movements of celestial or cosmic forces, in order to secure seasonal fertility for their gardens.

Less mystery and fewer questions are attached to a third earthwork tradition that covers the greatest geographical range of them all. Up and down America's midsection one can visit the remains of "platform mounds," which supported chiefly residences and "sacred fire" temples attended by priesthoods. Some were built during Late Woodland times. But most were arranged around geometric plazas to create "rurban" centers (communities that blend the features of the rural and urban) during the burst of cultural growth that lasted from A.D. 800 to 1200 and is known as the Mississippian Tradition. These mounds enclosed burials, allowed leaders to gaze down upon the throng and elevated priests closer to their principal deity, the sun.

Settlements that reflect this general Mississippian civic plan are so wide-spread that I could visit the remains of one of their earliest town squares in southern Wisconsin and then take a three-day drive to the last of them to survive, about fourteen hundred miles to the south, near the Gulf of Mexico. But in another example of early scholarly reluctance to credit North American Indians with sophisticated lifestyles, that northern outpost was not attributed to them initially. The fortified Wisconsin site we know as Aztalan was named because it was considered the limit of Aztec expansion. Enamored of Baron Alexander von Humboldt's theory of a correspondence between Mexican Aztec pyramids and North American mounds, an amateur archaeologist named Nathaniel F. Hyer adopted the nobleman's title for a mythical Mexican homeland that was said to lie somewhere to the north.

Situated alongside Wisconsin's Crawfish River, at the outpost Hyer called Aztalan you can conjure up a detachment of Indians dispatched to thankless duty on the Mississippian world's frozen frontier. This image is partly supported by the fact that in its heyday, around A.D. 1300, the twenty-one acres that compose Aztalan were surrounded by a stockade made of upright logs that were probably interwoven with saplings, then plastered with clay. At intervals of about eighty feet stood log watchtowers. What were they afraid of? is a question often asked. But one might also wonder, what were they protecting? What were the key symbols that were so important to this community, and which differentiated it from a transitory hunting camp?

Part of an answer may be found in Aztalan's principal flat-topped mounds, which archaeologists tell us were raised layer by layer over successive years, and part may lie in the conical-mound burial of a well-to-do Aztalan woman, whose body was wrapped in a mortuary shroud sewn from nearly two thousand perforated shell beads. For if you head south, to the site that has been labeled the "Leviathan" of Mississippian culture, you find similar examples of both multiple-staged building projects and high-status burials in abundance.

Comparisons may be odious, as Cervantes wrote, but when it comes to impressing Americans with the largest civic footprint that any Indian culture has imposed on North America, it is hard to resist them. I am referring to Cahokia, a Mississippian metropolis of roughly twenty thousand native citizens that thrived a thousand years ago on about six square miles of an East St. Louis suburb in southwestern Illinois. It was named by early French visitors after a subtribe of the local Illini Indian tribe, whom they found living in the vicinity in the late 1600s. Cahokia generates a stream of comparisons and analogies because, I suspect, we have no alternative when filling the void of what we can learn about a place of such overwhelming significance in its day. This is true of other archaeological sites, but it is especially maddening to think of all we will never know about Cahokian society—the tangle of kinship allegiances, religious pomp and devotion, sociopolitical commitments, key personalities and subsistence habits that mobilized an Indian citizenry to develop this spot as their religious capital for three times as long as the United States has claimed sovereignty over North America.

Cahokia was probably the Mississippian world's economic hub and spiritual nerve center. Its estimated 120 earthen mounds required the digging, loading, transporting and dumping of an estimated 50 million cubic feet of earth that were carried by laborers in baskets that weighed up to 60 pounds each. The city's size rivaled that of Paris in the same period. The major, central mound was the largest precontact earthwork in North America; its scale surpasses that of Egypt's Great Pyramid. Its 21 million cubic feet of earth are the equivalent of six of today's oil tankers. Erected in fourteen stages over about three hundred years (circa A.D. 900 to 1200), eventually it stood as tall as a ten-story building, on a base that was larger than a modern New York City block, and supported a wooden temple or royal residence on its summit that ran more than a hundred feet long.

Within Cahokia's city limits thrived a population twice as dense as that of Los Angeles County. The two-mile-long stockade protecting its sacred precinct was reconstructed four times and required, all told, an estimated eighty thousand logs. Cahokia's five circles of large, evenly spaced upright skinned trees, known as woodhenges, probably served as solar horizon calendars that marked solstices, equinoxes and the proper times for planting and harvesting corn, and possibly they functioned to align new earthworks as well.

Among the three hundred burials found within one ridge-top mound at Cahokia was a high-status male laid out on a blanket woven with more than twenty thousand marine shell beads; beside him lay copper from the Great Lakes, mica from the southern Appalachian Mountains, and seven hundred freshly chipped arrow points, presumably for use in the afterlife. Although this dignitary was interred in the mid-tenth century, Indians would return to Cahokia to bury their dead in her mounds until 1700. In 1989, Cahokia was recognized as one of only three archaeological sites in the United States to enjoy recognition as a World Heritage Site by the United Nations. It is the largest and longest-lasting sacred landscape that was created by human hands north of Mexico, and we will never know its original name.

To the south, however, we can fill in some of the gap between an overload of measurements about these mounded landscapes and our inability to know how human beings used them. Not all the tribes of this Mississippian culture dispersed after the droughts, overpopulation and depletion of natural resources that saw most of them abandon the sprawling middle-western plain known as the American Bottom in the mid-thirteenth century. Many of the survivors reconstituted themselves into the historical tribes we still recognize today: Cherokee, Choctaw, Creeks and the others encountered by Hernando de Soto in 1540.

But at least one pocket of mound-building and sun-worshipping Mississippians survived. Along the lower Mississippi River, not far from the subtropical habitat where marking the landscape with earthworks fifteen centuries earlier reached epic proportions at a site called Poverty Point, a chiefdom of nine towns continued to maintain a remarkably intact way of life right into the eighteenth century. We know them as the Natchez.

When French missionaries first arrived in Louisiana and visited the wattle-and-daub cabins and formal plazas of the Natchez in spring 1700, they saw priests and nobles who could have stepped out of the pictures engraved into the famous Black Drink cups that were fashioned from large Gulf of Mexico conch shells and which were uncovered by Harvard University from the Mississippian-period mounds of Spiro in eastern Oklahoma. Resplendent in full-body tattoos, copper jewelry, turkey-feather capes and headdresses, they descended the stepped ramps of low earthworks to show the foreigners around town.

Our ability to visualize flesh-and-blood Natchez coexisting with their temple mounds is a result of the two-volume *Histoire de la Louisiane,* which was written and illustrated by a Dutch-born engineer named Antoine-Simon Le Page du Pratz. As is the case with many Euro-Americans who have written about American Indians over the centuries, Le Page du Pratz had his unsung native collaborator, a nobleman by the name of *Olabalke-biche,* or "Tattooed Serpent." As principal war chief, he held a position that was second only to that of his eldest brother, the nation's overlord. The insult of being temporarily held captive by the French in 1716 did not harden Tattooed Serpent against them; for nine years his diplomacy helped to keep the lid on degenerating relations between the two peoples.

In early 1720, two years after Le Page du Pratz first landed at Mobile Bay, he moved to southeastern Mississippi and purchased from the Natchez a cabin, four hundred acres of tobacco fields and some slaves. Among them was a Chitimacha Indian woman, perhaps stolen in war, who became his ward and possibly his mistress. He met her friends, became conversant in Natchez and close friends with Tattooed Serpent.

During four years of relative peace, Tattooed Serpent invited the Frenchman to sacred pipe ceremonies, showed him the community's holy Osage orange tree and explained his people's unusual social system. And forty years after the death of the French Sun King back in Versailles, Le Page du Pratz enjoyed an audience with Tattooed Serpent's eldest sibling, the Natchez high chief who was known as the Great Sun.

Thanks to Le Page du Pratz's writings on the tribe, later anthropology would add a new form of social stratification to the world's roster of how humans organize ourselves. At the apex was the Great Sun himself as well as his select group of wives and immediate relatives. Next came the tier of high nobles, followed by lesser nobles, or "honored men," under whom stood commoners, who were known as Stinkards, and finally slaves, who were usually prisoners of war. What was unique about the Natchez class system, however, was its method of self-perpetuation. Upper-crust males *had* to "marry down," choosing mates from the Stinkard class. Since inheritance was through the female line, only certain offspring of mixed-class marriages might rise on the social ladder.

Mounds were an apt metaphor for this hierarchical structure. Wearing his swan-feather crown and borne by slaves on a litter, (his moccasins only allowed to touch woven mats), the Great Sun greeted *his* elder brother in the sky from the mound's summit every morning, whose elevation, it was said, enabled them to converse more easily. Balancing his divine power base was that of the priesthood, who occupied the community's other highest mound. After Le Page du Pratz gained Tattooed Serpent's confidence, he was led up to the fire temple mound at their Grand Village, near St. Catherine's Creek, a tributary of the Lower Mississippi. From the temple guardian he recorded the Natchez creation myth and the meanings of the sacred flame.

One can only imagine the pride with which Tattooed Serpent probably escorted Le Page du Pratz to another earthwork, only recently abandoned by his forebears. But it would have been hard for any of the French to miss Emerald Mound. Today one locates it about ten miles north of the present-day town of Natchez, near the beginning of the old Indian trade route that connected many river-bottom tribes to the faraway Tennessee Valley and that whites would transform into the Natchez Trace.

Some time after A.D. 1300, the Natchez took a second look at the promising hillock and saw an opportunity to improve on nature. Conscripting what had to have been many work gangs, the Natchez supervisors reshaped, graded and smoothened the natural loess into a raised plaza that ran for nearly 800 feet in length and a little over 230 feet in width—larger than two football fields. After the much earlier Poverty Point and Cahokia's central mound, the 35-foot-high Emerald complex—which Park Service director Kennedy once described in its present-day state as "untended, unexplained but astounding"—represents the third largest religious structure in North America.

At both ends of Emerald's eight-acre elevated platform, two additional temple mounds, sizable in their own right, were superimposed. Climbing up their ramped stairways, priests and ritual participants were lifted above the tree cover; in the distance they could even catch sight of the Mississippi. One of these constructions probably supported a temple with a sacred fire and attendants; the other perhaps housed the community's chieftain. While the compound was under construction and in use, between 1300 and 1600, the surrounding fields supported corn, beans and pumpkins.

The French honeymoon with the Natchez lasted less than four years. With a sinking heart, Le Page du Pratz watched his countrymen, clustered around Fort Rosalie on the bluffs of the Mississippi, attack his Indian friends in 1724. One year later, on June 1, 1725, illness overtook Tattooed Serpent. The funerary lamentations were overwhelming, as if his passing foreshadowed that of his nation. It was then that Le Page du Pratz watched what was possibly the last internment of a dignitary in an American Indian earthwork.

Four years later, as French encroachment on Natchez lands and rights reached the breaking point, the Great Sun led his Natchez warriors against them. Caught by surprise, Fort Rosalie was destroyed and hundreds were killed or captured. In furious retaliation, the French slaughtered most of the tribe. Within two years the Natchez as a people were no more.

Some Natchez escapees were harbored by the Chickasaw; others found shelter among Creeks and Cherokee. To their hosts, wrote anthropologist James Mooney, the Natchez were a breed apart, regarded with awe, "a race of wizards and conjurors." And as custodians of ancient knowledge, they led dances and brewed medicines. From an estimated population of at least four thousand in 1650, no full-blood Natchez were left by 1940, and only two individuals could still speak the language.

• • •

No American Indians construct full-size earth mounds today, but one tribe lives in the shadow of an earthwork that played a role in their history. To find them, you must leave Tattooed Serpent's burial mound in the Grand Village and head about 160 miles up the Natchez Trace. In the 1830s, with the encouragement of President Andrew Jackson, the U.S. government ordered the wholesale removal of the Choctaw tribe to new lands in the southern portion of Indian Territory, now the state of Oklahoma. But some Choctaw escaped removal and now live on Louisiana's Choctaw Indian Reservation.

Their cabins cluster near a Woodland period mound known as Nanih Waiya, which means "Leaning Mountain." When I scouted for the place, I got lost among Winston County's narrow, sandy lanes, which cut through thick underbrush. Ten miles southeast of the town of Noxapater (meaning "Dark Father") were warning signs that recent flooding had damaged the bridge across Nanih Waiya Creek. After pulling onto an unpaved driveway, I rapped on the door of a wooden house whose right wall was sinking into runny red dirt. The musical sounds of an unfamiliar language—Choctaw— went silent inside. Two men with bare feet and wearing coveralls stiff with motor oil stared at me, then broke into toothy grins when I leaned against the doorjamb in despair.

Once I'd followed their directions to the detour, the well-groomed mound was easy to find. Maintained by the state of Mississippi as a recreational rather than a historical or archaeological site, it abuts a rural mail route and adjoins a small park where non-Indians book their family-reunion picnics. The earthwork also stands only twenty miles from the hub of Mississippi Choctaw life, in Philadelphia, Mississippi. But local Indians visit the site only periodically, I was told, still wary of pickups bearing loaded-gun racks that seemed to materialize whenever unfamiliar dark faces showed up.

To the Choctaw, the earthwork is still gendered as "Great Mother." A wooden staircase leads twenty-two feet to the flattened summit. From there the glassy bayou waters reflect the splayed trunks of towering cypress and drooping foliage. The mound is not far from the merging of five

streams into the Pearl River, which drains the length of the lower Mississippi Valley before it empties near New Orleans. Until recently, white
farmers cultivated the mound nearly up to the summit. Still surrounded
by a patchwork of cornfields, one sees only an amputated remnant of its
former glory, when, shortly after the time of Christ, it overlooked an ensemble of plazas, mounds, moats and walls that extended for two miles.

In October 1540, Hernando de Soto's caravan of clanking wagons passed
a hundred miles northeast of the Great Mother. He burned down a nearby
Choctaw village and executed a thousand residents. By then the mound had
already been abandoned. The chronicler who first noted its spiritual importance was an Irish trader named James Adair. In the late 1760s he ascended a
structure he called *Nan-be Y-a*, the "Divine Hill, or Mount of God."

According to the Choctaw, the mound marked the end of a legendary
migration. At one time they had lived to the northwest, but population
growth, scarcity of game or weak soil forced them to find new homes.
Magical staff in hand, a man named Chahta led the migrants. Each night
he stuck his pole in the ground; each morning he inspected it. Whatever
direction it leaned, that way they headed.

For many months they traveled. One night, on a creek's western bank,
Chahta planted his pole and a heavy rain commenced. The next day, reports this version of the Choctaw migration narrative, "the staff had burrowed itself deeper in the ground and stood straight and tall." Chahta
proclaimed that the long-sought land of Nanih Waiya had been found.
"Here we would build our homes and a mound as the sacred burial spot
for our ancestors."

Some accounts have the Choctaw bearing a portable ossuary that contained the bones of important ancestors; perhaps they were the first to be
interred in Nanih Waiya. Europeans were fascinated by descriptions of
Choctaw "bone pickers," whose six-inch fingernails cleaned the meat off
rotting corpses to preserve their bones. Other stories tell of superhuman
inhabitants who were already living in the mound's vicinity and who soon
perished from disease. And one also hears that the Choctaw migrants were
led instead by two brothers, whose disagreement in the new land splintered the arrivals into the separate tribes we know as the Chickasaw and
Choctaw.

.   .   .

If only Choctaw stories ended there, but oral traditions are rarely tidy and uniform. For a second group of Choctaw narratives link Nanih Waiya to a different creation scenario. In an account narrated by Choctaw who were living in Louisiana in the 1930s, what was a man-made "mound" in the other stories becomes a natural "hill." Their narrative follows:

> In very ancient times, before men lived on earth, the hill was formed and from the topmost point a passage led down deep into the bosom of the earth. Later, when birds and animals lived, and the surface of the earth was covered with trees and plants of many sorts, and lakes and rivers had been formed, the Choctaw came forth through the passageway in *Nane chacha* [Nanih Waiya]. And from that point they scattered in all directions but ever afterwards remembered the hill from the summit of which they first beheld the light of the sun.

Some twists on this second story line describe all the major south-eastern tribes—Creeks, Cherokee and Chickasaw as well as Choctaw—emerging from this passageway. Like a newly born just out of a womb, their skins are damp with a protective film. Before heading for their destined homelands, they dry themselves on the hill's body. All but the Choctaw go elsewhere; their Mother mound says they must never leave her side.

Sometimes the inconsistencies of Indian chronicles hide deeper truths and subtler realities. Inside the caretaker's cabin near the picnic tables at Nanih Waiya park, I examined a hand-drawn map that provided directions to a *second site,* which is also named Nanih Waiya and lies about a mile and a half to the northeast. It was described as the "cave mound," to distinguish it from the "temple mound." Was this the location associated with the Creation myth of Choctaw origins, whereas the man-made mound only a few yards away was the site emphasized in their migration scenario?

One way to untangle the relationship between the two sites is to ask whether other aspects of Choctaw culture history reflect similar paradoxes and oscillations of identity. Names are a place to start. Although one finds general agreement that *nanih* means "mountain," interpretations of *waiya* conform to the different associations suggested by the two scenarios. To Choctaw scholar Muriel H. Wright, it meant "to produce," with the site's name translating as "mountain that produces." To others it meant "leaning," referring to the version of the migratory story of the leaning pole.

For the Choctaw of historical times, we have some evidence that the man-made mound had come to symbolize the bosom of their homeland, or as Choctaw writer Charles Roberts put it, "the center of the Choctaw universe." Faced with pressures to remove from the area, it was here at the old Nanih Waiya monument that the half-French, half-Choctaw leader named Greenwood LeFlore convened a grand council in 1828. Eventually the Choctaw signed the controversial Treaty of Dancing Rabbit Creek, which tossed most of the tribe on the road again. A glimpse of the emotional toll of this eviction comes from Choctaw writer W.E.S. Folsom-Dickerson. In his village the women "did not weep or mourn openly." But on the day of their departure, they "walked through their own beloved forests of oak and elm for the last time, and touched ever so gently the leaves of those trees which had sheltered them and their people for generations."

As for the Choctaw left behind in the vicinity of what they called "our good old mother mound," fewer than three hundred of them received any lands through the Dancing Rabbit Creek Treaty. On all sides they were hemmed in by white squatters who refused to move. After whites established the town of Philadelphia in the 1830s on the former Choctaw village location called Bull Frog Place, Indians were even less welcome. Some families quit the area to join fellow Choctaw in Oklahoma, where, out of nostalgia, they named their first tribal capital Nanih Waiya. By the turn of the century not more than fifteen hundred Choctaw remained in Mississippi.

With the clear-cutting of their old forests, including the Nanih Waiya tract, the holdouts had no choice but to find work as landless sharecroppers in cotton fields. When the influenza epidemic of 1918 swept the South, impoverished Choctaw were especially vulnerable. A federal delegation investigating their plight found most of the remnant Choctaw living illegally near the Nanih Waiya mound, "clinging hopefully," as a visiting folklorist put it, "to the legendary promise of protection."

To reach the second Nanih Waiya location, the so-called cave mound, I sought help from Kenneth H. Carleton, the tribe's archaeologist, whose analyses of Choctaw pottery had strengthened the theory that it was actually at least three earlier ethnic groups who had incorporated over time to create the sizable and powerful historic Choctaw of the late seventeenth century. Though a Winston County native, Carleton, like many locals, had never laid eyes on the less visited cave-mound site.

At the end of a gravel road, surrounded by pools of standing water, we saw the forested hillock. It was midwinter, and the gentle slope was carpeted with brown and yellow leaves. On its northern flank, the mound curved inward toward a soft dent in which lay a perfectly round opening about the size of a manhole cover. A damp, mossy rim softened the aperture that angled downward like a road culvert. The orifice seemed to incarnate the great womb caves of Meso-America, from which emerged new tribes like the Chocho and Chichimec.

With Ken's grip on my belt, I lay on the ground and dropped my torso into the darkness. Cool drafts swept up at me, smelling earthy, fresh and damp. From the blackness of a hollow chamber far below came a gurgling echo, as if seeps were dripping into a subterranean pool. It was hard not to imagine that what pressed upon my body and breathed back at me was some sort of living thing.

CHAPTER FOUR

BETWEEN RIVER AND FIRE

Cherokee

The ancient Romans recognized two kinds of sacred places. First were *loca sacra,* which meant sites that were turned over to religious use through human acts of consecration and dedication to ritual practice, places such as temples, graveyards and arenas for sacred dance. Second were *loca religiosa,* which referred to the locations that were revealed to be intrinsically holy or endowed with invisible powers through the miraculous events that took place there.

Sacred places of the old-time Cherokee of the Little Tennessee River region, located along today's states of North Carolina and Tennessee, suggest a similar distinction. Out in the mountains, forests and rivers were their *loca religiosa,* or places associated with the characters of mythology and magical forces. Within their well-organized towns were the *loca sacra,* the rectilinear plazas and round council houses where rules and ceremonies controlled the power emanating from sacred fires.

One goal of the American Indian Religious Freedom Act of 1978 was to protect both kinds of sites. But the first challenge to the act concerned a threat to drown every kind of Cherokee place, sacred or secular. A dam was being constructed over the Little Tennessee River near the North Carolina–Tennessee state line. No longer heralded as part of the 1930s crusade for providing electrification and flood control for rural poor, the Tellico Dam project was blatantly geared for the tourist industry. Along with creating a recreational lake, the ensuing spread of backed-up water would inundate a thirty-three-mile stretch of riverbank that supported a series of historic Cherokee town sites. Paramount among them was the principal "Peace" capital of Chota, the tribe's equivalent to colonial Williamsburg or Philadelphia. It would also flood much of the surrounding countryside.

Although the Cherokee had been removed from the valley for centuries, some traditional people among the tribe's eastern groups, who had successfully resisted being removed to Oklahoma in the nineteenth century, now fought against destruction of their ancestral lands.

The homeland of the Overhill Cherokee is found in Swain, Latour and Monroe counties in eastern Tennessee, just "over the hills" of the Great Smokies. Geologically this portion of the Southern Appalachians consists of the oldest mountains in North America. The lifeline for the cluster of Overhill towns was the Little Tennessee River, a stream which the Cherokee knew as *Yunwi Gamahida*, the "Long Man," a living being who granted energy and spoke to those who knew how to listen. This river was born more than two hundred million years ago. After the earth's crust buckled into mountains, it swelled from rain runoff in the Blue Ridge highlands and gathered speed as the waters cascaded down the northwestern slopes. Relaxing once it had achieved the valley floor, the Little Tennessee sashayed back and forth across the Tellico Plains. Every year its expansion and contraction left whiplash shadows of dried meanders as it fertilized the flood plain before merging into the greater Tennessee River just west of present-day Knoxville.

The valley drew generations of Native Americans. For at least nine thousand years they hunted, fished, foraged, gardened, built houses, raised children and transacted with spirits here. This tenancy reached a peak of sorts in the mid-eighteenth century with a string of nine Cherokee Indian towns that extended from Citico, nearest the eastern mountain range, to Tuskegee, close to the mouth of the Tellico River. Until the fall of 1979, one could raft its length and see on the southeastern shore the grassy hummocks that once supported temples and enclosed noble burials.

After the first flowers bloomed here ninety-five million years ago, the region became a botanical repository; in mountains surrounding the Little Tennessee Valley thrived the largest inventory of plants in North America. To the Cherokee hardly a cleft in the hills or a crook in the river was without its spirit (plant) occupant; a test for their healers and shamans was the extent of their knowledge of how to find and use them.

In early spring a few years ago, I drove through the tunnel of trees that shroud Route 129 from Robbinsville, North Carolina, and arrived at a memorial to the old town of Chota on the Bacon Bend of the river. Dusk glowed pinkly to the west, what the Cherokee called "the darkening land," the direction they associated with blood, power, success. Southeastward loomed the front ridge of what they described as the "wave upon wave" of the Great Smokies. Swathed in the bluish gauze of the largest mountain chain east of the Mississippi, the summits and slopes, forests, dells and rivers of those mountains were inhabited, they believed, by all sorts of spirit beings, some hospitable, others up to no good.

Through the Stony Grave Gap of Chilhowee Mountain I could still make out Thunderbird Peak, which stood at more than fifty-five hundred feet. And I was aware that another sixteen miles due east lay Clingman's Dome, the crown of the Southern Appalachians, its summit lifting yet another thousand feet. "Peak," "mountain" and "crown"—the vigor of those alpine terms seem ill fitting for this rounded, well-worn skyline. I appreciated why locals, whose cabins nestled in valley "coves," preferred the words "knob" or "bald," as if respecting the aged personalities of mountains that have seen it all.

According to Cherokee tradition, many of these mountaintop "balds" were considered to be "town houses" for the animal kingdom—circular structures that were identical to the council houses where the Cherokee met in communities like Chota. The story goes that when the animals became furious that Indian hunters were eating their flesh and striping their fur without due respect, their "tribes" convened in these mountaintop buildings. First gathered the Deer. The Bears met at "The Mulberry Place," near Clingman's Dome. On Gregory Bald, in North Carolina's Swain County, the Rabbits discussed revenge. Then the Deer sent rheumatism, the Fishes and Snakes unleashed bad dreams. Each species retaliated against humans with their trademark malaise.

But the plant world befriended people. As if as one, the trees, shrubs, herbs, grasses and moss spoke up: "I shall appear to help man when he calls upon me." That assistance came in the form of "medicine," the Cherokee antidote to every misfortune. Under the principle of reciprocity that governed Cherokee life, it became the job of trained conjurers, schooled in identifying hundreds of plants, to match animal-derived ailments with their wild plant cures.

Some were helpful personalities in their own right: Little Man, the beneficial ginseng; Talker, the bugle weed, which, when rubbed on their lips, made children eloquent; Fire Maker, the sticks of fleabane used in fire-by-friction techniques; and White Man's Footsteps, the white clover that always cropped up in the wake of Europeans. Within most Overhill towns were native herbalists who could "converse" with more than eight hundred separate plants, who knew which bled, bore scars and needed recuperation when their roots, bark, buds, leaves or shoots were harvested for concocting cures.

Living within these woods were other places and beings who helped those who behaved properly. South of the Oconaluftee River's headwaters lay a lake whose waters were the yellowish color of gall. To casual visitors, it looked like any highland bog; to respectful hunters who chanted and fasted, it became a clear, deep lake with flocks of ducks and pigeons.

Every Cherokee was aware that Little People inhabited rocky cliffs and gorges like the Nantahala and Tullugh. They knew that Thunder Beings traveled from bald to bald by means of invisible bridges. They were taught that Rabbit spirits burrowed within broom sage on hillsides, that Fish beings were found along river bends under the shadows of drooping hemlock, that Whirlwind spirits hovered in leafy treetops and that any of these mountains might hold the game that was dispensed by the mythic master hunter Kanati.

Also in the landscape lay powers for the mind and spirit, especially on nights slashed by lightning, when medicine makers sought it face-to-face. "If you want to know how long you'll live," confided one, "the conjure man will take you out on a night with an electric storm and strip you to your loincloth, and run you through some trees. The number of trees you run through is the number of years you'll live. . . . Lightning will part the trees for you, but just the right number of them." For the Cherokee, lightning was a positive power. Trees struck by it were sought after so that shamans could bury their blackened splinters in cornfields to assure healthy crops. Warriors and ballplayers rubbed the charred wood on their biceps and calves for strength. Everyone knew they were charged with "You, Ancient One," bolts of sacred fire from the sky.

The hills and streams around the Little Tennessee also harbored less benign spirits. To the west of the river, near Culhowee, the Thunderers holed up in a deep ravine; every spring one heard their resounding drums. In the inky darkness of Nantahala Pass lay the hunting grounds of Spearfinger, a man-eating ogress. In a pool about twenty-five miles downstream from Chota swam the Dakwa, a monstrous, sharp-toothed fish. Four miles above present-day Bryson City, a fearsome water serpent, the Uktena, left its crawling marks in the river bottom. Along the Cheoah River, just below Rock Creek Knob, an underwater buffalo caused a ravenous eddy. Above Caney Fork lived an unfriendly giant named Judaculla. The ominous lights that drifted up the hollows near Quallah were evidence of Rattlesnake's home. And just south of Chota, at the mouth of Hiwassee River, a red-and-white-banded leech who was as large as a house churned the waters into a cauldron.

Early Euro-American visitors were of two minds about this teeming vegetation, which matted hillsides, hid ankle-twisting obstacles, buried streams, and where venturing fifty feet into the woods could leave a tenderfoot tattered and disoriented. "I've been in Hell," stammered a mid-eighteenth-century white hunter, whom we know only as Jeffrey, when he emerged near Chota after days in the brush. That demonizing epithet would be hurled at the Blue Ridge wilderness more than once. But to naturalist William Bartram, exploring the same valley at roughly the same time, it felt like Eden before the Fall. Bartram sauntered down the Little Tennessee Valley, intoxicated by its "meandering river gliding through, saluting in its various turning the swelling, green, turfy knolls, embellished with parterres of flowers and fruitful strawberry beds."

Where rivers were concerned, the Overhill Cherokee also held two views. From what we might call a navigational perspective, they knew the Little Tennessee as the Pine River, one of a number of streams that drained into the Tennessee River. Paralleling its banks were trails by which they pursued whitetail deer, spied on enemies, gathered medicines and col-

lected the cobbles to pave their plazas. This aspect of the river was emi-
nently practical. It routed how the Cherokee got from here to there and
where they might find useful things along the way.

Yet the early British trader James Adair noticed that the Cherokee
seemed "strongly attached to their rivers, all retaining the opinion of the
ancients that rivers are necessary to constitute a paradise." The Little Tennessee was personified as a willful but benevolent superspirit named "the
Long Man," whose head rested near the Great Smokies and legs extended
downstream until his toes touched the Tennessee River. The Long Man
was said to "bear down" on all in his path, and his hand "held all Cherokee
lives." Only initiated singers could translate into human speech the mur-
muring of his cataracts.

For Cherokee who bathed in his body, who drank from him and invoked his curative powers, the Long Man always helped them out. For the
first two years of their lives, Cherokee children were washed in its waters
each morning. Into historic times, when medicinal incantations written
on bark or paper in the Cherokee syllabary lost their effectiveness upon
their owner's death, dunking the written scripts in this living river restored their potency.

At every critical turn in a man's life, the river's blessings were imparted through the "going to the water" rite, which required prayers that
were lent spiritual force with "new water" from free-flowing streams. Only
those waters were ladled for the Black Drink emetic, and preferably in autumn, when the distillate of falling leaves made them most potent. The
Cherokee spooned the river waters over their heads, limbs and torsos or
plunged in whenever they could.

Whenever shamans fought disease, during birth and death rituals,
prior to all hunts, war parties and ball games, before eating the powerful
first corn of the season, to avert threats foretold in dreams, or upon greeting a new spring moon, the Cherokee fasted all night and then "went to
the water." It was best to visit the river at dawn, when the rays of the sun
were purest and strongest. It was best to visit bends in the stream in the
company of a shaman, who would douse his patients four or seven times
and chant with each immersion:

O Long Man at rest. O helper of men, you let nothing slip from your grasp. You never let the soul slip from your grasp. Come now and take a firmer grasp. I originated near the cataract, and from there await me on the road. Now my soul stands erect in the seventh heaven.

As for the *loca sacra* category of sacred place, no Cherokee site epitomized it more than *Itsa'ti*, or Chota, which was the capital town for the entire Little Tennessee Valley. After construction of Tellico Dam, a memorial was erected where it had stood. Located on a man-made jetty that juts into the swollen reservoir about twenty-five miles south of the dam, the monument consists of eight squat pillars within a twenty-foot-wide concrete curb. Constructed in 1985, it lies twenty feet over the site of the actual "town house" that had once served as the Overhill Cherokee's Supreme Court, House of Representatives and White House wrapped into one.

By the mid-eighteenth century, the reputation of Chota as a civic center had spread through the word of travelers and written documents by European and American diplomats, traders, missionaries and travelers. It was the Cherokee Nation's "Imperial City," their "Washington and also their Rome," and their "Beloved Town, where the fire of Peace is always burning." To Cherokee, the town was addressed more affectionately as Grandmother. The council house, which is lost today under impounded water and riprap, held sway over about sixty acres of public plazas and thatch-roofed dwellings and a patchwork of gardens along the bottomlands.

Chota was the epitome of what the Cherokee called a white or peace town, which set it apart from those communities where red, or war-centered, town councils were held. In the years of swiftly shifting diplomacy between 1755 and 1778, Chota assumed an almost mystical influence over the Little Tennessee Valley as well as the wider network of Cherokee sub-tribes. And Chota also served as the ultimate "town of refuge," where fugitives, who faced strangulation under the tribe's stern legal code, raced for safety. Once inside her walls, where no blood could be shed, fugitives and guilty parties worked to "wipe away their victim's tears" and win pardon. Later in the eighteenth century, as this landscape darkened with Cherokee, French, British and American blood, Grandmother's arms also took in refugees from Lower and Middle Cherokee settlements in flight from the white invasion.

The security of the Cherokee civic realm spread from sacred fires. Considered genetic grafts from the sun, one burned in every town, lending light and purity to pomp and ceremony. To the Cherokee, their ritual fires were considered "human in thought, consciousness, intent, emotions," and a virtual "grandmother in kin terms." In the old days, Cherokee warriors carried coals from their sacred fires into battle and brought them in gunnysacks to their ball games. Into their flames they fed Indian tobacco, deer-tongue offerings and the season's first fruits. Fire was the medium of transformation, turning offerings into gifts for spiritual intercessors or the four quarters of the earth. And when their coals cooled off, fires left behind the symbols of charred blackness and death, along with the ashen whiteness associated with peace and the power of elders.

As one Eastern Cherokee told anthropologist Frank G. Speck, "Proper treatment of the fire was essential to the well-being of the family, good family life, mannerly and proper conduct and many rules about the conduct of the earth contributed to the health, strength and magical power of the old woman. Putting out the fire on the last day and [maintaining the] ritual new fire during the Green Corn was essential, as was the proper sharing of meals by burnt offerings to the fire." Weather permitting, the sacred fires blazed outdoors, drawing the dispersed citizenry to Chota's ceremonial grounds for the Green Corn, Great Medicine and Reconciliation and other national festivals. When it turned cold or stormy, designated fire keepers kindled them inside the council houses and fed them with fagots from the seven sacred trees: beech, birch, hickory, locust, maple, oak and sourwood.

In the late eighteenth century, momentous debates and tough decision making revolved around these fires. Once word spread that Chota had usurped Tenasi as the political hub of the Overhill Cherokee, a stream of white visitors—traders, missionaries, land speculators and diplomats representing England, France and the United States—arrived by horseback, bearing overt and hidden agendas. Emissaries from the Ottawa and Shawnee nations bent their heads under the h doorway of Chota's council house. Within the seven-sided interior, with deep-tiered seating to accommodate upward of five hundred guests, they displayed nine-foot-long belts of purple and white shell beads in their attempts to rally multitribal crusades against American homesteaders.

Chota relished its rising prestige. The walls of its council house glowed like pewter from a clay slip tinted with pulverized oyster shells. Civic officials, male and female, painted their faces and held swan-wing fans of office to greet visitors before sitting down to business. Prominent guests were feasted and regaled with Eagle Tail dances in the town plaza. Banners rippled from tall poles before its entryway; the flags of foreign representatives were raised whenever they were in town. In other Overhill Cherokee settlements, symbols of whiteness and redness would alternate, depending upon the shifting intrigues of international politics. Those displayed at Chota, however, were exclusively white. But when war was on Chota's docket, a military standard was erected outside the council house, and its interior posts were daubed red and black.

Outsiders were taken aback by the authority wielded by Chota's women. During the eighteenth century, seven so-called Beloved Women as well as War Women were assigned seating in the town house. Prominent among them was *Ghighau,* the "Supreme Beloved Woman," who, with a wave of her trumpeter-swan wing, pardoned condemned murderers and resolved disputes.

When the Reverend William Richardson entered Chota's council house on December 29, 1758, he wanted permission to hold Bible classes for the Indians. Over the months that Richardson rented one of Chota's cabins, he saw how its councils provided equal time for Beloved Women and Beloved Men. As Richardson made his case, the tribe's treasurer, Old Hop, sat to his right; two seats away was the famous Attakullakulla, "prince" of Chota, while five down the bench was Oconostota, the town's renowned "Great Warrior." But Richardson did not keep his seat for long. Once the Indians heard what was on his mind, they asked him and his religion to leave town.

Three years later another young colonist sat in Chota's bleachers. Hoping to strengthen Cherokee ties to Virginia, Lieutenant Henry Timberlake also took up temporary quarters in their "metropolis," spending hours in the same council house. To appreciate his mission, one must backtrack a bit. For nearly a century by then, the Lower, Middle and Overhill Cherokee divisions had bought into the white man's economic and political system. The imported goods that began as conveniences had now become necessities: axes, knives, hoes, rifles, black power and shot—and rum. As the Little Tennessee Valley became the focus of heated diplomacy, England won over most towns belonging to the Lower and Middle Cherokee towns; only the Overhills kept straddling the fence.

At the same time, the export of Indian-killed and tanned deerskin rose in numbers. Twenty years before Timberlake's mission, Cherokee porters were hauling fifty thousand hides a year across the Tellico Plains, through the Blue Ridge, to North Carolina and the coast. Then the Deer beings retaliated: between 1738 and 1739, a devastating smallpox epidemic wiped out half the Cherokee Nation, and the disease struck soon again. Many Cherokee healers died; others, their cures proven ineffective, committed suicide.

By the time Chota assumed supremacy of the Overhill region in 1753, it was a refugee depot for the scarred and displaced. On September 14, 1757, the Cross of St. George was unfurled at Chota's square during the annual Green Corn Dance; soon nearly seven hundred Cherokee warriors were fighting for the British against the upstart colonies. Declaring war on the tribe two years later, in campaigns against the Lower and Middle Cherokee towns, American soldiers from the Carolinas and Virginia burned their cottages and cornfields. More refugees fled over the mountains to join their Overhill kinfolk. And it was to halt these hostilities that Timberlake found himself in Chota's town house.

But his visit was too little too late. Unlike most of her sister Overhill towns, which strove for neutrality during the War for Independence, and despite their flirtation with the English, for the most part Chota remained partial to the Americans. But that alliance was ignored as the revolutionaries gained the upper hand and American reprisals against all presumed Crown sympathizers began. Indian town houses were burned, livestock were driven off or slaughtered, the Cherokee were killed and scalped or enslaved. Real estate speculators and immigrants, hearing that Overhill bottomlands were "equal to manure itself," looked greedily over the Blue Ridge. Despite a last-ditch attempt by the Cherokee to draw the line at Waya Gap in the Nantahala Mountains, the American juggernaut broke through, and William Christian's Virginia troops spilled into Overhill territory.

At first Chota was spared. But when the first treaties with the new republic failed to hold, the winter of 1780–81 saw the Americans tear across the Little Tennessee Valley. Ten of the Overhill Cherokee towns were leveled, and Chota's luck finally ran out. On December 28, 1780, ragtag mountaineers breached the town of refuge. Sweeping aside the Beloved Woman's appeals for mercy, they kicked apart her sacred fire and torched the council house. For a number of years, it was as if only the force of Chota's longevity kept hope flickering; Indian holdouts even had the temerity to complain to North Carolina's governor about white homesteads creeping to "within a day's walk" of town.

But by 1788, when old Chief Oconostota was laid in the burial mound that would be exhumed by archaeologists two centuries later, Chota was on its last legs. After the death of Old Tassell, its chieftaincy was taken up by Hanging Maw. Now the Cherokee capital officially shifted to the southeast, to Ustanali, along the Coosawattee River in northern Georgia. Exhausted from a century of fighting, disease and land grabs, most of Chota's occupants gravitated toward the new population center known as New Echota.

While still resisting the move, Hanging Maw accepted President George Washington's invitation to talk it over in old Chota. The conference was a trap. Fifteen Cherokee leaders, including Hanging Maw's own wife, were caught by surprise and shot to death. Now it was within the American blockhouse at Tellico that subdued Indians and U.S. representatives wrapped up what business remained.

By 1799, Chota was practically a ghost town. Five dwellings were occupied by lingerers like Old Bark, who clung to his 640 acres until 1819, and Toqua Will, who begged the Tennessee legislature to let him die in old Chota because "his long residence there caused him to esteem it as his appropriate home for life," explained his lawyer. "He felt as if the very land were akin to him. It contained the remains of the mother of his children, and some of them also."

As for Cherokee refugees putting down new roots in northern Georgia, their hopes for permanent homes dimmed after 1815, when a Cherokee boy discovered yellow mineral in the Chestatee River. Georgians did not realize the extent of the gold in their backyard until 1827, but they made up for lost time. New state laws opened up the resettled Cherokee lands and forbade Indians from resisting property seizures. When President Jackson assumed the presidency in 1829, he supported southern whites who called for wholesale removal of Southeastern Indians west of the Mississippi.

This removal trauma split the Cherokee people into western and eastern bands. Of the estimated sixteen thousand who were rounded up in stockades, marched west under armed guard and resettled in the broken country of eastern Oklahoma, perhaps a quarter died from brutality, exposure, disease and heartbreak. The smaller number who avoided the round up became the Eastern Cherokee of North Carolina's Qualla Reservation. The Overhills were divided between relocatees in Indian Territory and families who stayed put in the Great Smokey hamlets of Wolftown, Birdtown and Snowbird. Many became Christians and remythologized their landscape, comparing baptisms in the river to the old "going to the water" rituals and accepting the redefinition of their dark mountains as the Devil's abode.

But older sympathies persisted. "We wondered why white people don't hear strange things and see things like Indians do," an Eastern Cherokee told a white scholar in 1959. To still hear those strange things, some continued to ride wagons over the high passes and into the Little Tennessee Valley. When the great-granddaughter of the Cherokee leader John Ross was a girl in the 1880s, she visited her grandparents there. Not far from the site of old Chota, she came upon them camped at the mouth of Citico Creek, sleeping on brush mats in a lean-to that was roofed with split cane. She played in cornfields that white farmers cultivated on the Citico town house mound, and picked old Indian beads out of the mud for her grandmother to string into necklaces.

They often arrived in Model Ts and pickups, and these informal visitations continued into the twentieth century. Cherokee parents showed their kids the sites of old Tenasi and Chota, left offerings at the Nikwasi

Mound near Franklin, and scoured the brush for medicinal plants they could find nowhere else. Another old Indian who visited the valley recalled, "The first time I came here I felt as though I'd seen it before. I had heard my grandmother and other Indians describe it. 'Beautiful Chota,' they called it."

After 1900, aluminum mining interests penetrated the central Appalachians. In the 1930s, the Tennessee Valley Authority (TVA), seeking affordable electricity and flood control for neglected backwaters of rural America, instituted a public works program whose likes the world had never seen. Between George and Knoxville alone, eighteen dams went up. A facility for the Little Tennessee River was on the wish list of the U.S. Army Corps of Engineers, but World War II cut that short. For two decades the corps did not reset its sights on the river. In 1966, however, the U.S. Congress approved more than $111 million and soon the TVA began condemning lots and buying out farmers. The Fort Loudon dam was to be built at the junction of the "Li'l T" and the Tennessee River, near Lenoir City.

But flood control and two hundred million kilowatts of electricity for an estimated twenty thousand households along the way were no longer its driving purpose. Now its selling points were the flatwater recreation industry, which required stocked fish, boat pull-outs and slips, camping and RV grounds and shoreline housing. An estimated 16,500 acres would go under, with an additional 22,000 acres adjacent to the new lake's shoreline designated for support services.

The trapped waters would rise into the woods for thirty-three miles along the Little Tennessee's main stem and twenty-two miles up its tributary, the Tellico, obliterating ten thousand years of Indian heritage and culture and the sites of momentous events in North America's colonial history. To some Cherokee it struck closer to home. "If the water covers Chota and the other sacred places of the Cherokee," testified Ammoneta Sequoyah, a seventy-eight-year-old Cherokee herbalist, "I will lose my knowledge of medicine. If the lands are flooded, the medicine that comes from Chota will be ended because the strength and spiritual power of the Cherokee will be destroyed." Another elder remembered a medicine man who stood on a hickory stump around 1910 and envisioned the Little Tennessee choked with water. "Our forefathers would be on the bottom of the valley looking up through a wall of glass," he said. Tears rolled down his cheeks when he added, "One day the people would once again be put to the test of holding on to that which is sacred or giving up forever another part of our lives."

Environmentalists also went on the offense. At the location of old Chota, a delegation of Eastern Cherokee stuck a Plains Indian war bonnet on U.S. Supreme Court's William O. Douglas, a prominent spokesman for wilderness protection. From a rowboat in the Little Tennessee, the white-haired justice was photographed casting for trout, preparing his article against the dam, which had been commissioned by *National Geographic*. But TVA authorities persuaded the magazine to shelve his piece. Of foremost concern to Douglas were losses to outdoor recreation. "The lake resulting from the dam will forever ruin the "Little T" as Tennessee's finest trout river and as a picturesque free-flowing river enjoyed by canoeists," Douglas wrote, "and a host of others seeking an escape to an unspoiled natural setting." Only at the end of his piece did the dam's threat to Indian culture and history seem to sink in: "There were Cherokee towns near the mouth of the Little T to its headwaters . . . places as revered to them as Williamsburg and Plymouth Rock are to us."

On the heels of surveyors bent over transits and hard-hatted engineers carrying clipboards arrived bulldozers, dump trucks and cement mixers. Archaeologists from the University of Tennessee were given less than fourteen years to read the human history of a watershed that had begun with the Ice Age. Aided by eighteenth-century maps, they were keen to uncover about a dozen Overhill Cherokee towns, such as Toqua, Tomotley and, of course, Chota. For a while the valley featured a race: dam construction versus archaeological excavation.

Near the site of Chota they identified the very bones of its Great Warrior. Although Oconostota's final years were spent away from home, shortly before his death in 1783 he'd asked to be returned there. To ready him for the Cherokee afterlife, his corpse was laid in a dugout canoe, white beads wrapped around his right shoulder, an iron knife and a pair of eyeglasses laid alongside his right leg.

His grave was among more than three hundred other sites discovered in the late 1970s, as archaeologists worked with a haste usually abhorred by their profession. In the most ambitious salvage operation ever attempted east of the Mississippi, they backhoed deep trenches to reveal nine successively occupied river terraces. The Cherokee were only the valley's most recent native occupants, possibly entering the Little Tennessee from the north just a thousand years ago, but probably sharing with their predecessors their customs—burials in earthworks, social hierarchy, belief in sacred fires. Archaeologists worked down through dancing and ball-playing grounds that were paved with cobblestones. They cut into deeper layers of fire-and-grease-hardened house floors and refuse dumps. Farther down they unearthed chunks of charcoal associated with Indian cultures that predated the Cherokee by millennia.

Only a dozen miles downstream from Chota, for instance, lay the site named Icehouse Bottom. From a fifteen-foot pit, Dr. Jeffrey Chapman extracted burned remains from campfires kindled by Indians nearly ten thousand years ago. Since this silty deposit lay well below water level, Icehouse preserved the walnuts and butternuts that were side dishes to a mastodon main course. A nearby chert quarry, good for chipping into grooved projectile points, helped explain the location's long popularity. In lower strata, Chapman found evidence of women's work: the clay imprint of a vegetable-fibered textile that was dated at more than nine thousand years of age, our earliest evidence for weaving in the Southeast. Nor was Icehouse an isolated community—Chapman also turned up mica from North Carolina and stone blades from Flint Ridge, Ohio, which were evidence of a wide trade network.

Then environmentalists, archaeologists and Indians got a break. Biologists alerted them that a three-inch fish, known as the snail darter, bred only along the Little Tennessee; the Cherokee knew it as *dugalvina,* whose long nose they likened to the neck of a gourd. The threat to its survival drew national attention, initiated the Endangered Species Act of 1973 and delayed the opening of the dam's floodgates. The snail darter snag dragged on for five years, until the U.S. Supreme Court agreed with government experts that the little fish could be found in other streams, and the dam was on track again.

With environmentalists peeling off, the Indians were on their own. One year after the Supreme Court's decision, a coalition of Eastern and Western Cherokee, as well as three Cherokee individuals acting on their own, moved the issue into the legal arena, citing the recently signed American Indian Religious Freedom Act. The Tellico Dam threatened their "resettlement sites, cemeteries, rich farmland, forests and the river itself," testified Eastern Cherokee Jimmie Durham. "Our connection with the Great Spirit" would be broken, maintained plaintiff Richard Crowe, who recalled his parents using the phrase *diga tale nohr,* for the Little Tennessee region, which meant, "This is where we began." And Crowe warned, "If they are flooded, our spiritual strength from our forefathers would be taken from us, along with the origin of our organized religion." And another Indian witness, Robert Blankenship, stressed that the land and river were sacred "because they are the only tangible items left for me and other Cherokee to worship."

Lawyers for the Cherokee tried to build on the legal victory of Wisconsin's Amish community in the early 1970s. When that case had reached the U.S. Supreme Court, the justices accepted the argument that Amish resistance to the state's compulsory education laws was "rooted in religious belief" and not a matter of "lifestyle preferences." Government interests were not compelling enough to outweigh those of the Amish in their First Amendment appeal to freedom of religion. Unmentioned, of course, was the fact that as Christian pioneers, the Amish sect had been allowed to stick together for more than two centuries as separate, self-educating, self-sufficient religious communities. Along with the Indian Religious Freedom Act of 1978, the Cherokee legal team saw this precedent as their last weapon against TVA.

District Court Judge Robert L. Taylor took two months to mull over the Cherokee plea for the valley's stay of execution. When he turned them down in 1980, he highlighted the division between secular and sacred claims by questioning whether the Cherokee were fearing the loss of a cultural heritage *or* their religious rights. When Cherokee visited the area, he believed, most were not there for religious purposes but were "prompted for the most part by an understandable desire to learn more about their cultural heritage."

Taylor's distinction between ways of life and ways of belief drew from the Religious Freedom Act's stipulation that sacred sites had to be "central" to a living religion. Taylor was not persuaded that these thirty-three miles of the Little Tennessee watershed were "central, inseparable, and indispensable" to the Cherokee. Cultural history and tradition may be "vitally important to any group of people," he wrote, but they were "not protected by the Free Exercise Claim of the First Amendment."

The Tellico case was the first legal fight over American Indian sacred geography to divorce history and culture from religion. The Religious Freedom Act's criteria of "centrality" and "indispensability" were borrowed from the famous historian of religions Mircea Eliade, who sought to champion what he termed "primal religions" like those of the Cherokee. But in this case they proved too high and too general a standard.

Under the old Overhill Cherokee legal code, invading or "polluting" a sacred place was considered the equivalent of assaulting or merely touching a "peace priest." Whereas punishment was whipping or death for serious offenses, for violations of sacred places the spirits themselves executed the guilty, but at an "uncertain date or manner." But no one cited the consequences of old Indian laws when, on November 29, 1979, even before the Supreme Court delivered its verdict, the floodgates at Tellico Dam were shut. Foot by foot and hour by hour, the river sites went under. The river became a lake; as an ecological and cultural entity, the valley died within the next six weeks.

I wanted to see the Chota memorial in daylight and returned in late afternoon, a few weeks before the hemlocks leafed out. As an evocation of the landscape sensibilities that had nurtured the Overhill Cherokee belief system, the jetty's design failed. Perhaps an improvement over concrete riprap, its breakwater of dumped rock was too impersonal and defensive. Around the reservoir, where pooling undercut the limestone bedrock, few mossy banks invited one to daydream or stick feet into refreshing waters. The shoreline looked readier to drown you than befriend you.

Meant to symbolize the pine logs that once supported Chota's council house, truncated concrete pillars were hacked off and pitted from the cardboard tubing into which their wet concrete had been poured. An eye-shaped basin was a halfhearted attempt to symbolize a hearth that had warmed Cherokee souls three hundred years before. It was filled with dry gravel. The effect was invasive and industrial, more fitting as self-congratulation for the destruction of the Cherokee capital, the banishment of its people and the construction of Tellico Dam than as homage to a banished Cherokee presence. One longed for a more organic commemoration, for earthier metaphors to conjure up a profusion of wild plants in the mountains and an unencumbered river and smoke from a sacred fire.

Driving north and upstream, past the turnoff to the old town of Toqua and toward Fort Loudon, I pulled into the old Tenasi monument, where Chota's neighbor town and the state's namesake once stood. Now it was a perfunctory turnabout with minimal information on a small sign. My plan was a quiet pilgrimage to all the Overhill sites, but then reality intruded.

Guns and bloodshed may have been banned from eighteenth-century Chota, yet on every road shoulder were trucks with shortwave antennae whipping around and huddles of barking hounds. Groups of men in camouflage and greasepaint stomped out of the trees, shotguns bouncing on their shoulders and knife sheaths and .45 automatics swinging from their belts. They eyed my candy-red rental with undisguised condescension. Gunfire boomed through the woods. It was dusk on the last day of rabbit season, but it resembled a paramilitary takeover.

As I paid my respects at Oconostota's headstone, erected over his re-buried bones, it was hard not to sympathize with the old man's lament, recorded in July 1769: "The whole nation is filling with hunters," he had said, "and the guns rattling every way on the path, both up and down the river. They have settled the land a great way this side of the line."

I headed for the Knoxville airport without any more stops.

PART II

SOUTH

In 1979, when the U.S. Forest Service allowed a new access road for the Arizona Snow Bowl operation on the San Francisco Peaks outside of Flagstaff, Arizona, alarm bells rang among two Indian nations. For more than forty years the Hopi and Navajo tribes had come to accept downhill skiers and the road and lodge that had been constructed by the Forest Service. For the Hopi, this infringed on the homes of their rain-bringing spirits known as Katsinas. For the Navajo, the Peaks were known as Shining on Top, their sacred mountain of the West. From both tribes, trained practitioners came to renew shrines, to utter prayers and to gather herbs, minerals and spruce boughs. After the Forest Service ruling, a regional supervisor authorized construction of the new access road. Although at the time the two Indian nations were at each other's throats over the Joint Use Area dispute, they joined forces to fight this Snow Bowl expansion. Citing the 1978 American Indian Religious Freedom Act, they filed suit to stop the road in three consolidated federal cases. Essentially, they argued that the world that bulldozers and SUVs were about to invade didn't belong to them. It belonged to Hopi and Navajo spirits.

CHAPTER FIVE

A TALE OF THREE LAKES

Taos/Zuni

N ot all struggles over American Indian landscapes end in sorrow and loss. The following tales unfold in Pueblo Indian country; they revolve around threatened lakes, highlight pilgrimage as religious practice and end up with Indians still visiting their holy places.

Northern New Mexico witnessed the most unlikely victory of all.

Behind the tourist town of Ranchos de Taos looms the fourteen-thousand-foot-high backdrop of Taos Mountain—*Mawaluna* to the people of Taos Pueblo. Deep within the massif sits a glacial pool named Blue Lake. While visiting a friend who lived beside the crumbling mud wall that still isolates the old Indian pueblo from Ranchos de Taos and the rest of the modern world, I was hypnotized by the mountain's dark-green slopes and crown of thunderheads. Since outsiders are not allowed up there, I'd seen only aerial photos of the environmental shrine that Taos Indians know as *Paw'ia* or "lake," or what Taos Indian poet James Cordova calls "the little blue eye of faith, the deep turquoise lake of life." It is a steep oval basin with a thin, rocky shoreline crowded by spruce trees whose mirrorlike surface reflects the azure sky and those exploding clouds.

For six thousand feet, its runoff spills down pine and aspen mountainsides, passes scrub oaks and elders, and flows into Red Willow Creek, which ripples diagonally across Taos Pueblo's dance plaza before entering the Rio Grande about three miles farther south. Taos Indians say their earliest ancestors emerged from Blue Lake's cold waters; into them the dead return, to become spirits, known as "the ones who always believe." There they merge with cloud people, the rain-bringing Pueblo Indian spirits known as Kachinas, and circulate to other sacred lakes in the vicinity by means of subterranean "roads." About other meanings regarding Blue

Lake, the Taos people are famously tight lipped. Even the hostess of Taos's bohemian heyday in the 1920s, Mabel Dodge Lujan, who was married to a Taos Indian, was kept at arm's length. Why did his people believe it was wrong to point at rainbows? "That's enough" was all her husband Tony would reply. That was also his response when she asked why she couldn't join the "They Lake Go" (*Ipa'w'imeho*) pilgrimage of August, when most of the community repaired to Blue Lake for prayers and rituals.

Mabel gained respect for Pueblo traditions of secrecy, as one senses from her memory of an overnight on the mountain:

> It has never been surprising to me that the Indians call Blue Lake a sacred lake, and worship it. Indeed, at first I felt we should not camp upon its shore, but after I found out how they conduct the camp there I knew it was all right and fitting that one should sleep beside it and try to draw what one could for oneself from its strong being. . . . When the dishes are washed and all the scraps are burned and we are sitting in a circle around the fire, the Indians begin to chant, at first in faint, humming tones, that gradually grow strong and full. They look over to the lake and sing to it. Their faces show they are deep in communion with the place they are in. They experience it and adore it as we do not know how to do.

While Mabel was empathizing with Taos sentiments toward the lake, the tribe's access to it lay under siege. In 1904, the visionary environmentalist and U.S. Forest Service director Gifford Pinochet carved fifty thousand acres out of the Sangre de Cristo mountain range to create Carson National Forest. Two years later, his boss, President Theodore Roosevelt, dismissed Taos Indians as "a dozen squalid savages who hunted for long intervals" and signed ownership of the Blue Lake watershed over to Carson Forest.

First the Indians had to pay fees to graze their cattle. Then the lakes on Taos Mountain and Lucero Canyon were stocked with trout; logging roads were cut; hiking trails blazed and newly built cabins, outhouses and corrals soon accommodated sportsmen and weekend visitors. Fishermen,

lumberjacks and eventually miners entered the Taos Reserve. A private effort by Indian sympathizers to restrict grazing and timbering and protect
Indian shrines went nowhere. Then worm-baited lines plopped into Blue
Lake and beer bottles and trash washed up on the shore. Heartsick at the
desecration, the Indians launched a campaign to win back their lake.

The August trek of the Taos Indians to Blue Lake belongs to a devotional
practice by which societies around the world renew their ties to sacred
landscapes—the pilgrimage. Leaving humdrum roles and duties behind,
pilgrims light out on roads that link the domestic to the divine. Willpower,
religious fervor and the obligation to fulfill vows must overcome sore
muscles, uncertain company, homesickness and terrors of the unfamiliar.
On the one hand, pilgrims face the unknown; on the other hand, they
never really travel anyplace at all. For their sacred narratives have usually
forecast their itineraries and indoctrinated their eyes in what to see and
what it all means. Often they bed down at hostels or way stations containing images and routines that only reinforce the assurance that theirs is the
one true path. During their "time out of time," pilgrims satisfy old promises,
make new soul mates and create memories to cherish all their lives.

Of pilgrimage there is wide variety. Some take days, like the relatively
benign Taos Pueblo trek to Blue Lake. Others are more arduous and con-
sume weeks or months. Some pilgrims venture on their own to seek out
the spirits, gods, saints or ancestors in distant locales where they are
buried or are still believed to dwell. In an exchange of suffering, they pray
that their ordeals will lessen those of the dying or hapless back home.
Other pilgrims merge into mobile congregations, among whom a sense of
camaraderie may blossom. High or low class back home, pilgrimage becomes the great leveler. Equalized by blistered feet, aching muscles and
shared pieties, they form a motley crew stumbling toward paradise.

One requirement of a pilgrimage is space, usually lots of it. From the
familiar and safe home of departure unfurls the actual route, which may
include pilgrim inns and stopover shrines and go on for miles. Some pilgrims become semitourists who will return home with souvenirs for family altars and mantelpieces, or with restorative vials of water or packets of

earth. Others test their limits, hoping that the farther out they venture and sacrifice their comforts, the more receptive they will become to inner revelations. Their ultimate destination may be a lake, cave or shrine—some great repository of religious and social identity.

Along the way are appointments with mountains, springs, deserts, plants, rocks, and/or gods, saints, ancestors and sacred beings who figure in their mythology and history. Thanks to the narratives, liturgies and songs they have heard since childhood, the ground possesses a vague familiarity. *There* is where Coyote did it, *this* was left behind by the Great Flood, *here* was where grandfather talked with a bear or, as a Zuni Indian man told archaeologist M. Jane Young about a fight between the mythic Twin War Gods and a monster snake, "It happened over there, just beyond the place where the elementary school is now." Such locations may lie across foreign or enemy territories; political or ethnic tensions may make crossing boundaries a problem. But pilgrims believe they brandish a higher passport. Before anyone purchased a deed to these springs, mountains or caves, their devotees already belonged to this storied landscape.

Finally comes the destination, the climactic sacred place where offerings are given, deities witnessed, epiphanies experienced and blessings received. As they look back, however, pilgrims often realize it was as much about what they learned getting there that was the point. Praying with their feet, the act of pilgrimage allows American Indians to practice piety and self-reliance, and to experience their topography, cosmology and sacred history—all in one physically demanding, psychologically absorbing, socially reinforcing and mystically fulfilling fell swoop.

The Taos pilgrims go to Blue Lake in late August. From the following first-person account of the 1906 trek comes most of what outsiders know about the event.

Escorting youngsters who were undergoing their initiations into Taos secret societies, the Indian families walked and rode along twenty-seven miles of trail that led up Glorieta Canyon. The first night they sang and danced in a cottonwood-shaded campsite along Pueblo Creek. The next morning all the pilgrims washed their hair in yucca suds, imbibed a purifying emetic brewed from creek water, and donned their best, the men pulling on trade cloth leggings and wrapping their bare chests in blankets and the women wearing silk dresses with Mexican shawls tossed over their shoulders and everyone tying on the fine, white-tanned moccasins worn only for special occasions.

Progressing along the trail, they passed fields of white and yellow wildflowers, which the women wove into wreathes for their hair. They filed up steep, narrow defiles and passed pine trees bearded with Spanish moss. At a spring near Blue Lake, they listened for the rumbling sounds that rose from corn being pulverized in underground metates by the legendary Grindstone Women. Reaching its shores, they offered wild turkey plumes, cornmeal, bits of turquoise, and prayed "that the earth may be made beautiful to look upon and that she may be made fruitful by the rainmakers," according to anthropologist Matilda Coxe Stevenson, and "that they may be blessed with many children who will grow to be strong. They also ask that the men may be brave and the women able to grind corn and do other work." After eating together, singing, dancing and resting until the rise of the morning star, the pilgrims returned home with bundles of wilting flowers, basking in the afterglow of reaching their origins together.

Initially settled by migrants from southern Colorado around A.D. 900, Taos Pueblo offers a textbook introduction to Pueblo Indian notions of sacred place. First is the emphasis on "earth navel centers." Most Pueblo genesis stories tell of emergences from womblike underworlds through "navel" places in the land. Then comes the new arrivals' search for a homeland, a "center" place that can offer an unmovable pivot for collective security and geographical orientation. As one man illustrated this concept to anthropologist Alfonso Ortiz, a fellow member of San Juan Pueblo, "An earth navel is like an airport. You notice how airplanes, no matter where they go, always return to an airport. In the same way all things—game, people, and spirits—always return to the earth navel."

Next is the importance of four "directions," associated with different colors and mountains that stand as approximate corners of the Pueblo territorial domain. Connecting the multiple levels of the Pueblo underworld, earth plain, and sky world are vertical axes that are represented by the ladders by which one drops into the Pueblo's secret, socioreligious chambers

known as kivas. Sometimes Pueblo cosmology is characterized as a bas-
ketlike sky dome fitting onto a potlike earth bowl to form a complete
globe that is their container of sacred space.

To Pueblo Indians, however, this cosmology does not stand still; to
keep it dynamic and active, humans must play their parts. The sun is regarded as a male who, after the fall equinox, weakens and drops lower and
lower in the winter sky. Hence, this is when Eastern Pueblo Indians all
along the Rio Grande—from Taos Pueblo in the north to Isleta Pueblo,
south of Albuquerque—must lend the sun their strength. At Taos they do
this during the annual saints' day fiesta, on September thirtieth, by relay
running at breakneck speed back and forth on east-west "sun road" race
tracks under the supervision of eagle-feather-wielding shamans. To outsiders, Taos religious leaders stress that such rituals assist the rhythms of
seasonal change and fertility. "We are the people who live on the roof of
the world; we are the sons of the Sun, who is our father," said a Taos religious leader to psychologist Carl Jung. "We help him daily to rise and to
cross over the sky."

By the time Jung heard this in 1925, Taos Pueblo was in the thick of its
fight to recover Blue Lake. Pleas in governmental hearings during the
twenties, the forties and the sixties reveal a consistent effort to express in
English what could not really be translated, to portray what could not be
shown, to defend what could never be proven, namely, the inner powers of
place. With the help of white writers and supporters, Taos spokesmen
tried different approaches to resonate with Washington decision makers.
"We have no buildings there," said one tribal elder, referring to Taos
Mountain, "no steeples. There is nothing the human hand has made. The
lake is our church. The evergreen trees are our living saints. We pray to the
water, the sun, the clouds, the sky, the deer. Without them we cannot exist.
Blue Lake is the heart of our religion."

The Taos campaign to convey their lake's spiritual importance got
harder in the early 1920s as rumors spread of a secret Interior Department
"dance file," which contained sensationalistic accounts of Hopi handling
rattlesnakes, debauchery at Blue Lake, and Pueblo clowns running around
half naked and performing mock copulations. In 1923, Indian Affairs

Commissioner Charles H. Burke updated the old list of "Indian offenses" for which Indians could be punished, highlighting polygamy and ritual self-torture; Burke suggested maypole dances as a more positive substitute for Indian schools, apparently oblivious to the fact that they were survivals of European pagan fertility dances around phallic icons.

Organizing against Burke's anti-Pueblo agenda was John Collier, a feisty, bespectacled New York social worker. Collier envisioned a national Indian renaissance modeled after a utopian "Red Atlantis," which was the romantic impression imparted by Tony Lujan during Collier's first eye-opening visit to Taos Pueblo in 1920. Collier became a congressional gad-fly, drafting petitions and recruiting social scientists to bear sympathetic witness to Indian ceremonies. At Taos Pueblo itself, where school officials denied Indian kids release time for religious training in their kivas (wherein they learned, testified one tribal leader, "about God and the earth, and about our duty to God, to earth, and to one another"), Collier got the government to back off.

Running through the Taos statements about protecting their special places was the theme of obligations to the earth. Cowboy politicians like New Mexico's senator Clinton Anderson could not understand why Taos needed all that acreage to pray in; he was willing to grant them only three thousand acres right around Blue Lake. "Now may I ask a question?" he asked during a debate in 1943 over the Pueblo's yielding rights to mineral resources. "Do you have any place in that territory that *is* yours where you would not object to drilling?" Taos elder Ferlino Martinez shot back, "Every inch of our land is religious land, a place of sacred shrines."

But in their nonviolent effort to regain their Blue Lake watershed, the Pueblo nearly fell into the traps of oversimplification and broad comparison, which can be tempting during desperate efforts to translate one culture's beliefs into the terms of another's. At first the tendency of Taos elders to show similarities between their sacred places and those of world religions employed metaphor. In 1927, a Taos spokesman told Commissioner Burke that their Blue Lake region "is like a church to us, and if you look at it that way you will understand how deeply we feel." By 1960, one could hear Taos elder Seferino Martinez trying to avoid entrapment by the analogy to a single building or plot of ground: "We don't have beautiful structures and we don't have gold temples in this lake, but we do have a sign of a living god to who we pray—the living trees, the evergreen and spruce, and the beautiful flowers and the beautiful rocks and the lake itself. We have this proof of the sacred things we deeply love, deeply believe." Six years later, however, the Taos governor, John C. Reyna, was again embracing Euro-American comparisons: "The lake is our church. The mountainside is our tabernacle. The evergreen trees are our living saints."

When a sympathetic Christian priest, the Reverend Dean Kelley, heard this rhetoric, he realized that Pueblo leaders "had tried to find an analogy that would speak to the non-Indian mind. To some degree they had succeeded by comparing it with the European idea of a church." But Kelley also saw the danger of going down a road that "got them into the European idea of holy ground as being rather specifically located in an artificial setting, a building that you could build and then that's the sacred precinct, and outside of it is not sacred." Ecological setting and pilgrimage route, not just one specific site, were at stake.

Aware that evoking the kinds of sacred/secular, purified/polluted dividing lines, so common to academic theories about "primitive" or "tribal" religions, would actually support those who wanted to chip away at the Indian claims, Kelley wrote a magazine article emphasizing how, in Indian eyes, *the entire watershed* was greater than the sum of its sites. Here was an integrated, sacred ensemble, he argued. In the opinion of Taos historian R. C. Gordon-McCutchan, "Kelley's moving arguments played a central role in the hearings and debates that followed."

Had politics and fate not intervened, however, we might still be hearing those debates. But during the 1960s, quiet efforts by Taos spokespersons and their ardent supporters caught Washington's imagination; Blue Lake became a key symbol for the Nixon administration's new policy of support for Indian rights and sovereignty. From January 1970 through early spring that year, Washington buzzed with private discussions among sympathetic politicians, Taos supporters and White House officials. Inspired by the Taos cause, Vice President Spiro Agnew and presidential aide John Ehrlichman worked on their boss. For Richard Nixon, the stumbling block was risking the backing of two anti–Blue Lake senators for his Anti-Ballistic Missile Treaty initiative. When Ehrlichman first characterized the debate as a "cowboys and Indians" thing, Nixon allowed that he was "more of a John Wayne man himself." Then Ehrlichman confessed that they'd gotten involved in the Blue Lake cause as "more of an esthetic matter than a political matter," which also disappointed the pragmatic president; it should have been political from the start. But since they'd gotten this far, Nixon said, "we'd better tough it through."

After the proposal survived its legislative oversight, on December 15, 1970, President Nixon signed the order that reversed the one his hero Theodore Roosevelt had decreed sixty-six years earlier. By presidential fiat, Blue Lake, together with its surrounding forty-eight thousand acres, went back to Taos Pueblo, no strings attached. An unreplicable convergence of factors had jelled in the Indians' favor: the persuasive manipulation by Taos backers of picturesque images of blanket-swathed elders set against their pueblo-and-mountain backdrop; the absence of overriding energy or economic concerns; the advocacy of wealthy liberals and influential artists; the popularity of Frank Waters's novel *The Man Who Killed the Deer* (1942), based on Taos Pueblo; the sympathetic profile of Taos Indians as peaceful farmers and poetic environmentalists; the antiquity of their residence in situ; the adroit use of analogy and the shrewd recruitment of Nixon to a blue-ribbon support committee for the lake's return—and, of course, the prayers of the Taos people. Through the domestic equivalent of Nixon's maverick trip to China, the nation's chief had done the right thing on behalf of pre-Christian rituals that neither he nor anyone else in Washington really understood.

While Taos Pueblo was fighting for Blue Lake, another southwestern Indian pueblo was struggling to protect its treks to another sacred lake. To appreciate the emotional link between the people of Zuni Pueblo in western New Mexico and the dry basin they identify as Zuni Heaven, one must turn to unanswered questions about one of their earliest clashes with Europeans.

What was preoccupying the group of Zuni men who jogged by Francisco Vázquez de Coronado's soldiers on July 6, 1540? Why did the tribe send smoke signals into the sky and jump Coronado's scouts at Bad Pass later that night? Why were the Indians so insistent about banning whites from their village of Hawikuh the following morning? And what, only minutes later, sparked the first big flare-up between Indians and Europeans in North America? Some historians have seen it as a preemptive strike by the Zunis to forestall Spanish retaliation for their killing, about a year earlier, of a Moroccan servant—America's first black explorer, Estevan de Dorantes. But a second look at the tribe's ritual calendar suggests another scenario.

The Spanish knew all about pilgrimages. Back home, the Iberian namesake for the western Mexican village of Compostela, from which Coronado launched his expedition into New Mexico, was a destination for Christian devotees since the ninth century. Many of Coronado's 336 soldiers, largely recruited from the provinces of Extremadura and La Mancha, had suffered blisters and sunburn to earn the scallop-shell insignia of a Santiago pilgrim after walking the 350-mile road that ended at the cave shrine of Santiago de Compostela, where they knelt before the bones of the apostle James. But the idea of similar devotions in the New World never crossed their minds. If any of Coronado's soldiers had questioned their Indian guides, they might have learned that from the snowy tail of the Rockies to Mexico's sun-hammered deserts, the landscape was laced with native highways, trade routes *and* pilgrimage paths. And this might explain why the Zuni encounter with Coronado went so wrong.

In late February 1540, Coronado's expedition mustered in Spain's first settlement, on Mexico's west coast. Crowded into Compostela's tiny plaza, what one historian characterizes as "the most pretentious and spectacular exploratory expedition that ever set foot within the domain of the United States" bowed its collective head. Over the ensuing weeks, Indian marauders taught Coronado to watch his back and guard his supplies. Finally, he split from his lumbering caravan and led a faster party of eighty horsemen and thirty foot soldiers along old Indian trails that followed ridges or riverbeds.

After crossing today's Mexican–U.S. border, the advance guard forded the Gila River, surmounted the Mogollon highlands and pursued the Little Colorado River to a fish-filled stream where an infusion of ocher clay led them to name it Red River (Zuni River). That was when the bunch of Zuni hustled by with no time for small talk. Uneasy about the smoke signaling back and forth, Coronado sent scouts ahead. Bedding down beside an oxbow in the Zuni River, he awoke at midnight to Indian yells and a rain of stone-tipped arrows.

Coronado's fantasies of El Dorado evaporated the next morning, as he laid eyes on the Indian Pueblo of Hawikuh for the first time. Two years earlier, Father Niza de Marcos reported that he had heard from somebody who had heard from somebody else that the village was "richer than Mexico," a veritable "paradise on earth." But in front of Coronado on that morning lay a few hundred adobe huts "all crumpled together" beside patches of desert grass. No native royalty draped in mantles of songbird feathers. No jewels or gold. Only unsmiling Indians armed to the teeth.

Some Zuni men wearing bandoliers hastily sprinkled a line of cornmeal on the ground and gestured the Europeans to back off. When they didn't, the Indians let loose arrows and rocks. Spanish matchlocks boomed back. Before the Zuni fled into the hills, five of them lay dead. Coronado was lamed by an arrow and knocked unconscious. Nervously reentering the village, the natives arranged a shaky peace before scuttling to safety atop a huge mesa nearby. A precedent for Indian-white relations in North America had been set.

Was self-protection the only reason the village seemed so vacant? Were invisible sanctities and unknown obligations also at issue? One answer comes from the Zuni themselves. They maintain that early July in 1540 coincided with an eight-day ceremony, still held every four years, which celebrated the solstice and involved a pilgrimage to a sacred lake. Back in the mid-seventeenth century, the seven separate Zuni villages—today reduced to one—alternated in holding these observances. Spanish documents suggest that Hawikuh played host in 1540, during the summer season the Zuni call *iti'wana* or "middle." Much as Hawikuh itself represented the "center" of Zuni space, as anthropologist Ruth Bunzel has pointed out, these solstices were regarded as a "center" of time.

Coronado's movements through the high desert roughly paralleled the migratory route of Zuni ancestors; and, in fact, it's hard to find a sacred place his men didn't ride close by. When tribal consultants T. J. Ferguson and E. Richard Hart surveyed that corner of Catron and Cibola counties in the 1970s, they identified more than 234 sites that, for the Zuni, provided the setting for what Ferguson and Hart clarified as a "way of life" rather than a separate "religion." "To the Zunis," they explain, "the land-scape is considered a spiritual relative . . . because it provides the physical setting within which Zuni religion is grounded" . . . with certain "buttes, geological formations, lakes, mud ponds, ruins and religious trails" imbued with special powers.

Visiting the rim of the Grand Canyon, Coronado's men peered into *Chimik'yana'kya dey'a,* the Place of Origin, near the spot where Zuni ancestors crawled out of the underworld and where, the Zuni say today, light from the rising sun hits Ribbon Falls. And Zuni elders add, "The plants that grew along the stream that flows from Ribbon Falls of the Colorado River; the birds and animals that we saw as we traveled out into the world; the brilliantly-colored minerals in the rock walls of the canyon; all of these things are recounted sacred in our prayers, and have a central place in our ceremonial religious activities and way of life. . . . So, we believe that the Grand Canyon is alive and sacred."

Approaching the Little Colorado River, the Spanish surely spied a free-standing mesa to the west, but did not learn that the pinnacles of *To'wa Ya'lene,* or Corn Mountain, reminded the Zuni of the mythic children who were sacrificed to placate the great flood, or that it was home to their War God Twins, the *Ahayu:das,* who guarded the Zuni landscape. Its maternal associations ran deep—the mesa held fertility shrines visited by women desiring children; its summit first lent them refuge after the Hawikuh fight and did so again, in 1680 and 1693, after the Zuni joined multitribal uprisings against the Spanish.

In the far distance, outside today's Flagstaff, the Spaniards probably saw the outline of the San Francisco Peaks, a volcanic formation where the ancient Zuni wanderers were given medicinal plants. It, too, was considered alive. "All matter [to the Zuni]," explained anthropologist Bunzel, "has its inseparable spiritual essence . . . the whole world appears animate. Not only are night and day, wind, clouds, and trees possessed of personality, but even articles of human manufacture, such as houses, pots, and clothing, are alive and sentient." Each spring, grove and campsite encountered by those ancestors became what French historian Pierre Nora has termed *lieux de memoire,* or "sites of memory," numinous landmarks to which the Zuni return with prayers and offerings.

•   •   •

Before reaching Corn Mountain, the Spaniards noted the convergence of the Little Colorado and Zuni rivers—a blessing in this arid land. But they were unaware that from there on they were retracing a Zuni pilgrimage route, the *We:sak'yaya onnane,* or Barefoot Trail. A two-day walk, this sacred pathway links the river junction to the Zuni villages about eighty miles upstream. When pilgrims are afoot, no one is allowed to cross this "spiritual lifeline," for it leads to the holiest of Zuni locations, *Ko:thluwala;wa,* or Zuni Heaven, the lake bed whose waters are said to hide the six-chambered Village of the Dance Gods, where spirits of the dead live happily as Kachina beings.

When anthropologist Frank Hamilton Cushing came here in the 1880s to steal the wooden effigies of its protecting War Gods, this Lake of Whispering Waters still reflected the blue sky by day, whereas at night one saw light flashes and heard noises from Kachina spirits frolicking below. It was here, say Zuni stories, that a mythic sister and brother once committed incest, producing nine children with gaping mouths and protrusions about their heads—the ceremonial Mud Heads. To separate herself, the violated sister created the Zuni River. Later on, continue the narratives, when the early Zuni were hunting for a permanent home, they forded this stream. Some children fell from their mothers' arms and swam to the Kachina village, to be reborn as the moist tadpoles, frogs, salamanders and other water-associated creatures that existed before the early Zuni were transformed into "dry," finished human beings. "It is hard to overstate the lake's religious and emotional importance to the Zuni people, past and present," writes anthropologist Carroll L. Riley, "for it is the entrance to the Zuni afterlife and the residence of the kachinas."

So goes a Zuni explanation for the violence at Hawikuh. If its timing coincided with the solstice rites, when pilgrims returned to Zuni Heaven to renew shrines and pray for the universe's well-being, those preoccupied Indians who jogged by the Spanish were likely returning home. By transgressing the Barefoot Trail, the foreigners were obstructing an umbilical link between the Indians and their afterlife. Those smoke signals conceivably came from the youthful impersonator of the Fire God *Shu'la:witsi,* who accompanies these pilgrims, setting bushes on fire to release smoke, which the Zuni likened to rain clouds, while at the same time alerting villagers that they would soon be home. The bandolier-wearing officials who drew that line in the ground were very likely War Chiefs trying to keep the Spaniards from polluting their community at an especially vulnerable moment.

More than three hundred years later the sanctity of Zuni Heaven was threatened again. In 1877 President Rutherford Hayes signed an executive order that turned over the surrounding lands to the government (and opened Zuni shrines to looters). Yet that did not stop upward of sixty of the tribe's pilgrims who continued to hike or ride horseback to their Heaven every four years. In 1920 the tribe began negotiating with the Interior Department for the lake's return, and finally in 1984 the tribe was grateful to receive title again to eleven thousand acres surrounding the lake bed.

Getting the right to cross the intervening ranches, however, was another matter. One landowner was set against it. In 1985, Earl Platt, a former state senator and county attorney with an estimated four hundred thousand acres under his control, wanted the Apache County sheriff to arrest any Zuni who walked on his land during the upcoming pilgrimage. Forewarned, the tribe's lawyers got a restraining order, and the journey went on without incident. During the following years, the Department of Justice backed the Zuni fight for a permanent "easement," which would allow them unchallenged access. But the matter was still undecided when it came time for the next pilgrimage, in June 1989. Again Platt threatened to disrupt it, and another restraining order was signed.

On the pilgrimage's third day, as the Indians were heading home, Platt sideswiped his pickup into them, reportedly hitting one rider. Under strict orders not to pollute their mission with violence, the Zuni quickly withdrew. The eventual determination of court trials against Platt (September 1989) and for the easement (February 1990) were a tribute to other landowners, local law officials and dedicated lawyers who had joined forces on behalf of Zuni religious rights.

When I drove through unlocked ranch roads to the outskirts of Zuni Heaven it was hard to see what the fuss was about. The hardpan supported greasewood and stumpy cedars. Irrigation wells had sapped the lake of moisture; it was now a white-rimmed, grassless *playa*. Near rusty, leaking water tanks, a cow carcass dissolved into the ground. Windmills squealed like sad harmonicas. What went by the names of the Little Colorado or Zuni rivers were actually horse-crippling ravines that disappeared into the Stinking Spring Mountains.

When I got out of my four-wheel drive for a closer look, strange winds spiraling out of the hills moaned and buffeted the bushes. My eyes dropped from the unprepossessing landscape to find at my feet a magic carpet of stone shards from old Indian tool-making activities, broken geodes revealing their crystalline innards, agatized wood, the fragment of a rusty arrowhead cut from sheet metal—all signs of age and human usage. Feeling like an interloper, I retraced my tire lines and passed a farmhouse where a white couple squinted at me from their porch. "Tell 'im not ta' go back up 'err," the woman started yelling, "thasa Indin place. They don't want none up 'err." An improvement, I thought.

The future for a third sacred lake remains in greater peril. In contrast to the evocative public relations strategy that helped Taos recover Blue Lake, the campaign to save Salt Lake, which is revered by the Zuni, Acoma, Laguna, Hopi and Navajo tribes, did well to omit pictures. Drought had parched the land, located in the Carrizo Valley about sixty miles south of Zuni Pueblo, to a bleak gray-brown. Corroding metal sheds, broken grinding machinery and conveyor belts from the abandoned commercial salt mine turned the shoreline into a junkyard. Remnants of dilapidated piers extended across the murky water. A bulldozed berm ran around the salt flats to a collapsed picnic table. Near the opposite shore a large, black volcanic cone rose like an omen out of colorless liquid.

Unphotogenic as it might be, the lake is revered by these western Pueblo peoples for protecting their mythic Old Lady Salt after her flight from Black Rock Lake a little to the north. As the Zuni tell it, "The Salt Lady did not like being polluted with trash and debris, so she moved away from there. She moved to the southeast, going through a rock in the mountain, now known as the Pierced Rock." Catching up with her, the people "planted their prayer sticks, praying for her forgiveness for being so careless about keeping the lake clean and beautiful."

The granules from Salt Woman's skin are so flavorful that Coronado commended them to his king. Every year Zuni pilgrims head down the Zuni Plateau, ford Largo Creek and walk on to the lake's western shore. Along the way the land reminds them of Salt Woman's story—the boulders she left from her flight, the feather-shaped rock where she dropped a plume. Pilgrims can also identify locations from more recent history; for instance, the spring where, in 1680, after all the pueblos had risen in a successful rebellion against the Spanish, one thirsty Spaniard lay on his stomach to drink. Nearby are the spots where he misplaced his knife and lost his shoes and was finally killed. Reaching the best beach for collecting "beautiful salt flower" crystals, the pilgrims fill their sacks and soak ears of corn with brine to save for the harvest festival back home.

Between the late 1870s and the turn of the century, railroad, mining and farming interests seized lands that included both Zuni Heaven and Salt Lake. After some lobbying, the U.S. government finally traded acreage with New Mexico so that at least the Zuni could enjoy access to the salt. Then in 1987, the Interior Department allotted six hundred acres around Salt Lake for their use, only to have the state of New Mexico resist giving the tribe exclusive rights to the salt itself.

But a greater danger awaited Salt Woman. In the 1980s came plans for deep water wells to support an eight-thousand-acre strip mine approximately eleven miles northeast of the lake. Reports estimated that the wells would produce about eighty-five gallons of water per minute in order to wash crushed coal through tubes and down chutes to fill hundreds of coal cars that then transport this fuel to an Arizona-based public electrical utility. That would deplete the same Dakota Aquifer that services the springs that percolate through the salty lens under Salt Lake to produce the precious crust.

Against Indian prayers and opposition, on May 15, 2002, the Interior Department allowed the Salt River Project to pump around 1.5 billion gallons of water during the next forty years. But the Fence Mine also threatened the surrounding Salt Lake area by digging into Zuni shrines and burials, disseminating coal dust particles over the lake, and disturbing ancient trail systems as new railroad lines were laid to send the projected three hundred carloads of coal ore a day to Phoenix. In Zuni eyes, the same sort of disrespect that had forced Old Lady Salt to seek sanctuary there in ancient times would certainly drive her away again.

In the desiccated region of Zuni Salt Lake, however, where most locals are on the government's side, energy concerns could plan and lobby with lessened scrutiny, and the Zuni themselves were hesitant about going public with their private religious information. So it took awhile to win wider support. But in July 2002, tribal representatives testified in Washington on behalf of the lake, Pueblo and Navajo runners staged a protest run from Phoenix to Zuni, and a newly organized Zuni Salt Lake Coalition got the U.S. National Trust to include Salt Lake among its most endangered historic places.

No sooner had the Arizona power utility withdrawn its plan to mine the coal, however, and the Salt Lake Coalition celebrated their victory than the state of New Mexico revealed its intent to open more than a hundred thousand acres in the Salt Lake vicinity for natural gas and oil exploration. This would draw upon the very same underground acquifers in order to extract coal-bed methane gas. Once again, Salt Woman's home seemed bound for violation, and who knew where she would flee next?

The Hindus have a term for the destinations where pilgrims revisit their origins and deities to renew their sense of purpose and return home with blessings. The word is *tirtha,* and it translates as "a fording or crossing place." The meaning is more literal when one thinks of "crossing" sacred waters, like lakes or rivers, and emerging, as from a baptism or a vision quest, reborn. But its wider, figurative connotations include the possibility of crossing from one social status to another, one state of consciousness to another, one cosmological realm to another, or even this plane of existence to the one to come. At places like Blue Lake, Zuni Heaven and Salt Lake, pilgrims come the closest they can to those realities that are eternal, and return for a while renewed.

Who cannot appreciate the idea of Pueblo pilgrims visiting such lakes to celebrate how they originated out of them, to bear witness to the mists and waters that are imbued with the spirits of their ancestors, to offer blessings for the salt and moisture that maintain their lives and fields? And as Pueblo Indians often add, those journeys and their other ceremonies fulfill a broader mandate. "We do this not only for ourselves, but for the Americans also," Mountain Lake told Carl Jung about the Taos pilgrimages. "Therefore they should not interfere with our religion. But if they continue to do so and hinder us, then they will see that in ten years the sun will rise no more. . . . Then it will be night forever."

CHAPTER SIX

PLACE AS PERSONAL

Navajo/Apache

U nderstanding Navajo Indian history is a good test of F. Scott Fitzgerald's measure of a fine intelligence as the ability to hold two contrasting notions in the mind at the same time. Archaeologists claim that the peoples we know as the Navajo and the Apache sprang from bands of Athapaskan-speaking migrants who wended their way south from northeastern British Columbia anywhere from six hundred to nine hundred years ago. Navajo say they emerged from the bowels of the earth in the Four Corners area of the Southwest to find their sacred landscape, which they call *Dinetah*, ready and waiting and already protected by their four sacred mountains. And there, as Carl Jung once said of arguments over the validity of religious experience, the conversation often ends.

In laying claim to the high desert plateau of New Mexico and Arizona as their site of creation, however, the Navajo had a problem. Pueblo Indians, descendants of the "ancestral pueblo" ruins found in Mesa Verde and Chaco Canyon, were there first. From the start, little love was lost between the two peoples. One strategy that the Navajo employed to claim the Southwest as their motherland was to smother it with stories. Few American Indian nations have produced such a crowded atlas of place-names and localized narratives. One wonders if a certain insecurity may lie at the root of this tendency to leave no site untitled or unstoried, and whether the impulse to stake spiritual claims becomes stronger when those of historical residency are weaker.

But no one argues that the Navajo and their linguistic cousins, the Apache, did not develop profound, distinctive and durable attachments to their new lands. Unlike Plains Indians, they did not seek out lonely mountain ledges for vision seekers to suffer and pray. Unlike northwest coastal

Indians, they did not want the resting places of their dead anywhere near them—the farther away, in fact, the better. And unlike their new Pueblo neighbors, they preferred to live in dispersed, extended-family camps or "outfits," which were sprinkled throughout the Colorado plateau. Originally hunters and not farmers, they didn't cluster in condominiumlike apartments around ceremonial plazas, they lacked priesthoods and they didn't dance together in great congregations during agricultural festivals.

A subtler distinction was how Navajo and Apache stories came to emphasize their faith in the *protective* and *instructive* aspects of their special places.

Appearing among the juniper-and-piñon mesas as numerical underdogs, these newcomers were quick studies. Although the Navajo spurn the thought, some scholars say they borrowed from Pueblo Indians the ideas of directionally oriented and color-coded sacred mountains, of layering their hogan roofs with adobe mud, of making ritual sand paintings on the ground with colored minerals and of successfully growing crops in one of the continent's driest habitats. While eschewing the idea of "center" or "navel" shrines, the Navajo do identify one revered place, Huerfano Mesa, as something of a geographical pivot—"the mountain around which traveling was done."

Fluidity in thought and movement were vital to peoples so often on the run. The travel-hardened, settlement-raiding and semimigratory Navajo and Apache had a harder time than the Pueblo in winning white friends and influencing U.S. government policies. And over the centuries, it's as if these Athapaskans and Pueblo peoples came to define themselves—like Israelis and Palestinians, or Turks and Armenians—as each other's "other"— a way of defining who they were not. When Pueblo Indian friends of linguist Dennis Tedlock pondered the differences between the two peoples, one speculated, "Maybe the Zuni needed a center so they wouldn't be like the Navajos and so they would all stick together."

In place of proof of ancient occupancy, the Navajo offered another argument. They did not own their lands through ancestral experiences. Their gods had already done it for them. As the Navajo tell it, shortly after

First Man and First Woman climbed onto the surface of this "glittering" earthly plane, they used dirt brought up from the underworld to "plant" the four sacred directional mountains. Each peak had its mantle—white shell for the East, turquoise for the South, abalone for the West, obsidian for the North. Each peak also had its own inner life, as historian of religions Karl W. Luckert stressed to me, "Navajo mountains *are* gods; they are not only places at which gods live. The analogy of Jewish, Christian, or Muslim sacred sites is usually misleading. . . . Thus, to be exact, talking about the Navajo Holy People as if they are things or places may in itself be seen as a sacrilegious act."

Within the protective dominion of these greater-than-human mountain beings, the host of spirits whom the Navajo know as Holy People (*Haashch'eeh Dine'e*) then created the sky, the seasons and death—and established the Navajo distinctive practices: their sweat baths, *hogan* dwellings, moccasin gambling games and ways of healing and handling death.

Already prowling this new world were monsters who fed upon the First People. When First Man and First Woman discovered a girl baby on top of Huerfano Mesa, the Holy People raised her. Named Changing Woman, she gave birth to the Sun's twin boys, Monster Slayer and Child Born of Water. They slew the cannibals and performed legendary deeds, and the land remembered them. Their adventures and travels left behind place-names, geographical stories and altered topographies (the coagulated blood of one giant, for instance, created the *malpais* lava beds near today's Grants, New Mexico).

As they also learned, this high desert contained dangerous forces. Some places were trustworthy, others definitely taboo, or *chindi*—especially those contaminated by contact with the dead, for instance, and hence the cause of sickness and distress. Trees struck by lightning, whether of the zigzag, forked or flash varieties, were also avoided. Only trained healers handled wood struck by them, to counteract the illnesses caused by lightning. Navajo kids were warned not to eat corn during rainstorms lest they be hit by lightning, not to eat piñon nuts from lightning-touched trees, and never to collect firewood from them.

The gradual dispersal of Navajo clans beyond their Four Corners heartland yielded more extended-family homesteads, more hunting areas and spotty gardens, and more sacred places. "To give the People protection," say the Navajo, one Holy Person embraces them all—his rainbowlike torso curves around the terrain marked by the four Sacred Mountains. Just southeast of the volcanic plug known as Shiprock one finds *Dzilk' Hozhonii,* or Mountain Beautiful on Top. In Navajo belief this uplift is the feet of the Holy Person named *Yyo'di Dzil,* or Goods of Value Mountain, whose body curves southward along the Chuska Mountains until reaching his head, a pine-topped promontory named *Ch'oshgai,* White Spruce, or Chuska Peak. To complete the portrait, the jagged stump of Shiprock is imagined as his medicine pouch.

To survive, the new arrivals drew upon their prowess as hunters. Because the Holy People "presided over the circle journeys of their game animals," says Luckert, the Navajo were never far behind. Wearing hard-soled moccasins and firing sinew-backed bows, they stalked their prey in great walkabouts, and in this fashion, "the Athapascan hunter mind laid claim to the southwestern homeland."

Yet meat did not remain their main course for long. Further rooting these strangers in a strange land were the kernels they learned to raise into stalks. Rather than acquiring maize cultivation from the Pueblo, however, Navajo tradition says First Man gave them white corn; First Woman, yellow corn; multicolored ears came from Turkey; and Big Snake provided pumpkin, watermelon and muskmelon seeds. Because of these origins, a Navajo told anthropologist W. W. Hill, "When a man goes into a corn field he feels that he is in a holy place, that he is walking among Holy People, White Corn Boy, Yellow Corn Girl, Pollen Boy, Corn Bug Girl, Blue Corn Boy, and Variegated Corn Girl. If your fields are in good shape you feel that the Holy People are with you, and you feel buoyed up in spirit when you get back home."

Having learned to live off the land, the Navajo also knew where to hide by the time the Spanish arrived. During nearly three centuries, their relationship was mutually predatory: Navajo raiders snatched Spanish horses and sheep; Spanish slavers stole Navajo women and children. But as they gravitated to stock raising, pastoralism made Navajo life more predictable. Summers in mountain pastures, winters near lowland forage—this yearly round turned a culture of deer trackers into bands of shepherd farmers who became skilled at the tender science of herding, lambing and shearing.

Maintaining this cycle of sheep herding here, gardening there and raiding whenever the opportunity arose stretched the Navajo thin. In the 1820s Mexicans took over from Spain and pursued Indian stock rustlers more aggressively. The Navajo dodged and lashed back, but once the United States entered the region after the Treaty of Guadalupe Hidalgo (1848), making themselves scarce became harder. Unable to cramp the Navajo free-raiding style, the Americans bided their time for a dozen years before moving in.

Between 1863 and 1868, soldiers under Christopher "Kit" Carson, together with Ute Indian mercenaries, created what the Navajo still remember as "The Fearing Time." Families and livestock were hounded down, killed or rounded up and thrown into the three-hundred-mile treks that fused in tribal memory as "The Long Walk." Left behind were destroyed hogans, rock-stuffed wells, burned cornfields, mutilated peach orchards. Ahead lay a concentration camp, Fort Sumner, on the eastern banks of the Pecos River in the alkaline wastes of southeastern New Mexico. About eight thousand bedraggled Navajo were hauled to this dead zone they called *Hwelte*. A quarter of that number would perish before their four-year exile was over.

But a dozen or so Navajo headmen slipped through Carson's dragnet. For their followers, at least, the Holy People again came through. And gratitude to place became an abiding sentiment for descendants of the Navajo who followed a clan leader named Hoskininni, or the Angry One, as he evaded soldiers and Utes and led his small band into the narrow gorge behind the 10,388-foot peak the whites called Navajo Mountain in northern Arizona.

To the Indians, this mountain was actually a "she": *Naatsis'aan,* or Head of Earth Woman, or Changing Woman. Monster Slayer was one of her sons, born in a house made of flint and reared to maturity in a single day. He had defended his people against the ugly children of a monster, who, the Navajo say, were the ancestors of the Paiute. Atop the mountain is a spring that generated rain beings who became the waters that fill Aztec and Oak creeks.

No sooner had the Navajo escapees filtered into the greasewood ravines six miles behind the mountain than they discovered, or "recognized," that they were not alone. Already the area was occupied, one might even say "domesticated," by their Holy People. Fossilized into postures of stone, or bubbling up through green fissures, were rock and spring beings with whom they were already acquainted from their origin stories. Seeing the mountain's back side for the first time, the fugitives realized how Earth Woman and her flint-armored son had protected them from white pursuers. When they shouted into one of the canyon's alcoves, they even heard the mineralized embodiments of Talking God and his brethren talking back to them. "Time and again," says Navajo educator Ruth W. Roessel, "the Holy People come to the aid of the Navajos and are responsible for assisting them in returning home and being restored to the land."

Sometime after the Angry One's discovery, a medicine man named Blind Salt Clansman, tracking loose horses down this canyon, came upon the "rainbow that spans the canyon." At first it looked like a single being. On closer inspection it proved to be two rock rainbow people, a man and a woman, caught in flagrante. To the Navajo, the arch was a sexual union that produced the water babies who flowed beneath them and downstream into Navajo country. Over time they also understood how the springs of distant Navajo Mountain were visually aligned with the Rainbow Bridge Canyon spirits and, in turn, with the convergence of the San Juan and Colorado rivers ten miles away. Here the Angry One's clan folk waited in hiding.

For the majority of the Navajo, however, still imprisoned back along the Pecos, it was as if the landscape itself had turned against them. The dreary, broiling steppes made them long for the snow-crested, piñon-blanketed slopes of home. Instead of freshwater streams, the stuff running down their irrigation ditches tasted evil and caused killing cramps. Within the mud walls of Fort Sumner, food was in short supply. Their first harvest of shriveled cobs was riddled by cutworms. In winter they had to walk more than twenty miles to find mesquite with which to cook and stay warm. Then these former predators turned into easy prey as marauding Comanche picked away at the Navajo's dwindling livestock and stray children. Even their friendly wind spirits now behaved like enemies—hot and stinging and bearing the invisible evils of pneumonia, scurvy and syphilis.

In secret ceremonies they prayed to their Holy People and pleaded for Coyote's intervention. And some Navajo still maintain that it was performing the Coyote Way ceremony that persuaded the U.S. government to realize it had a disaster on its hands. With their prisoners dropping like flies, officials did an about-face. But when the Navajo treaty was finally signed on June 1, 1868, carving out the country's largest reservation in their Arizona homeland, it also stirred old animosities between the Hopi and the Navajo, whose new holdings surrounded the mesa-top pueblos.

As the Navajo refugees trudged homeward, however—finally crossing the Rio Grande near Albuquerque and entering the safer confines of their holy mountains—that hornet's nest lay in the future. "After we get back to our country," promised their leader Barboncito, "it will brighten up again and the Navajos will be as happy as the land. Black clouds will rise and there will be plenty of rain. Corn will grow in abundance and everything look happy." Strung out in a ten-mile convoy of exhausted Navajo, it is said that when the lead families first caught sight of Mount Taylor, they stopped and wept. "When we saw the top of the mountain from Albuquerque," recalled their chief Manuelito, "we felt like talking to the ground we loved it so."

Away from the Plains Indian wars boiling to the north and avoiding Apache insurgency to the south, the Navajo slowly returned to life. From sheep and horses provided by the government, their herds regenerated. For a little more than half a century, they and their landscape enjoyed a separate peace.

From this history arose the profound gratitude of the Navajo toward the homeland that Changing Woman had given them, which they thought they had lost forever in 1864 and, which unlike many of the world's refugee populations, they had won back four years later. "Outside my own country we cannot raise a crop," said Navajo leader Barboncito to General William T. Sherman in 1868, "but in it we can raise a crop almost anywhere." And a hundred years later, a Navajo medicine man, George Blue Eyes, echoed this sentiment of geographical dependency, "These mountains and the land between them are the only things that keep us strong. From them, and because of them, we prosper." Explained a Navajo woman to writer Emily Benedek, "This plant is going to talk to me; this rock is going to talk to me. You have to put your mind at that level." But this Navajo version of what theologian Martin Buber once described as man's I-Thou relationship with nature went deeper, and the following Navajo prayer should probably be taken literally: *Nahyasdzaan ts'ida biya nishli,* "I am truly, absolutely, without a doubt, a child of the earth."

When I first entered Navajo country in 1958, working for an Episcopal church orphanage outside of Farmington, New Mexico, I would have flunked Fitzgerald's test about retaining contrasting ideas in the mind. But as I learned to balance both the Indian and white sides of the tribe's history, understanding their land and all its elements became central to my education.

The exploitation of the tribe's natural resources centered in our Four Corners region, the old Navajo heartland. Some sacred sites, where Navajo medicine men gathered soil for their healing bundles, were already contaminated. That had happened to Shiprock, or "Wings of Rock," to the Indians, whose spiky profile could be seen to the west of our orphanage. Long ago the splintered volcanic core had elevated Navajo forefathers above enemy attack, but then the rock split apart in a thunderstorm. Left stranded on top, some Navajo families starved to death—their ghosts are said to haunt it still. Only trained medicine men could gather medicines there, but never past the point known as Lightning Struck Tree. However, those trips stopped after the California Sierra Club, contrary to Navajo requests, polluted it with a climb to the summit in 1939. I remember how the faces of old-timers tightened when they remembered that episode and other issues related to the Navajo earth and the 1930s.

For that was the decade when government officials forced the Indians in the Farmington-Shiprock area to face the results of generations of unchecked sheep breeding. After their return home in 1868, the Navajo reveled in their multiplying flocks of sheep and herds of horses, but they overlooked the grama grass nibbled to bare dirt and the late-summer rains sweeping topsoil down deepening ravines. Between 1868 and 1930, they lost nearly two thirds of the land's ability to provide forage for domestic animals. To stem the erosion, Commissioner of Indian Affairs John Collier imposed a massive stock reduction. Sheep were slaughtered by the thousands. Losing the prime symbol of their hard-won prosperity, the Navajo felt betrayed; Collier would be cursed as their Hitler.

Forty years later, the tribe had established a better balance between flocks and pasturage, but animal husbandry offered a precarious future for the nation's largest and poorest tribe, and Navajo leaders felt compelled to exploit the resources under their soil. My half-year sojourn on the San Juan River occurred during what some call their Golden Years, because of the $34 million in mineral leases earned in the late 1950s. Today we realize how much of that short-term income came at the expense of Navajo environmental health and harmony.

Petroleum came next. A few hours' drive from our orphanage lay the Hogback Lease, where the original strike had gushed in 1922, turning Farmington into a boomtown. As wages in the oil fields outstripped sales from sheep, blankets or jewelry, Navajo leaders negotiated deals with the government that brought new roads, drinking water and housing, but little financial security. And petroleum extraction brought an altered landscape: sulfurous smells, noisy machines, contaminated springs and no-trespassing signs. Outsiders were now "driving all over the place in automobiles and drilling," complained one Navajo. "Bulldozers tore up the land," said another. "We could not get a drink of cool, unpolluted water anywhere without getting sick."

Because of the San Juan basin's rich fuel deposits, our region underwent the ups and downs of numerous "rushes"—one shortly before my sojourn. These boom-and-bust episodes left itinerant Navajo families stranded in shacks and tents along irrigation ditches—where I dropped off their children after our recreation programs and stayed for coffee boiled over outdoor fires. Maybe tribal politicians at Window Rock reaped benefits from oil, the parents told me, but it hadn't improved their lives. Other Navajo resented the towering rigs and bobbing pumps. Klara Kelley and Harris Francis reported one woman's complaint about the Aneth oil fields of southern Utah, "She asked us to tell the company to stop the clearing because she collects herbs for her medicine from the spot, and she also uses the soil from there for sand painting for various ceremonies."

More promising to tribal coffers was coal, whose the subsurface deposits were also concentrated in the Four Corners area. Every day I saw the discharge from the hundred-foot smokestacks of the recently built coal-burning Four Corners Power Plant near Shiprock, which sent most of its electrical energy to Phoenix. A few decades later, when the Middle Eastern oil crisis fixated the Carter administration's attention on coal, the entire San Juan River Basin was deemed a "national sacrifice area" and opened to strip-mining.

One especially rich bed lay just beneath the surface of Black Mesa, about 150 miles southwest of Farmington. Although its promised revenues never equaled that of oil, by the 1970s they still proved substantial. For many Navajo, however, that did not justify the sight of their high desert being flayed alive, as gigantic steam shovels peeled off acres of ground cover, exposing naked rocks and leaving miles of dirt hills and rain-filled trenches behind them.

Negotiations for Black Mesa's mineral rights were tricky because it straddled the reservations of the Hopi and the Navajo—a strip of their overlapping territorial claims. This intractable problem began when establishment of the Navajo reservation in 1868 exacerbated ancestral tensions between the Navajo and the Hopi. In 1882, when this corner of the Southwest was officially dubbed Indian Country, President Chester Arthur set aside 2.5 million acres for the Hopi and "such other Indians as the secretary of the Interior may see fit to settle thereon." Lying low after their Fort Sumner ordeal, the Navajo families and their flocks spilled into lands the Hopi considered traditionally theirs. Friction between the two tribes escalated from disputes over fencing or fights in bars to lawsuits in courtrooms. In 1962, a federal panel finally ruled that 1.8 million acres of the contested land would be owned by both tribes, hence creating the so-called Joint Use Area (JUA). After twelve years of this unworkable solution, the Navajo-Hopi Settlement Act was passed, and in 1977 barbed wire was strung between the tribes. On one side, about thirty Hopi received eviction notices; on the other, some ten thousand Navajo were told to move. Each claimed loss of sacred lands in the process.

To complicate the picture, the fence cut across Black Mesa. This meant that both tribes had to negotiate separately with the Peabody Coal Company, but coordinate leasing their mineral rights to its coal—the Navajo in 1964, the Hopi two years later. For each tribe these decisions were the outcome of warring factions, political enmities and secret deals. Some of their members shared misgivings about strip-mining's impact on their spiritual ties to the environment. In the words of one elderly Navajo, "[Our] people were told by the holy ones to leave it [Black Mesa] alone. Now the coal companies who hired Navajos have come in and are strip mining the mesa, desecrating it. This coal is said to be the blood of the Female Pollen figure lying there. . . ." By 1963, the Four Corners plant had been identified as the largest source of pollution in the United States, yet three more coal-fired plants were built in the area in the 1970s. Added the old lady, "You hear about the people working in these mines become sick with cancer. The desecration of Black Mesa will burn out our souls one day."

Fights over water also endangered Navajo sacred places. Just below our mission ran our source for drinking and washing, the San Juan River, one of whose Navajo names is Old Age River. One hundred forty miles to the northwest, at the present San Juan side of Lake Powell (fifty-five miles from Glen Canyon Dam), it joined the Colorado, one of whose Indian names means River of Never-Ending Life. To some Navajo, the San Juan is imagined as an older man, with hair that is white like foam, who "mounts" the female Colorado at the juncture of these streams.

In the 1920s, as they projected the energy needs for Arizona's growing cities, U.S. government engineers envisioned damming the Colorado. But it took until two years before my sojourn in New Mexico for the U.S. Congress to pass the Colorado River Storage Project Act. As President Dwight Eisenhower approved flooding what environmentalists called "the place no one knew" (Glen Canyon), among the tributaries that would also go under was the little canyon that had shielded those fugitive Navajo led by the Angry Man back in 1863.

Work on the dam began shortly after I left the state, in the early 1960s. At the narrow gorge fifteen miles above Lee's Ferry, the shoreline was dynamited, the grade reformed and concrete was poured for retaining walls that rose six hundred feet above the riverbed. In 1963, the gates were closed. Lake Powell backed up nearly two hundred miles, creeping through 163,000 acres of creeks, springs, plant and animal colonies and Indian sites—and headed for the largest natural rock bridge on earth.

Nine years later a contingent of Navajo sought out the German-born scholar Karl W. Luckert, then at Flagstaff's Museum of Northern Arizona. They needed professional validation that the tributary of Forbidden Canyon, which led to Rainbow Bridge, was a hallowed place. Would Luckert accompany them there, record their prayers and document their associations with it? Thirty years earlier, author Wallace Stegner had hiked up this branch of Aztec Creek to see the 267-foot sandstone span. "This is the way things were," he wrote, "when the world was young."

Organizing against Glen Canyon Dam injected new vigor into the staid Sierra Club. Its popular run of large-format picture books was launched by photographer Elliot Porter's renderings of the Canyon's serpentine curves and scalloped hollows. The canyon's plight inspired wishful thinking by novelist Edward Abbey about radical environmentalists' blowing up the dam, which in turn incited the Sierra Club's shadow group, Earth First, to flirt with the romance of "ecotage." But no Indians were consulted when environmentalists cut a deal to sacrifice Glen Canyon in order to save Dinosaur Park, and no environmentalists rallied behind the Navajo fight to save Rainbow Bridge.

From the site's bronze plaque, hikers learned that its "discoverers" were a Paiute Indian named Noscha Begay and a local Indian trader, James Wetherill, who had guided archaeologist Byron Cummings there in 1909. But local Navajo from the Shonto community claimed that their forefathers had been familiar with it before then. Even after the U.S. government established the Navajo Reservation—and the Navajo Mountain refugees had come out of hiding—Indians returned to Rainbow Bridge for prayers associated with their Protection Way ritual. Too powerful for them to visit out of mere curiosity, it became a site of pilgrimage.

Luckert had to counter the white man's criterion for designation as a sacred place: antiquity. This standard was based on ideas and images from biblical sites in the Middle East, where holy sites were expected to have the patina and prestige of millennia. Excavations along the Colorado did suggest an Indian presence before A.D. 100, but little proof of occupation after A.D. 1300, although Rainbow Bridge was probably visited, as one report dismissively put it, "by nomadic tribes, such as the Ute, Paiute and Navajo, who have left little archaeological evidence of their presence." The Navajo whom Luckert interviewed freely admitted that their ancestors *first* saw the place in 1863; but their point was that those early visitors recognized that the canyon had *already* housed their Holy People, who had kept it ready for just such a crisis.

Luckert had no recourse but to offset the absence of time depth with a persuasive documentation of the devotion expressed in Navajo songs, stories and prayers toward the canyon. To demonstrate that their claims were not opportunistic inventions to stall development, he interviewed a crippled ninety-year-old medicine man named Long Salt, who'd lived near Navajo Mountain all his life.

Taking the forty-mile trail to the hidden canyon, Luckert then saw for himself the petrified Holy People who were stationed along the canyon walls. With Navajo guides, he poked into brush-covered springs occupied by other Holy People, who, Navajo Paul Goodman told him, were now violated because outfitters corralled their mules and tourists urinated near them, forcing the holy residents to flee. Finally, into view came the Rock Rainbow itself, which another Indian, Ernest Nelson, had warned Luckert not to disrespect by walking under it.

The collection of affidavits that Luckert submitted in the ensuing *Badoni v. Higginson* court case chronicled this visit. Appended to them were texts about Protection Way and chants he had recorded from ten different medicine men. All of the canyon's spirits, or "Holy children of Earth Mother," were "born and raised in one day in a miraculous and holy manner," Buck Navajo told him, "out of necessity and need, because there were many enemies [of the Navajo] in those days. . . . At the time of the creation of Rock-arch certain songs and prayers were given for us to use—to have and use in time of need. And a certain way was also given whereby we could give offerings to Rainbow, also to Water, to Earth, and to Sky . . . and yes, certain places in the Rainbow Bridge area have personal names.

"And certain offerings and prayers are given in these places," Buck continued. "I know about the prayer of the Rainbow, and that prayer has twelve parts. And one of the ways is Rain-requesting way. Another way is that of Talking Rock. These holy places must work together equally." He added, "If some part is missing, it will no longer be complete."

Luckert documented a century of Navajo visits to the Rainbow Bridge and Navajo Mountain area, and quoted their thankful prayers for escaping the Fort Sumner disaster. But on June 15, 1981, the Navajo suit to halt the spread of Lake Powell was turned down. Soon visitors were taking seventy-five-foot houseboats, sleek powerboats or Jet Skis to Indian ruins and slickrock canyons. Motor launches dropped tourists right at Rainbow Bridge as its status had devolved from that of a sacred place caught in an intimate act to what the courts insisted on labeling "the monument."

Uranium was the next mixed blessing. Radioactive residue from yellow-colored uranium oxide had been destroying my Indian neighbors' lungs ever since 1953, when the Kerr-McGee uranium-milling plant opened operations at Shiprock. We were mostly ignorant of this, even as I visited Navajo parents who worked there and saw the plant's plumes every day. One account of Navajo origins describes their ancestors arriving on this fourth world and being greeted with a choice between two yellow powders. Upon selecting the corn pollen as their medicine, they were advised to leave the yellow dust untouched in the rocks lest it bring death.

Breakthroughs in nuclear fission research in the early 1940s made "yellow cake" a hot commodity. Under the Carrizo Mountains just west of Shiprock lay one of the Southwest's four major beds; the area was nick-named the Saudi Arabia of uranium. As prices rose across the country, however, royalties to the tribe remained at less than half the national average. And during the late 1950s, an increasing number of Navajo miners began exhibiting scarred lungs, malignant tumors and other health disorders.

Back in college, I kept abreast of congressional hearings that exposed working conditions in the Four Corners uranium mines, crushing plants and refining mills, the dangers from their toxic dumps, wastewater ponds and loose tailings, and the shoddy treatment of Indian miners. Unlike their white counterparts, Navajo weren't promoted, received only minimum wages and were denied subsidized housing. Worse, some of them slept in housing where the Sheetrock walls were contaminated with radioactive dust, and they washed and drank from well or river water into which radioactive residue had leached. Their children, sheep and neighbors breathed particles that, by 1990, were declared the cause of some five hundred miners' deaths from lung cancer. The risk of Navajo miners' dying from the disease was twenty-eight times as great as for those Navajo not exposed to uranium.

Although the Shiprock pits were closed in the late 1960s, in other parts of the Navajo land, mining continued for decades. However, at the Navajo community of Cane Valley, located in Monument Valley, the Department of Energy decided to showcase its atonement. Attempting to rehabilitate the valley in 1992, they removed uranium tailings to another site. But first they hired a medicine man to bless the transfer. A daughter interpreted his Navajo speech: "He said it should never have been dug up. He believes in Mother Nature. To him, everything that has been taken out of Mother Nature has been harmful. . . . Back then those old folks like his dad [knew] that it . . . is poison and can kill. They knew it, but it was the white men that took it and it killed a lot of Navajos."

Then the medicine man commenced a two-and-a-half-hour abbreviated version of the Blessingway ceremony. Often described as the backbone of the tribe's ceremonial system, Blessingway asks the Holy People to return peace, beauty, harmony and all good things—aspirations summarized in the important Navajo term *hozho*. Central to Blessingway is a buckskin bundle that contains samples of soil from the tribe's four sacred mountains, gathered by the medicine man himself. The songs of Blessingway appeal to Earth Woman's restorative powers by reminding the Navajo of their connection to her: "As I stand along the surface of the Earth," one goes, "she says child to me, she says grandchild to me. . . ." And then, beginning with the soles of Earth Woman's feet, the verses lovingly guide everyone's attention up her corpus, describing body part after body part until they reach the top of her head.

In the Blessingway ritual, everybody is implicated; its pleas for a restoration of balance and health are universal and personal. The ceremony seeks to return everyone to an intimacy with the Holy People and their harmonious ways. But the participants' apologies must be sincere, their actions must match the words in its chants. So in his effort to decontaminate Cane Valley from uranium poisoning, and to restore *hozho* to its weakened landscape, a Navajo medicine man had "high-powered executives strip to their waists, dab their arms with corn pollen, and get down on their hands and knees to think good thoughts."

An overview of Athapaskan-speaking Indian attachments to southwestern land would be incomplete without a salute to a stunning example of what can be learned about Indian environments through acquiring a proficiency in native languages and an understanding of their storytelling traditions. This is the landmark work of linguist Keith Basso among the Western Apache of south central Arizona who live in and around the mercantile center of Cibeque.

Located south of Navajo country, these Indians do manage to keep two sets of ideas about the past at the same time. Knowledgeable leaders on today's Fort Apache Reservation preserve the mythic stories they know as "In the Beginning" narratives. Familiar to most of the six Athapaskan-speaking peoples known as Apache, one scenario has their ancestors crawling from the bowels of the earth to blink at the Arizona sun within the protection of such peaks as Mount Baldy and Mount Graham, which in turn prove to be the homes of mountain spirits called the *Gaahn,* who descend from their strongholds—as impersonated by heavyset, black-hooded dancers with distinctive lattice headpieces—to perform during fire dances and girls' puberty rites.

But these Apache, or at least scholar-rancher Keith Basso's neighbors in the thirty-five-square-mile western corner of the White Mountain Reservation country around Cibeque, also relate shorter, "historical" narratives. They concern ancestral times as well, but are set within a less mythical and more recent historical period—the oldest stories describe the migratory forefathers and foremothers of today's Apache trudging with all their possessions into an unfamiliar landscape, the full value of which they have yet to comprehend. Later tales recall early reservation days, the late nine-teenth century, when the Apache lived under the thumb of all-powerful government Indian agents and their deputized Apache police.

One way the first-arriving Apache made their new Arizona surround-ings their own was by looking them over intently and coming up with highly descriptive place-names. This discovery launched Basso's explo-ration into the philosophical and moral importance that Apache invested in their places.

Trained in anthropological linguistics at Stanford University, Basso started fieldwork at White Mountain in 1959. The U.S. government had established the Fort Apache Reservation in 1872, creating for their recent enemies a 1.5-million-acre realm between the Mogollon Rim and the Salt River, which encompassed red-rock canyons, soft-crested mountains and a mantle of pine forest. After making friends and acquiring conversational skills, Basso delved into the customary anthropological topics of kinship, religion and witchcraft, but then graduated into more offbeat subjects, such as the role of silence and humor in Apache discourse, and how Indi-ans used their psychological observations of white people's behavior as a way to correct their own. As if these studies were but an apprenticeship, tribal chairman Ronnie Lupe suggested in 1979 that Basso was ready to tackle Apache geography. White men needed maps, Lupe told him, the Euro-American labels which were soon seen by Basso as yet another "sub-tle form of oppression and domination." But his people's maps were in the place-names they kept in their visual memories.

To see these places that names helped to preserve in Apache minds, Basso accompanied Indian cowboys down creeks, over meadows and through the trees. To understand how they remained there he stayed alert to whenever place-names came up in everyday speech, and then checked his notes with notable elders, the "culture bearers" of the Cibeque com-munity, to tell him why. After five years, his maps had blanketed the thirty-five-square-mile area around the trading hub with over six hundred place-names, and his notebooks contained the background stories keyed into each of them.

A number of these names were so visually precise that Basso could recognize the places they referred to today. They described locations such as Water Lies with Mud in an Open Container, Juniper Tree Stands Alone, Green Rocks Side by Side Jut Down into Water and Gray Willows Curve Around a Bend. The stories of the historical-tale type, which were associated with these places, were also notable for their brevity. Taking seven or so minutes to recount, amounting to three or four paragraphs on a page, their formulaic opening lines anchored the story: "It happened at . . . [the place-name]," a line that was repeated at the end, "It happened at . . . [place-name]."

Small rural communities like Cibeque, whose two thousand or so inhabitants live in small houses or trailers and weed their family gardens strung along an irrigating creek, are sometimes labeled "face-to-face" communities because everyone knows everything about everyone else; through blood or marriage most people are even kin. But Basso discovered that Cibeque was also a face-to-*place* community; human links to well-known locations could be as intimate as those between fellow Apache. And those descriptive names that Apache applied to such places served as memory pegs on which were hung all kinds of historical experiences that they invoked for various reasons.

Reciting the place-names that were first spoken by their ancestors and evoking their oldest experiences, even in seemingly idle talk, was a way of reliving those early events and, more important, resurrecting their underlying lessons. So topographically precise were the names that speaking them placed the pictorial imaginations of today's speakers in their ancestors' footsteps; the "speech act" made contemporary Apache feel as if they were seeing these rocks, trees and waters for the first time—from identical vantage points—and internalizing their associated stories and parablelike lessons. That was one way that these place-names "worked on your mind," as Basso's friends put it. It was as if saying the place-names channeled the ancestors' courage and values as they had settled this habitat long ago, and revived their model of right action for their descendants.

The deeper Basso probed the common uses of place-names, the more he realized that this moral code governed their usage. One incident, included in his earliest essay on Apache place-names, concerned a woman who behaved inappropriately during a Sunrise Ceremony, or girls' puberty rite. Wearing plastic curlers in her hair, she had barged into a kitchen where the cooks were preparing the ceremonial feast. This was a major faux pas during a period when everyone is keenly aware of the heightened power of symbols. During Apache puberty ceremonies, the spirit of White Shell Woman hovers over the proceedings. Among the telltale attributes of their beloved deity and epitome of womanhood is a cascade of well-brushed, free-flowing hair.

At that point, the intruder's grandmother told a story, which she announced by the formulaic opening, "It happened at Men Stand Above Here and There." Her tale involved an Apache policeman who was supposed to arrest a fellow Apache who had killed a cow off the reservation. But standing with his prisoner before Fort Apache's commanding officer, the policeman drew a blank about why he was there. He returned with his prisoner a second time, but again his mind left him and he stood there looking foolish. The culprit went free. Everyone in the kitchen recognized the humor and the warning: don't behave like a white person or betray your kind lest you will open yourself (your mind) to witchcraft.

Even just telling Basso the story left the woman bothered by it, or more precisely, by the place where it had happened. To describe the feeling, she used a hunting term. "I know that place," she said, and even though the grandmother who had told the story was no more, she added, "It stalks me every day." When they referred to these stories and places the Apache often harkened to their old hunting heritage. One of Basso's teachers, Nick Thompson, extended the hunting analogy's reach. "Even if we go far away from here to some big city, places around here keep stalking us. If you live wrong, you will hear the names and see the places in your mind. They keep on stalking you, even if you go across oceans. The names of all these places are good. They make you remember how to live right, so you want to replace yourself again."

Sometimes people didn't need to tell the whole stories for their messages to come through. In a sort of communicative shorthand, they merely passed those place-anchoring first lines back and forth. Nearly always triggered by some problem of interpersonal or cross-cultural misbehavior, it was as if the place-names themselves, with which everyone was familiar, were doing the talking, the lecturing or the consoling.

Place-names helped the Cibeque Apache to remember what happened where and what it meant. Another of Basso's mentors, Dudley Patterson, reflected on how these names, stories and locations contributed to the development of a smooth, steady and resilient mind: "Wisdom sits in places," Patterson said. "It's like water that never dries up. You need to drink water to stay alive, don't you? Well you also need to drink from places. You must remember everything about them. You must learn their names. You must remember what happened at them long ago. You must think about it and keep thinking about it. Then your mind will become smoother and smoother. Then you will see danger before it happens. You will walk a long way and live a long time. You will be wise. People will respect you."

CHAPTER SEVEN

CHRIST IN THE FLOWER WORLD

Yaqui

I n Peru one hears the term *conpenetrado*, meaning "mutual penetration," to describe the merging of Indian and Spanish religious traditions. The context in which I first heard it concerned pilgrimages to sacred mountains. Caravans of villagers with rippling cloth banners and vows to fulfill climbed to peaks and caves in the central Andes, which their Incan ancestors knew as *huacas*, places that are still considered the living ancestors of social lineages but which Catholic priests rededicated to a host of Christian saints. "These two facets of miraculous shrines, Christian and Andean," says anthropologist Michael Snallow, "are locked in a perpetual embrace." Much as human relationships can get their zing from blends of attraction and antagonism, the term *conpenetrado* suggests two cultures gazing at each other with curiosity and surrendering through a mutual tumble, followed by a lifelong, if contentious, marriage.

In social science, the term for these sorts of hybrid rituals is "syncretism," but it loses the juice of *conpenetrado*. An anthropologist from Arizona named Edward H. Spicer preferred "collaboration" between cultures. Spicer coined it to describe what he learned after studying the Yaqui Indians, at first, in the 1930s, among their refugee hamlets around Tucson, Arizona, and a decade later, in the Yaqui motherland of western Sonora, Mexico. To his astonishment, there Spicer entered what he called a "medieval world" that had preserved eighteenth-century Indian beliefs. Behind the religious code that united the tribe's Ocho Pueblos, or Eight Sacred Towns, was the conviction that their Yaqui River landscape constituted a "Holy Land."

With that term Spicer was invoking the Judeo-Christian heritage, with its Middle Eastern deserts and three world religions. But the Holy

Land of the Yaqui meant something more. Even though the tribe had been Catholicized in the seventeenth century, their older, pre-Christian spirits continued to live a parallel existence in that portion of the Sonoran landscape that the Yaqui still call *huya anía,* or "the wilderness world." More remarkable, these Yaqui did not consider the Old Testament heroes and prophets to be Middle Eastern characters. They were Indians. The Garden of Eden, Noah's Ark, all the rest of it happened here. Nor did the Passion unfold in Galilee. Christ first walked the Americas. His miracles took place along the Yaqui River. This was not any Holy Land; here lay *the* Holy Land.

To glimpse this twist to an American Indian sacred geography, a few years ago I visited my graduate student Kirstin Erickson when she was studying women's roles in the Yaqui Indian village of Potam, in western Sonora not far from the Pacific Ocean. I went in late October for the Day of the Dead. After landing in Ciudad Obregón, we bussed to Vikam Switch, the most "Mexicanized" of the eight Yaqui towns that are strung along the desiccated, overgrown bed of the Yaqui River. While we waited in a bus shelter for the last local to Potam, coughing trucks and dented cars raised clouds of dust and the twilight softened into a mustard-colored haze.

Vikam lies near the center of Mexico's only Indian reservation, where a population of about thirty-two thousand Yaqui cling to their distinctive identity. After a battering century of intermittent warfare and forced exile, in 1937 the pro-Indian regime of President Lázaro Cárdenas established this 485,000-acre *zona indígena,* making the Yaqui the only one of the country's fifty-six ethnic groups to enjoy their own homeland. Although losses to agribusiness and non-Indian squatters have reduced it by half, to the Yaqui, this landscape remains the stage for all their mythological, historical and religious dramas.

Behind us Kirstin indicated *Kawi Omteme,* the Angry Mountain, no more than a mile away. On its summit originated the tribe's central story about itself; hardly a visitor escapes having the Talking Tree tale drummed into them, with its message of territorial autonomy and spiritual duality. Kirstin's version came from a descendant of Juan Maldonado, the late-nineteenth-century freedom fighter known to his people as *Tetabiate,* or

Rolling Boulder. The tale is set in the days of the *Surem,* a mysterious band of Little People who are ancestral to today's Yaqui. Atop the Angry Mountain a leafless tree began to vibrate, and its message was interpreted by a prophetess. Strange things were coming from distant lands: new kinds of people, cows and horses, seeds to plant, people flying through the air and talking over long distances. "Guard your territory," warned the tree. "Mark your borders."

To do that the Surem archers fired into the air. Wherever their arrows landed—on the border of Mayo Indian territory and up to the Rio Colorado—determined the breadth of Yaqui territory. Then came the predicted troubles: the establishment of New Spain, the despotic regimes of Porfirio Díaz and Lorenzo Torres. "They all wanted this land of the Yaqui," the Yaqui man told Kirstin. "They sent us to Yucatán, Oaxaca, the Valley of Mexico. Many fled to Tucson. But they couldn't finish them off. The Yaqui Tribe has never left the Yaqui River."

Nor were the Surem gone for good. Each one was said to wrap up a section of the Yaqui River, as if safeguarding their lifeline from all invaders. With the arrival of Spain and Christianity came the prophesied divisions in Yaqui life, belief and land. Those who chose baptism faced mortality. But the Surem slipped into a parallel "enchanted" realm of eternal existence where they still live today. Among their band was Omteme, namesake of the Talking Tree's hill. When Christopher Columbus arrived, another story goes, he occupied its summit. Upon hearing the Tree's prediction of European takeover, Omteme was beside himself. After killing Columbus, he joined his Surem kindred and the countryside swallowed them up. But sometimes you stumble across their miniature grinding stones and clay pots hidden where they still dwell along the *yo vatwe,* "the enchanted river," the scrub, or the mountains.

In verses that she'd heard in the Deer Dance songs the previous Easter, Kirstin learned the river was considered part of *yo ania,* the "enchanted world" of untamed nature. These songs celebrated how, come springtime, you could experience this enchantment for yourself as the colors of blooming thorn trees and desert cacti fulfilled another key Yaqui phrase, *sea ania,* "the primeval flower world." Through the repetition of vivid descriptions in song, accompanied by a skilled dancer mimicking the animal's mincing steps and head movements, the Deer Dance offset the Passion of Christ with the environmental allure of a pre-Christian paradise:

> You are an enchanted flower wilderness world.
> You are an enchanted wilderness world.
> You lie with see-through freshness.
> You are an enchanted wilderness world.
> You lie with see-through freshness, wilderness world.
>
> Over yonder in the middle of the *seyewailo* wilderness,
> In the enchanted wilderness world.
> Beautiful with the dawn wind, beautifully
> You lie with see-through freshness, wilderness world.
> You are an enchanted wilderness world.
> You lie with see-through freshness, wilderness world.

That "enchanted world" seemed far from the sun-scorched trees and prickly plants catching torn plastic in their spines that surrounded our bus shelter, and the urine-soaked newspapers and gas fumes that were stinking it up. The arrival of a derelict with unzipped fly and drink-fired eyes made us shuffle over on the bench. He was a Mayo Indian, and Kirstin knew him—a venerated Pascola dancer, the ritual character for the Yaqui and Mayo whose powers derive from compacts with the Devil but who also perform sacred duties for their people. Leering at her, he complained that she'd been ignoring him. No Deer Dance, no true fiesta can happen without the Pascolas, known to the Yaqui as "elders of the Fiesta." At public events they may goof around, but they are honored as ritual hosts and religious authorities. Much like the Surem, they speak the language of the "little animals of the desert." It is said that when they converse with Saint Bullfrog, Saint Horned Toad, Saint Turtle, Saint Lizard and Holy Cricket, the Pascolas receive special skills—the frog's gift of staying both under and on top of water, the turtle's self-confident pace, the lizard's heat-resistant skin and ability to burrow into desert sand, the cricket's endurance for singing all night and the horned toad's protective crown, which is shaped "like the Virgin of Guadalupe" herself. Our visitor was a nuisance, but too powerful, even half crocked, to dismiss.

Until this trip, my awareness of Yaqui culture stemmed from writings by Edward Spicer and Carlos Castaneda. The bench onto which our Pascola squeezed us recalled the celebrated passage in Castaneda's *The Teachings of Don Juan,* which launched my generation on a thousand trips. Early in Castaneda's supposed memoir of his apprenticeship to a crafty Yaqui shaman, our nerdy author is led to his "power spot." It was 1961, Castaneda was a UCLA graduate student in anthropology studying medicinal plants, and in the Nogales bus station on the Arizona-Mexican border he'd run into Don Juan Matus, a mysterious old man. Carlos begged to be treated "as if I were an Indian."

Don Juan took him home, then abandoned him on an eight-by-twelve-foot porch all night so Carlos could locate his *sitio*—his "spot." All night Carlos shifted position, suffering a gamut of emotions that he associated with subtle shifts of color in the darkness: fear, panic and peace. By dawn he'd crawled to the extremes of threat and safety and finally fell into a deep sleep. Both poles were necessary, said Don Juan, for searchers after wisdom. The "Yaqui teachings" that Castaneda poured into ten books had begun. The episode's influence was summarized a quarter century later by essayist Nicholas Bromell, who remembered how "Castaneda learns from his Yaqui shaman that each person has his 'spot' in the world, a place where the strength of the earth wells up and protects him from the demons of the psyche." Like thousands of his generation, to Bromell the scene's appeal drew upon his own aching rootlessness. "I'd come from nowhere," he bemoaned, "and have no spot."

Critics questioned Castaneda's spiritual romanticism and his guru's warrior ethos. "The sorcery in Don Juan is Western sorcery," challenged his fellow South American mystic Oscar Ichazo. "The idea of a warrior is not an Indian idea. It is a Chinese idea, because if there were a warrior thing in the Indian culture, there would be a martial art and there is none." As for Don Juan's trick of "stopping the world," Ichazo felt that it was lifted from Buddhism. "Nobody can stop the world. But you can really stop your mind. But you know that is the trick of Castaneda—trying to say something new about something very old. . . . One thing with concepts, and mostly with mystical concepts, is that they don't allow you to manipulate them at random."

Regarding the book's authenticity about Indian ways, the hunch of Lakota Indian author Vine Deloria, Jr., that "the absence of references to sacred lands causes me to wonder" was insightful. The individualized sense of space that Don Juan used as a mystical exercise for opening Castaneda to the world of "non-ordinary reality" contradicted everything we know about Yaqui sacred landscapes. Indeed, what makes their Holy Land so fascinating are the very collective, tribal and Christian features that amount to a greater "separate reality" than Castaneda ever imagined.

Our converted school bus bounced over potholed roads for a half hour before dropping us on a chilly, dark street in Potam village. Suddenly alert, Kirstin clipped down the rutted road. Her Indian "sisters" had insisted she never walk alone after sunset. Beyond one's gate loitered teenage *chamacos,* whose sexual teasing could get out of hand; sinister *vagos* high on beer or weed who might rob you; the *malas palabras,* or gossip, which loose behavior earned you; even the *chonim,* little goblins who watched you from the rooftops. Our eyes adjusted to starlight. We cut corners at smoldering trash piles, kicked aside Tecate bottles and steered around horse droppings. Bordering the spooky shortcuts were fences wired together from carrizo cane. From the shadows came scraps of radio music, growls of dogs pacing the perimeters, smells of mesquite cooking fires, glints of lightbulbs illuminating families quietly laughing under *ramadas* that were roofed with boughs. The silhouette of a horseman floated by with a squeak of leather, a jingle of reins. When we reached her compound, Kirstin tilted her head. From the direction of the Yaqui River, a half hour's walk away, came cries of coyotes.

Twenty years before Carlos Castaneda was smitten by his Don Juan, another American anthropologist ran into a charismatic Yaqui by the same name. The Indian was fifty-five-year-old Juan Valenzuela, but everyone knew him as Don Juan, a *pueblo yo'otui,* "respected old man." To Edward Spicer, then a postgraduate student from Arizona renting a room in Potam village, the old man exuded a "feeling of unearthliness which he gave rise to in all of us."

By now Spicer knew the painful arc of Yaqui history. Seven years before the Zuni Indians of New Mexico had laid down their cornmeal line to
prevent Coronado from entering their village, a slave trader named Diego
de Guzmán and his soldiers crossed the Yaqui River and faced its residents.
It was October 1533. Carrying his bow and arrows, the rising sun made
the Yaqui leader's pearl-studded robe "blaze like silver." Then the old man
grabbed his ceremonial staff and "drew a line on the ground as a demar-
cation, threatening death to any intruder who dared cross it."

Like Coronado, the newcomer crossed the line—to his regret. Never
had Europeans tangled with such foes, a "nation of witches," they branded
the Yaqui. Badly bloodied, Guzmán's forces withdrew. Seventy years later
the Spanish hit back, their forces bolstered by a few thousand Indian
mercenaries and forty mounted Europeans slashing at the Yaqui with
cutlasses. Again the Indians whipped them. Regrouping—doubling their
native allies, throwing in more cavalry—the Spanish tried once more. The
Yaqui delivered a third knockout. Around this point, something exceptional in the history of Indian-white relations seems to have transpired.
Starting a pattern of fiercely standing fast and then backing off and ac-
commodating, the Yaqui sued for peace. A treaty was sealed on April 15,
1610.

With their boundaries secure, the Yaqui invited a few Jesuits to cross
them. Much like those Algonquian Indians of northern New England who
developed loyalties to solitary French missionaries who learned their language and gave them some respect, the Yaqui accepted the Padres Andrés
Pérez de Ribas and Tomás Basilio when they entered Yaqui territory in
1617 without soldiers.

Until the 1680s, during nearly three generations, a relative peace
reigned over the Yaqui River Valley. There is sparse documentation on
how the more relaxed atmosphere allowed for cultural interactions that
blended aspects of Spanish and Indian worlds. It was then, however, that
the eighty or so spread-out Yaqui *rancherías* were consolidated into eight
mission towns, the Ocho Pueblos—in the Yaqui tongue, *Ume Wohnaiki
Pueblom*—which were strung together for fifty miles along the flood plain.
Over these decades the Indians learned to tend sheep and cattle, plant, irrigate and harvest fields. The biannual harvests from their communally

owned flood plains along the Yaqui and Muerto rivers yielded so many baskets of corn, beans and squash that they had surplus to export.

Something about the less coercive pace of this period fostered a fusion between cultures. Somehow the Yaquis wove Catholicism into their pre-existing system of beliefs and rituals, but with such intensity that their Mexican neighbors would consider them "religious fanatics." To Mexican poet Ruben Dario the souls of Latin America's Indians were the spoils of a war "between the Cathedral and pagan ruins." But the analogy that began this chapter may be more accurate. In western Sonora, jihad was replaced by something more like an embrace.

Through cracks in the wattle-and-daub walls of Kirstin's hut, slashes of sunlight woke me, then crowing roosters and splashing sounds shot me upright. The cool, rammed earth floor felt good to my bare feet. Entering the freshly sprinkled yard, I blinked around the irreducible cell of Yaqui territory—the family compound.

At its root the religious festival of All Souls, or the Day of the Dead, is a form of ancestor worship. It is a tricky time—the usual distance between the living and the dead is transgressed. Every family yard becomes a transitional zone as their deceased, the *aniimam,* return to savor the large Yaqui flour tortillas and their favorite delicacies. Every home preserves their names in its book, which is treasured as a genealogical talisman. One always treats the dead respectfully, but especially today. So the ritual *must* be celebrated here first, not in the thicket of graves that cluster around Potam's church. Those will be spruced up tomorrow, when the dead return to their own kind. Today their personalities are remembered, along with their favorite dishes—I could smell them from the kitchen.

Alongside the recently splattered whitewash gleaming off the yard's three-foot white "house cross," I met the family. Men were lashing together the altarlike *mesita* in the open yard, soon crammed with Yaqui treats: caramel-flavored beans, steaming beef in mole, *elotes* of maize. Erecting the structure on rickety mesquite saplings, the relatively short men stood on chairs while they worked. Flies thickened above the steaming bowls coming out of the kitchen. Soon would arrive the lay ministers, *maestros,* with their entourage of old women *cantoras* in tow, droning nineteenth-century hymns in off-key, mournful Latin, joining the dead at the table.

After breakfast Kirstin walked me through the next ring of Yaqui space: the barrio. Of the four neighborhoods that make up Potam, her's lay just east of the oldest, Santiamea, named after a prominent hero of the Yaqui wars and also closest to the river. In every yard I noticed the freshly white-washed crosses that protected families against disease and misfortune, and that alerted lay brotherhoods who made the rounds during Lent that here were folks to tax before Holy Week.

Kirstin stressed that Potam's apparent poverty had fooled her at first. People helped each other out and wild foods and natural medicines still came from the land. She regularly picked fresh lemons from her family's bush camp, or *ranchito,* found closer to the river, where goats, pigs and cattle were corralled outside of town. Shadowing most family compounds were large *guamuchil* trees, their limbs full of gray-yoked Sinaloa crows feeding on seed pods. The tree bark was boiled to stop diarrhea, and the fruit's whitish pulp dulled toothaches. The spreading boughs brought each yard's temperature down by ten degrees. Cartloads of mesquite firewood, gathered near the river, kept passing us. On nearly every block people were setting up wooden-crate stands of homemade *tacos dorados.*

As for hints of the pre-Christian "enchanted flower world," a bicyclist in a beaten-straw cowboy hat pedaled by on an ancient black single-speed. Sitting sidesaddle behind him balanced his wife, the train of her cobalt-blue rebozo lifting in the wind. Her skirt! Kirstin whispered. Between patent leather shoes and a dark overskirt peeked out a white cotton slip that was embroidered with purple, yellow and hot pink *sea hiki,* or "fantasy flowers," a visual quote from the flower world Kirstin was learning to recognize.

Today's Yaqui country approximates the territory the Surem's arrows outlined in mythic times. A few miles into the mesquite scrub, we neared the Yaqui River, once called Chief River, now reduced to a trickle. Draining the southern Sierra Madre Mountains, it turns west near Ciudad Obregón and runs for about sixty miles before emptying into the Gulf of California, thirty miles south of Guaymas. At one time, that last stretch of fertile valley bottom was a farmer's Eden where, in a patchwork of flood plain farms, the Yaqui families simply waited for the spring overflow to subside before being assured of a bountiful crop of corn, white beans, pinto beans and melons.

But in 1930, a dam project sent a tracery of irrigation canals into the desert. Wheat rather than corn became the "winter vegetable." A second dam in 1945 drowned a half million acres of tribal lands. What fields were left—as visiting bass fishermen and dove hunters plied the new thirty-five-mile-long artificial lake—were tilled by struggling Yaqui who marketed their wheat in Cuidad Obregón. With construction of the huge Alvaro Obregón Dam in 1952, however, even that option was lost. The semiyearly overflows that once layered the banks with organic loam and threw precious water into hundreds of natural channels were no more.

Yaqui hopes to survive as subsistence farmers on the river's northern bank weakened in 1976, when President Luis Echeverría confiscated 106,666 acres for landless non-Indians. The little Yaqui family plots were recombined into immense wheat and cotton fields run by large corporations; now the Indians drove tractors for wages or worked as field hands. The impact on the enchanted desert was not ignored. "We feel sorry for the wilderness world," said their kinfolk in Arizona, "but what can we do?" A Mexican Yaqui lamented to writer Felipe Molina, "They are hurting our land, they are destroying our beautiful wilderness world. What are we going to enjoy once it is gone?" And an older woman reminisced to Kirstin, "How beautiful the countryside was" before the days of agribusiness and crop spraying. "Sweet smelling, there were many trees, many flowers."

On the gulf coastline, about fifteen miles away, Kirstin had visited beach shanties where teenagers from her compound found seasonal work at the tribe's fishing cooperatives at Las Guasimas, nearby Los Algodones, and the shrimping hamlet on the Bay of Wolves, an estuary at the river mouth. To the northeast, beyond the fringe of paloverde trees, across the Rio Muerto and the Ferrocarril del Pacifico tracks, she pointed out the Bacatetes, the rugged stronghold sliced by plunging canyons that had so often protected Yaqui freedom fighters. Her hope was to go there next month.

· · ·

Cracks in the detente between the Yaqui and the Jesuits appeared in the late seventeenth century. Spanish cattlemen coveted Yaqui grass and released their stock across the tribe's western borders. They opened the Alamos silver mine and began taxing well-to-do Yaqui and confiscating Indian land for their burgeoning ranches. During the next hundred years, this trespass by Spanish and Mexican settlers swelled into an invasion. In 1740, the Yaqui warriors bared their fangs again, but it was only a delaying action. When the Jesuits were withdrawn twenty-seven years later, the more institutional Franciscans, never sympathetic to Indian ways, stepped in. What Edward Spicer called the "typical Spanish frontier situation" of land usurpation, racial intolerance and anti-Indian lawlessness, which had been held at bay for a remarkable century, now swept across Sonora. Between 1767 and about 1825, the split in Yaqui identity began, with some Indians migrating north of the border, others staying put. When Mexico won independence from Spain in 1828, the nation's new lawmakers stepped up their redistribution of Yaqui farms.

Under a series of hero martyrs, many Yaqui rearmed. While in the United States Indians were surrendering on battlefields and removing to reservations, here in Mexico, from 1876 to 1904, the Yaqui Nation was still at war. Hundreds of Yaqui rebels and their families hid out near mountain water holes, lived on agave cactus and small game and in tight spots were even forced to suffocate their own children, says tribal folklore, lest crying reveal their hideaways. Only after 1900 were most of their people subdued, as permanent Mexican garrisons turned the Eight Towns into an occupied zone. From about thirty thousand Indians a century earlier, the Yaqui population fell to fewer than three thousand.

When his own village was overtaken by Federales, Spicer's friend Don Juan Valenzuela sought refuge in the Bacatete Mountains. Word came of friends tortured and relatives strung up on gallows. His generation never forgave the terrors of the Porfirio Díaz years, when Yaqui ears or hands brought bounties of one hundred pesos each, aerial bombing of Yaqui hamlets kept families on the run, their fields were incorporate haciendas and deportations of Yaqui began in force. Betwee

1910, their diaspora reached its peak. Thousands of Yaqui were shipped by train and boat to fishing communities near Tehuantepec on the Oaxacan coast and to hemp fiber plantations in Quintana Roo and Yucatán, two thousand miles away, to be sold as indentured laborers.

By the 1920s, hundreds of undocumented Yaqui immigrants were scraping together their livings in the United States as cotton pickers, ranch hands and house maids. Their shacks filled new barrios on the outskirts of Tucson and Phoenix. Although it would take until 1978 for this Arizona satellite community to win U.S. designation as a federal Indian reservation, unofficially their rituals began doing just that. In 1909, a few families dramatized their traditional Easter Week ritual scenario, *Waehma,* in the Tucson barrio of Pascua, now known as New Pascua. Starting before Ash Wednesday and continuing through Easter Sunday, the remembered landscape of Sonora still comes alive not far from the city's airport. Pascolas, Chapayekas, Matachinis and Deer Dancers, the custodians of the Yaqui of environmental memory, play their parts. It may be during Christ's Passion when the Deer Dancers and their musicians perform, but their thoughts are on the Flower World. Say the Yaqui of their lyrics, "We sing to honor the great mountains, the springs, the lakes. We sing of our father the Sun, and of creatures living and dead. We sing of trees and leaves and twigs. We sing of the birds in the sky and of the fish in the ocean."

Our walk circled back to where the bus had dropped us the night before. Another block and we stepped into Potam's sprawling *Llano,* or "plain," a windswept area that seemed too dusty, rambling and rural to deem a plaza. In the middle stood the unadorned, humble red-brick church, rebuilt in the 1940s, slightly elevated on an earthen knoll. Around it crowded the humped graves, as if the spirits of bygone Yaqui were hoisting the building on their shoulders. Tomorrow streams of dutiful relatives would filter among them, shoring up their mounds, repainting and pounding back down the askew crosses, replacing cracked and sun-faded plastic flowers, taking breaks to chat with neighbors and to remember loved ones.

Kirstin took me to the *Konti Vo'o,* or Way of the Cross, which was shaped like a horseshoe and encircled the Llano. At its opening stood the

Easter *ramada,* whose simple mesquite posts and thin cane walls belied its significance as the "wilderness home" of the Deer Dancer. During the days when the Easter drama is enacted, the songs and dramatizations associated with the figures of Deer Dancers, the Pascolas and the legions of Christ's enemies, the Chapayekas, bring the wider magical pre- and post-Christian landscape of the Yaqui directly into the plaza. Then is when and where, according to scholar Richard Schechner, the Yaqui continue to work out their own drama of "how to be simultaneously Yaqui and Catholic . . . the major problem of Yaqui history."

The few hours before sunset offered a quick run to the neighboring village of Rahum. During his fieldwork in the 1940s, it was in Rahum that Spicer first learned of the narratives that had supported the Yaqui through their troubles. In the custody of Don Juan's circle of elders, he found, already transcribed into Spanish, the "Rahum Land Texts," a charter for the tribe's Holy Land.

Our pickup sped by the boundary marker set up in the seventeenth century between Potam and Rahum, a miniature Calvary of three short crosses hacked from stout mesquite. Not a soul stirred in the village as we slid into the grassless arena of its *llano* and unremarkable church. Getting her bearings, Kirstin remembered the scrubby paloverdes to the northeast. About eight months before, on the Friday following Ash Wednesday, she'd paid a visit. A wisp of salty humidity from the gulf hung in the air. All was quiet at first, then a *maestro* clanged the three large bells that stand in front of every Yaqui church, and she saw frightened children pointing toward those trees.

Darting in and out, dramatizing his stealthy approach, a solitary masked man in white and black was carrying a wooden sword. He was a Chapayeka—along with Pascolas one of the key players in the miracle plays through which early Jesuits taught Catholicism to the Yaqui and encouraged them to internalize its messages of death and resurrection. Each Chapayeka is a Judas, a soldier of the Pharisees and an antagonist to Christ. Playing this role is risky. It asks participants to embrace the split personality familiar to actors: someone who wants to do right playing characters intent on doing wrong.

Their regalia echoes those contradictions. The masks, called *sewam,* or "flowers," are powerful and good and equated with Christ's blood. So the performer is not evil, nor is the spirit they enact, but they represent evil. They also lampoon undesirables: Mexican police, U.S. soldiers, hobos and other lowlifes. To counteract this playing with fire, underneath his mask the dancer clenches his rosary crucifix in his mouth. He must follow the mask's rules carefully, finally burning it on a pyre lest it stick to him or he return as a ghost after his death.

With his ridged helmet, black cape and vest with shiny gold buttons, he reminded Kirstin of a conquistador, and maybe that was another double message. Later, when the church emptied out for a stately procession to the stations of the cross, the Chapayeka crept after them, as if pursuing Jesus and Mary. Of all their villages, Kirstin learned, the Yaqui preferred to attend Rahum's religious processions and Deer Dances—fewer whites and Mexicans, lighter crowds and more like family.

Only a stone's throw away from us was the store where Spicer met Don Juan Valenzuela in 1941. Rahum's former governor, he had been a prominent conservative in a town noted for its old ways. But a certain "mystical" and "humorous" charisma set the man apart. Looking into his eyes, Spicer wrote, you glimpsed "the passage from our world to the other." Even when he was nowhere around, Spicer had the feeling he was "sitting in the rafters up there looking at us and listening to what we said." Spicer's earlier research in Phoenix taught him how the Jesuits had encouraged the Yaqui to embody their religion through miracle plays and folk performances. Now Valenzuela and his friends revealed how this spirituality was experienced geographically.

The expulsion of Jesuits in the 1770s left a vacuum in Catholic leadership, which was filled by Indian lay ministers known as *maestros*. They fine-tuned the fusion of Yaqui and Christian ritual calendars into a faith they could truly call their own. Having internalized stories about primordial floods, sacred trees, Edenic flower worlds and the travails of hero-saviors, they reached deeper into Christian traditions to extract the ingredients for a new territorial ideology. They were the authors of the Rahum Land Texts, the three-part, culturally mixed mythology that would substantiate and sacralize Yaqui claims to their sacred Eight Towns.

The first part spoke of the Flood, the second about the Singing of the Boundary, the third concerned the Talking Stick. In Yaqui calculations, fourteen days of rain produced a deluge that submerged the world in the year 614. Only a "just and perfect man" and his small following of Yaqui were saved. Don Juan showed Spicer the very hills in Yaqui country that had lifted them above the raging waters. After that, "Two angels arrived at the hills of Sinai at the break of dawn," bringing the word of God.

Unlike what Kirstin had been told, Valenzuela's version of the Talking Tree story featured a mythical flower woman who hired a giant to string his bow and stake it out. His first arrow landed near present-day Guaymas, a second struck the peak named Ba'apoosi; the third a mountain named Takala'im, the Crotched Peak, north of Guaymas. Within these three points, which took in the Yaqui River, lay the "wild" and "lost" beaches, deserts and foothills that Yaqui nostalgically knew as their "enchanted world."

Then Spicer learned about the Singing of the Boundary, in which heavenly angels joined ranks with Yaqui "inspired men" and walked around western Sonora singing and preaching the tribe's Holy Land into existence. Beginning at an arroyo named Cocoraque, beneath a mountain that lay between Yaqui and Mayo Indian territories (but which has since disappeared into the Gulf of California), they headed northward. En route they encountered evildoers and turned northwest, crossing the Yaqui River and arriving at the Crotched Peak. Their great journey covered 375 miles and embraced a region of about 650 square miles, including 200 miles of coastline, the heartland of the Bacatetes, and the mineral-rich Ostimuri district and fertile flood plains that would arouse the envy of Mexican miners and ranchers. Once the holy band had established this perimeter, the land itself was ready for Yaqui settlement.

Moving from east to west, wherever each of eight Yaqui prophets had a vision, there arose a sacred town. Potam was created when one of the prophets had an apparition of the Garden of Eden. From Cocorit to Bacum, Santa Rosa to Torim, Potam to Vicam, Rahum to Huirvis to Belem—at each town a founding prophet performed "ceremonial labor" (*tekipanoa*, from an Aztec word) to consecrate the place. Through this series of visions and ceremonies, the distinction drawn by the ancient Romans between places made sacred through supernatural revelation or those consecrated by human ritual was erased.

Then Jesus was born in the Yaqui community of Belem, and played as a child in this desert. Equally at home in the enchanted wilderness and the sacred towns, he grew into a poor man in a straw hat and ragged clothes who walked "among the flowers all the time, seven years, in the foothills and in the mountains; and then he went to the deserts." Following river bottom footpaths between settlements, he ministered to Yaqui sick and suffering, gaining a reputation as a *hitebi,* or "curer." His time on the cross became the Yaqui calendar's peak event. That his sacrificial drama climaxed here in northern Mexico still lends Yaqui Easter the sort of immediacy that pilgrims experience when they retrace the stations of the cross along Jerusalem's Via Dolorosa.

Now the Yaqui viewed their watershed and its towns as predestined. The Surem ancestors and their flower world were also recruited to support their nationalistic claims as older rituals were integrated into the Christian ritual cycle. The King of Spain even joined their roster of supernatural figures. "Even when he [the Indian] borrows from Christianity the idea of a supreme and universal spirit," wrote Francis Parkman in 1866, "his tendency is to reduce him to a local habitation and a bodily shape." By the 1880s, Spicer believed, "the Yaqui conception of sacred common cause with the land" was locked in their hearts. As Yaqui refugees moved to the Arizona barrios of Pascua, Guadalupe and Barrio Libre, the Sonoran landscape never left their hearts. During Semana Santa, when singers and drummers backed the Deer Dancers, its enchanted flower world came to life.

Weeks after returning home from this trip, I received an excited phone call from Mexico. Kirstin had finally been to the Bacatetes; she'd entered *huya ania,* the "wilderness world."

Joining a small group of ritualists, including the old *maestro* who had blessed her compound's *mesita* during our Day of the Dead, and his train of old *cantoras,* they piled into pickups near Potam's church. Their destination was the grave of the martyred nineteenth-century resistance leader Rolling Boulder. For hours they were tossed around as the vehicles followed cattle paths and rocky trails and waddled across arroyos washed out by flash floods. The mountains were beautiful, covered with paloverdes, boulders the color of henna, dark mesquite and pillars of deep-green organ pipe.

A *cantora* pointed out the hill *Hiapsi,* or "Heart," named after the shape of a gash in its side. They skimmed across a flat covered by low-lying cholla and dry, yellowed grass. Again they bucked uphill until, just before dark, they reached an adobe ruin, one of the Mexican garrisons for soldiers who were hunting fugitive Yaqui a hundred years before. Here Tetabiate was executed in 1901.

Reddish-brown rocks were piled over his cement tomb. They lit a bonfire and hundreds of candles and after scooping *frijol y hueso* stew with tortillas from shared bowls, began their vigil. The Matachini Dance Society danced by the light of the fire. A half-moon rose as they waited until, after midnight, the Pascolas and the Deer Dancer arrived to pay their respects. There was a stunning meteor shower. Coyotes yipped closer and closer up the arroyos. The mournful chanting of old women lulled Kirstin to sleep.

Around three in the morning, she was startled by the banging of tambourinelike drums. The sky was mantled with stars. "Coyote Dancers are here," someone whispered. Military society members materialized like ghosts, solemn in the firelight. Beside them stood three dancers in sandals, jeans and button-down shirts, with coyote pelts draped over their heads, the dark noses and eye sockets pointing above their foreheads, the puffy tails down their backs; they carried strung bows and short cane sticks. Also known as "bow dancers," their specific duty was to protect *Hiakim,* the sacred lands of the Yaqui. Only here would this military society show itself. *Cantoras* droned their chants. Coyote Dancers bowed toward the four directions, conducting the *kusaroapo bwiata teochiawame,* or "blessing the earth in the way of the cross." Side to side they moved, acting out the Latin verses: "You soldier leaders beautifully side by side are walking, together playing, together playing. . . . Here on the flower road side by side you are walking, together playing."

Hours later she woke again with aching hips and stiff knees. The Coyotes were gone. Under the cold purple sky, dozens were huddled around her, wrapped in rebozos, snoring under sombreros. She smelled coffee.

They roused and stretched, ate and ambled, waited for return rides; some gathered medicinal plants found only up there. She didn't get home until late afternoon. Everyone was a little giddy, joking about being thrown around like dolls in the trucks. The *maestro* confessed to being proud of another "completed fiesta"—the ninety-sixth anniversary of a Yaqui who had sacrificed himself in defense of their Holy Land.

CHAPTER EIGHT

DRAINING THE SACRED PLACES

Hopi

I f one strays off the beaten path in northern Arizona's Hopi Indian country and clambers around the three mesas that elevate its sandstone-and-adobe villages above the marbled floor of the Painted Desert, it's not uncommon to come upon bushes or rock piles that from a distance look possessed by an inner agitation. Walking closer, one realizes that the impression comes from dozens of what the Hopi call "breath feathers," which are fastened to willow wands with hand-spun cotton cord. Fluffy and light as air, this down from eagles' breasts is associated by the Hopi with the mists and clouds that are the homes of rain-bringing spirits known as Kachinas. Under the old principle that like attracts like, the Indians pray the fluttering plumes will appeal as gifts and invitations for these spirits to mediate between human beings and the wider cosmic forces.

Breezes across the Colorado Plateau may make these plumes shiver, but the Hopi have already granted them life and purpose by exhaling on them. When greeting respected elders, it is customary to cup one's hands and breathe a blessing upon them. Given the spiritual importance of holy winds in Navajo culture, it is tempting to see here yet another contrast between the two peoples. A sensitivity to wind, to its shifting directions and moisture levels, was critical for Navajo hunters, whose skittish prey are keen to the odors it carries. Wind is a person, say the Navajo, whose presence everyone can see perks up at sundown. And when morning first appears, "beautifully becoming white-streaked through the dawn," as Navajo say, "it usually breezes" once again. Our fingertips bear the imprint of whirling winds, Navajo point out; the wind that is within and without all bodies is "holy."

But among farming Pueblos, to the contrary, it is the domestication of wind by sending it through the lungs and heart that turns it into living prayers. Breath confers that blessing, and the wild, untempered winds are surely not Hopi allies. All farmers know how they tear away the thin soil, wither the tender corn shoots (which is why Hopi farmers provide them each with little tipped-rock shelters), twist melon vines into knots, blind the men weeding or irrigating with their sandstorms and, worst of all, hasten evaporation.

In this land where every drop counts, Hopi have always sung for rain, prayed for rain, danced for rain, run for rain, dreamed about rain. "You ask why all our songs are about rain," a Hopi once said to a white anthropologist. "All yours are obsessed with love—is that because you never have enough?" If keeping the sun on its annual cycle is a ritual preoccupation for Eastern Pueblo peoples like the Taos Pueblo, who enjoy proximity to the Rio Grande or its tributaries, for Hopi villagers on their hot, dry mesas maintaining the cyclical movement of moisture through subterranean conduits up into the air and ensuring that it falls back down again is the overriding concern.

Hopi prayer feathers also petition for all the good things that rain evokes: healthy and resilient crops, relief from personal problems, the well-being of the Hopi as a people, a calm pace to human affairs, and the proper cycling of the seasons. Under the principle of reciprocity that governs the world, such offerings and prayers are the duty of responsible human beings.

Hopi place their shrines and prayer sticks so as to catch the attention of rain beings. From the village of Walpi on the narrow prow of First Mesa, a glance in most directions falls near one of them. There is the *Wala* spot, alongside the precarious road up the mesa, containing the fossilized cast of an ancient seashell. Close by is *Wukomaasaw,* a shrine to "earth father," the great god Maasaw, a rock smothered with twig and branch offerings that are left by firewood collectors. To the east is Heart-Contained-Here, said to hold the heart of a mythic runner who won a famous footrace, where aspiring track stars still leave offerings. Also in the foothills to the east is a spring shrine for the Sky Serpent, whereas to the west lies the more elaborate Kachina Society shrine.

Some of these shrines sit on innocuous ledges or in brush-clogged clefts. Others are so spectacular one is inclined to say, as did Oedipus upon first seeing Colonus, "Clearly, this must be a sacred place." Or as territorial historian Sharlot Hall wrote in her diary on August 30, 1911, in the thrall of her first visit to the Grand Canyon, "No wonder the early Mormon explorers believed that God had revealed to them a land to be all their own. . . ." To ancestors of the Hopi people, however, an all-powerful deity delivered the same message about that same canyon, but to them exclusively, and much earlier.

During the past century, an increasing number of sensitive Hopi sites have fallen under the shadow of other men's skies, and therefore are harder to renew. As the Hopi dispute with the Navajo over their overlapping territories heated up, and mineral extraction heightened the threat to sacred places, the strategic importance of these shrines as tribal boundary markers deepened. Renewing their prayer sticks became a means of reviving claims to a traditional landscape that the Hopi associate with two groups of stories.

One body of narratives features Maasaw, the supernatural figure who bestowed the Grand Canyon to them. A deity of multiple personalities, and associated with death and war, he sometimes wears a face like Medusa's; sometimes he's handsome as Apollo. Protector and caretaker of the Fourth World, in which we all live now, he is "the autochthonous proprietor," write Michael Lomatuway'ma and Ekkehart Malotki, who have devoted two books to him, of all "land and life" and "water and life." Stepping like a furious giant, he outlined Hopi territory with his wanderings.

To the early ethnographer Alexander Stephen, whose daily journal of a two-year sojourn at First Mesa in the 1880s provides an inside look at Hopi environmental thought, an elder said, "Maasaw first traveled south, then circuitously toward the east until he reached his starting point. He called this area his land." It was a hefty claim: from today's Fort Mojave on the California-Arizona border, south to today's Panama Canal, up along the Gulf of Mexico, tracing the Rio Grande into the Colorado River and following its tributaries back to Fort Mojave.

When the Hopi ancestors first emerged out of the netherworld, Maasaw was there to greet them. Becoming proper Hopi wouldn't be easy, he warned; ahead lay a life of poverty and hard work. Yet it would be a good life—a true Way of Life. Before they embarked upon their clan wanderings, Maasaw handed them tablets. These sealed his covenant with them; now the country was theirs. "Once your children have multiplied throughout this land," he said, "lead them with care. Guide them in goodness. When it rains and crops grow, strive in life for old age as you sustain yourself with food." And another version has Maasaw adding, "You and your people are strong of heart. Look in the valleys, the rocks, and the woods, and you will find my footsteps there."

Those footsteps defined Hopitutskwa, the sacred lands of the Hopi people.

By tracing the converging travels of the separate Hopi clans, a second body of narratives yielded a somewhat smaller homeland. Historians may want to avoid dealing with Indian stories about mythic emergences from the earth, but archaeologists identify the so-called Basket Maker culture of the San Juan Valley of southern Colorado as major Hopi forefathers; and they concur that the Hopi Nation we know today then cohered in piecemeal fashion, clan by in-migrating clan. To the Hopi, their history constitutes this braiding together of separate clan journeys hailing from cultures as diverse as Paiute, Plains Indian, Apache and Piman, which would meta-morphose into some thirty matrilineal "clans" who started, stopped and then picked up again. Wherever they halted, it is said, they buried canteens— basketry jugs that were waterproofed with spruce gum. Like plants from seeds, the life-giving springs one finds in the Painted Desert derive from these deposits.

These springs emerge from the southern base of Black Mesa because its sandstone cap tips in that direction, sending precious moisture beneath the crests and depressions of the sand dunes that fall below. Entering this arid world, the early Hopi put up rock-and-adobe homes near these springs and within running distance of their cornfields. Their creative exploita-tion of the springs, the washes that caught seasonal rains, the subsurface waters under the dry sands, as well as corn with unusually long roots pro-ded patchy gardens in what looked like an American Sahara.

Every spring contained its own water serpent, the Hopi believed, who poked its head above the surface only at noon. The young learned how to behave correctly around these pools. Instead of slurping up water with their mouths they were taught to use gourd ladles and to leave prayer feathers at the springs, to cleanse them of mud or debris, and to refrain from having sex near them lest those serpents seize the opportunity to impregnate Hopi girls. Care and feeding of springs still remains an obligation for today's dozen Hopi villages, whose members consider their springs, old village sites and places where miraculous stories took place as "steps" in the migrations of their constituent clans. The process by which the clans converged in the legendary region known as *Sichdukwi,* or Flower Mound, has been labeled "Hopification" by native scholar Hartman Lomawaima. By the term he highlights a process of unification not unlike that which produced the United States, creating for Hopi people "a promised land where they would follow good teachings and a good way of life. A prophecy held by many clans was that Sichdukwi would eventually be settled after centuries of migrations."

To commemorate where these forebears left their "footprints," the Hopi leave prayer sticks at ruins that remain, they believe, under the protection of clan ancestors. They do this, according to Hopi scholar Armin Geertz, "to keep the spirits alive as boundary guardians *and* to notify them whenever major ceremonials were to be performed at home." Ever since the nineteenth century, according to land-claim researchers who have worked with the tribe, Hopi priests have led pilgrimages to renew the shrines.

Were it not for the Joint Use Area dispute between the Hopi and the Navajo in the late 1970s, outsiders might not have learned about these journeys. By establishing the Navajo reservation, however, the U.S. government pitted these two American Indian holy lands against each other. The Navajo's attachment to their Dinetah landscape, which saved them after the exile at Fort Sumner, was up against the Hopi's covenant with Maasaw, who had created their sacred Hopitutskwa.

Visiting the "guard" village of Hano on First Mesa in 1979, I snaked my vehicle up the dirt lane that leads to the mesa. Drawings on a slab of sandstone caught my eye. Despite pickups tearing downhill, I yanked my hand brake. A square house with windowpanes and a chimney was sketched in charcoal alongside a smaller, dome-shaped hut. Scrawled underneath: "All Navajo live in bread houses." It was something of a cultural putdown: the Hopi graffitist was likening traditional Navajo houses, or hogans, to their own adobe *hornos,* or bread-baking ovens, which Pueblo Indians had borrowed from the Spanish. Like most cultural slurs, the message was evolutionary: the Navajo were wild and uncouth, not too bright and none too clean.

Until a hundred years ago, Navajo hunters and herders and Hopi farmers were uneasy trade partners at seasonal rendezvous, and sometime enemies whose warriors occasionally went after one another's scalps. But after the Navajo Treaty of 1868, they managed to coexist on adjoining properties—the sprawling Navajo reservation surrounding that of the Hopi—with mutual tolerance if not great affection. When the court issued a partition order in 1977 decreeing that the Navajo must leave the Big Mountain region, the nervous truce broke down. The ideological importance of pilgrimage, for the Hopi, and of inventory, for the Navajo, reached new intensity.

In the pages of the Hopi's own newspaper, *Qua' Toqti* (*The Eagle's Cry*), and then in full-color layouts for *National Geographic,* the Hopi went public. In the summer of 1982, they invited authors Jake and Suzanne Page to join eight of their priests on an eleven-hundred-mile trek to their major boundary shrines. Normally the trip takes anywhere from four to eight days and involves a mix of hiking and bouncing over fire trails in four-wheel drives. "The elders say that the shrines are our standards," Abbott Sekaquaptewa explained to the Pages, "the way white people raise flags over their territory. Without our shrines, our inheritance, we simply cannot continue as Hopi."

Following a counterclockwise itinerary, the priests took pains to descend to the great *Sipaapuni,* a natural travertine dome that stands alongside a tributary of the Little Colorado and bears striking similarity to old Basket Maker pit houses, down to its perfect-circle opening on top that resembles the old smokehole for an entry ladder. As a depiction of a world-womb navel, no sculptor could have imagined it better. From this geological phenomenon, the Hopi say, the first human beings emerged.

Not far away is a salt seep with crystalline stalactites the Hopi scrape off to use in their rituals—the destination of their salt pilgrimage.

The Hopi priests also stopped at Grand Canyon, or *Ongtupqa,* where rain spirits are known to reside, and numerous ruins, such as the National Park Service's Betatakin, which they call *Kawestima,* where they themselves once lived. At places as far apart as the Apache Descent Trail along the Mogollon Rim; Bear Springs near Flagstaff; Navajo Mountain in southern Utah; and Lupton, southeast of Gallup, they cleared brush and released puffs of smoke from mountain lion–shaped clay pipes to alert the cloud spirits that they were there and that they cared. Although not enclosing the grand domain claimed by Maasaw's mythic odyssey, the trip encircled a homeland of Hopi memory in northeastern Arizona that is more than four times the size of the reservation the United States gave them and enfolds half the Navajo reservation as well.

The final stop for this Hopi boundary pilgrimage was a boundary marker south of Holbrook, Arizona. Whites call it Woodruff Butte, after the Mormon founder of the white settlement at its base. To the Hopi, it is *Tsimontukwi,* or Jimsonweed Butte, named for the plant with white trumpet-shaped flowers, the potent roots of which are sought for medicinal purposes by both Hopi and Zuni. Unlike most of the harder-to-reach sites, one can see it from Interstate 40, just east of the Holbrook turnoff.

Outwardly it doesn't look different from other cinder cones in the area. When I was a teenager hitchhiking across the country, this was Route 66, and the road signs along this Holbrook-Flagstaff stretch hustled travelers to rattlesnake farms, faux western saloons, ancient ruins and Indians weaving blankets at trading posts. The current attraction is the gradual razing, from the top down, of a sacred place.

Nor are the Hopi alone in considering Woodruff Butte an ancestral spot. "You used to find flint arrowheads, stone axes, corn grinders and pottery shards all round here," said one longtime resident as we walked its eastern side. Around us were stone circles, possibly structures or corrals left by Navajo, whose medicine men knew the promontory as *Tooji' Hwi-idzoh,* or "Line Extends to the River." It is featured in their Coyote stories;

after holding ritual "sings" in the natural amphitheater, also on the eastern slope, Navajo gathered datura, the "plant that kills things." On the south slope lay shrines visited by Zuni pilgrims, who called the place *Dematsali Im'a* and remembered their ancestors gathering plants (probably the same Jimsonweed) used in divination.

Once rising like a five-hundred-foot nipple from the plain, Woodruff Butte is visible today largely because of its flag of billowing plumes of dirt. A few years after the Pages' trip, it was bought by a gravel-mining operation, which began blasting it apart for the sharply faceted granite rocks that are mixed with boiled used tires for highway pavement.

On the northern slope, past NO TRESPASSING signs near the beheaded summit, I was shown where Hopi had maintained a boundary shrine, with rock art associated with travel narratives of their Bearstrap and Water clans. Shortly after the tribe went public about their shrines, Woodruff residents noticed increased bulldozer activity on the butte with loaded dump trucks rolling downhill day and night. By the time Hopi priests showed up after a resident's phone call, two sites had already been crushed and the pictographs defaced by rifle fire. In a final insult, the bulldozer operators stared from their bucket seats at the Indian visitors, gunned their engines and demolished the place before their eyes.

At the same time that the two tribes were at each other's throats over the Joint Use Area conflict, Hopi and Navajo found common cause in a fight for another piece of sacred geography revered by both of them.

Though not a Hopi boundary shrine, the San Francisco Peaks, a volcanic mountain range just outside Flagstaff, Arizona, plays a pivotal role in their everyday and religious lives. On clear mornings, you can see the Peaks from the kivas of Walpi Pueblo, on First Mesa, eighty miles to the north. Closer up, the serrated, green-brown mass of the Peaks seems to suck power from the surrounding dry gulches and wizened trees before lifting into four promontories that are joined at their hips and extend for two and a half miles. They support ponderosa forests and alpine meadows and contain the steep, aspen-fringed basins known as *cirques,* or bowls. Their highest spot is also Arizona's tallest, Mount Humphreys, where one can hike across the state's only patch of arctic tundra. Often muffled in the snowpack that hides their mantle of loose scree, the Peaks gather great clouds that swirl and shred and recombine around their uppermost crags. Their task, like the Taos Mountains', seems to be to take and give moisture, in all its myriad forms.

In Old and New Testament stories, prominent mountains like the San Francisco Peaks serve patriarchs, saviors and saints as personal sanctuaries and retreats for spiritual renewal and direct communications with the Almighty. But that was not the only reason that in 1629 early Franciscan missionaries named them after their patron saint and his known affinity for solitude and wild creatures. Throughout the Americas, habitats as much as their inhabitants became targets for Euro-American religious conversion. It was as if the new landscapes themselves had to be annexed to the white man's heaven—or demonized and deeded to the white man's hell—before Christianity could attend to saving souls. By conceiving of the Peaks as a sort of geological cathedral, perhaps the Franciscans thought they could better subvert Hopi land beliefs. And one even hears the story that early missionaries forbade the Hopi from uttering their name for the Peaks: *Nuvatukya'ovi,* or "Snow Lying on the Top."

If it was actually tried, the edict didn't take. When Hopi worry in public about the fate of the earth, some dismiss their warnings as coming from a New Age–influenced fringe of the tribe. But this ignores the fact that monitoring their natural surroundings is a venerable Hopi tradition. For centuries, their appointed calendar watchers kept track of the sun's yearly movement from his summer "house" in the northwest until it reached his "winter" house, the cleft on the Peaks' profile known as *lahavwu chochomo,* about ninety miles away, in order to schedule ceremonies and work in the fields. During an archaeological dig in 1990, at an ancestral Hopi village that dates to around A.D. 800, excavators working in a kiva noticed discoloration on the lower half of the walls. At first it was attributed to leakage of desert salts, but once the entire surface had been scraped—the discolored shapes covered half the room, with apparent dots at some notches—the outline looked familiar. Back at ground level, the archaeologist gazed west and realized why. The forms on the kiva walls were practically a photographic reproduction of the skyline of the Peaks, and the dots were very likely calendrical markers for various positions of the sun throughout the year.

As children, most Hopi heard about the warrior gods Pokanghoya and Polongahoya, who first molded the Peaks to relieve the earth's monotonous flatness. The Peaks are also revered as homes for the One-Horn and Two-Horn societies, which still maintain shrines. Older Indians can still identify the ridges and meadows that fed the last stand of antelopes. Once their large herds darkened the lower slopes, but now their movements are recalled only in the winter animal dances.

Throughout the year, the Peaks are featured in Hopi ritual. In December, young Hopi run considerable distances to deposit prayer sticks and cornmeal at shrines on their slopes. Two months later they are visited for the gathering of the Douglas fir boughs and small trees that are used during the Powamuya Festival, when Hopi children are initiated into the Kachina Society, with prayer "breath" feathers tied on branches left in exchange. In spring and summer, ponderosa logs are cut for roofing vigas, sections of oak and holly-grape branches are measured for tool handles, mountain mahogany is collected in order to brew a dye for coloring leather, bee balm is sought for food flavoring and to add to tobacco mixtures whose puffed smoke is said to foster rainfall, like the clouds it resembles. In July, the Peaks are visited before Niman, the bittersweet farewell festival to the Kachinas. Again the Hopi harvest fresh evergreens from them for dancers to wear, symbolizing the moisture that sustains life, and another cadre of foot runners returns to make sure the winter prayer sticks are safely in place.

But Snow Lying on the Top is also a participant in daily life. Driving to work, Hopi check out the San Francisco Peaks as if they were a combination of clock, barometer and calendar, gauging the direction and velocity of their clouds to assess tomorrow's weather, noting the spread or density of the snowpack to estimate how much runoff their spring plants can count on. And there remains another related reason for Hopi watchfulness. From July through February, the San Francisco Peaks are the home of their rain-bringing spirits, the Kachinas.

The clouds that gather around the Peaks are the physical embodiment of Kachinas, who serve as messengers between this temporal world and the timeless cosmic forces. Two or three hundred strong, each identified by individual regalia, style of movement and distinctive voice, the Kachinas control all good things. For the betterment of Hopi people, Kachinas mediate between the way things are and the way they ought to be, reminding young and old how to hew to the Hopi Way, chastising in endlessly amusing fashion those who fall short. The company of Kachinas also includes dead Hopi. Hence, the clouds *and* the Kachinas *and* their ancestors have shared inner identities that flow back and forth through one another.

Deep in the San Francisco Peaks lies the Kachinas' own kiva. For the months when they shift their base of operations to the man-made kivas up on the Hopi mesas, its entryway is shut tight. That is when hundreds of the Kachinas are impersonated by male members of the Kachina Society who mingle with their people. They throng and perform in the open plazas, going door to door to donate *tihus,* the miniatures of themselves carved from cottonwood root. They admonish the lazy and adulterous or those who behave too much like white folk. They appear when the "children of cottonwood," the sacred puppets, come alive in the kivas during the Powamu initiation ceremonies for new members of the Kachina Society. But in July, the Kachinas return to the Peaks, pull back the cover of their secret kiva and rest.

Whenever cornmeal is strewn during ceremonies when prayers or songs refer to the Peaks, when cedar boughs cut from them are stuck into armbands and belts, or when wooden altarpieces are repainted with their image, it is toward the San Francisco Peaks that the Hopi turn their heads. And those glances probably linger a few minutes if a sunset is saturating the snows with a sequence of pinks, purples, indigos and, abruptly, a darkening ivory—all of which can pulsate through the span of ten minutes.

The health, identity and survival of Hopi people are wrapped up in the Peaks' well-being, which explains their anxieties after 1937, when the Civilian Conservation Corps cleared an access road and erected a timbered lodge to attract downhill skiers to a 777-acre bowl between two of the Peaks. As lift cables were strung in 1958 and 1962, word got around and more visitors showed up. A decade later the U.S. Forest Service reviewed plans from a new entrepreneur, Northland Recreation Company, to expand their Snow Bowl operations. After more public hearings and back-and-forth revisions, Northland was licensed to build a new day lodge and three additional lifts and to widen and pave the road so that five times more skiing enthusiasts could use the slopes. Said one tribal witness during hearings in 1978 regarding the proposed development, "We shall encounter hardships if we desecrate the kingdom of the Kachinas." And five years later, the chairman of the Hopi tribe warned, "If the ski resort remains or is expanded, our people will not accept the view that this is the sacred Home of the Kachinas. The basis of our existence as a society will become a mere fairy tale to our people."

On the other side, the all-white Flagstaff Chamber of Commerce, meeting in the Ramada Inn at the southern feet of the Peaks, was elated at the prospect of more tourists pounding their sidewalks. In the prevailing probusiness euphoria, neither the Flagstaff nor Tucson newspapers, and certainly not the rapid-fire commentary of local TV newscasters, took the time to explain to ordinary people why the prospect of the Peaks' crawling with out-of-towners and gasoline-driven towlines troubled not only the Hopi, but also many Navajo.

To the Navajo, the Peaks are known as *Do'ko'oslid,* or "It Was Not Melted Off" or "Abalone Shell Mountain," their sacred peak of the west. In a painting by the Navajo artist Harrison Begay, he calls the "Peaks Shining on Top" and depicts it as the home of their Holy Person named Yellow Corn Girl. Begay shows the mountain fastened to the earth by sunbeams. We see an abalone shell on the summit that contains two yellow warbler eggs and the yellow cloud that spreads over the mountains (although Begay doesn't paint in the Peaks' black clouds and their heavy-falling "male" downpours, which Navajo contrast with more veillike, diaphanous, "female" rain). A key boundary for the Navajo homeland, on their slopes medicine men collect herbs for healing ceremonies.

Six years before they joined forces with the Hopi to resist the ski-lift expansion, the chairman of the Navajo tribe, Peter McDonald, declared, "The peak which you have named in honor of St. Francisco, patron of the wild birds and animals, is truly a sacred place to the Navajo—a place where nature can be respected and revered. On behalf of all the Navajo People, I pray it can remain that way." In testimony against the development that rang like an incantation, Navajo Frank Goldtooth, Jr., said, "This peak was made by the holy people in the beginning. At that time when it was made only by the holy people, not by the white people nor any Indians, it was made just by the holy people and this thing here, this San Francisco Peak is prayers, is a prayer and it is sitting there with prayers and it has white shell beads and turquoise and Apache tear drops and abalone and that is what is sitting there with also plants of life, sitting there with life."

In what resembled the same governmental response to the defense which Taos Pueblo made on behalf of their sacred mountain, a forest ranger asked, "Just show us on this map which parts of the mountain are sacred so we can protect them." And like the elders of Taos twenty years earlier, the Hopi answered, "How can we point on a map to a sacred place? The entire mountain, the land surrounding the mountain, the whole earth is sacred."

Another Hopi explained the Peaks' importance in a more metaphysical way. To Emory Sekaquaptewa, it was his people's songs and prayers that had made this home of their Kachinas the closest outward visible symbol they had of "a perfect mountain with perfect beings in their perfect balance with each other." Untouched by the imperfections human beings might lay on the Peaks, they provided daily proof of such perfection as well as the inspirational model, reinforced for the Hopi by their Kachinas, in how to live properly. But if Sekaquaptewa saw new lodges and trash bins and Day-Glo vests and heard the grinding of ski-lift gears and shouts of patrons in line for hamburgers, he argued that this "spiritual satisfaction" would become impossible. "I have a right," he insisted, "to believe in the things I have been taught to believe in and this should not be interfered with."

Because the Peaks belonged to Coconino National Forest, and therefore lay on public U.S. government–owned land, lawyers for the Hopi and Navajo consolidated their three cases in federal court in 1983 to prevent the U.S. Forest Service and the U.S. Department of Agriculture from allowing the expansion of the ski lifts. Rippling like a banner of hope above their arguments was the five-year-old American Indian Religious Freedom

Act, part of whose intent was to safeguard precisely these sorts of locations. With files full of ethnographic, folkloric and historical confirmation about Indian beliefs regarding the Peaks, it was hard to imagine a more compelling case.

In the district court's response, however, came the double message that often meets Indian religious lawsuits that raise issues of constitutional rights. On the one hand, said the judge, the planned expansion of the ski bowl did not violate the Indians' rights to free exercise of religion, a First Amendment right. On the other, if the court were to uphold the Indian claims, the government would violate the Second Amendment by singling out one religion and hence "establishing" or "managing" it, which it was forbidden to do.

When the Indian appeal moved to a circuit court, the site for making a final decision shifted farther from the Peaks, as if to prevent the mountain cluster from hearing about its own fate. In Washington, D.C., the judges agreed that the Indians had not proven that the Peaks were "indispensable to their religious practices." Perhaps their religious attitudes would be "offended" by the expansion, but that was insufficient reason to stop it. The court expressed satisfaction that the Forest Service had "faithfully met all the Indian Religious Freedom Act's provisions."

When I visited the Peaks two years later, road scrapers were lowgearing up the western slopes to widen access to the Snow Bowl; an expanse the size of a football field had been graded to red earth for future asphalting, with RV and SUV parking lots already staked out. By then, however, the mountains were threatened by new intrusions: the Bahai'i Church had sued for the right to conduct its open-air religious ceremonies near the homes of the Kachinas, and the sudden popularity of stonewashed jeans had caused a Phoenix-based company to quadruple its mining of pumice nuggets on the eastern slopes.

Perhaps skiing was untouchable because it had grown in popularity and suited the New West's self-promotion as an outdoor playground. But many regarded the phony aging of western wear for suburban high schoolers as too much. With the Sierra Club weighing in to oppose the country's exploitative mining law of 1878, which allowed mining companies to make killings on federal land, the government took action. In the summer of 2000, the Interior Department exempted seventy-five thousand acres on the eastern slopes of the San Francisco Peaks from further mineral exploration, and a locked metal grate was installed in front of the pumice shaft.

But only a year later, Hopi vigilance about the perils of digging into their landscape caused tribal members to take up the drums again. More ominous than the scenic nightmare of gutting Black Mesa and plunking on it what looked like a New Jersey landfill were inklings of deeper side effects. Scientific soundings concluded that sucking up three million gallons of underground water a day in order to flush the mesa's coal in a slurry mixture from northwestern Arizona down 273 miles of pipeline to the 1,570-megawatt Mohave Generating Station in Laughlin, Nevada, was depleting a subterranean network of watery pools known collectively as the N-aquifer.

The studies showed that Black Mesa and its surrounding countryside were dying of thirst. Underwater reserves that had taken the earth thirty-five thousand years to purify and store were being reduced by 3.3 million gallons a day—two and a half times as much water as was drunk, boiled and washed in by the city of Flagstaff in the same twenty-four-hour period. Already 40 billion gallons of irreplaceable water, which might have replenished human bodies and cornfields, had been mixed with pulverized rock, turned into a polluted slush and pumped out of state.

But the Hopi didn't need studies to tell them that something was amiss. They were trained to watch the sky, the horizon, the animals and insects and water. At the springs that had risen from the canteens their wandering forefathers had planted in the ground, at wells and seeps, they were well aware that water levels had been dropping for years. The earth's blood bank was thinning. Something was shriveling the streams that ran like veins under their feet. The land was cracking like an old man's hands. "Hopi culture and religion," a Hopi farmer from Moencopi village told a Senate committee that was eliciting testimony on tribal lands, "is one of stewardship, a responsibility to take care of mother earth and her life's blood: water." To the Hopi, the natural and proper circulation of moisture was going the wrong way, with ominous consequences. Industrial extraction of water upward, from under the ground, had produced these clear and present signals of mother earth's weakened ability to attract rain from above by "sucking" it down from the clouds.

In 2001, concerned Hopi organized an advocacy group called the Black Mesa Trust, with former tribal chairman Vernon Masayesva as its executive director and leading spokesperson. Soon the trust was supporting highly visible, symbolic "runs" by young Hopi couriers to publicize what Masayesva and a growing number of supporters were describing as an emergency. "It is our tradition to send messages through running," said organizer Lillian Hill, "and the planting stick, gourd of water, corn, sage and other herbs we presented to Hopi and Navajo leaders carried a spiritual message. . . . We care about our futures, our lives, and our culture."

Seeing itself as representing "grassroots Hopi people," the trust challenged the more business-oriented Hopi Tribal Council; opposed its surprise announcement that it was considering becoming partners in another power plant on Black Mesa; and promoted new water-saving technologies of drip irrigation, waterless urinals and solar-powered water pumping to alleviate conditions in a region that, in a good year, receives only ten inches of rainfall. In the struggle to preserve their rights to the lifeblood of their lands, survival of both body and soul were at stake. "No longer," Masayesva wrote the U.S. Office of Surface Mining in March 2002, "will we tolerate unchallenged cultural imperialism that exploits our natural resources and destroys our sacred lands."

More than human vigilance, the delicate responses of amphibians, with their vulnerable membranes and blinking wariness, are for Pueblo peoples like the Hopi the best readings on the earth's state of health. But dwindling numbers of frogs and lizards are not the only signs of a life out of balance, of soured relationships with the water serpents. There are others in their moist company.

The Hopi know that they flourish wherever fog flows or mist rises and whenever liquid comes down in the form of rain and snow, and as water streams down mountains and rivers and seeps into springs or mossy cracks in the rocks and collects in marshes and muddy pools. On the ceramic bowls made by Pueblo potters and on their painted wooden altar pieces, as well as on the headpieces, or *tablas,* worn by women during Pueblo harvest dances, one sees a company of creatures whose darting, jerky presence is an indication of the liquid that must circulate in some measure for all other kinds of life to survive.

Everywhere in the Pueblo arts of pottery, basketry, weaving and song, the creatures associated with water are invoked: dragonflies, butterflies, lizards, frogs, toads, turtles, snakes, tadpoles, storms and rainbows. Ever since childhood the Hopi have been delighted and attracted by these little creatures, even if as children they had to be reminded not to pester them.

They flit about as if they are very busy, or sometimes they remain as still as stones. Some have a way of blending in. Some of the water beings curve overhead as miracles of moisture and color and then are gone. Some crack and shiver the earth. They frighten, awe or delight. Yet of this there is no doubt, human survival is bound up with theirs. There are fewer of them these years, people say. The disappearance of any of them is a sign of the condition the Hopi dread and that they call *paanaqawu,* or "fatal lack of water."

PART III

NORTH

In 1965, an elderly Teton Lakota holy man, who'd been vision questing since the age of thirteen, returned to one of his favorite fasting sites. It was the pine-speckled hump immediately east of the Black Hills known to his people as Mato Paha, Bear Mountain. There it was revealed he would tell his life story to a white man. In that autobiography, Frank Fools Crow described what happened in 1982, when, two years after the U.S. Interior Department leased the Black Hills for coal mining and nuclear power development, the South Dakota state parks department made plans to construct access roads and parking facilities at Mato Paha and imposed restrictions on Indian vision seekers in the meantime. In what became the third major case to test the powers of the 1978 American Indian Religious Freedom Act, ninety-one-year-old Fools Crow became the key plaintiff, on behalf of both the Lakota and Cheyenne tribes, to fight against this infringement of Plains Indian rights to one of their premier sacred places.

CHAPTER NINE

A GEOLOGY OF POWER

Plateau

Painters call it *pentimento;* writers use *palimpsest.* The first refers to the layering of oil renderings on a canvas, the second to rubbed-out and written-over drafts on a slate. In both cases, one detects traces of the earlier efforts underneath; in both, the surfaces embody and benefit from what has been tried before. The terms offer analogies for one way that religious beliefs and concepts of sacred place can build up, layer by layer, over time.

This process contrasts with the fusing of religious geographies, as happened among the Yaqui of Mexico, where Catholic and Indian beliefs produced a brand new Holy Land. It also differs from the compartmentalization one sees among the Southwestern Pueblo, whose sacred lakes and cloud-spirit shrines keep their distance from Catholic churches and convents. With such an accumulation of layers of beliefs comes the stacking of the stories that fix them in tradition. "I was just endlessly fascinated by the notion that a landscape is a palimpsest," writes environmental historian William Cronon, "that [there are] these layers that can be peeled off."

One American Indian region where these layers of land concepts can be peeled off to reveal a record of evolving spirituality is the Columbia Plateau, where two mountain ranges lock up an area the size of France and a quilt of ecological zones: arid steppes, river-cut gorges, dense forests, greasewood deserts, reed-fringed lakes, crashing streams, rugged mountains. To the east run the towering Rockies, to the west Oregon's Cascades. The Fraser River marks its northern terminus; to the south the Snake River plain merges into the northern Great Basin.

It is no surprise that Plateau Indian stories seem obliged to explain these highlands, crusted by cooled lava over half of its 175,000 square miles, which emerged out of violent eruptions, shaken earth, drowned peaks and trapped or unleashed waters. The Columbia Plateau may lack the visual glamour of the Southwest's pastel mesas, and the names of its dozen or more Indian tribes are on few American lips. But its native history carries a big secret. In the late-nineteenth century, this was a hotbed of messianic creativity, whence the messages of its native prophets kept hope alive for tribes from the Missouri River to the California coast.

To Indians, those geological transformations were the work of Coyote, culture hero and slayer of fire-snorting monsters. He carved the rivers Snake and Columbia, which served Indians as gateways to buffalo-rich grasslands (eastward) and the trade-promising seacoast (to the west). Along their river valleys, he created shoals, narrows and marshes, with natural pools and spills that rose steplike into higher elevations. Add Coyote's other gift, five species of salmon fighting upstream by the millions, and these Indians were handed one of the finest inland fisheries in the world.

Native peoples have lived there for a long time—possibly back to Kennewick Man, the individual who died about ninety-two hundred years ago and whose bones fell out of a Columbia River bank in 1996. By the American Revolution, the Plateau was home to twenty or more tribes belonging to four different language families but sharing much in common: fishing for salmon, hunting mountain sheep, picking huckleberries, digging for camas and bitterroot, trading for everything from Puget Sound shells to Plains Indian dried buffalo, and practicing a spiritual life that fixated on seeking visions. "Perhaps nowhere in America," wrote anthropologist Verne F. Ray, the dean of Plateau Indian studies, "did the guardian spirit play so great a role in the lives of people."

For a look at one spot where members of the Kootenai tribe sought such spirits, I headed for Flathead Lake in northwestern Montana. No sooner was the tourist trap of Polson behind me than on the far horizon an escarpment rose like a tidal wave. Its steep terminus, Chief Rock, faced east, as if about to crash into Big Arm Bay. Blushing with violet-colored napweed, its flanks promised a break from Polson's seafood bistros, tackle shops, clothing boutiques and the forest of metal masts in the marina. Under fast-moving clouds, Chief Rock kept changing moods—glowering in shadow, uncertain in mottled cover, beaming under direct sunlight.

"There's Indian legends about that old Indian place," volunteered a retired accountant, but he couldn't recollect a one. Then I geared down through the Indian hamlet of Elmo—windbeaten government-built houses, TV antennae falling from roofs, grinning kids and their dogs daring me to invade the road shoulders, buckled roofs of dead cars in the high grass, hand-lettered signs pointing to health clinics and advertising local powwows.

I was paying my respects at Chief Rock because I knew that around the month known as "When Berries Ripen Even in the Night" in the summer of 1884, a thirteen-year-old boy named Lasso Stasso had left his mat-lodge village and walked up there. It lay between Flathead Lake and the smaller Black Lake a mile or so north, an area still stocked with Indian signs—open quarries where earlier generations had mined gray argillite for carving into pipe bowls; burial pits; rock alignments for trapping deer; and rock art drawings of hands and lines that seemed like tabulations and depicted men with animals inside circles. Down the lakefront were glacial terraces that for centuries had supported generations of Kootenai villages until the waters dried up. Offshore lay the island once inhabited by their oldest ancestors.

For a series of nights on that stony hump, Stasso prayed for a visitation from the spirits known to the Kootenai as *nupeeka;* to the Salish, *sumesh;* and to the Nez Percé, *weyekin.* For a generic term to describe these supernatural helpers, scholars use "guardian spirit." Among indigenous cultures of Mexico, the animal spirit, or "one's twin," that guides people through their lives is called *nagual,* meaning both companion and sorcerer; a virtue of the old English term one's *familiar* is its reminder that these magical associates become as intimate as other members of one's immediate family.

Some years earlier, on the banks of Finley Creek near present-day Arlee, Montana, Lasso Stasso had been startled by a bear splashing in the water. That became his first *nupeeka* spirit and marked him as quick minded and gifted at aiding women in childbirth. Now at Chief Rock he received more "helpers." As an older man, relishing his renown as the *Wamu* (shaman) of Elmo, Stasso recalled the "little circle of rocks" on its windblown crest. "All kinds of spirits dwelled up there, like birds, animals, rocks, everything. Coyote spoke to me up there one night." The *nupeeka* of Deer arrived by means of a song that mysteriously entered his body and bestowed the instincts of a successful hunter. A year after these apparitions, a Fawn *nupeeka* added gambling and love medicines; during his lifetime, Lasso Stasso was known to cure the sick and charm women. His success at Indian-style "hand games" was also famous, along with his skill at locating wild game and lost objects and telling the future. Luck seemed his middle name, but he confessed to never having attracted the spirits who made one a tribal leader.

By the 1920s, the circle of rocks that had enclosed Lasso Stasso on Chief Rock had been kicked apart by high school kids on Saturday-night beer busts. Any religious mystery Elmo residents attached to Cliff Rock had more to do with a suggestive outline of the Virgin Mary and Jesus, which some Indians claimed to have made out on its slopes. But until his death in 1951 (a fact of life caused, the Kootenai believed, by the waning powers of one's *nupeekas*), whenever Lasso Stasso sought to access his Deer or Coyote spirit powers, it was as if his very essence was swept back to Cliff Rock. The place was as central to his autobiography as the mysterious creatures who had stamped his character and career.

It has been argued that beseeching vegetal, animal or mineral spirits for support grew out of a still older Plateau Indian belief about reciprocal relationships between hunters and prey, or foragers and plants. To feed one's people, it was necessary to go to the top, transacting with those "bosses" of the different plants or animals. When negotiations went smoothly and respectfully, animals "allowed" themselves to be killed and plants and roots let themselves be plucked. If they didn't, stomachs went empty and people looked around for a new, luckier leader.

But I suspect that vision questing was taking place all the while. And we know that by the early 1800s, venturing into the wild to contact spirits had become the foundation of Plateau Indian spirituality. How totally these Indians relied upon the bonds created through these solitary epiphanies is clear from a famous Salishan leader from western Montana, Chief Moise. "Before the Black Robes came," he said, "each year we used to choose a boy and send him to the top of the mountain, and he fasted there and made Medicine for the people. Then he came back and we were well." Referring to the white man's insistence that Indian kids go to school, Moise added, "That was all the studying we had to do then. . . . The valley was our home. If we had not learned to think, we would not have been driven out." Explained another Plateau Indian to scholar Marius Barbeau, "Without guardian spirits, an Indian is like a fish without fins. He cannot live very long; he is nothing but a fool. For it is through them that we really know the sun, the moon, the mountains, the dawn and the night; it is from them that we get the strength of the earth, of all nature."

The true events of mythic times made this land and peopled it with these spirits. Plateau Indian stories told of the rock near the present-day town of Nelson, in southeastern British Columbia, which contained the imprint of Grandfather, who helped Coyote perform his earth-transforming deeds; the boulder that another superhuman being made from a young mountain lion's heart; the thermal spa where Four Brothers boiled meat in a "pot" between the Kootenai and Columbia rivers, thereby creating the streams that flow in opposite directions and wrap their steaming "veins" around the world, which sometimes bubbled up into hot springs for the benefits of human health and pleasure.

But after this turbulent era all was still not peace and love. Coyote may have rid the earth of many giants and mysterious beings, but some avoided death and retained their ancient powers—those that harmed as well as healed. Escapees from Coyote's age of transformation remained at large: giants in the highlands, spirits haunting pine forests, rock beings in mountain passes who crushed the lost, evil forces in the waters who drowned the unwary. They inhabited their own villages and went about their parallel lives. Although leery of humans, Spirits and their destiny were entangled with them.

Through stories, place-names and ordinary conversation, every Kootenai child knew their whereabouts and chosen lairs. Around the age of six, children were made to deal with the spirits in earnest by relatives and friends. They came to expect them in dreams, where they would appear as animals, trees, winds, even insects. Because human smells and sounds were repugnant to these spirits, the seeker took purifying sweat baths and was smudged in juniper smoke before heading out for their places with the appropriate offerings: tobacco and, later, cloth or even coins. For two, three or more days and nights, the seekers took no food or water and focused their prayers. Then, if they were lucky, these beings turned their undivided attention on them.

The centrality of vision questing to the Plateau Indians impressed the Jesuits who showed up in the 1840s. Wrote Father Urban Grassi to a fellow priest in 1873: "One will go rambling alone in the woods, abstaining from food and drink, for ten, fifteen or even twenty days. . . . Then, whether in trance or waking he does not know, the *genius loci* appears to him if he wishes to be lucky in something or other, such as fishing, hunting, trapping or curing of diseases. On the man's answering in the affirmative he becomes a bondsman of his visitor, from whom he receives a badge. It may be a feather, or a clam, or a ring of the rattlesnake."

With that Latin term, Father Grassi got it right; few of these Plateau *genii* lacked their preferred *loci*. Across the sacred geographies of all Plateau tribes were the spirit places the scholar Deward Walker calls portals, where Indians had the best chances of gaining entry to that "other world." For the eight bands of Kootenai, these included White Swan Lake, whose floating spirits helped anyone brave enough to hold his breath and dive into their icy underwater caves; the pothole on the Tobacco Plains; the incised boulders in the Bull Lake area; or the famous "big camp of spirits" between present-day Libby and Rexburg. Exceptionally tall trees lent other Kootenai boys the gift of flight, so they learned to hurl themselves from the uppermost branches and land without a scratch. These spirits might appear without warning, revealing themselves in bluish patches of moonlight shining on the ground or in the rasping of dry branches rubbing together. One Salishan man woke up to the voice of a tree named Wind in Dead Timber: "He told me I was soon to be a man and would no longer be afraid; I would always be protected if I sang this song which he taught me. . . . Sometimes I used it for curing other people who had been injured."

When it came to accounting for the attraction of spirit seeking to Plateau Indians, some scholars have emphasized the experience's "thrill." But this devalues the mutual relationships and ascent to adulthood that were affirmed through these crossings into "other worlds." No one stood proxy for these young people; no one shielded them from the grown-up terrors of hunger, thirst and a foretaste of death. In this school there were no secondary sources, no textbooks, no incompletes.

From a normal existence dominated by sunrise-to-sunset time, which theologian Paul Tillich has termed *chronos,* they were lifted into an "interval of sudden unfolding," which he called *kairos,* in which everything their society told them about the deep nature of the world was proven true. They received special skills, learned how to transact with inhabitants of the nonhuman environment, and often acquired new names, songs and talismans. Here their individuality was stamped and supernaturally affirmed. From now on, they called upon their spirit guardian, as they would upon a godparent, for a prayer or a boost and for success in life. In the afterglow of such peak experiences, thankful for the "edge" they now possessed—what we may call luck—they might commemorate the mythical encounter by drawing on the rock, as if returning the gift. For a remarkable time out of time, they had lived in that other zone and returned to tell about it. They were never the same again. Some part of that "inner world out there" was now permanently inside them.

In the nineteenth century, another layer of Plateau Indian sacred geography emerged from horrendous times and the doctrine of the Earth Mother, which arose to deal with them.

All Plateau peoples were aware that spirits were especially plentiful along the cataracts and stepped falls of their great rivers. At foaming defiles and sucking pools along the Columbia, the Snake and the Fraser, from April through June, the Indians congregated by the thousands to fish, trade, gamble, court and dance. The shorelines were jammed with plank lean-tos and rickety platforms that leaned over their boiling waters for men to net and spear. Today most of these sites are lost to Indian ownership, their channels reformed by dynamite and concrete into hydroelectric dams. But their former status may explain why an influential prophet, who sought to give Plateau Indians a new lease on life, originated at one of them.

Just before the Columbia River pulled out of its downward roll through Washington State and barreled for the Pacific, it ran over one turbulent nine-mile stretch. In the days before dams pacified them, seven shoals

dropped eighty feet, and water surged around an island. To whites this became known as the Priest Rapids of the Columbia's "big bend"; to Wanapum Indians it was a prized location, with each cataract individually named.
Its abundance of ancient burials, old abandoned house pits, stone piles indicating vision-quest spots, and engraved "power" rocks, where Indians
fished and prayed for more than two thousand years, mark it as their Mecca.

   In the 1870s, on the western banks of the lowest rapids, stood a Wanapum village of A-frame lodges named *P'mna,* or Fish Weir. By then, the
Wanapum and their Plateau neighbors had been through a biological
holocaust, losing nearly 90 percent of their population to smallpox,
whooping cough, influenza and measles. The very real possibility of ex-
tinction loomed as the Wanapum were pressured to give up their hunting
and fishing way of life in favor of farming, to send their kids to government boarding schools and to evacuate from the riverbank.

   Among local officials the conservative holdout of P'mna village aroused
particular consternation since it was the stronghold of a mystic named
Smohalla. His message was spreading from there to the interior: a brand-
new earth, free of white people—it was the regional expression of a universal impulse, in times of crisis, to turn back the clock and restore the world.
In the 1880s, a veteran of the Sioux Indian wars, E. L. Huggins, who'd
heard rumors about this rabble-rouser, was escorting freight wagons
through eastern Washington and asked to meet the prophet. One autumn
day, while Huggins camped on a tributary of the Yakima River, "Three
mounted Indians in gorgeous red and yellow turbans" emerged from the
trees. Unhurriedly the leader drew his pinto alongside Huggins. "I'm Smohalla," he said. After they'd dismounted, Huggins faced a strangely de-
formed man about sixty years old. His teeth were worn to the gums, he
was so nearly neckless that some called him a hunchback, his oversize
head was "almost Websterian," but his eyes shone with intelligence.

   Smohalla was born shortly before 1820, among the nearby Nez Percé
people. His early name was said to have been "Arising from the Dust of the
Earth Mother." Like the Priest Rapids, his own birthplace, Wallula, was a
communal fishing grounds and favored spot for tribal rendezvous, where
tribes shared news and the boy heard about the white man's god who rose

from the dead, along with horror stories of villages strewn with bodies that had perished from the white man's diseases.

For his own vision quest Smohalla had chosen La Lac mountain, a three-thousand-foot peak in the Rattlesnake Hills located between present-day Prosser, Washington, and the Columbia River, where spirits of the dead were known to ascend into the sky. There the Crow and Coyote beings passed on their songs and special powers. Later he acquired additional names: "Rock Carrier" and "Big Talk (or Shouting) on Four Mountains," referring to the belief that Smohalla's revelations derived from a mountain that spoke within his chest. Almost beaten to death in a brawl with another Indian, he dropped from sight. Some say he sojourned with the Mormons of Utah or even traveled into old Mexico. In the 1840s, however, he reappeared on the Plateau bearing a message from "the other side"—a doctrine of hope, resurrection and faith in the earth herself.

At first Smohalla believed his white visitor was after the Rapids. "You didn't come to see me about the land?" No, said Huggins, but if the Wanapum people accepted agriculture, they'd have a better chance of staying put, he suggested. That launched Smohalla into a harangue about whites who fenced land and then failed to farm, and against "book Indians," who cut their long hair, wore white man's clothes and wound up despised by both races. As for crops, Smohalla then delivered one of his famous quotes: "Men who work cannot dream, and wisdom comes to us in dreams."

When Huggins pointed out that surely Wanapum "worked" during fishing season, Smohalla said that only lasted a few weeks, and besides, "It is natural work . . . but the work of the white man hardens soul and body; nor is it right to tear up and mutilate the earth as white men do. . . . We do no more harm [to the earth by digging out edible camas roots] than would an infant's fingers harm its mother's breast. But the white man tears up large tracts of land, runs deep ditches, cuts down forests, and changes the whole face of the earth. . . ." Here the old man looked Huggins "searchingly" in the eye. "Every honest man knows in his heart that this is all wrong," he said. Smohalla also hinted to Huggins of "help from a stronger power" that would soon create a "sudden and powerful" deliverance for his Indian people.

As he rode the twenty miles back to his camp at Fox Canyon, Huggins confessed to himself, "If I were an Indian, I should be tempted to be thy disciple."

Central to the revamped creed of Smohalla and other Plateau prophets of his era was an apparent paradigm shift in the personification of landscape. His singular emphasis on the earth's gender appears to be something of an innovation. In Smohalla's revised cosmology, one heard less about evil beings in the forests, whereas the old wilderness spirits, such as Blue Jay or Owl, were relegated to the sidelines. With their ecological future in jeopardy, the old First Fruits rituals, which the Plateau people conducted each season, took on heightened importance. Giving thanks for the first berries, the first salmon and the first camas root now became overtures to sacramental feasts. And instead of normal gatherings at the Winter Spirit or Blue Jay dances, when people were permitted to manifest their spirit guardians, an urgent, intensified communal emphasis now surrounded Smohalla's new Prophet Dance.

Likewise transformed in the scheme of the Smohalla-inspired Dreamers was the familiar power balance between a trusted culture hero, sometimes named Sweat Lodge, and the loose-limbed trickster Coyote, who had originally wrested their topography from domination by monsters. Now this generation of prophets spoke of a spirit-being named Chief, who functioned as a sort of god. "Coyote and myself will not be seen again until the Earth-Woman is very old," said this Chief through the Dreamers. Smohalla's message bore the ring of biblical prophecy: "Then we shall return to the earth, for it will require a new change by that time. Coyote will precede me by some little time. . . . When I return, all spirits of the dead will accompany me, and after that there will be no spirit land. . . . Then will the Earth-Woman revert to her natural shape, and live as a mother among her children. Then things will be made right, and there will be much happiness."

The Plateau Dreamers also spoke of this male Chief and female Earth almost as a divine pair. Perhaps the hint of hierarchy was borrowed from Catholicism, as was the prophet's prohibition against working on the Sabbath or exhibiting one's supernatural guardians in the Winter Spirit gatherings. "For now they convened every Sunday to honor the Earth-Mother."

Word of Smohalla's teachings spread up the streams and across the meadows of the southeastern Plateau. His stronghold at Priest Rapids became a sanctuary for holdouts against white society, a magnet for Indian pilgrims. Followers gathered in bell-ringing congregations and committed to this new Indian way, distilled from old Plateau traditions and more recent Christian ideas, which outsiders, predictably, branded as being "cultish."

In July of 1884, Smohalla was visited by a second white solider. Unlike Huggins, Major J. W. MacMurray had direct orders to make the Wanapum accept "civilizing influences." In plain language that meant carving their tribally owned lands into individual family homesteads and living off their farms rather than the land and rivers. To reach P'mna village, the major bounced in his wagon until the terrain got too rough. Then Indians led his pack train over a three-thousand-foot pass until they dropped into the Columbia's big bend and MacMurray trained his field glass on the Indian camp.

"I discerned a number of houses stretched along the margin of the river, and from several flag poles fluttered in the wind." A few hours later he was greeted by Smohalla "all attired in gorgeous array and mounted on their best chargers. We wended our way through sagebrush and sand dunes to the village street, not a soul being visible; but from the mat-roofed and walled salmon houses there came forth the most indescribable sound of bell-ringing, drum-beating, and cat-surpassing screeches."

Smohalla told the major that the street had been swept and wetted down "in my honor, and to show that his people had cleanly tastes . . . he had constructed a bench for me, having sent to Ainsworth on the Northern Pacific railroad, more than ninety miles distant, for the nails." The visitor noticed the whitewashed fence of driftwood planks that protected the sacred assembly grounds, the row of ritual participants in red-and-blue-trimmed vestments, which reminded him of a Christian mass, the ringing bells and beating drums, and the spellbinding impact of Smohalla's oratory upon his followers. Fluttering from a flagpole was the religion's banner. The yellow in the flag stood for grass; green, for the mountains; blue, for sky. "This is my flag and it represents the world," Smoholla explained. "God told me to look after my people—all of my people. There are four ways in the world—north and south and east and west. I have been all those ways."

Using a board for the game of checkers, MacMurray explained the government's idea of land allotment. If Smohalla let his people apply for little squares for each family, he advised, they might beat white settlers to the best plots. That set Smohalla off; the idea "was against nature." As for the "checkerboard," he cursed it as "a bad word that comes from Washington." Then MacMurray heard the quote that would become a manifesto of American Indian ecology:

> Those who cut up the lands or sign papers for lands will be defrauded of their rights and will be punished by God's anger. It is not a good law that would take my people away from me to make them sin against the laws of God. You ask me to plough the ground? Shall I take a knife and tear my mother's bosom? Then when I die she will not take me to her bosom to rest. You ask me to dig for stone! Shall I dig under her skin for her bones? Then when I die I cannot enter her body to be born again. You ask me to cut the grass and make hay and sell it, and be rich like white men, but how dare I cut off my mother's hair? It is a bad law and my people shall not obey it. I want my people to stay with me here. All the dead men will come to life again; their spirits will come to their bodies again. We must wait here, in the homes of our fathers, and be ready to meet them in the bosom of our mother.

Despite dams, harassment from Indian agents and threats of eviction, Smohalla's colony refused to budge. For years his wooden effigy of an oriole swiveled atop its sacred pole in the Priest Rapids assembly ground, and parishioners pounded their seven sacred drums beneath it. Leadership passed to Smohalla's son, and a generation later to that man's nephew. Under the name of the Washani Faith, through the 1920s and 1930s, its sacred center remained in place. In the 1960s, the last families finally reached agreement with Grand Country power company and relocated across the river on a forty-acre site with new homes where they could fish and hunt at will.

Today the core ceremony of their Earth Mother doctrine remains their First Fruits activities. When bitterroot and camas are collected, or berries and wild greens harvested and spawning salmon caught, elders carry these traditional foods to their longhouses. No longer do they believe that the Creator will destroy the whites. Instead they express gratitude to Earth and Sun for regenerating the earth, and renew their devotions to Mother Earth and God the Father.

Then a third incarnation of Plateau Indian sacred landscape emerged from a fight over another riverbank.

Kootenai Falls, a series of watery tiers just west of Libby, Montana, is a time-honored Plateau Indian fasting location, where powers, spiritual and potentially electrical, come from the rapids that rush over its smooth-worn bedrock. The Kootenai Falls dispute of the late 1970s, which centered around construction of a hydroelectric dam, saw local Indians and their academic allies amplify their old belief systems in order to influence the non-Indian world.

Driving north from Chief Rock took me about two hours to reach Libby. Some ten miles later, between the populated Libby Valley and the undeveloped Lynx Creek flats, through a curtain of pine trees, I glimpsed the falls. What caught my breath was the river's stately pace as it spilled over those elegant terraces and shallow pools. I waded out to the middle, dropped to my knees and surrendered to the weight and sound around me. Looking downstream, I noticed how the flow splintered through a fan of chutes to boil around three stubborn little islands and combined again under a single-file suspension bridge that looked almost Andean in its high arc across the river. From there the river runs through the white sturgeon-spawning grounds and the thickly forested Purcell Mountains toward the Canadian border.

The falls are within earshot of logging trucks bound for Kalispell. They are cramped between the steel tracks of the Burlington Northern on one side of the river and China Mountain on the other side. They have been domesticated by the Lions Club picnic tables and metal-railing overlooks and are reined in by engineers controlling the Libby Dam spillways upstream. But in spite of these intrusions, they hold their own. Conversations are muffled by the rapids. From high ledges bighorn ewes check whether it's safe to try the grass along the northern banks. Sooty-colored dippers shoot through watery explosions, and I saw a rare pair of harlequin ducks bob in the upper eddies. An osprey spun into the riffles, twisted for a split second, then beat into the air with a six-inch rainbow in its talons.

The issue that threatened this place in 1979 was an old story for the Columbia River drainage. A consortium of six rural energy cooperatives wanted to build a 925-foot-long dam controlled by six hydraulically operated floodgates so as to generate up to 144 megawatts of electricity. Ninety-seven percent of the Kootenai River would be diverted around the falls, its flow reduced from 13,000 cubic feet per second to 750 feet. The trapped waters would back up into a 232-acre reservoir at 2,000 feet above sea level and would extend four and a half miles into the woods. The last undeveloped waterfall on a major river in the American northwest would become history.

Over the last seventy years, nineteen major dams and some sixty hydroelectric projects have harnessed and rechanneled the Columbia's main trunk, branching tributaries and secondary streams like the Kootenai. Where a million fish once fought their way up the Columbia and Snake and into central Idaho, not a single sockeye or chinook swims today. Along with blocking the old fish-spawning runs, these projects obliterated a string of traditional Indian fishing encampments that had been established along the 1,214 miles of the Columbia River system. In the process, the dam builders wiped out untold numbers of spirit "homes" and associated rock art remains.

But the Kootenai Falls proposal was made in an environmentally conscious day and age. Assessing what were described as nonutilitarian consequences was now mandated by law. Although most of the falls' environmental impact study went into forecasting the project's effect on non-Indian fishing, hunting and recreation, some native commentary was allowed. But since no money was earmarked for original research, the study relied on recent archaeology and older ethnographies. By now some thirty-seven cultural or historical sites had been identified close to the falls; at least two of them (the Kootenai claimed five) suggested vision questing in prewhite days. Not far away were quarries of soapstone from which old-time Kootenai carved pipe bowls. The study also agreed that the falls had been a major native trail stopover, a boundary between hunting grounds of Upper and Lower Kootenai tribal divisions, and that native trade had taken place there for more than a thousand years. But scholars hired by Northern Lights Electric Cooperative were not so sure. Perhaps the "river and rocks are frequently important locales for spirits and/or contact with the spirit world," but they were unable to confirm "the significance of the Kootenai Falls to Kootenai religious practices."

The written record on Kootenai religion was not much help, nor were contemporary tribal members, for whom it was a point of honor to prevent outsiders from poking into their beliefs. And if archaeologists had to prowl around or elders were to be interviewed, the Indians insisted on choosing who made the queries, and on keeping all findings under wraps. Already they were upset that the Libby dam, completed in 1972 about twenty-six miles upstream, had reduced sturgeon spawn and destroyed some four hundred historical and archaeological sites, burial grounds and other places dear to tribal memory.

Maintaining a wall of silence about the details of their religious practices, the Kootenai would declare only that both banks of the river for a stretch of six miles constituted their "holiest of temples." Skeptics suggested that it was a matter of the tribe's "new clothes," that the Kootenai were hiding the fact that they had no traditional associations with the place. Quite the contrary, Indian advocates responded, the falls were the heart of their cultural universe; the dam "would cause the irretrievable loss of the Kootenai religion, culture and way of life."

After their tribal council voted on July 6, 1979, to fight the dam, they engaged an old ally, anthropologist Deward E. Walker. At first, the writings of nineteenth-century French sociologist Émile Durkheim seemed relevant. "By sacred things," Durkheim had written, "one must not understand simply those personal beings which are called gods or spirits; a rock, a tree, a spring, a pebble, a piece of wood, a house, in a word anything can be sacred." But the line drawn by Durkheim's writings between the "sacred" and the "secular" struck Walker as precluding many sacred places described by his Plains and Plateau Indian friends. More effective was showing how Kootenai Falls fell into a "worldwide religious pattern involving visions and sacred sites." To help him do that, Walker turned to his University of Colorado colleague, David Carrasco, whose relatively new discipline to North America, history of religions, applied universal religious patterns and ideas to specific cases.

Without benefit of fieldwork, Carrasco declared that since the falls was the "center, pivot, axis and foundation" of a religious system, Kootenai Falls was like "Jerusalem, Mecca, Tepeyac, Bethel, Blue Lake, Lourdes, Cholula." To the Kootenai Indians, they were a "primal" ground "where the first and/or most important revelations from God took place, the foundation for the people and the center of the cosmos." Citing examples from Judaism, Christianity and the institutionalized state religions of China and Aztec Mexico, Carrasco wrote that "the claims about Kootenai Falls do not reflect the idiosyncratic tendencies of local malcontents but the authentic religious inspiration of Montana tribal people which is shared with religious peoples throughout history."

These analogies between tribal and world religions drew on the work of the prolific religious scholar Mircea Eliade. Born in Bucharest in 1907, Eliade studied in Benares, India, lectured in Paris, Rome, Munich and Strasbourg, and eventually occupied an influential chair at the University of Chicago Divinity School. Almost single-handedly he shifted his discipline's older focus on Christianity, Judaism and Islam toward an incorporation of eastern mysticism, the occult, shamanism and the belief systems of those he classified as "primal" peoples. Eliade's terminology for embracing them all reverberated through the Kootenai defense because two of his favorite topics were so relevant—sacred space and sacred time.

But the strategy of validating Kootenai Falls as a major shrine by appealing to patterns shared by "high" or "world" religions put the tribe in a bind. Comparisons between rushing waters and Gothic cathedrals found the Kootenai facing the same risks that Taos Pueblo barely skirted when they equated Blue Lake with temples and cathedrals: in focusing on one single place, they undermined protection of the larger watershed whose streams fed and purified it. Also, as Kootenai from Idaho, Montana and British Columbia mobilized against the dam, they were hard put to keep secret their rituals and where they practiced them. The courts made them pin down where and what they did, and codify their beliefs in terms that justified that their religious feelings were like those of "the most devout practitioners of the Moslem Faith at an attempt to destroy the Holy Mosque in Mecca."

In the checklist of cosmological features that Eliade and Carrasco identified as universal were preoccupations with an *umbilicus mundi*, or "sacred center"; an *axis mundi*, or "world tree"; the four sacred directions; and a dome of heaven over it all. The Indians had to provide documentary support for the statements of these well-intentioned supporters, which included the Boulder-based Native American Rights Fund, that "at issue is their *holiest* of temples or shrines where the most central ceremonies are practiced."

Through the same sort of theological readjustments by which the Plateau Dreamers had synthesized their trinity of Chief, Coyote and Earth Mother, the Kootenai lawyers began talking about a "creator and his divinities—now known collectively as Nupika." Kootenai Falls was classified as what Eliade had called a *hierophany*—where the sacred manifested itself, erupting into our visible world. Nor did the lawyers attempt to hide the Christian overtones of condensing the diversity of Kootenai spirits into a single Creator being, or of the falls' becoming his "home." They argued outright that "the visions which are sought and received are closely comparable to those described in the Bible. . . . The divine revelations obtained from Nupika actually form the basis for the life of the vision seekers and have far-reaching impacts upon the Tribe's religious life and welfare." If "Nupika is disobeyed," they declared, a "sacred covenant" between the tribe and their creator would be destroyed.

This synthesis of Plateau Indian religion retained the older Plateau Indian faith in visions as the conduit for ultimate truth, supernatural assistance and personal guidance. Of that, Lasso Stasso would have ap-

proved. From the prophet doctrine of the late nineteenth century, however, it took the reverence for the Earth Mother as a central religious tenet.
Of that Smoholla would have approved. And when the Kootenai-Salish
Culture Committee encouraged the harvesting of natural foods and medicinal plants, they were reviving Smohalla's preachings about the inter-
dependence between his people's social identity and their old traditions of
surviving off the land.

What was new was turning these beliefs into "articles of faith," like
those associated with the large-scale, "founder" religions that focused
upon creative visionaries like Jesus or Mohammed. Instead of the omnipotent pair of Chief or Old Man and his female partner, Earth Mother,
revered by Smohalla and the other Plateau Dreamers, now the Kootenai
spoke of the Creator and his female counterpart, Mother Earth. The tribe's
official culture committee clarified the relative status of the two in a simple injunction: "Give thanks to our Creator for the things Mother Earth
provides and ask that whatever you take be put back again next year."

With such statements the Kootenai joined national Indian demands for
respect for this new sacred pair, and in insisting that the places where Indians communicated with them deserved protection. Adopting the generic
English term "Creator" across the spectrum of American Indian tribes
positioned a nativist supreme being on a separate but equal footing with
the imported Christian one. But it was clear which deity took precedence
in Indian hearts. The white man's "God" might relax on his throne, and
looking at the finished job, be pleased with himself; but the Indian's male
"Creator" kept working in partnership with his female equal, "Mother
Earth," in seasonally renewing their universe on behalf of their peoples.

The times were responsive to the spin the Kootenai Indians, their
lawyers and loyalists were giving to Indian spirits of place. During their
fight, the tribe scored a supportive victory in persuading the regulatory
commission to keep their testimony under wraps. The transcript that described locations of sacred places and how they were used were stamped
"limited distribution status," to be destroyed once the case reached a "non-
appealable decision."

In 1982, the Federal Energy Commission released its findings. Only
two pages were devoted to the dam's impact on Indian religion, but they

were forcefully worded. Paraphrasing Patrick Lefthand, a medicine man and cultural liaison between government and tribe, it said, "The terms of the Kutenai covenant do not provide any compromises. The Kutenai could not arbitrarily change the creator's home or agree to conditions under which the project could be built in the area. . . ."

Although the tribe had brandished President Carter's Religious Freedom Act in their favor, two years later, when presiding judge David W. Miller gave eight reasons for denying the power company a license to build the dam, he never mentioned the act or Kootenai beliefs. Without compelling evidence that existing facilities could not meet energy demands up to the year 2000, Judge Miller simply felt there was no justification for threatening the "aesthetic" and "recreational" appeal of the falls. "If the Kootenai project was built," he wrote, "it would result in a surplus of power and this surplus would have to be achieved by the sacrifice of unique values associated with the Falls."

Three years later, Northern Lights' final appeal of his decision was turned down, but neither Kootenai religion nor the sacred status of the falls was credited with being the reason why. Yet it did not matter to the Kootenai or their lawyers if the falls' reprieve was largely for economic reasons; they believed that the spirit of the falls had spoken. Drums were beaten and victory dances were held in the reservation towns of St. Ignatius and Elmo.

On second thought analogies to the fine arts of painting and writing may not be the best way to imagine this process of religious evolution on the Columbia Plateau. Perhaps geology offers a more organic and rooted stratigraphic comparison.

As occurs after shifts of tectonic plates, volcanic eruptions and cataclysmic earthquakes, underlying beliefs buckle up, stick out or thicken layer by layer. Sometimes the oldest elements retain their worth, as the practice of vision questing remains central to Plateau Indian belief, like a diamond in the rough. New credos may catch the eye, like the Earth Mother Doctrine of the Plateau Prophets. But fissures, flows and slides maintain all sorts of relationships with strata underneath. Embedded with old beliefs, today's Indian rituals, like the revised and revitalized beliefs about Kootenai Falls, emerge from this constant cutting into and churning up of ideas—as with the histories of religious systems the world over.

Plateau notions of sacred geography grew out of early faith in a landscape alive with localized spirits. Then came reliance upon an authoritative Earth Mother and a sky-dwelling Creator who could hold their own against a non-Indian Almighty God. Next, one heard equations between Plateau sacred places and those of world religions. Just as the Earth Mother ideology of the Dreamers was no substitute for vision questing, so today's emphasis upon a central "home of the creator" still retains elements of the Dreamers' Mother Earth rhetoric. If Plateau Indian religion and its special locations remain relevant, dynamic and worth protecting today it is *because* of the layers of spiritual energy and creative purpose that have been folded onto them over the centuries.

CHAPTER TEN

PRIESTLY SKIES, SHAMANIC EARTH

Pawnee

I n 1962, a young urologist named Lou Gilbert, from Lincoln, Nebraska, heard about a piece of property about an hour's drive from the city. At one time, the river valleys of eastern Nebraska were dominated by earth lodge villages of Pawnee Indians. But since the tribe had been forcibly removed to northern Oklahoma in the 1870s, there were no Indians around to tell Mr. Gilbert that the parcel contained their people's most important sacred place—the site known as "Mound Sitting on (or over) the Water," or *Pahaku*.

During the previous years, Lou and his wife, Geri, had joined a circle of up-and-coming Lincoln professionals who shared interests in the arts and the outdoors, and vacationed together with their kids. But now the spiritually inclined Geri sought a getaway for her peace of mind. To her pragmatic husband, a weekend place seemed a sound investment as well as a break from Lincoln's faster pace. A patient had mentioned 160 acres for sale on the southern banks of the Platte River at Cedar Bluffs, just outside of Fremont. One Saturday they drove over for a look.

Lou's forebears were German-French, and his family had lived in Beatrice, about fifty miles south of Fremont, for three generations. Geri's background was Swedish-Irish; her father was a printer in Columbus, some thirty-five miles west of Fremont. The designation "Pawnee" had never left an impression upon young Geri or Lou, whether around the dinner table or in their classrooms.

Since at least the fourteenth century, their corner of Nebraska had nurtured a complex hunting and agricultural Plains Indian culture, which historically had become known as Pawnee. With their Caddoan linguistic origins traceable to the south, this Indian nation comprised four separate bands. From April through September, the Pawnee cultivated gardens along the flood plain, living in villages of round, mud-roofed lodges located on bluffs overlooking their fields. In fall and early spring, they packed their portable tipis on buffalo hunts toward the west. Supporting this lifestyle was an elaborate system of rituals that viewed their survival and social well-being as dependent upon gods among the stars and magical animals in the earth.

By the mid-nineteenth century, the Pawnee homeland found itself threatened on two fronts. A war machine of Sioux Indian tribes pressed from the north while white settlers from the east eyed their fertile river bottoms. In the 1870s, all their bands submitted to treaties of removal and relocated to Indian Territory, in what would become northern Oklahoma. Left behind were flats pockmarked with grassed-over house pits—but no Pawnee families. Aside from a few historical markers at the town of Genoa, where the tribe had consolidated shortly before its departure, the state of Nebraska had erased that chapter from its past.

Even though she had been raised near the Omaha and Winnebago Indian reservations just to the northeast of Columbus, to Geri any mention of Indians evoked the tomahawk-wielding villains of motion pictures. To Lou, whose birthplace was not far from the Kansas reservations of the Sac and Fox, Kickapoo and Prairie Potawatomi, the term was identified with the occasional brown-skinned hobo rapping on the kitchen window for table scraps.

The morning drive to Fremont was bright and promising, corn and soybean fields streaming by. They turned off an unpaved country road and headed down a half-mile lane to a forlorn cabin. Junk lay piled about, paint flaked from the walls, and without front steps you had to hoist yourself inside. The family of the talkative proprietor, Edgar Cullin, had owned the place for generations. About him Geri had her doubts, with his patter about something the locals called Elephant Cave. "He went on about Indians living here, there were caves, and I thought, so what." Absenting herself from the men, she found a path through some big old oaks and made for the river bluffs.

Beneath her feet lay a six-foot blanket of silty earth, which blowing winds had taken two million years to distribute over a series of ancient glacial deposits. Soon she reached the highest point in Saunders County and gazed down eight miles of the dried-up channel of the Platte River, the Todd Valley. She didn't know it, but this was a geological and botanical wonderland with a cultural heritage just as exceptional. The path she took had been trod by generations of Pawnee, who once occupied sizable villages only a few miles away, both up- and downstream. Yet this overlook they had apparently left alone, taking pains to detour a major trade route around its cedar trees and a peculiar rise near the river.

Glad to be alone under the hickories and hackberries, Geri couldn't have cared less about that. The path curved down to a sandbar. From overhead she heard songs of birds she was learning to identify from Audubon Society outings. Above arched the robin's-egg blue of a Nebraska sky. The November air was crisp and redolent with decaying leaves. Memories of childhood flooded back as the winds that tear down the river basin carried the scent of cottonwoods up the slope. Through the trees she caught silvery flashes of the Platte. "I came back from my walk and said, Lou, we've got to buy this. And after we bought it, three days later, he said, what are we going to use it for? And I said, I just want to walk in the woods, I just want to be here."

Three years after the Gilberts purchased their property, a twenty-five-year-old graduate student in the Department of Linguistics at the University of California, Berkeley, went knocking on doors of older Pawnee in northern Oklahoma. Douglas R. Parks was looking for surviving speakers of the old Caddoan language and guidance on how its grammar worked.

In 1876, the U.S. government had resettled the Pawnee on a 283,000-acre reservation in the rocky, scrub timber of northern Oklahoma's Payne County. Even after five generations of struggling to adapt to a life of dependency and to restore their decimated population, a few old-timers remembered tales of their homeland.

Among Parks's favorite storytellers was a blind man in his midseventies named Harry Mad Bear. A stalwart Baptist and member of the Native American Church, the pan-Indian religion that uses the peyote cactus as its sacramental food, Mad Bear lived alone in a small house on the northern edge of Pawnee, the tribe's commercial center. His father and grandfather had been prominent Pawnee medicine men, "doctors" who'd sung their songs for earlier scholars. An exacting informant, after each session with Parks, Mad Bear would press his ear to the tape recorder to check the jaw-breaking words and intricate syntax that are lost to today's generation.

Back home, Parks played back the thirty-six stories he'd taped during five summers to extract words and verbal constructions for a Pawnee dictionary and grammar. Then the tapes slept in his files. But in 1977, teaching at St. Mary's College in Bismarck, North Dakota, he took them for a summer's fieldwork back to Pawnee and listened with another fluent speaker, Nora Pratt. First they translated stories from a man named Roaming Scout, then they tackled the Mad Bear narratives.

A by-product of Parks's focus on the cultural background that emerged from Mad Bear's stories was his curiosity about the Pawnee's Nebraska. Few of Parks's consultants remembered anything about life along the Platte and Loup rivers, but the narratives did. They revealed how those ancestors interacted with the natural world; each story sent Parks back to the library in search of earlier versions. Of all the tales, the story of a boy brought back to life at a sacred place known variously as Pahuk, Pahuku or Pahaku was recorded most often. When Mad Bear began his account of young Pacha, he said it concerned the "last time our people had the good fortune to enter the lodge at Pahuku."

But where was this place? In writings by Melvin Gilmore, an early-twentieth-century historian, ethnobotanist and story collector from the Nebraska Historical Society, Parks discovered the most extensive version. Obtained by Gilmore from an old man named *Letekots Taka*, or White Eagle, it told of a father who had murdered his son and thrown his corpse into the Platte River. A kingfisher noticed the body, then flew downstream to the place Gilmore called "Pahuk," an underground chamber where the sacred animals met in council. "This animal lodge was under the hill," White Eagle told Gilmore, "and entered by a secret passageway which was hidden by bushes and vines." Every species of bird, beast and reptile had their assigned seat. The kingfisher pleaded with them to bring the boy to life.

The council was unable to reach a consensus, so the kingfisher went to other animal meeting places for their opinions. (Outwardly these natural sites resembled Pawnee earth lodges—round mounds with a side hill like an entryway.) Collectively, wrote Gilmore, they were called *Nahurak.* Finally, the animals reached consensus: the boy should be brought back to life.

With his curiosity piqued about these "animal lodges," Parks noticed them cropping up in many accounts of the Pawnee—before long he tallied fourteen separate sites. But none turned up as often as what a linguist would write as *Pa;haku,* "Mound on the Water," whose reputation extended to other tribes as well. To the Sioux it was *Paha Wakan,* or "Holy Hill," and to the Omaha, *Pahe Wahube,* "Hill Sacred." In the 1890s, environmentalist George B. Grinnell collected its story, and pioneer anthropologists Alice C. Fletcher and George A. Dorsey also cited its importance. From Pawnee friends, historian Marie Sandoz heard of its power—which Nebraska historian A. E. Sheldon likened to that of Mecca for Muslims or Mount Sinai to Judeo-Christians. Conducting fieldwork among Oklahoma Pawnee in the 1930s, the husband-and-wife team of Alexander Lesser and Gene Weltfish were struck by Pawnee nostalgia for the place called Pahaku.

Then Parks reviewed the work of veteran archaeologist of the Central Plains Waldo R. Wedel. Unlike his crustier colleagues, who mostly trusted hard facts derived from what they had extracted from the dirt, Wedel was also intrigued by Pawnee religious imagination and its focus on gods in the night sky. Now Parks wondered how it extended to spirits within the earth as well.

To novelist Willa Cather, the storm-whipped winters and overcooked summers of her native Nebraska inspired good stories but bred a suffocating social climate for writing them up. Old-time Pawnee felt quite differently. Those skies and flood plains liberated their cultural imagination. Its spirits taught them to love it and use it. Well before Coronado met them in the mid-sixteenth century, they had learned to exploit its "edge zone" ecosystem, where the Republican, Platte and Loup river bottoms proved excellent for growing corn, beans and squash, and the buffalo plains were only a few days' ride away.

Given the sophisticated levels of Pawnee philosophy, astronomy and the ritual arts, it is curious that American popular culture so often stigmatizes this tribe as ghouls and bad guys. From the "red rascals" whom a Nebraska newspaper editor in 1856 urged the U.S. government to exterminate to the Sioux enemies in the 1990 film *Dances with Wolves,* the Pawnee are often identified by their trademark Mohawk-style hairdos, black striped leggings and garish face paint. They are portrayed as villainous updates of James Fenimore Cooper's evil Iroquois who terrorized the French and English—almost condemned for *not* being your stereotypical war bonnet-wearing, exclusively buffalo-hunting Plains Indians.

From lance and arrow points in western Nebraska, we know that numerous different Indian groups lived there for more than eleven thousand years; some archaeologists wonder if one mammoth skeleton was butchered by Indians six centuries before that. Better understood are the foraging cultures dating to around 200 B.C., the artifacts of which remind us that the region's earlier residents were rather cosmopolitan for they used stone from eastern Wyoming, marine shells from the Atlantic or Gulf of Mexico, mica from North Carolina or the Black Hills, copper from near Lake Superior and olivella shells from the Pacific.

About twelve hundred years ago, floodplains along the middle Missouri River tributaries began attracting Indian gardeners. The seminomadic patterns of life they established would be elaborated farther south by the Pawnee—women raising corn along the river in summertime and overseeing the permanent earth-lodge villages, men venturing west for buffalo during the two annual hunts, in fall and winter. Although there's no certainty that the Pawnee were here before 1600, Francisco de Coronado wrote that in central Kansas he met some visiting "Harahey" Indians, who may have been Pawnee.

After the late seventeenth century, however, the material record of Pawnee life grows overwhelming. Numbering perhaps ten thousand strong, they built upward of twenty villages that contained cemeteries, council grounds and hundreds of forty-foot-wide domestic earth lodges. With narrow alleys winding between their lodges, the villages were surrounded by earthen berms and overlooked rivers in present-day Kansas and Nebraska.

But Pawnee origins remained mysterious. They spoke dialects of Caddoan, somehow linking them to a southeastern heritage. Their calumet, or Hako ceremony, was distantly reminiscent of mound-building Mississippian rituals. Their villages had ball fields, like the pre-Spanish Hohokam of the Southwest. Among their other rituals was sacrificing a virgin to the Morning Star, which recalled the rites of Meso-America. Their shamanistic dramas employed elaborate stagecraft and puppetry, rivaled only by Southwest Pueblo or Northwest Coast Indian ceremonies. Their stellar astronomy, the poetry of their ritual liturgies, the aristocratic nature of their priesthoods all added up to a culture of considerable antiquity with a root system clearly extending far afield.

With Lou's urology practice thriving in Lincoln, he opened a satellite office in Fremont, nearer the hideaway where he and Geri now camped on weekends. Pulling in on Fridays, they ate sandwiches and watched the sunset before rolling into sleeping bags on the lawn. Waking to jays and chickadees, they dug a garden, composted, cut brush and trimmed trees. Come the cool of late afternoons, they explored the wildlife that seemed particularly abundant.

They also researched their investment. The previous owner's mother, Lucy Cullin, lived there in August of 1914, when historian Melvin Gilmore brought the eighty-two-year-old Skidi Pawnee named White Eagle up from Oklahoma to revisit his people's homeland. The man had served with Captain Luther North's famous Pawnee scouts, been wounded and then survived on his veteran's pension. White Eagle was especially excited about seeing Pahaku.

Making a beeline for the riverbank, White Eagle pointed down the 150-foot embankment. Down there, he said through interpreter Charles Knifechief, was where the magical animals had convened in their secret cave. In his notebook, Gilmore wrote that the old man "identified the place as confidently as I would identify my childhood home." White Eagle also remembered wagon trains rolling down today's Highway 30, and as a boy he kept lookout for suspicious Indians riding up the Platte Valley.

But every spring the flooding river undercut the bank; by the 1940s, the cave was but a slit. When a squatter reported two kids caught playing inside, the cliff was dynamited to eliminate a safety hazard. Locals filled the resulting gully with cast-off ice boxes, broken stoves, garbage; Edgar Cullin himself added two dozen trashed cars.

Geri was still more absorbed by the land than with Indians or history. Belonging to a food co-op in Lincoln, she'd talked with herbalists and exchanged natural food recipes. Here was a perfect home for a large organic garden. The new environment drew something else out of her too. "We'd had guests here; it was a Sunday," she remembered. "They'd left and it was quiet. A beautiful evening. I was standing by the pond watching our black-and-white cat. And I don't know really what happened. The light was right, it was like a trance, as if *I* had disappeared and became part of the scene." On another weekend she returned to Pahaku "and I looked at those oak trees and it was as if I was that oak tree, like they were alive, as alive as I was."

Lou also focused on the ground, but on a grander scale. A new patient, the architect Emiel Christensen, became his accomplice. Reseeding native grasses, reintroducing meanders, sloughs and beaver dams into rivers, and even raising a few buffalo, had become a popular topic in environmental magazines, catching the imaginations of Sierra Club landowners and their counterculture offspring. Both his wife and Christensen were inspired by writer Aldo Leopold's call for a new "land ethic"; specifically, by Leopold's belief that it was on private land that the restoration of original ecosystems had its best chance for success. Sitting astride this dramatic ecotone, where hardwood floodplain gave way to western grassland, Pahaku seemed a good place to try it.

Out went the rotting garbage, smashed-up car bodies and busted refrigerators. Following the dim traces of what geographers call the "desire lines" left by former residents, they cleared five miles of hiking trails around the property and cleaned a pond left by railroad construction in order to once again attract migrating wild fowl. Since this was the western limit of walnuts, hickories, lindens and mulberries, Lou cleared and pruned around them. They sought to restore unique adaptations that plant life creates at the frontier of its normal distribution range with the compass plant, big blue stem and Indian grasses not found farther west. Without clearing by the fires that the Pawnee used to set every fall, some plants needed thinning; the reborn meadows cried out for sun and air.

Realizing Geri and Lou's vision of Pahaku as a restored environment would have been simpler if there hadn't been that nagging cultural dimension to the place. Every now and then its older presence intervened. Yellowing newspaper clips fell into their hands—overripe local features about the exotic "rituals of the Pawnee" and the "mysterious hill" where they had taken place. They discovered that their property was linked to four other Pawnee sacred sites, also on bluffs, overlooking streams, supporting little rises. Sometimes strangers—some part Pawnee or a scholar studying the tribe—showed up at their front door, inquiring if this was the place the Historical Society in Lincoln had told them about. In Melvin Gilmore's book *Prairie Smoke,* Geri read that it had been a place of pilgrimage to more than one Prairie-Plains tribe. "When I learned the Indians had used it as a ceremonial hill, especially when I heard the Pawnees had this great knowledge of astronomy, my attitudes began to change, and it also seemed that I was feeling some of the sacredness here that they had felt."

In the 1930s and 1940s, the Smithsonian archaeologist Waldo R. Wedel compiled a time line for early Pawnee settlements. In the libraries he found accounts of the tribe by an educated, half-Pawnee Indian scholar and writer named James R. Murie, which prompted him to ask about the religious ideas that lay behind these villages. Their great gods, Wedel learned, were the stars. Pawnee priests looked to the Nebraska sky the way Catholics gazed at the history of their faith in the Sistine Chapel. Despite one nineteenth-century Presbyterian missionary's opinion that the Pawnee astronomy was "very limited," their religious specialists, known as *hu'rahus,* were on speaking terms with the heavens. To bestow blessings and health on their villages, they transacted with the Pleiades (associated with winter), Lyra, Ursa Major, Cassiopeia (known as the turkey's foot), Ursa Minor, Coma Berenices, the Big Dipper, Andromeda, the Milky Way (the cloudy trail followed by spirits of the dead) and the Corona Borealis (known as the Council Circle of the Chiefs).

Every Pawnee village boasted its origin story, which told how their patron star or constellation had bestowed a medicine bundle—sacred objects secured within a leather binding—upon their founding father. Like satellite dishes picking up flares from outer space, these sacred bundles brought the sky powers down to earth. Passed down through the male line and set upon altars, they served as conduits for rising prayers (accompanied by smoke) and descending benefits.

So intimate was Pawnee identification with the stars that they tried to lay out their villages to approximate their positions in the sky. Ideally, farthest north lay the village in charge of the North Star bundle, the female star "which doesn't move," whose gardens always had green corn and larders of fresh buffalo meat. To the west should stand the Evening Star village, with the moon considered "her" helper, and the community's bundle dedicated to Tirawa, the Pawnee creator god, who stood above all stars, humans and living things. Eastward you located the Morning Star village, with "his" helper, the sun.

As on the macro level, so with the micro: the celestial order was projected into the Pawnee dwelling. In photographs taken by William H. Jackson along the Loup River in 1871, their earth lodges look like great turtles buried in a mud slide. But inside, each one was swept clean and symbolized the universe. The walls represented the surrounding hills; the domed roof, the sky; and the lights that twinkled through the open smoke hole drew in the strength of the celestial powers.

Much like Pueblo Indians, the Pawnee associated each of their four sacred directions with its own tree, animal, weather condition and color. These symbols were assigned, in turn, to cottonwood posts holding up the lodge roof (matted with finer sticks and brush, then covered with earth or sod), which stood for the four semidirectional stars that had been instructed by omnipotent Tirawa to prop up the heavens. At the building's rear was the realm of the Evening Star and a family altar, "the place for the wonderful things." The lengthy tunnel entrance, a trademark of Pawnee lodges, faced the Morning Star. Sightings of the sky through doorway and smoke hole turned the dwelling into a home observatory.

All this symbolism did not dampen the pleasure the Pawnee found in common beauty. In late winter their women brightened the earth lodges with redbud and evening primrose blossoms; summer had them watering yellow and red gallardia daisies around the perimeter. But special moments lifted Pawnee aesthetics toward the transcendent. From Alice Fletcher's early account of the tribe's Hako ceremony—an elaborate ritual for bonding families, clans or tribes in friendship and peace—archaeologist Wedel read about a journey undertaken by a "Father" group of celebrants to a "Children" group.

Before setting off, the lead priest explained the inner significance of water, the winds, fire and the earth, and blessed the landscape ahead. As the party caught sight of a stream, he led their praise song "to the river glistening in the sunlight in its length." Standing on its bank, they chanted to "the water in it that ripples as it runs." Before crossing, the priest instructed his charges in how to turn the act of fording a stream into an action meditation. Timed to a sequence of stanzas, the travelers waded across. On the opposite shore, he had them stand still. "We are wet with the water through which we have just passed," he said. "But we must not touch our bodies where we are wet, for the running water is sacred. So we will sing the first stanza of this song, and call on the wind, Hotoru, to come and touch us that we may become dry." As the breeze worked on their legs, the participants were reminded to feel it "touching us here and there, completely enveloping us." The song climaxed as the evaporation was complete and their journey resumed.

But Wedel knew that these highlights of Pawnee ritual told only half the story. Neglected were the equally important activities of acquiring mystical powers and healing the sick. Those practices left few traces in the ground. And they were the business of the mysterious Pawnee "doctors," the brotherhood of shamans, healers and magic makers whom Mircea Eliade once dubbed "technicians of ecstasy." Whence came their powers?

Sixteen years after Doug Parks first heard about Pahaku from Harry Mad Bear, he and Wedel saw it for themselves. Over three days in mid-August 1982, Parks joined the Wedels, noted Plains anthropologist Raymond De-Mallie and Gayle Carlson of the Nebraska Historical Society on a road trip down the Pawnee's memory lane—the linkage of sacred places which Parks said they referred to as *rahurahwa:ruksti:'u,* or "(being) holy ground." Cramming into a Nebraska Historical Society van, they retraced White Eagle and Melvin Gilmore's route back in 1914. This meant cutting through the muggy heat along the lower Platte River, detouring up the thicketed Loup River, popping back south to locations along the Nebraska-Kansas border, and finishing with a swing back to the final cluster of upper Platte sites.

It meant pursuing the ghosts of ghosts.

Near Wahoo Creek not a trace remained of the old Leshara village, whose hundreds of earth lodges rang with life in the late 1860s. Its burial ground was eviscerated for the Saunders County Courthouse. En route to the McClean village site close by, they watched the river bottom glide by, knowing its eroded and plowed banks once supported other bygone Pawnee communities. Next they learned that not only had the Woodcliffe housing project erased McClean's burial ground, but also that a promised museum had never materialized. Except for one rusty gun barrel, its trove of old Pawnee axes, pots, beads and even skulls lay hidden in the garages and trunks of local collectors.

About six miles upstream came the heavy woods of Pahaku Hill, or Mound on the Water, the loftiest point on the Platte's south shore. Not having received prior agreement from the Gilberts to hike the bluff for their photographs, they crossed the river at Fremont, doubled back on gravel roads and gingerly stepped halfway across an abandoned Chicago and Northwestern railroad trestle. Here was the first animal lodge, the origin place for the Pawnee doctors' fraternity; stories described it variously as an island in the Platte or a cave under its overhang.

Continuing south at North Bend, they rolled by feed lots, cornfields, housing projects and yard landscaping, which everyone in the vehicle knew were superimposed on Pawnee village sites that their profession had memorialized on site maps as 25BU1 (Linwood), 25BU4 (Barcal), 25BU2 (Bellwood) and 25CX1 (Schuyler). In his mind's eye, Dr. Wedel recalled sunken house pits from his surveys in the thirties. Buried or bulldozed, they were long gone, together with the enigmatic earthen ring just past Barcal, and no markers indicated that any Indians ever called this their home. "Dr. Wedel was not interested in stopping," his driver said tersely.

The following day was rainy along the Loup. At least at Genoa, where the four tribes composing the Pawnee lived shoulder to shoulder from 1869 until their forced departure six years later, the shell of the old Indian boarding school reminded tourists of a native presence. From there it was a bit north of Fullerton where they searched for the elusive White River

Bank Site (*Ahkawita:ka*), finally noticing its whitish ridge opposite the mouth of the Cedar River, now hidden by hardwoods and cedars. By the time I visited a decade later, the landowners were handing out leaflets summarizing a lovers' leap legend that glorified white pioneers who committed suicide rather than fall into the hands of the devilish Pawnee; one owner recalled playing in the cave that, he was surprised to learn, once housed magical animals who cured earlier Pawnee.

At their last stop, the oversized Palmer village, the proprietor was better informed. Walking them over to the bowllike lodge depressions, he was proud of his pledge to leave them untouched and preserve a portion in old Nebraska sod. Despite a chunk of riverbank lost to an irrigation pipe spilling into a nearby cornfield, this stop gave the group a taste of days when at least the land remembered its native occupants.

On the third day, the van dropped south. Without a guide like White Eagle, it was a guessing game as they looked for more elusive places where tribal stories described hills that resembled giant earth lodges and subterranean chambers under water or inside islands and earthen cliffs in which needy Pawnee once received healing powers from spirit animals. They visited Dark Island, or Lone Tree, near present-day Grand Island; "Girl Hill," (*Curaspa;Ku*), near the old Clark's village site; and Hill That Points the Way (*Pa:hu:ru*), on the Republican River's south shore; and the old Hill village.

Pulling into Lincoln around midnight, they hadn't been able to make the southernmost sacred place: Spring on the Edge of the Bank (*Kicawi:caku*). It was better known as a popular tourist draw called Waconda, or Great Spirit Springs, and Parks wasn't the first to suspect that its folklore might be bogus. "To make tourists fully appreciate a high bluff or picturesquely dangerous spot," wrote W. E. Webb back in 1874, after a stop at these springs, "it is absolutely essential that some fond lovers should have jumped down it, hand-in-hand, in sight of the cruel parents, who struggled up the incline, only to be rewarded by the heart-rending finale." It was the same plot one hears so often: white stories about Indian places drawing sentimental tears over the suicides of brave Indians whose life and times are sadly past. These folk variations on the nineteenth century's wishful thinking known as the Myth of the Vanishing Indian became self-fulfilling prophecies. They replaced Indian memories of the land as alive and the animals as their teachers and rationalized their takeover by white homesteaders and the forces of progress.

Writing up their trip, Parks and Wedel also challenged academic myths. Popularized by such scholars as Joseph Campbell and Mircea Eliade was the notion that priests and shamans never mix. Either they were viewed as mammoths and elephants, in which case you first found shamans overseeing the healing and economic needs of hunting tribes; whereas only much later, with agriculture and seasonal rituals, they were replaced by priesthoods. Or they were seen as cats and dogs, with mystical conjurers rejecting the priests' institutional role and rote rituals in favor of direct, ecstatic communication with the powers that be. In this popular dichotomy, priests were portrayed as domineering bureaucrats who suppressed individualism, but shamans were romanticized as "ancient America's superheroes," mystic humans associated with animal powers who went into trances and worked alone.

But this trip had visited villages protected by priests *and* sacred places tied to shamans. The Pawnee case suggests they could coexist and complement each other; it was a matter of different job descriptions. On behalf of entire communities, Pawnee priests transacted with deities in the heavens—the star gods. On behalf of individuals, their shamans relied upon spirits found within the earth—the sacred animals. Rather than being separated by evolutionary phases or as spiritual adversaries, in Pawnee society, at least, priests and shamans seemed to work in partnership to bring earth and sky closer together, and here were the places where they did it.

Folklore leaves few dates. Pawnee oral narratives don't pinpoint exactly *when* that original boy, near death, was saved by the animal powers at Pahaku, or when the boy Pacha became the last Pawnee to seek help there. Behind the bare bones of Pawnee written history, in fact, their secret religious life rarely peeks out.

And a century and a half after it collided with the white man, Pawnee history turned into a tailspin of suffering, loss and dependency. Picky about their white contacts, by the late seventeenth century the Pawnee were trading with the French from Canada and exchanging buffalo robes for horses with Spanish trade outside Santa Fe. But that connection soured after the

Platte battle of 1719, when Pawnee warriors, serving as French allies, beat the Spanish all the way back to the Sangre de Cristo Mountains. By the time Zebulon Pike's American expedition visited them in 1806, they had settled on the easier-going French as their preferred trading partners.

Then they experienced the first downside of white contact; on the heels of Pike's arrival, a third of their number was lost to smallpox. And that other product of the white world proved to be a mixed blessing. At first horses allowed for increased populations and a wider buffalo-hunting range. But when white settlers began competing with the Indians for wood and buffalo, the old ecological balance broke down. And soon those wonderful horses were mowing their way through ground cover and munching rings around cottonwood trees. The Pawnee mounts became their masters, as the Indians were forced to shift camp much more frequently in search of fresh pasturage.

Next came a third threat. The first Pawnee treaties with the United States sought only special bonds of friendship, agreement of protection by American troops and trading rights. But after the Louisiana Purchase, the pressures on the Pawnee to move multiplied. The bustling market of St. Louis attracted land speculators and their neighborhood became a dumping ground for Indian tribes evicted from east of the Mississippi. The Oregon Trail, which paralleled their Platte River for a spell, soon rumbled with wagon trains. The second round of American treaties was more demanding. Now the Americans wanted Pawnee land, with payment in monthly cash installments, tribal renunciation of hunting and Indian acceptance of white schools, cottage industries, Christian churches and control by military police.

The Pawnee domain shrank and their bands and villages consolidated. Confined to the Platte for the first time in their history, they suffered not only smallpox, but also measles, diphtheria and cholera contracted from pioneers passing through. And then a fourth peril raised its head. Ever their blood enemies, the recently confederated and emboldened Teton Sioux vowed to wipe them out. Relentless raids saw Pawnee corn and dried-meat stores looted, their earth lodges burned to mud-caked shells, their buffalo hunts too perilous to undertake, their families defenseless and starving.

In 1846 they were forced to bid farewell to their old villages along the Loup River and put up new earth lodges along the Platte. And when one looks at the location of these last three hastily built communities, they seem to be reaching for the protective high ground of Pahaku. Twenty miles downstream lies Leshara village, seventeen miles upstream is the Linwood site, while the McClean village is only an hour's walk away. With an aggressive and unfriendly world closing in around them, it is as if the last Pawnee Indians in Nebraska were clinging to their old sanctuary like seamen around the mast of a sinking ship.

With Nebraska Territory opened to homesteading that year, it wasn't long before U.S. emissaries demanded yet another land-cessation treaty. Soon the entire tribe was hemmed into a fifteen-by-thirty-mile stretch of riverside back on the Loup, adjoining the Mormon settlement of Genoa. Here the U.S. "civilization" campaign descended in earnest. Quaker overseers pressured the Indians to slice and dice this acreage into single-family plots, to put their kids into uniforms in school and to recruit their fathers as U.S. military scouts against the Sioux, Cheyenne and Arapaho. But these capitulations still couldn't satisfy the land-hungry families stepping off the Union Pacific passenger trains. By the end of 1875, the browbeaten Pawnee had accepted a reservation between the Arkansas and Cimarron rivers in Indian Territory. Their worldly goods packed on wagons, the fewer than two thousand Pawnee that were left alive traveled in three groups to the south. Nebraska was rid of its first settlers at last.

After three years, the Gilberts were feeling more at home along the Platte than they were back in Lincoln. Their weekends of vegetable and herb gardening and fixing up the cabin stretched into four or five days. Their membership in the country club lapsed, their show home was traded for a modest town house, bridge luncheons and golfing afternoons fell by the wayside. With Lou's Fremont practice up and running, they finally abandoned the city altogether for the place they now called Pahaku. They were remodeling the hundred-year-old farmhouse when other occupants entered their lives.

First was a baby raccoon, an orphan from Lincoln's Nature Center, which sensed that Geri was a soft touch. After the hairless thing had been affixed to one of their nursing German shepherd's nipples, he graduated to hackberries and pond frogs. Geri loved watching him, now masked and furred, scrub everything before putting it in his mouth, including the boiled eggs and graham crackers he stole from the cupboard. Soon he was spending days at a time outside, then he disappeared altogether. Early the following October she noticed the German shepherd staring at a hollow tree, tail wagging. The raccoon showed its head, and waddled after them to the house. For an hour or so it accepted some berries, as if for old times' sake, then left for good.

Another summer evening, Geri was gardening at Pahaku when she saw her prized hen in the jaws of a reddish blur half its size—her first fox. In the commotion, the hunter dropped its prey, but Geri got a second chance. Again the Nature Center in Lincoln phoned, this time about a fox with a broken leg. No more than six pounds, he acted twice his size in energy. It took a week of outstretched finger feeding before Geri could touch his pelt. At night he lived in a wire cage on the back porch, which she placed under a box elder every morning. Geri worked around him, talked to him and hand-fed him mice and berries.

Then came two abandoned baby horned owls. Geri lifted them into the barn's hayloft and began a regular feeding of ground horse meat. The larger was particularly antagonistic and made sure the Gilberts' cat stayed clear. Even when a violent storm blew the birds out of the barn and into the outdoors, the smaller bird wouldn't separate. Later that summer, Geri woke to wings slapping against her window screen. It was the more aggressive owl, who'd spurned the house since achieving freedom. Some disease had got him. When he now allowed her to hand-feed him, he couldn't swallow it down. Wings slightly extended, he just stared at her. He'd come home to die.

As the oak leaves turned, Geri was relieved when the needier owl made herself scarce. But then she got anxious with the cracking noises of hunting season. One evening she heard hooting from the barn. Climbing the ladder to the loft, she saw talons gripping the rafter. When she brought meat, it was ignored, and she heard baby cheeps. She stroked the new mother's vest. "Often at sundown I've heard her sound," Geri told me, "and I know who it is and whom she's calling to."

Their readings, and Nebraska Historical Society contacts, satisfied the Gilberts that the former owner's yarns about Pahaku and its significance to the Pawnee were true. But Geri was too modest to realize the irony of the Nature Center's implicating her in their mythology. At the site where the Pawnee believed animals with special powers healed injured human beings, she'd come closer to their world than ever before and had returned the favor.

One rainy day in the early spring of 1997, my son and I had joined those strangers who drop into Pahaku without warning. We were heading for Montana and visiting Indian sites along the way. An admirer of the prize-winning Parks and Wedel essay on Pawnee sacred geography, I had to see the place. A few dives through willow thickets and sandy access roads brought us to the banks of the Platte, but not the bluffs. Nor was the name Pahaku familiar to some teenagers leaning on cars smoking joints and angling for catfish. Then I called the Nebraska Historical Society in Lincoln just before closing time: a doctor was the present owner. From a phone booth in Cedar Bluffs, I rang and Geri answered. She was silent while I apologized. "Come on over," she said, with a soft laugh.

In borrowed slickers we were led by Geri on an abbreviated version of her regular evening walk. As we dripped back into the house, Lou drove up. They kept us for buffalo burgers and steamed vegetables. They were open, unguarded, enthusiastic and, except for a certain patrician grace, almost latter-day hippies. They pulled out some recent newspaper articles—a few Crow Indians I knew had recently dropped by.

By this time, changes had come to Pahaku. In 1973, Lou managed to get it on the National Register of Historic Places. A bigger decision came ten years later when an interstate highway threatened to nip off a corner and bring strangers, clamor and pollution to their front door. That was when Lou and Geri "locked up the land" by granting to the Nebraska Historical Society a "conservation and preservation easement," which protected it from farming, grazing, timbering, subdividing, resource extraction or housing development forever. For stewardship of what was now publically acknowledged as "one of Nebraska's greatest cultural treasures," the Gilberts received the Historical Society's 1991 Preservation Award; the next year they won the Nebraska Statewide Arboretum's Blazing Star Award for "restoration of native plant communities in Nebraska."

Three years later the Pawnee returned to Pahaku. In the spring of 1994, descendants of old White Eagle and his translator Knifechief walked the cedar-shadowed bluffs. Cooling her feet in the Platte River near Pahuk Hill, Mary Louise Waubonsie recalled her grandmother's stories of trekking from Nebraska to Oklahoma back in 1876. Theodore W. Morgan had also heard about the place, but never hoped to see it in his lifetime. With his eagle wing fan, he took smoke from burning cedar, purified the Gilberts and their guests, cleansed Pahaku of dangerous spirits, and voiced thanks "to you folks who are keeping the legend of Pahuk alive and the sacred grounds, like it was in the past."

My son and I last visited Pahaku in early summer, five years ago. We gave a good afternoon to exploring the banks. We passed bur oaks and fragile ferns, ground cedar and eastern cottonwoods. Lou pointed out a badger hole, probably the same sort of starter burrow that water and time had widened into the fragile legendary caves that opened and collapsed along the base of those porous cliffs. Around us were stately elms and small mushrooms, walnuts and catalpas. Somewhere else on the property a Lakota family, having driven over unannounced from an Indian symposium in Lincoln, were taking a less strenuous walk, praying by themselves. Lou had me taste his Indian toothache tree, the prickly ash whose pulp numbs the gums. Under the high canopy we approached the sunken ravine where a fresh slump had added more dirt over the supposed location of the famous mythic cave of the animals.

We kept moving and moving until my son had enough. "Dad, let's just stop. Stop!" Bless him. We sat slightly apart from each other and went silent. I glanced over to smile my thanks at Lou, but he was scanning the upper branches for birds.

There is no necessary correlation between Indian spiritual beliefs and environmental ethics, no automatic or easy translation from one to the other. This was about as close as it got.

CHAPTER ELEVEN

JOURNEYS TO PROMISED LANDS

Hidatsa/Crow

This is the story of how a cluster of Indian bands known as the Hidatsa of North Dakota were befriended by a tribe called the Mandan, and how some of them eventually broke off to emerge in the historical record as the Crow Indians of Montana. It is the story of how the Hidatsa's Sacred Land, located along North Dakota's Missouri River, gave birth to the Crow's Promised Land, which they finally found in the shadow of Montana's Big Horn Mountains. The distinction is something like that which author Diane Johnson draws between cultures that rely on "foundation myths"and those that are still focused on "arrival myths"—the first emphasizing the establishment of a fixed society in place; the second, the yearnings of an emergent community for independence in a new environment.

This scenario of the Hidatsa and the Crow is not unusual. Reviewing the deep history of Native America, one runs across many ethnic groups or tribes undergoing painful rifts or clean breaks, launching epic journeys, adapting to new habitats, wrangling over territories, merging migrant populations, reinventing tribal identities, adopting new names, enshrining homelands or experiencing revelations that seal new covenants with their surroundings. Through these ordeals and adventures, they became our continent's original Pilgrims, Pioneers, Founding Fathers and Mothers, and Sons and Daughters of their own Native American Revolutions.

This exploring and humanizing of North America began ten to twenty thousand years ago, whether Indian ancestors walked east over the Beringia Land Bridge, boarded sailing canoes across the Pacific or even, as Vine Deloria, Jr., once half humorously proposed, headed the other way, leaving North America for Asia. The native settling of America's nooks and crannies went on before, during and after the following story of some Plains Indian migrants of the sixteenth and seventeenth centuries who, before Lewis and Clark, sought their fortunes in the uncharted west and emerged as the Crow Nation.

No less than *Mayflower* families in their bid for religious freedom, these Indian pilgrims were looking for places to call their own, which they believed, or would propose, were predestined in stories or foretold in dreams. As with Anglo-America's veneration of that hallowed granite boulder that supposedly greeted the footfalls of its forefathers at Plymouth, Massachusetts, the three Native American peoples in this chapter still revere locations that commemorate their mythic origins or the launching of their dreams of becoming new nations.

The first major tribe to fully exploit the Missouri River ecology was the Mandan. Emerging from waters to the east (some traditions point to Devil's Lake, to the northeast), their forefathers ventured west to find themselves on its banks. Archaeologists identify their earliest communities, at around A.D. 750, by the presence of black pottery vessels, horn and bone tools for working their gardens, depressions left from earth-roofed lodges—first rectangular and then circular—which grouped around central plazas. The area where today's Heart River empties into the Missouri River became *Natcompasahah,* the "Heart of the World." South of this stream, said Lone Man, their mythic culture hero, his people should never dwell. Instead, as times progressed (and white settlement advanced), they would have to relocate ever northward. "Before they came," say the Mandan, "we lived at the center and thought with our hearts."

For nearly a thousand years, with dogs their sole transport, these newcomers met the challenges of the Middle Missouri ecosystem. The hot months brought fewer than seventeen inches of rain, which meant drought, scorched grass and treeless flats carved by flash floods. With winter came freezing storms and blanketing snows. Only under the prodigious cottonwoods lined along the tributary valleys did one find shade in summer and windbreaks in winter. Their inland sea drained a sixth of today's United

States: from the Continental Divide, the Missouri River ran for nearly twenty-four hundred miles across the Dakotas, dropped down the Nebraska and Kansas border and joined the Mississippi just north of present-day St. Louis. Along the way, it splintered into thousands of channels and meanders; carried sediment that formed marshes, sandbars and sloughs; and provided nutrients for the willows, cottonwoods and the reeds where migrating birds nested by the millions. Dangerous and unpredictable, its soupy brown surface could pile into ten-foot waves while hiding tree stumps, rocky snags, prehistoric-looking fish like the pallid sturgeon and paddlefish and whirlpools that sucked buffalo out of sight.

The Mandan became one of more than twenty tribes who would adapt to the 513,000-square-mile Missouri River Basin. Every spring the runoff from snowmelt spread a rich mulch for their corn, squash, beans, sunflowers and tobacco. In its muddy waters they trapped fish in wickerwork weirs and caught turtles with their bare hands. They dug clay from under lignite strata near the river bluffs and collected the eggs of whooping cranes, wild geese and whistling swans along its banks.

Overlooking the Missouri River or its tributaries, their villages occupied a middle zone where the Missouri Plateau, elevated on the remnants of old glacial moraines, drains either north or west, in contrast to those streams that run, as common sense would dictate, southward. Hence the French name for the region, "Knife of the Missouri." To the Mandan, the river was divided by male and female banks, whose contrasting ecologies were established by their two culture heroes, First Creator and Lone Man.

Along the well-silted floodplain lay their gardens. Nearby were grassy slopes where their menfolk would later breed and trade horses. The women weeded and hybridized crops, sang to their gardens, raised children, molded pottery, wove burden baskets and participated in the female-only religious societies. The men hunted, fished, built saucer-shaped boats, told stories and fulfilled their busy round of religious activities.

Their highest ritual, a dramatization of their origins and the exploits of their culture hero Lone Man, was the multiday Okipa ceremony. Its dancing took over the central plaza, and revolved around a barrel-shaped shrine that was the hub of every Mandan village. It symbolized the enclosure into which Lone Man was said to protect his Mandan children during the Great Flood.

Next to arrive in Mandan country were a trio of bands we know collectively as Hidatsa. One trailed in from Devil's Lake, another dropped on a magical arrow from the sky, a third entered later from the east. For these newcomers the Mandan had sage advice: live close enough so we won't become enemies, and far enough away so that we'll remain friends. The Mandan made sure to command the upstream position but shared their knowledge of magical locations. Among them were the "baby" places—one was a hill shaped like an earth lodge not far from present-day St. Mary's College in Bismarck, North Dakota, where after a rainfall people noticed the footprints of infants. Childless women headed to them to pray, leaving a girl's clothing and a ball for a desired daughter, or small bows and arrows for a son.

The recent arrivals perpetuated their own customs. "We thought our fields sacred," said a Hidatsa woman named Waheenee-wea, or Buffalo Bird Woman. "A family's right to a field having been set up, no one thought of disputing it. If anyone tried to seize land belonging to another, we thought some evil would come upon him; and that one of his family would die or have some bad sickness." Each family garden was delineated by piles of stones; the same went for the separate pits dug by their men on distant cliffs in which they hid while trapping eagles.

One important Hidatsa deity had her home about seven miles from the present-day Four Bears Bridge, on North Dakota's Three Affiliated Tribes Reservation. She was Grandmother Who Never Dies, but usually just called Grandmother. Mice and moles tilled her fields of corn, beans and squash, and the deer and blackbirds guarded them. She taught the Hidatsa how to "open" their gardens when the migrating swans, geese and ducks swept up the Texas-to-Canada flyway, accompanied by the corn spirits, and how to "close" them at harvest time when the flocks flew back south. Beside her earth lodge lay a basketball-shaped rock that her grandson had once thrown down from the sky, which remained an object of veneration to the tribe.

The uppermost echelon of Hidatsa sacred sites drew their prestige from renowned vision quests. On lonely buttes with wide views and deep fissures in their rocks, stomach-grumbling, dry-mouthed and light-headed vision seekers fell into dreams that were clearer than waking life. Of all these promontories, twelve buttes in central and western North Dakota came to assume such prominence to the Hidatsa that prayers to spirits living in them were consolidated into a major Hidatsa ceremony known as the Earthnaming. Chief among the sites was Singer butte in the Killdeer Mountains, where a magical Speckled Owl convened meetings of other spirit animals.

Their vision experiences were embodied in leather-wrapped "medicine bundles," which might contain eagle talons, feathers, animal or bird skins, skulls, beads or dried roots. Only those trained in their upkeep and associated stories and songs could decipher these emblems or activate their powers. But everyone knew the reputations and places of origin behind the tribe's most potent bundles and anticipated their regular openings during the year's turning points: the first thunder of spring, the first snowfall of autumn.

After the late eighteenth century, these so-called Village Indians, especially the Mandan, became the darlings of white travelers. Unusually tall, stunningly dressed, aristocratic in bearing, they played host to Meriwether Lewis and William Clark; German prince Maximilian du Weid and his artist Karl Bodmer; painter George Catlin and ornithologist John J. Audubon, among others. As agriculturists, traders and builders of bowl-shaped boats that looked suspiciously like Scottish coracles, they seemed unlike the stereotypical horse-riding, tipi-dwelling and settler-threatening Plains Indian. Some visitors even discerned a fairer shade of skin; were these Mandan actually Welsh explorers gone astray or remnants of one of Israel's lost tribes?

But this privileged status did not inoculate the Village Indians against a ghastly fate. Waves of smallpox came upriver in the 1780s, but the third epidemic lasting eight weeks in the summer of 1832 and centered at Fort Clark, wiped out hundreds of Hidatsa and more than 90 percent of the Mandan. Despite this trauma, the survivors regrouped at a hook-shaped

bend in the river about forty miles farther upstream named Like a Fishhook
Village. Here the Mandan remnants rebuilt their Lone Man Shrine, the
Hidatsa set their medicine bundles back on family altars and the tribes gave
sanctuary to a third group of earth lodge-dwelling refugees, the Arikara.

But the Hidatsa never forgot their old sites. This was clear when, just
as Like a Fishhook Village was being established, its leaders were invited to
a grand get-together. Around 1849, a white trader and mountain man
named Tom "Broken Hand" Fitzpatrick first proposed dividing the Great
Plains among its respective tribes. There was urgency behind his idea: wagon
trails blazed by white pioneers to California and Oregon were quickly becoming highways. Fitzpatrick saw rising friction between whites and Indians ahead. Unlike the earlier friendship treaty at Fort Laramie in 1825, this
council would stipulate which Indians belonged where and how to keep
them all out of harm's way.

Getting funds from a U.S. Congress more disposed to exterminating
Indians than negotiating with them was not easy. But Fitzpatrick's confidence was high; even before the reduced congressional appropriations were
passed, runners were delivering his invitations throughout the Plains; each
tribe was asked to produce its territorial estimates and boundary lines. The
date was set for early September 1851; the place was again Fort Laramie.

How tribes prepared for this grand assembly is mostly a mystery. But
a story that anthropologist Alfred C. Bowers recorded from a Hidatsa
friend named Crow's Heart offers one glimpse. Although the council occurred five years before he was born, Crow's Heart had heard about how
his tribe was invited and their initial fears that the meeting was a Sioux
trick to lure their leaders away and kill them. First, their chief at the time,
Four Bears, huddled with trusted white fur traders. The treaty would stipulate every tribe's territories, they explained; offered protection against
the fearsome Sioux and couldn't hurt future relationships with whites.
"Four Bears thought it was a good idea, too," remembered Crow's Heart.
But then the old chief wondered, "What boundaries should I claim?"

The question was reasonable. Measuring the outdoors was a mark
of the invaders' legal system; maps based on grids and scales had little
meaning to Indians. How to tell these ignorant whites which subbranch of
which tribe you were was hard enough; to locate yourself on their maps,

to pick out where you *wished* you were or what you thought was *yours* was another matter. In the months prior to gathering delegations and picking their flashiest outfits, the tribes mulled over the question. Instead of pulling out surveyors' chains or compasses, however, Four Bears and his friends asked around about who owned the privileges of having access to and stories regarding their sacred places.

"I don't have the rights to the sacred places our people go to," Four Bears said, "for my Gods [guiding spirits] are the Sunrise and Sunset Wolves." Someone piped in, "The people who have the medicines in the Earthnaming Ceremonies are the only ones who can speak for us, for they know just which spirits reside in the different buttes and other places. There are several people here who have rights to speak for a few places and there is Big Cloud and Poor Wolf who can speak for all of us for they have gone further than any of us in learning about these places."

In this way the Hidatsa leaders pieced together their geographical knowledge—bundle owner by bundle owner, power dream by power dream, sacred place by sacred place. The pedigrees behind the points on the landscape around which the Hidatsa could draw a boundary line were recalled and linked. "While some of the people were getting the list from Poor Wolf," Crow's Heart continued, "others were getting names from Big Cloud. Poor Wolf's rights had come down to him through Raven Necklace, an Assiniboine boy who was so grateful for the good attention the Hidatsa had given him that Raven Necklace fasted often and knew of many places."

But Crow's Heart said that "Big Cloud's knowledge came not only from his own dreaming of the sacred buttes but also through his wife, Bluesnake, whose former husband had been taken prisoner when Nuptari village had burned. He had made his pledge shortly afterward and his mother had escaped that he would revenge his people's massacre by getting the right to pray to all the sacred places on the prairie."

Compiling a list of these "praying places," Four Bears went back to his white trader friends. Together they "made his own map on a piece of white hide with charcoal," and Crow's Heart added, "Now days we are being paid for the lands that Four Bears got for us with the help of the Earthnaming bundle owners."

.   .   .

With the map of Hidatsa boundaries safely in his saddlebags, Four Bears embarked on the five-day ride to Fort Laramie to join representatives from about twenty tribes who were also bearing their deeds of territorial right. Over the course of August 12–14, 1851, in the vicinity of Horse Creek, they joined the cream of Plains Indian society. Upward of ten thousand Plains Indians were on display at the pinnacle of their prereservation power—chiefs and band leaders and their entourages, proud, beaded and feathered from head to toe, wearing their finest buckskins and digging their heels into thousands of combed and adorned horses.

It was the mother of all powwows; the world would not see its like again.

Already the Plains Indian time in the sun had been like a snap of the fingers. Less than a century and a half earlier, the trading and stealing of horses had begun across a region the size of Europe. Not long after these weeks at Fort Laramie, the power of the Plains Indians would start its decline. In forty years their populations would be decimated, scattered and psychologically shattered, their survivors living on handouts within government-run compounds that were designed to change everything that had made them so cocky at Horse Creek. The process of treaty making and gift giving and public display that had lured them to Fort Laramie would start their descent into confinement and oppression that would reach its symbolic climax at Wounded Knee in the winter of 1890, and its demographic climax around 1910, when the continent's onetime native population of more than a million would be reduced to 210,000 hungry men, women and children.

But this hot August weekend all of that was still around the corner. Rather than deploring what might be lost, this weekend the Hidatsa were hopeful about what had been saved. Thanks to the hierarchy of sites already consolidated for their Earthnaming ceremony, they could hand the U.S. commissioners their boundaries. These became the core of the territory that was assigned on September 17, 1851, to the Hidatsa, Mandan and Arikara, henceforth known as the Three Affiliated Tribes. Starting at the mouth of the Heart River, their line went up the Missouri to the Yellowstone mouth, ran up the Yellowstone to the Power mouth, extended southeast to the Little Missouri headwaters, followed the Black Hills to the head of Heart River and returned down the Heart to the "place of beginning"—a surveyor's cartographic term whose mythic resonance for people like the Mandan and the Hidatsa was surely lost on the white negotiators.

Nor did they realize that the native document that helped the Hidatsa establish this territory—the charcoal-on-hide drawings that have since disappeared—was the map of a North American *holy land.*

One well-tailored group of a hundred or so chiefs and warriors arrived at Fort Laramie fashionably late. Escorting the Crow Indians was their trusted friend and translator Robert Meldrum, a thirty-year-old trader who'd married into their tribe.

Quite likely the Crow stage-managed their entry for maximum effect, as they did on triumphal returns home after successful war parties, and as they still do for morning parades during the tribe's August fair at Crow Agency, Montana. Hushed and secretive throughout the previous day, they had probably overnighted beyond neighing and scent range of Horse Creek. One can imagine them rising before dawn, painting their horses, pulling on form-fitting leggings and war shirts fringed with scalp locks, strapping tight their high-pommeled elkhorn saddles and draping them with mountain lion pelts. At hand signals from their "pipeholder" leaders, they headed out.

That day, September tenth, the actual meetings were set for 9:00 A.M. Around that hour the Crow filed into view on their horses, their war songs piercing the air—"the finest delegation of Indians we have yet seen," gushed a *Missouri Republican* correspondent. Despite having ridden eight hundred miles, their steeds "showed more mettle," their riders "were dressed with more taste, and their dresses, especially the head dresses of the Chiefs, made more display than any of the other tribes." In the lead, chiefs Big Robber and Mountain Tail held their ceremonial pipes like royal scepters as they parted the crowd. Many onlookers were longtime enemies, from whom these Crow had only yesterday been stealing horses and taking scalps. But not "the least disturbed or alarmed," the Crow, identifiable by their trademark hair bangs that stood straight up with bear-grease stiffening, dismounted.

Who were these people?

One mark of their identity and background lay in how warmly the Crow greeted the Hidatsa and how well the two conversed in a tongue both could understand. For they were more than friends. Sometime in the not-so-distant past the Crow ancestors had broken off from the Hidatsa along the Missouri, to venture west and become a separate people.

To the Crow, Fort Laramie was something of a lark. Their traders helped them articulate their lands "from the Continental Divide on the west to the Musselshell River on the north," as historian Frederick Hoxie puts it in his history of the tribe, "from the mouth of the Musselshell to the Powder River on the east and south to the Rattlesnake range in what is now central Wyoming."

But after turning in these boundaries and strutting their stuff, the Crow grew restless. Too many Sioux and Cheyenne were milling about the mammoth camp for their comfort. Although they'd given up lands east of the Powder River, which they had once considered theirs, the Crow sensed that this truce was iffy. Another possible reason they were anxious to get home was the autumn tobacco-harvesting rituals, which was a seasonal opportunity to honor the guiding spirit that had led them to central Montana in the first place.

The origin story of the Crow tribe is one more narrative with contradictory versions that compete in the misty yesteryear where myth gives way to legend. When I first came to the Crow reservation in south-central Montana as a welfare worker in the summer of 1962, the predominant accounts of the Crow genesis in books boiled down to a mundane quarrel between two Hidatsa women. Possibly the wives of opposing clan leaders, they were butchering after a hunt and began arguing over the semidigested vegetal contents of a buffalo's stomach, a prized delicacy. Their husbands took sides; others joined the fray. To avoid bloodshed, one group split off and headed west, emerging as the *Gens de Corbeaux* encountered by the French in the late 1700s, which was probably a mistranslation of *Absaroka,* or "Children of the Large-Beaked Bird," from a type of raven now believed extinct. To the major scholar on the tribe, anthropologist Robert Lowie, the schism occurred around 1500, and that was that.

   Dissatisfied with this received wisdom, two decades after that summer I devoted three years to puzzling out Crow beginnings. From neglected sources came evidence of *two* migrations to present-day Montana. The first may have been triggered by internal strife, but a second group of Hidatsa split more than a hundred years later, and not under any cloud. Accompanying this second contingent was a priestly cadre whose rights and duties were associated with planting sacred tobacco. It became my hunch that the uniting of these two migrant peoples—numerically vulnerable, closely related, speaking the same language and adapting to a new landscape—jelled as the Crow. This scenario might also explain why every historical account described the Crow's unusual exaltation of a rare species of tobacco plant, a talisman they elevated to the status of what the Romans called a *palladium,* a national symbol, a tribal totem, whose function was to safeguard an entire society.

   Then it dawned on me that a third version, closest to Crow hearts, had been also staring me in the face. Its credibility did not stem from finding a place in white men's books. It derived from songs and narratives that the Crow still sang and told. It came from the ceremonies of tobacco growing, harvesting and initiation that enacted this version, which the Crow believed had shielded them—who served as white scouts—under a kind of spiritual ozone layer throughout the Plains Indian wars. Their Tobacco Society rituals also protected their stream-watered, game-filled mountain stronghold and produced new crops of Crow babies each year. For this orphaned tribe, outnumbered by enemies yet graced with a new territory that would be the envy of all comers, this plant became their symbolic parent and national patron. And much like other clan totems to which prohibitions were attached, this rare species of tobacco had its taboo: smoking it was absolutely forbidden.

   Although upon arrival the early Crow had abandoned their old gardening traditions and transformed themselves into a buffalo-pursuing Plains Indian tribe, in these ceremonies they continued to honor their agricultural ancestry. Every spring they planted their sacred tobacco; every fall they harvested it; and when "birds gave birth to their young," they initiated new members into their Tobacco Society. Only in Tobacco Society ceremonies did women share with men the rights to sacred medicine bundles and participate as equals.

To learn about this third Crow story of origins, I had only to open my ears. The Crow themselves still clung to this version, as I discovered from the dozen or so I interviewed. Returning to overlooked archives, even to Robert Lowie's own field notes, I turned up additional clues. And under the 1970s spirit of tribal self-assertion, Crow elders began writing about it in their own books. Opening his account of Crow separation from the Hidatsa, tribal educator Barney Old Coyote claimed the episode began with a vision quest and unfolded in harmony.

"No Vitals and his brother were on a vision-quest fast," Old Coyote said, "during which they experienced very similar visitations . . . of corn, which was already grown by the Hidatsa. But in No Vital's vision he also saw wild mountain tobacco growing in the foothills of the mountains." Pursuing this vision, No Vitals led his followers on a great odyssey that touched all corners of the Great Plains—to the Canadian Rockies in Alberta down to the Arkansas River near Oklahoma. "To this day," Old Coyote claimed, "the Crow still sing lullabies of the mountains of Glacier Park and the fowl of the Arkansas." Returning to the Missouri without any luck, No Vitals finally journeyed to the Big Horn foothills, some say the slopes of Cloud Peak outside present-day Sheridan, Wyoming. Like twinkling stars, one story goes, there the tobacco blossoms were waiting for them.

As the hallowed mistletoe in Diana's oaken grove in Italy was to her priests, described by Sir James Frazer in *The Golden Bough,* so became the fragile plants of sacred tobacco to the Crow. They developed into full-time hunters, driving buffalo over cliffs for food, exploring the mountains and streams between the Bighorn and Yellowstone rivers, and this landscape became their salvation. Believing the survival of the sacred tobacco plant to be synonymous with their own, they cultivated it religiously year after year, so that "the Crows would multiply and grow stronger." And when U.S. government suppression of Indian rituals in the 1920s led to the demise of their gardens, each spring they still initiated new members into the society, "cultivating themselves," as it were, and still ensuring Crow survival.

Yet the Crow never turned their backs on their old Hidatsa heritage. Trade between these born-again mountaineers and their old parent tribe along the Missouri River brought buffalo robes tanned white as ivory to the Hidatsa and dried squash, corn balls and pouches of Hidatsa smoking tobacco to the Crow. During these visits, Crow traders would make a point of paying homage to the lodge site of Old Woman [Grandmother] Who Never Dies, whose grandson remained one of their folk heroes.

Much as the Japanese in the eighteenth century turned their backs on Western progress and "returned to the sword," the Crow rejected agriculture and "returned to the hunt." Twenty years ago their story would have delighted the deep ecology school of fringe environmentalists who insisted on the fundamental incompatibility of farming and hunting and wanted Americans to turn back the clock. They believed, as mythographer Joseph Campbell framed the contrast, that the "Way of the Animal Powers" had little in common with the "Way of the Seeded Earth." In Campbell's interpretation, the "charmingly boyish" hunting myths did not hold up in gravity and sophistication to farming rituals that embodied "the whole mystery of women's range of life experience."

Accepting this contrast between hunting and farming societies but reversing the value judgments that Campbell applied to it, environmental philosophers like Paul Shepherd and Calvin Martin argued that the shift from a Paleolithic worldview founded on personalized ties between humans and animals and plants to the settled, agricultural Neolithic way of life had actually signaled the decline of healthy human-environment relations. It wrought a technological and moral rupture between humans and their landscapes and opened the door to a materially advanced, environmentally ruinous and spiritually empty existence that was available to fewer and fewer people.

But a closer examination of *specific* American Indian lifestyles suggests that some tribes bypassed this logjam and came up with a third way. Through the energy, time and creativity that the Mandan and Hidatsa along the Dakota floodplains put into a balance of male and female rituals that kept buffalo plentiful *and* gardens flourishing, they developed a formula for sustainable coexistence with their surroundings that included the diversified and low-tech exploitation of both wild and domesticated resources.

When the Crow split off from the Hidatsa, the mixed blessing of the horse soon allowed them to "return," as Martin or Shepherd might put it, to full-time hunting and greater mobility. But these activities hurled them into territorial conflicts with their Plains Indian neighbors who were undergoing a similar lifestyle revolution. Their fixation on raiding and hunting on horseback would prove more short term and less viable than the old Mandan and Hidatsa adaptions to living off the land, which took centuries to perfect.

But the mountain-dwelling Crow in Montana never shared the disdain for their old agricultural heritage that one picks up from white writers who romanticize nomadism, shamanism and getting your meals by the bow and arrow. When the Crow undertook nostalgic pilgrimages to their North Dakota roots, it was with a sort of awe, as if they were reentering a world of origin myths, legendary ancestors, sacred sites and cultivated foods. Here people spoke their Siouan language equivalent of, say, Latin. Here were the old powerful medicine bundles and the original settings of *their* oldest narratives.

During the last quarter century I have paid my respects to a number of places that figure in this many-stranded epic of Mandan, Hidatsa and Crow origins. First, in 1979, I visited a Mandan site in the Twin Buttes section of North Dakota's Three Affiliated Tribes Reservation. In my arms were bolts of red calico cloth I'd been told were the most appropriate offering for the Lone Man Shrine, which was hidden in bushes on the Missouri's southern bank.

Coming into an overgrown clearing, we laid eyes on a circular stockade about the width of a hot tub and constructed of upright cottonwood planks lashed together by thick strips of old cowhide. Called the Mandan Ark in nineteenth-century accounts, it symbolized the enclosure built in mythic times by the tribe's culture hero Lone Man to protect his Indian children from a great flood. Around older versions, a hoop of willow indicated the high-water mark before the waters subsided.

With long-handed scythes we whacked away the brush, said prayers and enshrouded the little structure with red cloth. Since the day in 1837 when artist George Catlin made this shrine the center of his panoramic portrait of the Fort Clark Mandan village, it had been rebuilt numerous times. Each new residence pushed it upstream, marking yet another step in the tribe's divorce from their beloved Heart River territory, in whose center it was always supposed to reside.

The shrine's last relocation came with the government's final blow against these old village Indian remnants. In 1956, the U.S. Army Corps of Engineers closed the gates on the world's largest rolled-fill dam. Extending two miles across the Missouri River channel, the Garrison Dam produced a hundred-mile-long reservoir and fifteen hundred miles of bulldozed lakefront. When waters behind the dam ripped out five-foot-thick cotton-wood trees, the debris that churned up in the dirty waters seemed to fulfill an old Mandan prophecy: at the end of the world, trees would grow their roots in the air.

That dam stripped the bottoms of these old cottonwoods, killed three fourths of its fish, rotted the marshes that provided refuge for wildlife, drowned the shallow pools where paddlefish and catfish spawned, liquified the riverbanks and sandbars where tern and piping plover laid their eggs, and sent 155,000 acres of prime farming, timbering, fishing and hunting acreage underwater. The new lake split the Three Affiliated Tribes Reservation into five sectors, forced 90 percent of the Indian families to relocate away from the river for the first time in a thousand years and caused local Indian unemployment to rise to 85 percent.

But before that happened, the Lone Man Shrine was disassembled and secreted to this spot, and the bones of Mandan and Hidatsa ancestors were exhumed from community graveyards for reburial on the wind-exposed uplands. These days the Three Affiliated Tribes scrape their living on the alkaline heights and brew coffee with bitter water from deep wells. They drive hundreds of extra miles to reach reservation hamlets chopped off from easy access by man-made bays. And the Army Corps of Engineers is still campaigning to bulldoze new shorelines, to add more buffer zones to the reservoir and, despite the environmental damage, to maintain high water levels for commercial barges and power plants.

After our visit to the shrine, we headed for the reservation's Four Bears Lodge for lunch. A guy drinking at the bar took one look at me and lurched out. Over his shoulder slipped the words "These white people are drowning me out."

A few years later I visited a Hidatsa place of origins. It was August 1982, and a retired scholar named Alfred C. Bowers had come from Idaho to the mouth of Charred Body Creek, near the North Dakota hamlet of Washburn. Forty years before, older Hidatsa Indians had told Bowers that this was the spot where their culture hero, Charred Body, had descended from the skies on a flaming arrow with thirteen sections—one for each of the tribe's clans. Then he cleared this land of its monsters, and allowed the Hidatsa to prosper.

Rarely do archaeologists put much faith in Indian oral traditions, preferring scientifically dated chronologies compiled in laboratories from objects they unearth from the ground. But the man directing this student crew, University of North Dakota archaeologist Stan Ahler, wanted Bowers on hand as he tried to link those Hidatsa stories to this place. Test pits had turned up stone chips; enough stories mentioned the Charred Body or Turtle Creek site as a onetime village that testing seemed worth the expense. As the dig proceeded, Ahler grew nervous, hovering over students as they brushed off dirt from one trench whose coloration had grown markedly dark. A rotten chunk of something emerged, pits were extended and branched and the outlines of a rectangular dwelling emerged. Radiocarbon would date this chunk of house post at about A.D. 875, proving to be the earliest Middle Missouri date ever recovered.

Next I wanted to see one of the Hidatsa vision-quest locations that the tribe had included on the map they carried to Fort Laramie in 1851. With my friend Tim McCleary, I drove east from Montana's Crow Indian Reservation in a general retracing of the original Crow migration path. Tim's goal was to leave offerings at the rock that had stood at the lodge of Grandmother Who Never Dies. In the 1960s, when that site was about to go underwater from Garrison Reservoir, this rock had been saved by a Hidatsa named James Holding Eagle and reinstalled above the flooding waters. Now it was safely in storage at Bismarck's North Dakota Historical Society.

When the rock was still on the reservation, Hidatsa left gifts for it, as did Crow on pilgrimages from Montana back to their North Dakota roots, even holding their children over it—much as Thomas Faunce, a second-generation Pilgrim, would suspend his sons over Plymouth Rock to imbue them with its power and remind them of their sacred history.

As we drove on Interstate 94, Tim pointed out numerous Crow sites. His current project was redrawing the Montana map with Crow place-names for these bluffs, hills and coulees. Near Forsyth we passed the rocky pinnacle known as *Buattaaile,* or Old Man Coyote's Penis. About an hour past Miles City Tim recognized the first butte with a Hidatsa place-name, *Apaa;iiatish,* or "Porcupine Den," indicating that we'd crossed the old Fort Laramie Treaty boundary line into Hidatsa country.

Past the North Dakota state line, we headed north for the Killdeer Mountains and hiked to the top. It didn't take long to find the natural opening to the cavernous limestone home of the magical Owl who presided here. We left tobacco, prayed for our families and friends. By the time we got back to the car it was nightfall. At the Bismarck museum the following morning, we were invited into a collection-and-assortment workroom. Two curators looked sheepishly at each other. One of them handed over xeroxes, perhaps as a consolation prize, of earlier records of Indian items the society had acquired in haphazard fashion. But they'd looked everywhere; the sacred rock was nowhere to be found.

The last of my trips was to Crow Indian country in south-central Montana. Outside the reservation town of Lodge Grass, in the backyard of an elderly Crow woman, lies a garden plot. Three years earlier she'd planted tobacco seeds here that had been extracted from an old medicine bundle. An East Coast collector of Indian art, who'd paid thousands through a dealer for this woman's old planting dress and assorted regalia, had lent it back to her for the occasion.

Nor were they ordinary tobacco seeds—they were direct descendants of the old Crow sacred tobacco, which had been found or planted near Cloud Peak. It was identified by botanists as a rare subspecies, *Nicotiana multi-valvis,* and all Crow have always been forbidden from smoking it. To obtain tobacco suitable for smoking they used to trade with their old parent tribe, the Hidatsa. In the Crow tribe's origin story, their creation is bound up with the career of the chief No Vitals, with his vision of this tobacco and with his people's subsequent travels in search of it that led them here.

For years, even under the shadow of religious suppression by the U.S. government in the 1920s that banned non-Christian rituals and such "animal dances," the Crow managed to perpetuate their Tobacco Society initiation rituals. But they had found it harder to re-create the sacred garden and conduct their planting rituals—until recently. This weedy plot was where that happened. During that ceremony it became the tribe's holy of holies, a miniature version of the slopes of Cloud Peak in the southern Big Horns where No Vitals first found the sacred tobacco and their homeland.

Yet about Crow Indian culture today there still lingers an air of "becoming," as if the tribe remains in anticipation of achieving its full identity, which they are still patching together in true American fashion. Like some northern Plains version of the Navajo, the Crow seem able to absorb outside influences into their ken (competitive sports, multiple religions, tough politics), while retaining key aspects of language and culture—two steps forward, one step back. Yet their rich body of place-names does not emphasize mythic events; they are primarily descriptive of historical battles, famous personalities or odd landmarks. And although Crow sacred places include vision-quest sites, and they leave offerings at springs and sites where their Little People saved lost orphans and they replanted from North Dakota the old concern with sites where women might pray for fertility and healthy babies, they boast fewer sites of cosmic origin or locations where culture heroes pacified the land for them.

A people still "parading through history," as scholar Fred Hoxie represents them, the Crow retain the restless energy of immigrants whom destiny brought to Montana around the same time that the Pilgrims established their City on the Hill. Noticing this parallel, the tribe was dubbed by Joe Medicine Crow, the tribe's senior historian, as a "Chosen People." Divine assistance led the Crow into the west, shepherded them to all four corners of the Great Plains and ultimately guided them to the center of it all, the Big Horn Valley, what Medicine Crow also characterizes as his people's "Promised Land."

CHAPTER TWELVE

THE HEART OF EVERYTHING

Lakota/Cheyenne/Kiowa

T he first time I experienced the immensity that early wagoners and homesteaders described with some trepidation as the Great American Desert was in the spring of 1958, when I followed in their wake. I took an all-night train from Minneapolis to Pierre, South Dakota. Our coach was so packed that I gave my seat to a beautiful nun from India and rocked to sleep on the floor.

A glow through curtains woke me, and over a coupling I leaned into a slipstream pungent with diesel and sagebrush. Never had I seen a land so broad or a sky so huge. Far to the east the curve of the earth was brightening by the minute—purple to violet to pink until a blast of sunlight streaked across the stretch of space that the Lakota evoke in their phrase *obleyaya dosho,* "the wideness of the world." In many ways, I was just starting out. For Indians as well as whites, the Great Plains have always been the place for that.

During the ensuing decades I've entered this landscape from all fronts but like it best from the east, usually homing on the Black Hills. On both flanks of Interstate 90, running past Pierre, the land beyond the roadside kitsch and oversized billboards (still shamelessly advertising gold in the Black Hills) is flat as a rug and, to the untutored eye, nondescript. Soon after a sign says that Spearfish is seventy-two miles away, a blue-gray silhouette materializes in the distance. Within ten minutes the sawtooth profile claims the horizon. This high plains country has a number of mountain oases that erupt out of the flatlands, but here is their patriarch. Even a NASA satellite image taken from outer space evokes the shape of the Hills as the continent's *wamakaognaka e'cantge,* "the heart of everything that

is," situated within its enclosing ridge of protective muscle, which is com-
puter enhanced in molten red.

Geography texts describe the Black Hills of South Dakota as an isolated,
elliptically shaped uplift of granite crags and well-watered meadows
whose name derives from its darkish ground cover of pine, spruce and fir,
all of which stand in sharp contrast to the surrounding sagebrush prairie.
Lying between the Belle Fourche River to the north and the Cheyenne
River to the south, the forty-five-hundred-square-mile "inland island" is
enclosed by that rim of reddish sandstone known as the Hogback Ridge.
Reaching for an adequate description of the Black Hills, earlier white writers could not resist "spiritually inspiring language," says Patricia C. Albers,
an anthropologist who spent years researching the Hills' cultural background. They characterized them as a "sacred fastnesses," an "earthly paradise," and an "Eden in the clouds."

Well before white explorers, geologists, gold prospectors, townsfolk,
tourist entrepreneurs and writers began waxing poetic and overrunning
the Hills, Indians from over a half dozen tribes lent the sanctuary their
own designations—the Comanche called them "Red Fir Place," the Kiowa
"Black Rock Mountains," the Cheyenne "Island Hills," the Ponca, Omaha
and Arikara "Black Hills," while to the Sioux tribes they were alternately
Paha Sapa, the "Black Hills," the "Meat Pack," referring to their value to
hunters, and *O'onakezin,* or "Place of Shelter."

And for upward of thirteen thousand years before these named tribes
were drawn to them, earlier Indians traveled near the Hills, hunted among
them and possibly wintered within them. Near here they probably slew
pre-Pleistocene mammals, while their successor cultures pursued buffalo
and antelope, harvested lodgepole pine, foraged for wild fruits and medicinal plants, sought power visions and held ceremonies. In this small orb
thousands of archaeological sites testify to the Hills as a magnet for subsistence and spiritual activities—the remnants of ancient campfires, sur-
rounds for corralling game, locations for butchering meat, circles for
ceremonies and carvings and paintings on stone.

The density and variety of these rock art sites alone, writes rock art specialist Linea Sundstrom, who was born near the Hills and is the reigning expert on their archaeology, "many illustrating recognizably religious themes [such as episodes from mythic narratives, portrayals of power visions, depictions of eagle-hunting rituals, images linked to game-increasing ceremonies, motifs associated with enhancing female fertility, shields and other symbols tied to battle exploits, and markings of places where human and spirit worlds intersect] dating back thousands of years, suggests that the [Black Hills] area has had considerable religious significance for much, if not all, of its human history."

A French fur trapper named Jean Valle, who in 1803 camped just north of the Cheyenne River, may have been the first white man to gaze upon them. Until 1851, when the first Fort Laramie Treaty introduced the concept of tribal homelands, the written record on the Hills is thin. But out of that council the Lakota emerged with a fairly good deal: within the sixty million acres assigned to them lay the Black Hills. Despite that treaty's vows of peace and friendship, however, the next seventeen years saw flareups between Indians and settlers. In an effort to pacify the Powder River country for the emigrant wagon trains heading west, U.S. officials convened the second Fort Laramie Treaty of 1868. It granted to the Sioux tribes a twenty-six-million-acre reservation that drew in the present-day landscape of South Dakota, together with the Black Hills, for the Indians' "absolute and undisturbed use." Such a conciliatory turn was rare in the course of Indian-white diplomacy, and it did not last long.

Following a lull in hostilities, the rising numbers of new pioneers, miners and land speculators flooding into the territory soon snapped it back to reality. Pressured by the demands of these new arrivals for land and dominion, in 1873 the Dakota Territory legislature asked the U.S. Congress to approve a survey of the Black Hills as a prelude to their exploitation and settlement. General Philip A. Sheridan wasted no time dispatching Lieutenant Colonel George A. Custer on a sixty-day expedition "for the purpose of reconnoitering the route from that post to Bear Butte in the Black Hills, and exploring the country. . . ."

But by July of 1874, when expedition member James Calhoun was entering the Hills, a grander usurpation was already on his mind. "In this wild region," wrote Calhoun in his diary, "man will ultimately be seen in the full enjoyment of true pleasure, in the possession of happiness obtained by honest labor. For the hives of industry will take the place of dirty wigwams. Civilization will ere long reign supreme and throw heathen barbarism into oblivion; . . . Christian temples will elevate their lofty spires upwards towards the azure sky while places of heathen mythology will sink to rise no more."

As word of the trespassing expedition and shattered treaty sped through the Indian camps, photographs of the gold-laden Hills and maps of the expedition's route flashed across the pages of national newspapers. With greater invasion by whites now unstoppable, in 1875 President Ulysses S. Grant formed a commission to tempt the Sioux, Cheyenne and Arapaho with a $6 million offer for the Hills. When the Indians turned it down the following year, Congress passed "sell or starve" legislation, threatening to cut off all subsistence to Black Hills tribes, whose buffalo herds white hunters were rapidly exterminating, unless they agreed to the deal. Although one warrior warned his chiefs, "I will kill any among you that will sell the Black Hills," very soon some tribes caved in, abandoning their claims in exchange for $4.5 million. In another decade the region was officially opened to a rush of grubstakers and a greedy future.

For a half century this betrayal and loss remained an open wound for Indians. Then, in 1923, some activist Sioux filed a case with the U.S. Court of Claims to recover the Hills. In 1950 the Indian Claims Commission, which was established in 1946 to resolve such disputes, determined that the 1877 Black Hills settlement was indeed a "dishonorable chapter" in Indian-white relations and pushed for a cash settlement. But in 1976 the Sioux turned down the offer; they wanted the land back plus damages. Two years later the court of claims proposed a $105 million settlement, forcing the Lakota to reiterate that no amount of cash could substitute for their sacred lands.

In 1985, a bill promoted by New Jersey senator Bill Bradley stated that "a more ripe and rank case of dishonorable dealing will never, in all probability, be found in our history." But Bradley's proposals of 1985 and 1987 only talked about returning federally owned acres in the Hills; private ranches and businesses and Mount Rushmore were untouched. Furthermore, the Sioux would receive only 1.3 million acres out of the roughly

256 million to which they laid claim, the rest to be held in trust for their exclusive use. In the face of what they felt to be insincere negotiations and paltry offers, some key Sioux spokespeople, like Frank Fools Crow of the Pine Ridge Reservation, preferred to turn down the cash and wait the government out.

They are still waiting.

A question hanging over decades of disputes regarding the Black Hills was how "sacred" they really were to Plains Indians. Skepticism about claims that the Hills were revered came from local non-Indians and distant academics alike. These doubts stemmed, in part, from concerns about upsetting a century of tourist investment in the Hills. As much gold was dug out of the Hills, even more money went into turning them into what historian Donald Worster has called "a single jumbled pantheon of our heroes and heroines peopling the half-truth history of the celebratory mind."

Few places in America are as inundated with patriotic and cultural symbols—from iconic representations of presidents on Mount Rushmore to resting places for military heroes and at Black Hills National Cemetery to rendezvous for antiheroes at the Sturgis motorcycle rally, to reenactment of the Savior's sacrifice at the Spearfish Passion Play, to dramatization of epic shootouts in reconstructed Deadwood, to specialty museums devoted to everything *except* Indian life in the Hills, to the endless jackhammering on a massive sculpture of the martyred Crazy Horse, which many Indians felt to be a ludicrous continuation of the nineteenth-century tradition of Europeanized sculptures of the Indian as "Vanishing American." It was as if the Black Hills became some giant piece of cultural luggage plastered with decals from every major narrative of American triumphalism and religious nationalism. A new visitor to the Hills might suspect that nowhere else was the United States so shaky about its tenure to a particular habitat, so crowded had these overlays grown, as if to cover up its illegal takeover in the first place.

Resistance to take Indian claims about the sacredness of the Hills at their word also came from the fact that they stemmed from *oral cultures* and were often not written down. Rarely of the definitive "smoking gun" variety, these facts were not found in the archives customarily probed by academic historians, nor even in standard anthropological studies of the Sioux, Cheyenne or other tribes. Despite the millions of dollars spent on legal research on the Hills, no major study was devoted to unearthing the host of hidden, local or overlooked sources that, judiciously assembled and cross-referenced, might better reflect the Indian side of the story.

Historians filled the void with piecemeal efforts to provide a balanced picture based upon official documents, but some remained skeptical of the antiquity of Indian devotions to the Hills. Foremost among the doubters was Donald Worster, an eminent Yale University-trained specialist on American environmental history and the West. In his 1992 overview of the Black Hills dispute, Worster concluded that "the Hills were an imposing feature of the landscape, and the Lakota were an impressible people. But the historian cannot find any evidence that in the nineteenth century the hills were in fact regarded as sacred by the Lakota." To Worster, the Sioux position as expressed in court documents and position papers was "less the presentation of a legal case for sacredness as it is the awakening of a new or revitalized religion." Yet while he was unwilling to credit the Hills as a native "holy ground," Worster nonetheless felt that the equally weak legal grounds for their seizure by non-Indians meant that "the Black Hills, or some significant portion of them, should be returned to the Lakota people."

These assertions about the lack of earlier documentation on the Hills were based on insufficient research. Worster seemed uncertain about the authenticity of an old bison robe, for instance, supposedly kept secret on South Dakota's Cheyenne River Reservation until recently, which superimposed Indian maps of the Hills and the night sky and which, for the Sioux, "established solidly the historicity of sacredness." But he failed to mention another native mapping of sacred places in the Hills whose provenance was impeccable. For visual documentation on Lakota history nothing equaled the folder of drawings by a former U.S. Army scout named Amos Bad Heart Bull.

An Oglala Sioux from the Pine Ridge area that lies within sight of the Black Hills, Bad Heart Bull was born in 1859. Thirty-one years later he began depicting his people's history—based on what elders taught him as a youngster and on what he personally experienced during the great Sioux wars. Working in a mud-chinked cabin, Bad Heart Bull completed more than four hundred pictures by his death in 1913, but they were not discovered until 1926. When his sister, Dollie Pretty Cloud, died in 1947, the ledger book of his drawings was buried with her. By then, however, all the drawings had been photographed, among them a map of the Black Hills, which emphasized its sacred sites.

The Bad Heart Bull map was extremely helpful to Dr. Sundstrom, the specialist in the prehistoric rock art of South Dakota. In fact, the map was not unlike rock art on the page; its pictographic symbols for eight key places in the Hills were central in countering insinuations that the Sioux had "invented" these sites in order to bolster their court cases. Almost as an oval frame for this map, Bad Heart Bull idealized the encircling corridor that demarcated the Hills, a curving valley between the outer Hogback Ridge and the Hills proper around which today's trucks and cars stream on Interstate 90. But every collection of Sioux folklore labels this beautiful valley as the Race Track.

That name derived from a mythic story, told by Sioux and Cheyenne alike, about a Great Race between the winged and four-legged creatures to decide who would rule the world. To gain speed, the flying contestants in one version of the story wore magic colors: the crow in black; the meadowlark, yellow; the magpie, white earth and charcoal. They tore around the track until the ground was stained with the bloody froth that streamed from the nostrils of buffalo and deer. By the time magpie and crow had come in first—on behalf of the two-legged beings—the track had been ground into the wide trough one sees today. Whenever the animals held their councils in the Hills, hunters were supposed to leave them alone.

As for the lack of nineteenth-century written testimony regarding the sanctity of the Hills, Worster overlooked numerous statements by whites and Indians; for instance, the letter from Episcopal Bishop William H. Hare to a New York newspaper in 1880, in which he attempted to communicate the environmental feelings of his Indian parishioners: "The Sioux, like Naboth in sacred history," Hare wrote, invoking the Old Testament story of a farmer who was stoned to death so that a bad king might steal his vineyard, "own something very dear to them which a more powerful neighbor covets. It is the country known as the Black Hills of Dakota. The Indians' attachment is a passion. And well it may be, for this district is the kernel of their nut, the yolk of their egg."

Referring to the 1805–1834 period in Oglala Sioux history, the early historian George E. Hyde wrote in 1937 that "during these years the Oglala camps were almost always within sight of the Black Hills," and Hyde reminded his readers that "a whole epoch in the life of the Tetons has been lost through the failure to record in writing at an earlier date the tale of Sioux migration to the Black Hills and their early life in that region. Here and there we catch a glimpse of the rich materials that we have lost. . . ." And as an example, Hyde recalled the chiefs who testified in 1876, when they were forced to surrender the Hills, as saying, "We give up the lands as far as the Race Track, the Bears Lodge Medicine Pipe mountain, the Old Woman's Hill and the Buffalo Gate . . . behind each of these names lies a story of those early times."

Although Hyde seemed unaware of it, some of those very sites were depicted on Bad Heart Bull's map, especially the breach in the Race Track known as *Pte Tali Yapa*, or "Buffalo Gap," which served as a gateway to the mountain sanctuary. Through this opening, wrote Sioux author Luther Standing Bear back in 1928, "the wild animals came in . . . for protection from the icy blasts of winter; and the Sioux likewise went there . . . [Here] nature seemed to hold us in her arms." Like a drawbridge to a castle, the gap welcomed humans who entered the Hills to find a safe, well-watered, game-stocked place, and released the game animals to the plains beyond. In their environs the Cheyenne remembered cultivating corn, the Kiowa applied place-names to key locations and humans and animals found shelter.

Bad Heart Bull also noted *Kagha Paga*, or "Evil Spirit Hill," what whites called Harney Peak. Rising to 7,242 feet, its spires were the highest in the Hills (and the geologically oldest in North America) and provided an opportune place for the seer Black Elk to fast in 1872, where he received the healing vision of the Six Grandfathers so powerfully described in his 1932 classic autobiography, *Black Elk Speaks,* edited by Nebraska poet John G. Neihardt. This was the mystical experience when Black Elk saw "the hoop of the world . . . and in the center grew one flowering tree to shelter all the children of one mother and one father. And I saw that it was holy." All his life Black Elk felt an obligation to protect the Black Hills. Yet in an irony familiar to many old native territories, by the time of Black Elk's death in 1950 the peak where he received that vision was named in honor of one of his people's harshest antagonists, U.S. Army general William S. Harney.

According to Indians, other sites in the Hills were apparently interconnected in mysterious ways. On older maps the Belle Fourche River was identified as the Sun Dance River, and Sioux stories suggest that the four-day ritual of prayer and self-sacrifice originated here. Those narratives also symbolically tied other Hills locations to key constellations whose changing positions in the night sky were used to time other Sioux ceremonies. But due to the exclusion of tribes from their seasonal visits to the Hills, some places on Bad Heart Bull's map were harder to fit into tribal beliefs and rituals, such as *Wapiya Oblaye I'ha,* or "Plain of the Rocks That Heal," Black Buttes, *Hinyankagapa,* or "Ghost Butte," *He Ska,* or "White Buttes," and *Re Sla,* or "Bald Place," among other spots.

One particularly important location was *Washu Niya,* or "The Breathing Place." Known to whites as Wind Cave, it was not on Bad Heart Bull's map, but many testimonies, not only from the Sioux, portrayed the vapor-exuding cavern as the portal where First Man emerged from the underworld, the place where the Sacred White Buffalo originated and the outlet from which buffalo and other animals emerged to provide sustenance for human beings. Not far from Wind Cave lay the gaping Vore pit—a cavity that resembles a Mayan *cenote,* the natural limestone wells found in the Yucatán where human sacrifice was practiced. Positioned between opposing lanes of Interstate 90, into this sinkhole Indians drove buffalo for thousands of years. Archaeologists even uncovered a ceremonial ring of horned skulls, perhaps an offering to the animal species that fed them so well. But other doorways to nether realms were also noted on Bad Heart Bull's map, especially *Mnikahta,* or "Hot Springs," whose steamy waters were cherished for their comforting heat, the medicinal plants that grew near them and the health benefits of imbibing them.

. . .

Until the end of the twentieth century, many historical references to the
Hills remained scattered and unnoticed. Aside from Dr. Sundstrom's pio-
neering work, no systematic study had fully fleshed out the story of Indian
relations to the region. Then, in 1999, into this informational gap stepped
a well-respected Plains Indian scholar named Patricia C. Albers. An anthropologist by training and chair of American Indian studies at the University of Minnesota, Dr. Albers was fifty-six years old when, after cutting
her teeth on contract-research projects helping the Rocky Boy Cree, the
Shoshone-Bannock and the Northern Ute recover water, fishing and other
treaty rights, she was invited to delve into the culture history of Wind
Cave National Park and the southeastern Black Hills.

Hesitant at first to plunge into such a volatile topic, Albers was persuaded that the project might advance Indian interests as well as provide
research experience for her students. The job began in midwinter; Albers
visited the labyrinthine cave, turned up interesting materials in the park's
own archive and began guiding her team through the standard ethnographic studies. Over the years, only a few of them stuck with the project
to the end. And Albers discovered that instead of turning up material in
familiar sources, she was forced to become more imaginative, treasuring
the fragments of information that had been collected during the 1930s by
fieldworkers for the Works Progress Administration, the oral testimonies
recorded in the 1950s under the Doris Duke Oral History project, the upright files accumulated by small-town libraries and the fascinating details
she found by leafing through the centennial volumes of local community history put together by amateur historians in Wyoming and South
Dakota. Although Albers's assignment left the central and northern
sectors for another day, researching her sector's legal and political background necessitated a general understanding of the entire forested island.
And that included two sites whose cultural significance to the Black Hills
was legendary.

Best known of the Black Hills outlier sites was what Indians called Bear
Lodge Butte, but which whites, in offensive contrast to its heroic role in
Indian mythology, came to name "Devils Tower." Remembered by most

Americans, this volcanic upthrust, located to the north of the Hills that jutted into the sky like a great horn with its tip lopped off, was the Mother Ship's landing pad in director Steven Spielberg's 1977 science fiction classic *Close Encounters of the Third* Kind.

But to the Kiowa tribe the 867-foot promontory was revered as *T'sou'a'e,* or "Aloft on a Rock." Here was the embarkation point for that early period in Kiowa Indian history that the Pulitzer Prize-winning novelist N. Scott Momaday called "the setting out." From these high plains their ancestors migrated south, to ultimately reach the area of Rainy Mountain in western Oklahoma, where their reservation is found today.

Like a number of Plains Indian tribes, the Kiowa never forgot the Tower's place in their mythology. They told of the seven sisters and a brother who were playing together. Transformed into a monster bear, the brother attacked his sisters, who ran for their lives. When they reached a giant tree stump it told them, "Climb up on me." Once they were on top the stump began to grow, leaving the bear pawing at them and raking its sides with his claws—those vertical grooves remain to this day. On the summit the girls were finally safe, but the Kiowa say the sisters then ascended into the sky, to become the constellation we know as the Big Dipper (other tribal versions say the Pleiades). Every Kiowa remembered the place and knew its story; in a high-end Indian curio shop in Beverly Hills, for instance, a proprietor recently showed me an old ledger book drawn by a famous Kiowa warrior named Big Bow, veteran of nineteenth-century battles between his people and white soldiers. Among the penciled images of mayhem was a picture of a spiderlike bear climbing a butte, with the sisters twinkling safely in the sky.

Although in 1858 an early cartographer put its Sioux Indian designation, *Mato Teepee,* on his map, ever since Colonel Richard Dodge called it "Devil's Tower" in his 1876 book on the Black Hills, so it has been known to photographers, tourists and mountain climbers. Seventeen years later the giant rock began attracting those energetic visitors who conceived of wilderness as an obstacle or opponent against which to test themselves. A rancher named William Rogers hammered wooden pegs into fissures in its basalt walls and planted an American flag on the 1.5-acre summit. The irresistible temptation of Rogers's Ladder introduced what Indians would derogatorily call a "multiple abuse" policy. The Tower won presidential anointment in 1906 when Theodore Roosevelt, a notorious trophy hunter in the Black Hills, decreed it the country's first national monument.

It was painful for tribes like the Lakota, Cheyenne, Kiowa, Arapaho and Crow to watch their mythic place of refuge taken over by outsiders. But after Indians protested that they had prior interests in the Tower, the National Park Service hired an anthropologist to compound the insult when he asserted in 1934 that "it is extremely unlikely that any one tribe has been in the area of Devil's Tower National Monument for a sufficiently long time to have occupied an important place in their lives or their religion and mythology."

Over the years the Tower continued to attract white daredevils, like the parachutist who, in 1941, dropped on the crest but had no idea how to get down. For six days airdrops fed and clothed him until he gingerly descended into a crowd that laughed him out of the park. Then Spielberg's film raised attendance significantly; while only 312 climbers ascended in 1970, a dozen years later more than sixty climbing routes, requiring metal pitons and rings hammered into the rock, guided more than 12,000 enthusiasts up its sides. Complaining about the climbing craze, some environmentalists cited the ecological sage Aldo Leopold: "The trophy-recreationist has peculiarities that in subtle ways contribute to his own undoing. To enjoy he must possess, invade, appropriate." At the same time the Black Hills proper became a prime venue for workshops on wilderness canoeing as a religious experience, vision quests for juvenile delinquents and other self-improvement enterprises.

In the early 1990s talks between park officials, Indians, environmentalists and some climbers produced a voluntary climbing ban for the month of June, out of respect for Indian desire to save the place for prayer and ceremonial gatherings. But when park officials tried to enforce the shutdown—so the site might also enjoy what Vine Deloria, Jr., has called "time of its own"—commercial guides, supported by a states' rights foundation, sued for the right to climb whenever they wanted. In June 1996 a district court judge in Cheyenne, Wyoming, decided in their favor. Unlike the restrictions on the heads carved into Mount Rushmore ten miles away, where climbing was forbidden, now park rangers could only implore sportsmen to voluntarily respect Indian religious attitudes. In the opinion of Dave Ruppert, a National Park Service ethnographer sympathetic to Indian sentiments, both Rushmore and the Tower were better characterized as crucial *cultural* sites. "The judge and the climbers see it as 'religion,'" he said, "but Native Americans don't make a distinction between secular and sacred. They call it 'sacred' because they figure it will make more sense to us—it fits our lexicon."

The second major outlier site that Patricia Albers came to know well lay closer to Wind Cave. This was Bear Butte, a fourteen-hundred-foot, pine-speckled bulge that stands just to the east of the Race Track. To geologists the double-summited hill is a classic *laccolith,* which means it's a volcano that never managed to reach eruption, as if still storing its energy within. For Plains Indians from the Mandan to the Lakota, it reigned as "the power place among power places."

When they were yet in the formative stages of achieving a separate tribal identity, the Cheyenne described their early ancestors as camping in "a foreign tall grass country." Surviving on fish and birds, they were also close to starvation. In desperation they sent a shaman named Sweet Medicine and a female companion to "a blue mountain with a body of water near its base." As the couple entered the butte's hollow, lodgelike interior they were greeted by "keepers of the animal spirits" who taught them healing rituals, granted them permission to hunt and then released the game animals.

To seal this "gift of the earth," the two also learned how to perform the "wonderful dance," the Massaum ceremony, which authorized them to lure buffalo into camps and game traps and affirmed their new identity as a distinct nation—the *Tsistsistas,* or Cheyenne—with sacred rights to their Plains landscape. Thereafter tribal members undertook pilgrimages to Bear Butte, which Albers found often described in oral testimonies recorded since at least the 1930s. Every Cheyenne acknowledged the sacred mountain as their birthplace; all considered themselves its descendants and custodians. "For those who climb [up Bear Butte]," wrote Father Peter Powell, an Episcopal historian who had also been invested as a Cheyenne sun-dance priest, "glimpses of the Cheyenne past lie all around . . . the prairie colors flow towards the four directions where the sacred beings dwell."

But the Lakota likewise held Bear Butte in pious esteem. Although their bands may not have arrived in their vicinity until the 1700s, the site quickly entered their mythology through much the same retroactive thought process by which late-coming Navajo claimed attachment to Rainbow Bridge in northern Arizona; Bear Butte, and the Hills for which it stood almost as a guardian, was already inhabited by their spirit world. Whether or not they learned of its powers from earlier Indians, they certainly regarded it as predestined to their sense of spiritual unity.

Before their twentieth-century generations paid homage, leaving its trees and bushes festooned with many-colored prayer cloths and strings of tiny tobacco pouches, the spirits had readied it for them. Here a primordial monster fought a great bear, who licked its wounds until it convulsed, expired and became the hill. Mysterious childlike beings made it their home, and spirit eagles circled its summit. In the stories of Lakota medicine man Pete Catches, when the "seven spiritual people" first visited the Hills, they chose Bear Butte as their altar.

Only later, apparently, was a layer of historical significance added to the place. In 1743 the explorer Pierre de la Verendrye, venturing west from the Badlands, was possibly the first white man to see Bear Butte. And six years after the Treaty of 1851 it was here that the Sioux held their *Oyate Kiwitaya*, or "Great Reunion of the People," the occasion when Crazy Horse pledged to resist any more white encroachment upon their lands.

The impetus for Bear Butte to test the new American Indian Religious Freedom Act began in 1962, when the state of South Dakota turned it into an 1,845-acre recreational park. Roads were soon installed, along with a machine shop, campgrounds, parking lots and a visitors' center. Non-Indian marathoners were encouraged to work out on its paths. Tourists were given maps to its trails and provided with viewing platforms and signs (now removed) that indicated where Indians could be spotted fasting for visions.

Then Indian privileges at Bear Butte were limited still further. In February 1982, Cheyenne and Lakota religious leaders in Oklahoma, Montana and across the Dakotas received an identical letter from the manager of Bear Butte State Park. No more gathering of sage, hackberry or wild rose. No use of sweat-bath grounds while visitor parking was expanded and new access roads were resurfaced. From now on Indians would be required to purchase five-day permits to fast and pray. Already irritated by tourists' clicking their telephoto lenses at praying Indians, the two tribes teamed up much as the Hopi and Navajo had joined forces to defend the sanctity of the San Francisco Peaks in Arizona.

Their suit, which pitted plaintiff Frank Fools Crow, a leading Lakota medicine man, against defendant Tony Gullet, the park manager, claimed loss of First Amendment rights to the Indians' free exercise of their religions. When the district court in Rapid City turned the Indians down it reminded the petitioners that the American Indian Religious Freedom Act of 1978 was only intended as a "general statement of federal policy," not a clear directive to the states. So agreed the Eighth Court of Appeals, and in June 1983, the U.S. Supreme Court saw no reason to second-guess either of them. Thus died the third major Indian legal effort that sought redress under the Religious Freedom Act but which only exposed its impotence where sacred lands were concerned.

Nearly four years after she began her work in the Hills, Patricia Albers mailed a document of almost a thousand pages to the National Park Service. Her patiently assembled "patchwork quilt" of hundreds of resurrected facts, lost quotes and neglected references provided the most complete reconstruction ever attempted of the historical, legal and cultural context of a portion of the Black Hills. Albers and her team had documented the early use and occupancy of the Black Hills area by upward of fifteen different Plains Indian nations; chronicled the Euro-American penetration and multiple uses of the Hills from the 1740s to the present day; clarified how the Indians' seasonal food-gathering practices interlocked with cycles of animal and plant availability; provided a clear narrative time line for the Hills' diplomatic, legal and political history; inventoried in minute detail the mineral and plant resources in the Hills that were exploited by various Indian tribes; put the Lakota and Cheyenne views of the Hills into understandable cosmological frameworks from their religious perspectives; made a strong case for the Black Hills as a "sacred landscape"; and with great subtlety articulated under what historical conditions they might become "contested ground" among tribes and also the circumstances that allowed them to follow a more "live and let live policy" that might turn the forested oasis into something like a "shared commons" or "neutral ground."

And having devoted so much of her professional training and fourteen-hour days to making sense of this corner of the Black Hills, Albers also felt ready to speculate about deeper meanings. This was around the time that she and archaeologist Sundstrom "shared an epiphany of sorts," as they simultaneously were struck by the important connection in Lakota consciousness "between winter, bison and breath." Their next step involved piecing together the larger puzzle of Sioux metaphysical thought.

Five of those pieces were Caves, Bison, Breath, Fertility and Stone. From her research Albers knew the Lakota considered caves more than holes or animal dens; they were likened to "birthing chambers or wombs of the earth, where certain animals and humans underwent their gestation before emerging on the earth's surface." Another important aspect of caves, of course, was their mineral nature. Stone, or *Inyan*, was a primal, immortal element to the Lakota, whose medicine bundles often contained special rocks. Albers believed that one kind of mineral, gypsum, found in the limestone cracks at Wind Cave, was associated with ice. And the behavior of Wind Cave, especially in winter, only fortified that connection, for that was when its colder interior released clouds of condensation that rose like mysterious breath.

As with caves, buffalo were viewed as more than animals or even the Indians' dietary mainstay; they symbolized existence itself and were even likened to the "breath of life." Originally the buffalo's home lay far down in the underworld, where they existed in a holier and miniaturized state. Small as ants when they emerged upwardly through such caves, upon passing through Buffalo Gap and feeding on the prairie grass beyond, they grew to their present size.

Buffalo were also linked to the feminine principle; indeed, some tales told of how a sexual union between a "buffalo woman" and an aspiring warrior might impart magical powers for hunting and raiding. "In being able to generate visible breath in the wintertime," Albers came to believe, "bison and caves became active co-agents in the process of life's revivification." And since the Lakota perceived such a close link between their own identity, the procreative principle and the esoteric significance of buffalo, Wind Cave served as their own place of emergence as well.

At the same time, Albers gathered from more than one source that the Lakota often chose such caves as the place to bury their dead. Standing at the nexus of life and death, as doorways through which spirits entered and left the world, this made caves "very holy places where special care must be taken in their presence." The further Albers probed, the more convinced she became of the cultural logic that linked these metaphors. Now she was learning what the Lakota really meant when they insisted that "spirits belong to places." It was as if her years of painstaking research to reconstruct the outer cultural epic of this section of the Black Hills had prepared her to descend into Wind Cave and explore the contours of their very soul.

PART IV

WEST

In the 1970s, the U.S. Forest Service planned to pave a twenty-six-mile section of logging road through the Six River National Forest in Northern California. Connecting the mountain hamlets of Gasquet, in the north, and Orleans, in the south, the extension would invade the so-called High Country of local Indian tribes. Its pinnacles, outcrops and trails were key places in Yurok, Karuk and Hupa Indian mythology; here their people still sought shamanic training and spiritual solace. Citing the First Amendment and the 1978 Religious Freedom Act, the Indians' lawyers tried to stop the GO Road. When elders told U.S. District Court Judge Stanley Weigel about the area's importance in early 1984, he was impressed; in late May, he agreed that the road would "seriously impair" Indian religious practices. Realizing that Weigel's action could endanger earlier court decisions related to sacred places—Tellico Valley, San Francisco Peaks and Bear Butte—the U.S. Justice Department pushed its appeals on Lyng v. Northwest Indian Cemetery Protective Association *all the way to the U.S. Supreme Court.*

CHAPTER THIRTEEN

SINGING THE ORIGINS

Colorado River

L
ate one night in 1982, I shared an airport van with an Indian woman from the tip of Washington State's Olympic Peninsula. She was Makah, from Neah Bay, whose people had hunted whales, clubbed seals, snagged salmon and gathered huckleberries along the Pacific Rim for thousands of years. Her child was fretful. She would stand it on her knees, relax her grip and let the child topple forward. Then she grabbed her, let go again, and the whimpers would turn to giggles. "I'm teaching her about edges," the mom said. "We live at the edge of the world; she'd better learn about that." She knew what she was talking about. Around three hundred years ago, one of five Makah villages, named Ozette, became an American Pompeii—suffocated within minutes by a mud slide, possibly triggered by a tidal wave brought about, in turn, by an earthquake.

Back then the West Coast presented this paradox. Whales, dolphins and swordfish out at sea; tuna, yellowtail and rock cod closer to shore; seals, otters and sea lions in the kelp beds; abalone, clams and mussels in tidepools and beaches; birds deafening marshy wetlands; salmon and eel spawning in rivers; lupine, poppies and seed grasses coloring the hills; deer, timber and wild fruits in the mountains; the shade from eight species of edible acorn-bearing oaks almost everywhere.

But then there were also earthquakes, volcanic eruptions, tidal waves, monsoons, flash floods, dissolving cliffs, lightning fires and parching droughts. In old Indian days, this roster of dangers included grizzly bears, mountain cougars, rattlesnakes, scorpions, a host of malevolent water and forest imps, homicidal "bear doctors" who haunted the woods, invisible pathways where one bumped into easily angered spirits bent on their evil missions, and "poison places" where sorcerers gained access to injurious powers.

And California Indian history is likewise one of extremes. For more than ten thousand years it has been a cul-de-sac for migratory cultures. Hailing from a range of cultural backgrounds, Indians adapted to a mosaic of habitats. By the seventeenth century, California boasted America's only challenge to the language diversity that scholars in the early 1950s would find in the New Guinea highlands. Seven of the nine American Indian linguistic stocks were represented there; at least a hundred mutually unintelligible tongues could be heard. By 1750, the mountain-bordered region harbored an estimated 310,000 Indians, also giving it the continent's largest aboriginal population.

Yet California Indians would also become the most decimated, dispossessed and denigrated in North America. During the Spanish and Mexican years, from 1769 to 1848, the coastal Indian population was reduced by 90 percent from disease, malnutrition, depression and outright slaughter. In 1833, three fourths of those coastal natives who had survived eighty years of Spanish domination perished in one summer's malaria epidemic, probably contracted from white sailors. A quarter century later, from 1848 to 1860, upward of fifty thousand more Central California Indians died from starvation, disease, overwork in mines and vigilante killings by bounty hunters; and thousands more were sold into slavery south of the border. Over little more than a century of disregard by Spaniards, Mexicans, Russians and Anglo-Americans, in the public mind California Indians were demoted to the lowly status of insect-eating "root diggers." First, the Spanish missions confiscated their land, next Mexican colonists converted it into immense ranches and then the Anglo-Americans refused to protect them with federal reservations of their own.

The state's Indian numbers kept dropping until 1910, when there were fewer than 16,000 of them left alive. Then, only four generations later, the tables turned. Looking at the recent decades of rising casino revenues, political clout and population increase (up to 333,000 Indians in the 2000 California census), one must ask if a trickster god could have written into the human comedy a plot twist of greater poetic justice?

During the last century, the lifeways of California Indians were studied by the most eccentric, dedicated collection of scholars in American history. From the academic generalissimo of California Indian studies Alfred L. Kroeber to the workaholic, loner-linguist John Peabody Harrington to the protohippie writer-scholar Jaime de Angulo, the practice of California Indian studies is replete with oddballs, amateurs and activists. And since the 1960s, their ranks have been enriched by a critical mass of American Indian scholars, elders, lawyers and artists.

At one time or another, nearly all these observers have noted stories, beliefs or rituals related to sacred Indian places. From the Colorado River peoples to the Southern California Indians, up the broad central province, thence to the Northwest and Puget Sound, the spirits of their stories inhabited mountains, knolls, oddly shaped rocks, coastal overlooks, river whirlpools, slit caves and seepage holes, special trees and almost everyone's dreams. As Alfred Kroeber ended a 1954 legal brief that described Indian land-owning traditions, "There must have been literally tens of thousands of such natural features or spots throughout California having magical or religious or legendary meaning and significance. . . . Allied to this, in turn, is the tremendously strong attachment which all California Indians had for the place in which they were reared and had lived most of their lives. They did not poetize about this or become romantic and make speeches, but the feeling was perhaps for that very reason all the more powerful."

Animals, plants, rocks and nature's forces were considered alive. The abodes of their spirits came in all shapes and sounds—the Wintun Indians of Northern California say power places were detected by audible buzzing around them. A tally in 1980 by the California Indian Heritage Commission counted fifty-seven thousand old village, rock art, burial, food-and-plant collecting, spirit homes and prayer sites located across 70 percent of the state. The continued importance of California's numinous geographies is an abiding theme in contemporary native arts, rituals and tribal politics.

Like that mother in the van, the West Coast tribes who coexisted with these spirits of place were well aware of their proximity to some sort of continental finality. As the Haida of the Queen Charlotte Islands imagined it, their villages sat "on the edge of a knife cutting between the depths of the sea, which to them symbolized the underworld, and the forested mountainsides, which marked the transition to the upper world." The Yurok of Northern California viewed their land base as a floating island, wobbling uncertainly in a vast ocean, anchored down by ropes, with sheer edges on all sides. On ground paintings they drew with colored minerals to instruct pubescent boys in their tribe's sacred geography, Southern California elders portrayed the world as a giant disk. Inside were their mountains, stars and creatures; beyond the coastal rim lay only islands and mysteries. And from the Costanoan Indians of Central California, about whom so little has remained, comes this tantalizing song fragment: "Dancing on the brink of the world."

For the southernmost cluster of California Indian tribes, however, it was the edge of the lower Colorado River valley, not the Pacific Rim, which dominated their creation stories and held their sacred places. Focused upon a cultural corner of California, this chapter looks eastward upon an aboriginal world so different from everybody's image of American Indians that it is still underappreciated: the Yuman-speaking terroritories of the lower Colorado River.

Tallest of America's Indians, inveterate dreamers, the region's major farming tribe, fierce warriors and epic voyagers who left home for months at a time, the Mohave and Quechan were also California's only natives, contended anthropologist Alfred Kroeber, whose clans clung to a "national" identity and could mobilize five-hundred-member armies in defense of their homeland.

Their front yard was the broad river—swimming pool, fishing hole, highway, garden strip, orienting direction and site of creation and revelation. Their back fences were the sun-hammered peaks that rise behind the river's eastern and western banks. Scholars have noted how Mormon pioneers projected their biblical holy land of burning bushes and wilderness sojourns onto the softer, sensuous high desert of southern Utah, but the tougher sacred geography of these sea-level lower Colorado River Indians seems a better fit with the Sinai Desert and the Jordan River. Yet like many comparisons between American Indian and Judeo-Christian traditions, such analogies to the Middle East can lead one astray, especially since in this case the revered locations for the Mohave and their Yuman-speaking neighbors were less where the son of god was born than where the world was created and their all-powerful Creator was *cremated*—most notably on the pinnacle thirty miles from present-day Needles, which is known to the Mohave as *Avikwame,* or White-Striped Mountain.

In late July, this environment can be hellish. White sheets of sunlight leach color from every place except the floodplain, which these days sports a grid of green squares from the irrigation water pumped out of the Colorado's dams and aquifers. The only escape from killing temperatures are the thickets of arrowweed, willow, mesquite, wild hemp and cottonwoods along its banks. Even the rocks get overcooked, acquiring the metallic sheen known as desert varnish. But the desert floor is also as fragile as lace. One treads with care lest a rock be dislodged and leave a light-colored spot for years—like the enduring scrawls of old burro paths, power facility access roads and off-road vehicle tracks.

Indian attitudes toward the lower Colorado yield more evidence against the equivalence that is often drawn between scenic appeal and spiritual depth. As anthropologist Howard Campbell remembered from his years with the Tarahumara Indians in northern Mexico, south of Mohave country, "Almost anything I consider beautiful is not considered so by the Tarahumaras. They fear the rainbow because it steals children and marries women and causes them to have babies. Deep pools of water are where huge snakes live which will make you sick if you get too close. And Tarahumaras are sometimes scared to walk through a lovely forest for fear of the 'little people' who live under the ground. The word for beautiful is often heard in their sermons, but always in connection with such good things as good crops and good health."

To those virtues the Yuman Indians would only add, good dreams and great battles.

Before it was beaten into submission by the Hoover and four subsequent dams, the Colorado River ran unfettered for seventeen hundred miles. Engorged with snowmelt every spring, it drew from tributaries in Colorado and Utah and drove their payload of organic matter down present-day California, Nevada and Arizona. From a drainage basin of a quarter million square miles, the runoff inundated the lower river terraces with brown waves before spewing nearly twelve million tons of silt into the Gulf of California. During the season the Mohave Indians called *aha homee,* "high waters," the Colorado brought ten times the sediment carried by Egypt's Nile and seventeen times that borne by the Mississippi, and left a loamy deposit that extended five miles across.

By 1698, when an Italian Jesuit named Eusabio Kino walked these riverbanks, the tribes known collectively as Yuman speakers lived in sand-roofed houses, which were half dug into its eastern banks. Northernmost were the Mohave, or *Pipa Aha Macav,* "People Who Live Along the River." Down the riverfront oases created by the Colorado's wiggles and meanders were found the Chemehuevi, Halchidhoma, Maricopa, Quechan and Cocopah. All these tribes had wrestled over the upriver position, with the Mohave ending up on top. All of them eagerly anticipated the weeks following the spring floods, when they cast their corn, bean, melon and pumpkin seeds upon the organic residue.

In 1900, the future dean of California Indian scholarship, anthropologist Alfred L. Kroeber, first learned how this landscape played into Mohave Indian stories. A twenty-four-year-old graduate student, Kroeber was initiated into the California Indian world by a field trip that fall. Twenty-five years later he would synthesize his research into the monumental *Handbook of the Indians of California.*

While Kroeber's ethnographic energies went into the two river-dwelling tribes who were bookends for the state—the Mohave along the Arizona border and the northerly Yurok near the Oregon coast—for most of the first half of the twentieth century his organizational skills made Berkeley's University of California the West Coast hub for American anthropology's last golden age. Kroeber inspired dozens of scholars to leave no California Indian tribelet, food-gathering skill or vocabulary word unrecorded, and he packed their findings into fifty University of California volumes.

But on this trip, in late autumn 1900, the novice field worker just wanted to get it right. In his room at the Depot Hotel in Needles, California, Kroeber opened his lined notebook and put questions to Jack Jones, a lantern-jawed, long-haired and exceptionally bright Mohave. (Of Jones, Kroeber wrote, "He lived relaxedly in both American and Mohave cultures, had helped kill a witch-shaman, lost three wives in one day, did not receive schooling but as an adult learned his letters by looking in from the rear of a first-grade classroom.") When reading their exchange in Kroeber's handwriting at Berkeley's Bancroft Library, I wondered whether I was making too much of the Old Testament mold from which it seemed struck.

"What is your name for 'man'?" he asked first. And then, "What's your name for 'woman'?"

Thinking one was beginning afresh, and subconsciously referring to how one's own culture pictured a supreme being sequencing his creation, perhaps it was natural to fall back on the Genesis checklist. As if in god's stead, Kroeber made the ultimate beginnings of the Mohave follow *on the page* what is called the Adamic narrative of the Old Testament. No sooner had Kroeber tried orienting himself in the Mohave behavioral environment, however, than he was torn out of this Judeo-Christian orientation and thrust into the Indian notions of landscape and territoriality that would hound him all his life. After obtaining Mohave names and locations for neighboring tribes, Kroeber inquired about the four directions.

Instead of answering directly, Jones talked about "downstream," some twenty miles away, toward *Avi Kvoverkvier,* or the "Sand Hills," associated with the three spires on the Arizona side of the Colorado River, which whites called the Needles. Behind them lay the dunes "where the dead go," he said. As for "upstream," Jones mentioned an even more potent place, *Avikwame,* or "White-Striped Mountain"—the 5,939-foot granite outcrop on the Colorado's western banks (now known as Spirit or Newberry Mountain)—where the great god Mastamho ended his life and turned into an eagle.

During his field visits to the Lower Colorado between 1900 and 1908, Kroeber absorbed these new orientations—*up*stream, *down*stream and *across* the desert. The doors to the Mohave's semisubterranean, narrow weed-and-mud–walled houses faced south, which was also the direction traveled by dead souls and where people generally headed to visit other tribes; whereas their mythic origins lay to the north, while they usually journeyed east or west to trade. The long-haired, sun-shriveled old-timers to whom Jones introduced Kroeber would recite epic narratives and chants that described, in minute detail, movement up, down and around hundreds of named sites. They provided a different script of origins than the one Kroeber carried in his head.

A drop of rain falling from the male Sky upon the female Earth conceived a son, the Mohave's great god named Matavilye. In a time, as the Mohave expression goes, "when the world was still wet," Matavilye formed the land and created the animals and birds and first humans. From his own body he produced a daughter, Frog Woman, and a son named Mastamho. In Black Canyon, just upriver from the present-day Mohave reservation, he built a sacred structure, the Great Dark House.

But it was the significance of Matavilye's death that was stressed by Kroeber's new acquaintences. When that day occurred, his Great Dark House was burned, together with his corpse and possessions. Instead of evoking sadness, the spot was thereafter revered as the prototype for what became the Mohave's central ritual, the Karuk cremation ceremony. But now they can no longer pray there; the site lies under Lake Mead.

Where the father had created nature, it was left to the son to create culture. Mastamho instituted the Mohave religious practices, taught his people how to fish and garden, to make tools and pottery, cook food and raise children, to interpret dreams, and become shamans, warriors and travelers. He differentiated their neighboring tribes, designated their territories and bestowed their distinctive dialects. What cosmic work his father had left unfinished, the son took on, creating the sun and moon and starting the Colorado River by thrusting his staff into the land. With his people he piled into his huge boat, headed south and formed the various bends and flow as he went. Much as his Mohave children would scrape lines on the desert floor to portray his gigantic likeness, he gathered dirt into the pile that became Avi Kwame, the Mohave Olympus, where he lived out his days. That mountain remains the most important Mohave landmark not under water. Either because he was focused on transcribing the Mohave stories that kept pouring in or in sympathy with Indian warnings that those who climbed the peak would be struck dumb and meet an early death, Kroeber left Avi Kwame alone.

But its ascent was made by a maverick personality who for the next fifty years would stand as Kroeber's shadow. Eight years his junior, the linguist John Peabody Harrington also visited Indians of the lower Colorado in the century's first decade, and hired the same Jack Jones as his translator. Except for a common dedication to documenting California Indians, however, their careers were a study in contrast: Kroeber the institution builder kept his subjects at an objective distance; Harrington the pathologically secretive loner longed to become one of them.

The Mohave were never Harrington's major focus, nor were many of the Indian communities he visited for years until, in Santa Barbara's Riviera Hotel in 1961, he died—a forgotten old man eating beans from a hot plate under his desk and taking elderly Chumash Indian women out for coffee before toiling over texts with them. But in the following decade, as his field notes cropped up in trunks, attics and storage places, it became evident that Harrington's material on Indian language and culture constituted the largest archive amassed by any American scholar in any academic discipline.

Gifted at transcribing obscure languages, and reputedly able to speak forty California Indian tongues, Harrington was appointed in 1915 by the Smithsonian Institution as a roving collector of linguistic and cultural information which left him free rein that he stretched to the breaking point. Not that he was hustling his superiors; his Washington paychecks often went uncashed, but as an obsessive on a last-ditch crusade, Harrington was often too busy or out of touch tracking down the last native speakers of some almost-forgotten tongue. What Kroeber was accomplishing with the prestige of university endorsement, this driven man characterized as an "angry god" by an ex-wife was achieving on his lonesome. They studied the same cultures and interviewed many of the same native elders, yet their paths failed to cross so often that it had to have been on purpose. Exasperated by yet another example of Harrington's mercurial independence, Kroeber finally blurted out in 1916, "There is only one word [that] fits you: crazy." But by then Kroeber had turned from his Mohave work to the broader challenge of his *California Indian Handbook* and to dispatching scholars to salvage whatever scraps remained of the state's native heritage.

.   .   .

Over the years some writers have looked for resemblances between Californian and Australian hunter-gatherers. Both wrested their livings from tough environments, ate larvae and dug rodents out of burrows, collected roots and seeds, endowed their landscapes with mythic significance, and suffered condescension from whites. Through their dreams and songs and a similar passion for travel, both peoples also touched places of creation from their mythic Dreamtime (Australian Aboriginal) or First Times (Colorado Yuman). In fact, it was in dreams, particularly the all-powerful *Sumach Ahot*, or "Great Dreams," that the lower Colorado Indians lived to the fullest.

The Mohave believed that persons began dreaming even before they were born—as six-month-old fetuses in their mothers' wombs. Those were the dreams that foretold, even "fore-*lived*," their personal character and professional skills. So it was that sorcerers, who were known to have lost their taste for life, would "dream up" tricks for failing to complete the birth process, such as sticking themselves crosswise in the uterus and dying along with their mothers. If this failed and they emerged as babies, then they dreamed of causing such evil through their toxic saliva or their fingernails that their victims would dream in advance of their killers' faces and experience beforehand the fear and pain of their own murders.

Lower Colorado Indians almost raised the application of the existence each of them lived through dreams to an art form. Dreams brought their myths and topography to life. In feats of reverse time travel, the dreamers even participated in primordial events. One of Kroeber's prized Quechan storytellers explained how this worked.

> Before I was born I would sometimes steal out of my mother's womb while she was sleeping, but it was dark and I did not go far. Every good doctor begins to understand before he is born. When I was a little boy, I took a trip to Avekwame Mountain [in a dream] and slept at its base. I felt of my body with my two hands, but found it was not there. It took me four days and nights to go there. Later I was able to approach even the top of the mountain. At last I reached the

willow-shade in front of the darkhouse there. Kumastamho [the cre-
ator] was within. It was so dark that I could hardly see him. He was
naked and very large. Only a few doctors [shamans] were in there
with him, but a crowd of men stood under the shade before the
house . . . I now have the power to go to Kumastamho any time. I lie
down and try, and soon I am up there again with the crowd . . . It
takes four days to tell (the origin myth) about Kwikumat and Kumastamho. I was present from the very beginning and saw and heard
all. I dreamed a little of it at a time.

Following this prenatal exposure to the sacred mountain and its deity,
the narrator was actually born, but he kept dreaming about the mountain
and other First Time sites. Dream by dream, episode by episode, he *personally experienced* the world's creation as if *in real time.* And as the stories
revealed themselves, his growing account was confirmed through consul-
tations with older, experienced shamans, who had undergone the same
extended dream life. "That is right," they said. "I was there and heard it
myself." Or they might say, "You have dreamed badly. That is not right.
It didn't happen there or in that way." This way, one Quechan friend told
Kroeber, "They would tell me right, so at last I learned the whole of it
right."

A second similarity to Australian Aboriginal culture was how Yuman
myths unfolded in song. Given the dream's power of making everything
happen in the "presentness of timeless myth," what other medium could
suffice? Song is channeling of direct experience, a gathering, summarizing
and conjuring into the present of events and emotions that otherwise are
safely distanced and fixed in another time and place. Extraordinary regis-
ters and rhythms and archaic vocabularies allow songs to "break into" the
here and now with their evocations of the there and then.

"What impressed Kroeber," believes linguistic anthropologist Donald
Bahr, "was not the sheer frequency of Mohave dreaming," but how they
used it to create songs as omens, clues for pragmatic action, "librettos for
myths" and literary works purely for their own pleasure. The prose supplied the drama, set directions, witness testimony, place-names and de-

scriptions and scene transitions. But as they carried "the supernaturals' very words," Bahr believes, the songs lent them a convincing magical realism. This collaboration between human artistry and divine intervention brought to life a topography more tangible and reliable than anything one saw before one's eyes.

One reason Kroeber did not move far from his hotel room during those early years was the sheer volume of these song-story *Ich-kamava,* or "Great Tellings." Transcribing day after day, he and Jones worked through the thirty or more song cycles, each of which contained 150 to 200 separate songs. Including the narrative tissue that linked them in sequence, each cycle might take a full twenty-four hours to recite. Peppered with precise locations and place-names, the songs recited the deeds of mythic personages and legendary heroes; they told of war, heroism, travels, curing and magic. Some were ancient, some seemed dreamed only yesterday, but most manipulated their time frames so that no one knew *when* was being sung of, though *where* was always clear. With the detailed itinerary and repetitious topography of each dream they had or heard about, everybody, young and old, became *more* Yuman.

A third similarity between Australian Aborigines and these Yuman-speaking tribes was their yen to get up and go. In great walking pilgrimages, Australians retraced the "dreaming tracks" of an earlier assembly of ancestors who had "sung the land into being," as British author Bruce Chatwin put it, creating a "spaghetti of Iliads and Odysseys, writhing this way and that" across the landscape. A throwback to the great nineteenth-century tradition of writer-walkers, for his book *The Songlines,* the charismatic Chatwin twisted the ethnographic data to conform to his romantic obsession with nomadism. The Mohave love of the open road tempts one to do the same.

In their dream sagas the gods were inveterate travelers—constantly adding new names to their oral maps or ticking off detailed itineraries. The lower Colorado River was as stacked with names for ancestral exploits, village sites, crisscrossing trails, dance circles and battlegrounds as the Hudson, the Seine or the Danube. On the heels of their mythic forebears, the Mohave were also incessantly on the move. One minute, early white visitors complained, they were indolent good-for-nothings, feet stretched out and dozing by their houses. The next they were nowhere to be found. By the evening of the following day they had covered more than 100 miles.

These Indians walked, swam, jogged, ran and, some of them claimed, even left the ground altogether to teleport by magical means. They traveled to retrieve people missing in war, to scout enemy territory in advance of a war expedition, to seek their doom on suicide missions (much as the fey deer in one of their myths headed straight for a mountain lion's den), to undertake raids of vengeance, to "travel for a name" like knights-errant and to undertake what anthropologist George Deveraux called "aimless traveling," which sounds much like the Aboriginal practice of "going walkabout."

A vivid account of such an impulse comes from an Indian group to the north. If Bruce Chatwin had a California soul brother, it was Jaime de Angulo—another nonconformist whom the staid Alfred Kroeber came to dislike for his bohemian ways. Born in France in 1888 to a semiroyal Spanish émigré family, he was breaking horses in Wyoming at the age of sixteen. When Kroeber met him on a pack trip into the Big Sur backcountry, he was struck by the man's language skills; hearing of Angulo's friendships with Pit River Indians, he signed him up. But Jaime was also a terrific writer. In his memoir of hanging out with Pit River natives, *Indians in Overalls,* he got the inside take on their roaming habits from an Indian named Robert Spring:

> Well, there come a time when a young fellow starts to feel uneasy, kind of sad, kind of worried, that's just about the time he's getting to be a man grown up. Then he start to "wander," that's what we call it, wandering. They say: Leave him alone, he is wandering. That's the time you go to the hills, you don't come home, you stay out all night, you get scared, you cry; two three days you go hungry. Sometime your people get worried, come after you, but you throw rocks at them: Go away, I don't want you, leave me alone.

The Mohave indulged in this wayward urge, but they also took business trips. Following well-beaten foot roads for hundreds of miles to the Pacific Ocean or east to the Hopi mesas, their runners exported reddish-colored pottery and dried vegetables. From the Los Angeles Basin and the San Joaquin Valley they brought back abalone shells, while from Hopi country they returned with woven blankets of homespun cotton.

In other ways the comparison between Aboriginals and the Yuman breaks down. Australian cultures were complex webs of interlocking clan relationships, with their Dreamtime stories stipulating each clan's inherited rights to territory. In Yuman society, however, clan affiliation was eclipsed by a higher allegiance. The need to protect their people as a whole leads to a second difference—the lower Colorado people's passion for warfare.

Along with their creation stories, these Yuman recited great battle epics. Their traditions of training young warriors, and their ability to marshal large forces, set them apart from most California tribes. Their strong sense of national identity and homeland certainly account for their confident and strident reaction to foreigners. When the foreign cattle trampled their gardens and mesquite groves, they raised a substantial army and went after the Spanish missions, settlements and forts, and drove them out of the valley for good.

And last, the Yuman ways of marking the landscape were more ambitious. Australian Aboriginals painted on rocks to renew the Dreaming experiences of mythic ancestors who had become their clan totems, but only among the effigy mounds of the Wisconsin piedmont or the Nazca lines on the Peruvian coast does one find "public art" to rival in size the earth drawings of the lower Colorado. Also described as *figured landscapes, geoglyphs* or *intaglios,* over 150 of these immense, representational and abstract forms still lie along the river terraces and nearby mesas at over twenty-five locations from Hoover Dam down to Yuma, Arizona.

Fashioned at various times between A.D. 900 and 1200, they extend to lengths of one hundred feet or more. Apparently their manufacture was the opposite of earthworks; rather than piling and shaping dirt, Indians scraped away the desert hardpan to "draw" with the exposed, lighter-colored subsoil beneath, occasionally adding rocks to borders or special features. Explorer Lorenzo Sitgreaves reported the Twins intaglio in 1852; thirty-four years later a Mohave Indian showed early ethnographer Captain John Bourke another image that commemorated a chapter from his people's Genesis; today a power-line access road has destroyed most of it.

Aerial photographers began shooting these forms in the 1930s, and I still find looking through the window of a Twin Cessna from about five hundred feet the most efficient if not exactly meditative way to appreciate them. Staring into the sky are bent-legged humans, animal and reptile forms, ceremonial or "dance" circles, rock alignments, stone cairns and pale lines of ancient trails that remind one how thoroughly this landscape was "taken in and thought through" by earlier Indians. Starting with downward spirals over the so-called Ripley Complex, where more than a dozen abstract designs encircle a large humanoid lying atop a mesa near Ehrenberg, my pilot coasted over a half-dozen figures near Blythe, including one fellow who lay over 95 feet long (seventy-five miles west of Phoenix a Bureau of Land Management researcher named Boma Johnson found another human figure who stood 297 feet tall).

Beside Parker Dam we floated over the sinuous Rattlesnake, and not far off lay the exquisite Fisherman, with two fish pictured within reach of his white quartz-tipped spear. Near Bullhead City we swung low over the sixty-foot-high twins of Mohave lore, one representing the good brother, the other evil. At Black Point appeared the Dance Circle, the Lizards, and near Pilot Knob, the incised Stone Horse, where writer Barry Lopez, who took the time to meditate upon it at ground level, was reminded of "huge horses carved in the white chalk downs of southern England by an Iron Age people; Spanish horses rearing and wheeling in fear before alligators in Florida" and also of the "vandals, the few who crowbar rock art off the desert's walls, who dig up graves, who punish the ground that holds intaglios . . . [who] devour history."

Near Needles we made out the butchered remnants of what was once the Topock Maze, eighteen acres of winding, parallel windrows scraped from the desert floor. Possibly a gigantic anthropomorphic figure, it is said to have served the sick, who ran along its furrows in a ritual that restored them to health and is also believed to have purified the souls of the dead as they traversed this threshold on their way to *Avikwal* ("Pilot Knob"), the land of the dead that lay just over the Needles.

To Colorado Indians these landforms are said to be the work of the "Ancient Ones." They portrayed "guardians of the land," identified "places where gifted Mohave go to receive instruction from the spiritual world" or commemorated the conquest over evil monsters that had terrorized their ancestors. To Boma Johnson, the now-retired researcher who spent most of his career puzzling over them, they incarnated various Mohave, Quechan and even Hopi origin stories and associated beliefs and, moreover, were linked through pilgrimage. From around Yuma, Johnson maintains, a sacred path known as the *Xam Kwatcan Trail,* whose traces remain today, ran north for more than 180 miles to end at Avikwame. With its north-south orientation symbolizing the Milky Way, and its route forcing Indians to walk directly through an intaglio representing the body of Mastamho, their creator, Johnson believes the trail allowed them to experience kinetically their culture's core beliefs about the nature of human existence.

At the end of his career, Alfred Kroeber returned to his Mohave notebooks. Leafing through those narratives of sacred landscapes was he only curious about what the places looked like or was he nagged by the thought that conducting his interviews in downtown Needles had deprived him of a more tactile appreciation for why the Indians so loved them? All his wife, Theodora, could add was that he "sometimes dreamed of checking the geography of a Mohave myth against the actuality from which it grew." With retirement, that became possible.

Scheduling a cool February for their trips in 1953 and 1954, the Kroebers drove south from Berkeley and turned east across the Mohave Desert toward Boulder. From there they followed the river to Parker, on the Arizona side. Times had changed. Hoover Dam had gone up. A few Mohave still grew corn on the river terraces; others were paid to drive John Deere tractors down endless furrows of cotton. Before long, Kroeber was sitting on an upended washtub transcribing a Mohave epic from an old man with mud-daubed dreadlocks who sang a myth he owned "with the expectable specificity in matters of geography."

Then Kroeber dusted off a lengthy tale he'd recorded forty-seven years earlier. With an old Mohave guide, his graduate student at the wheel and survey maps from the 1930s in the backseat, he revisited the story-measuring distances between the tale's campsites, pinpointing springs, mountains, hills, swales, villages and places where song cycles had been sung. "Thus it was mapped," his wife wrote, "this long ago myth from a man dead many years, who had lived into old age and throughout whose adult life, night after night, year after year, had dreamed its parts until at last he had come to the end of his dream journey."

That assignment complete, the couple took a side trip. Poling a light flat-bottomed boat about twenty-five miles below Hoover Dam, they veered west to push a few miles up the shallow wash of El Dorado Canyon. One pinnacle thrusting out of the water seemed a key location from Mohave myths—it was the "Middle of the Earth," or *Ha'avulypo*, also called Water House Post. Stories described it as what remained of his father's ashes, bones and cremation house, which Mastamho commanded the river to wash away, but also as the pillar of red sandstone into which his father had transformed *before* his cremation. Theodora saw it as "a silent sentinel guarding the river which his son, Mastamho, had caused to gush forth with a single plunge of his powerful cane made of spittle."

At the end of his life, working on his third volume of Mohave narratives, Kroeber still seemed like a man on an unfinished mission. "I have long pondered to whom we owe the saving of human religious and aesthetic achievements such as are recorded here," he wrote in its preface, which would come out after his death. Then, with a characteristic blend of paternalism and humanism, he asked, "Why should we preserve Mohave values when they themselves cannot preserve them, and their descendants will likely be indifferent?" His answer was ponderous and unsatisfying. "It is the future of our own world culture that can be enriched by the preservation of these values, and our ultimate understandings grow wider as well as deeper thereby."

How enriched? Which values? What understandings, and for whom? Kroeber never answered. A few days after writing those words he left for Paris, where he died in his sleep. As if the questions still rattled around the family attic, Theodora kept addressing them, and her artistic temperament let her push beyond her husband's skepticism.

She, like an old-time Mohave dreamer, in one book assumed the voice of Mastamho as he once assigned portions of the Colorado River to various Yuman tribes, until one last group of Indians stood before him. "To them Mastamho said," Theodora wrote, "'you are children, You shall stay with me, here at the Center of the World. You shall be the Mohave.' Thus was the World created and made complete." In a second book she recalled the boat ride up the river with her husband, with the flooded portion of the origin site of *Ha'avulypo* lying just over the gunwales. "The peaks reach almost to the surface and are ultimately deposited down river, forming the delta," she recalled, "building and renewing the Imperial Valley, a garden which will go on feeding a good many of the world's peoples, unless the greed of cities and power companies is allowed to destroy Mastamho's unique work."

But the impulse to formulate Mohave environmental "values" remained, and she argued in a third book, "The Yumans have kept much of the 'real' look because there are still among them their Old Ones to take the young to the sacred mountain and river sites, to repeat to them the old epic tales of their people, and to teach them to dream. . . . The inner life survives—despite the damming of the river, despite the threat to the canyon to the north, which their own God Mastamho created and into which he put the river, and despite the threat to the great fruitful delta of the river."

If Kroeber himself had probed his Mohave storytellers how they *felt* about the storied places he inventoried so faithfully, he might have understood how their values of *home* were part of those universal "understandings" to which his wife appears to have been more receptive. In his account of the great *Satukhota* narrative, for instance, all Kroeber dutifully noted was that an old woman heads south from *Avikwame* mountain and is impregnated not far from *Avir-qorotat,* the pinnacles which the white man knows as Monument Peak, before continuing on her journey.

About two miles away, in 1942 the U.S. Army Corps of Engineers built Headgate Rock Dam in order to irrigate lands cultivated by Indians from the Parker community. An old Mohave named Otasa never liked that dam, or trusted the motivations of its builders. Living and farming by the river, he preferred its original flow as his highway. As a boy, Otasa would run for fifty miles along its banks, covering the distance from Parker to Needles and returning the same day. On occasion he also took two- to three-day jogs between Parker and Yuma. And before any dams, he'd swum with friends all the way down to Yuma, while the women floated beside them buoyed by logs.

In 1945, Otasa received a white man who admired the dam's engineering. The old Indian listened patiently, then turned the conversation to Monument Peak, not far away, which had barely escaped flooding behind Headgate. What he said brought Theodora's words down to earth. "Many ages ago," Otasa told his visitor, "the Mohave God drove a great wooden stake into the earth. He told Mojaves this marked their land. Today that stake has turned to stone but Mojaves are still here. This is our homeland. We never want to leave it. My fathers lived here before the first white men came. Always to the Mojave that great rock means home."

CHAPTER FOURTEEN

BEYOND THE GODDESS

Southern California

In 1974, the phone rang in the office of Charlotte McGowan, a teacher of anthropology at Southwestern Community College, south of San Diego. A recent brushfire had swept over a ranch out in the Lyons Valley, about thirty miles due east. What the fires had exposed, said the caller, looked like eyes carved into rocks. Would she take a look?

Charlotte had gotten hooked on California Indians as a girl. Her father was a labor organizer who put venison and squirrel on the dinner table and let her tag along on his visits with Kumeyaay Indian friends at their Barona Ranchería. When her three children became teenagers, she launched a second career. Receiving an M.A. in anthropology from San Diego State (SDS), she organized a summer field school shortly after landing the Southwestern job. For twelve years her students had excavated in the nearby Otay Valley on an old, twenty-eight-thousand-acre Spanish land-grant ranch strewn with artifact-rich sites. Locally she had gained a reputation as the one to ask about Indians; when she couldn't answer, she would call her scholarly friends: her mentor at SDS, archaeologist Ken Hedges, or a new friend, anthropologist Florence Shipek, who specialized in Kumeyaay Indian studies.

Taking along four students, she drove to the ranch and walked around. Clearly visible on the ground were bedrock mortars, pottery shards and broken stone tools. Also revealed were a number of granite outcrops and bulges, some of whose exfoliating crevices seemed indeed "enhanced" by human hand. Yet Charlotte strongly doubted they all represented eyes. During the next months she returned several times, finding more engravings and a quarter mile away noticed a jutting stone. She consulted with Hedges, an expert in Indian rock art, reviewed his notes about similar-looking sites in the area and visited a few.

A number of these pear-shaped forms, with pit holes near one end, were also grooved into large rocks at Anza-Borrego Desert State Park, the Cahuilla Indian homeland that lay between the Colorado River and coastal Indian territories. Boulders resembling them were known to have significance to the Maidu Indians, farther north. And east of present-day Santa Barbara stood a thirty-foot-diameter rocky amphitheater in the Carrizo Plains, the Painted Rock site, which some scholars linked to these same oval-shaped sites.

Charlotte did her homework, but she never had much doubt what the forms in the Lyons Valley were meant to represent. Add the tangle of singed shrubbery, and their appearances were enough to make even her students blush. There were rock vulvas everywhere.

The homeland of the Indians now calling themselves Kumeyaay originally extended from around Ensenada, in Mexico's Baja California, up to the San Luis River drainage. Here an estimated ten thousand of these Yuman-speaking Indians fished, hunted and foraged across familiar terrain as far east as the Sand Hills, along the western edge of the Imperial Valley. Today only a dozen small *rancherías* of Kumeyaay descendants remain in San Diego County. Their survival is something of a miracle. For this is where the catastrophe known as the California Mission system began.

During the past thirty years, as California Indian descendants have demanded respect and cultural recognition, how they talk about themselves has changed too. Only twenty years earlier, the tribe that Charlotte McGowan visited as a girl had recouped its old name, which some say meant "Those from the Cliffs." Shortly before they proudly affirmed themselves as Kumeyaay, however, scholars had begun distinguishing their northern and southern groups as Ipai and Tipai, respectively. Since the early nineteenth century they had been commonly known as Diegueños. But conversationally they were generally lumped with neighboring tribes as Mission Indians, which was the catch-all term for Southern California tribes whose names derived from whatever Catholic mission had corralled and sheltered them. Mission Indians associated with San Luis Rey de Francia thus became Luiseños; those with Mission San Gabriel Arcangel, Gabrielinos; whereas converts at San Diego de Alcala were Diegueños. Over time the Mission Indian label, repudiated since the 1960s as a stigma, had conjured up poor, landless natives who had conveniently disappeared or been passed by, while their Mission-derived names had come to connote subservience and conversion.

In 1769, near San Diego Bay, Father Junipero Serra and the governor of Baja California broke ground for the first of twenty-two mission forts, which Franciscan priests would erect during the next fifty years along seven hundred miles of coastline, ending up north with San Francisco Bay. Attached to each were presidios, or military garrisons, housing the soldiers who defended Spain's assets and brought from old Mexico the policy for dealing with Indians known as *reduccion,* which meant stocking a string of church-fortress factories with Indian converts, laborers and field hands who had been cleansed from the wider countryside.

"Oh, what a heathendom so docile," gushed Father Francisco Garces in 1774, in his first impression of native California. But he was wrong. Encouraged by how Colorado River tribes had resisted the Spanish, one month after the San Diego de Alcala mission went up, Kumeyaay Indians tore it down. Although it was rebuilt, a year later not one Indian name had been added to the baptismal ledger. And in 1775, the Kumeyaay struck again. Up and down mission country, other rebellions would defy the image of those "docile" Mission Indians.

But soon Kumeyaay lands were confiscated, and most of the Indians' farms and granaries were burned. Hunger and desperation left many of them no alternative but to accept serfdom. At the San Diego mission, the Kumeyaay hauled rocks, built buildings, worked the fields, boiled fat for tallow, made wine. Church records tell the rest. At the height of their enrollment, say historians Rupert and Jeanette Costo, 6,036 Indians were baptized. But during the same time period, 4,146 converts died—1,575 of them children.

The mission system wreaked havoc among the half dozen Southern California Indian groups who were nonconfederated, outnumbered and already weakened by European-derived diseases. Soldiers snatched Indian families from outlying hamlets to convert them, change their social habits and turn them into an American peasantry. Molding their adobe bricks, the Indians then built their own environment: the chapels where they learned to chant in Latin, the stables where they groomed horses, the workrooms where they processed tallow and hides from cattle, the sexually segregated dorms where they slept. Days ran by the bell, rules were strict, punishment for breaking them severe. Thanks to the California climate and fertile earth, the missions enjoyed a brief commercial success. Indians ran cattle and sheep, grew wheat, maize, beans and grapes, and processed olive oil, bales of cow hides, and wine.

A by-product of this colonial crusade was a caste system that divided Indians who remained heathens and at large, known as *gentiles,* from those who underwent conversion and lived within or near the missions, called *neophytes.* Mexicans were labeled *gentes de rason;* offspring between them and neophyte women became *mestizos.* Indians who fled were *bravos,* fugitives lurking in the backcountry and fair game for military patrols. Upon their recapture, men, women and children faced the stocks, floggings or worse.

Missions never became the tranquil islands of happy Indians insulated from the historical currents swirling around them. With Mexico's takeover from Spain in 1834 and the secularization of the missions, their adobe compounds shut their doors and crumbled into picturesque dilapidation, leaving bell towers with sprouting weeds, cracking plaster and sinking walls—perfect for the sappy romanticism of novelists and filmmakers.

Of the estimated 53,600 Indians who underwent conversion, about 15,000 were alive in 1833 to enter a world where they had little preparation for how to get their next meal. Some rejoined their brethren in mountain-hidden hamlets; others were left disoriented and homeless. Even their chaparral-covered habitat, now transformed into sprawling grasslands managed by Spanish-Mexican ranchers, no longer looked the same. Few could read or were prepared for a relatively lawless frontier that did not run by the bell. A lucky few found work as vaqueros; most scrabbled to survive as domestics or day laborers.

Then, a dozen years later, the country fell under the control of the United States. The 1848 Treaty of Guadalupe Hidalgo stretched a new border from the Gulf of Mexico to the Pacific Ocean. For old Mission Indians like the Kumeyaay, who were official citizens of neither country, these international maneuvers meant being dispossessed squatters first and illegal foreigners second. In her life history, a Kumeyaay elder named Delfina Cuero remembered that at least Mexico held out the hope of survival. Originally from Mission Creek near San Diego, Delfina's family kept getting kicked out of their temporary shelters. "We went farther and farther from San Diego," she said, "looking for places where nobody chased us away. My grandparents crossed the line first. . . . In those days the Indians didn't know about a line. This was just a place where nobody told us to move on." But that left her stranded away from her kinfolk and beloved places. "Is there room for us in America?" she asked shortly before she died. "Can we come home legally?"

Thus tightened the American noose around Southern California Indians. Their favored spots, such as hot springs and river mouths, caught the eyes of settlers and entrepreneurs. Lacking land titles, any Indians in the way were easily evicted. Never receiving the publicity or sympathy accorded the better known removals of Southeastern tribes, the forced dislocations of California Indians further divorced these vulnerable *rancherías* from traditions about their lands.

The tale of the Cupeño, a minuscule tribe north of Kumeyaay country, was typical. In 1903 they were pressured to leave their spalike Pala Valley, known as Warner Hot Springs. One old Cupeño woman spoke on behalf of dozens of *rancherías* in similar predicaments when she told pro-Indian author Charles F. Lummis, as they watched people loading their horse-drawn wagons, "You see that graveyard out there? There are our fathers and grandfathers. You see that Eagle-nest mountain and that Rabbit-hole mountain? When God made them He gave us this place. We have always been here. How can we go away? We will go into the mountains like quail and die," and so she did.

These were the blood memories of the Indians whom Charlotte McGowan visited as a girl. With her finds in the Lyons Valley, she turned her studies to their secret places and to beliefs she had yet to understand. To discuss these sites, which featured what she daintily called "natural geological formations which resemble the female generative organ," Charlotte sought a term "that was impersonal and not overly medical." Borrowing from Hindu tradition, a friend suggested the word "yoni," which had the appeal of being "more esoteric and mythological."

As to explanations from Indians, the older women Charlotte approached professed ignorance or turned their backs. But a few years earlier, her friend Ken Hedges had talked with a rancher on whose Canebrake Canyon property appeared more yoni formations. Around 1935, some Kumeyaay rode into their father's ranch to ask if they could bury their grandmother there—where she'd been born. The oldest horseman was a shaman, whose skills included curing rattlesnake bites.

"He told us about those fertility stones up here," the rancher recalled. "He said that when a young girl acquired a man and she didn't have any children right away they would take them up and show them the magic stones." Nearby stood an old Indian shack, possibly where the visitors stayed overnight. Learning of similar sites south of the U.S.-Mexican border, Charlotte drove to Ensenada and learned that Mexico's Kumeyaay women were less reluctant to confirm that they were indeed fertility spots where childless women sought the power to conceive.

No sooner had awareness of Charlotte's graphically illustrated writings gotten around, however, than she found herself decried as "the dirty old lady of archaeology" or sought after as a resource on female-dominated religions. The 1970s were a propitious time for her discoveries. Much as psychologists Freud and Jung, as painter Frank Stella once put it, had generalized that "the mother's body is the primal landscape," spiritual feminists in Europe and America were arguing that belief in a fertility goddess had prevailed during Europe's late Paleolithic period. But her prominence had been usurped by patriarchal priesthoods and ignored by male scholars. These yonis were reminders of her global reach.

But these sites never quite fit the theory. For one thing, there were just too many of them—a scattering of local female entities across hundreds of miles rather than a single female substitute for a male High God. The earth might be female, but she was many yonied. Also, most power spots for the Kumeyaay and their neighbors were associated with shamans who animated places like Taquish Peak, in the San Jacinto Mountains; Bear Shaman Rock near Big Bear Lake; and Mount Kuchumaa, south of San Diego—and they were all male.

One might also expect this feminine dominance to be reflected in puberty rituals. To be sure, Southern California tribes put great importance on rite-of-passage ceremonies. But they paid *equal,* one might even say *complementary,* attention to girls and boys. It was as highly selective and half baked an appropriation of Indian beliefs for today's San Diego running clubs to take Kumeyaay puberty initiations for boys as models for their "wild men" ideology, racing through the Torrey Pines on full moon nights, as it was to turn their female puberty rites into fodder for a goddess ideology imported from old Europe.

During the Indian ceremonies, the youngsters entered brush-enclosed sanctuaries to endure the harangues of elders. This was a time for imparting guidance for proper hunting behavior in separate sessions for boys, for healthy childbearing practices exclusively for girls, and for the locations of the tribe's sacred places for both. These lessons accompanied other instructions about living "straight" rather than "crooked" lives in order to nurture what Alfred Kroeber once characterized as the Southern California Indian ideal: an "open, even, unruffled, slow and pleasant existence."

Initiates were positioned before circular drawings of the cosmos that, with powdered minerals on the sanctuary floor, depicted their cosmologies and important stars, mountains, islands and sacred animals. And in striking contrast to Socrates' warnings to the young, as Plato quotes him in the *Phaedrus,* that "trees and open country" could not teach them anything, that they needed schools and texts, these Indian boys were told, "The earth hears you, the sky and wood mountain see you. If you will believe this you will grow old." Pubescent girls received similar instructions: "Pay heed to this speech, and when you are old like these old people, you will counsel your sons and daughters in like manner, and you will die old. And your spirit will rise northwards to the sky, like the stars, moon and sun."

Straddling the invisible, arbitrary line that was drawn by diplomats in 1848 between Mexico and the United States is a large mountain. On maps,

the 3,885-foot peak is known as Mount Tecate, but to the Kumeyaay Indians on both sides of the border, it is *Kuuchamaa,* alternately translated as
"Exalted High Place" or "The Ones That Cure." Its three-peaked profile is
the background of Tecate beer labels, the brewery of which perfumes the
air over the border town of the same name, about fifty-five miles southeast
of San Diego. Running like a skunk's stripe across its slopes is a mowed
swath with a high barbed-wire fence that is patrolled by the U.S. Department of Homeland Security's four-wheel-drives and helicopters. This
mountain is a prime symbol of the politically divided identity with which
the Kumeyaay have coped for many years.

For Indians from the four states who stand shoulder to shoulder from
the Gulf of Mexico to the Pacific Ocean the international border cut their
societies in two. This increasingly tense border zone, usually defined as one
hundred kilometers (62.14 miles) north and south of the U.S.-Mexico
boundary, holds approximately sixty indigenous nations and communities. To their confusion and dismay, the Kickapoo, Tohono O'dham, Apache
and Kumeyaay, accustomed to crossing freely to visit kinfolk, attend fu-
nerals, gather plants or visit sacred places, were turned back if they lacked
proper documents. In the 1990s, Operation Gatekeeper, a U.S. effort to
clamp down on illegal immigration from Mexico, strengthened patrols
and toughened this screening; after 9/11 and under the Department of
Homeland Security the border began to feel more like a war zone.

If a sacred mountain like Tecate had to be owned by a white man, one
could hardly find a more sympathetic proprietor than Walter Evans-Wentz.
Born in 1878 in New Jersey, he moved with his family to California when
he was a boy. Of a mystical, romantic turn of mind, Evans-Wentz joined
California's School for the Revival of the Lost Mysteries of Antiquity when
he was in his twenties. At Stanford University, he studied with William
Butler Yeats; at Oxford, in England, his dissertation was a sympathetic study
of the Celtic fairy faith. Trapped in Greece by World War I, a former class-
mate, T. E. Lawrence, steered him to Sri Lanka and hence north India,
where he encountered theosophists, gurus, western seekers and Tibetan
monks. There Evans-Wentz lived and traveled for years while translating
texts such as the Tibetan Book of the Dead.

Although free of financial worries, upon returning to the United

States, Evans-Wentz holed up in a dingy hotel in downtown San Diego. Soon the mountain he called Cuchama became an obsession; ranch by ranch, acre by acre, he began buying it up. Mystics and friends wended their way to the stone retreat he built on the American side of Mount Tecate. During his final days in the 1960s, Evans-Wentz championed his property as a New World counterpart to the great peaks and pilgrimage centers he'd visited in the Himalayas and south India. Like Kailas in Tibet, Emei in China and Arunchala in India, believed Evans-Wentz, Tecate was supposedly positioned on the grid of magnetic lines that carried peaceful vibrations around the earth. From one interview with an old Kumeyaay he also got the impression that it was one of the tribe's four sacred mountains and the site of creation itself.

But strong exception to Evans-Wentz's New Agey generalizations was taken by anthropologist Florence Shipek. Having interviewed Kumeyaay elders since the late 1950s, in connection with the tribe's land-and-water-rights cases and petitions to win U.S. recognition (which finally came to the Jamul community in 1981), Shipek argued that nowhere in the literature on the tribe was Kuuchamaa associated with flood myths; none of her consultants made it central to their cosmology, and it was never depicted on those ritual sand paintings.

Undoubtedly it was highly "sacred" to them, but its power was double edged; Delfina Cuero, one of Shipek's most knowledgeable Kumeyaay friends, remembered would-be "witches" heading there to acquire danger-ous powers. Only trained Kumeyaay shaman-priests (*kusiyaay*) knew how to access the mountain's healing powers. For her 1981 dossier supporting Tecate's candidacy as a National Heritage Site, Shipek elaborated on Ku-uchamaa's role in Kumeyaay beliefs.

During the world's creation, their Creator, Maayhaay, placed the moun-tain in its present location. Assigning it as the home of a paramount male spirit and shaman named Kuuchamaa, he designated its powers be used for healing and peace. There the seer Kuuchamaa taught his people the *horloi* dance, whose practice ultimately wore a circular groove into the moun-taintop, and in its hidden caves shamans sought their power dreams. There they competed in demonstrations of their extraordinary powers (one such duel left a sharp split on one slope), and there they preferred to be cremated after they died. Among the secrets that the Kumeyaay shared with Shipek about Mount Kuuchamaa were place-names which suggested a broader land-body association. On the southwest lay a healing spring called "God's Tears," a slope to the west was named "Meadow at the Base of the Nostrils," a sand bar on its seaward side was called "the Mouth," east of that meadow and at right angles to Mount Tecate lay Otay Mountain, known as "the Nose." As Shipek imagined herself looking down on this landscape from on high, "One can conceptualize a face represented by these mountains," she wrote, "with Tecate Peak, or *Kuchamaa,* as the forehead, containing the brain, and to the Kumeyaay, the place of power as well as knowledge."

To see Mount Tecate for myself, I drove to the border one July morning, parked on the American side and walked into Mexico and down Avenida Cardenas to the main *zócalo.* Under the tree canopy, mariachis in unbuttoned *charro* jackets milled about wiping their brows with large handkerchiefs, their *guitarrones* propped on park benches. Nobody was buying from displays of toy windmills or plastic versions of the Virgin of Guadalupe. Some kids licked cones around the *helado* carts. A few gringos in Bermuda shorts furtively slipped into *farmacias* for cheap prescription drugs. Strolling past a table heaped with silvery geodes, I talked with the vendor, an unshaven old man in torn serape, straw sombrero and one good eye. He pointed to his handwritten sign announcing an upcoming gathering of *tribus.* In the shadow of La Sagrada Montaña del Cuchama, it said, come to four days of dance and oration to honor "the ancient tribes, mother earth, the great spirit." He shook a finger at me, "You go, you go."

Three weeks later I crossed the border again, taking the Ensenada highway for about nineteen miles to the Rancho Viejo turnoff. From various books, I knew that all around me were old Indian village locations and hideouts from which, two hundred years earlier, Spanish soldiers had dragged out Indians and taken them to San Diego. Following red arrows painted on rocks, I twisted along thinning dirt roads until I pulled alongside a pack of old cars and pickups. Enclosed by surrounding hills that resembled piles of house-sized boulders, booming sounds came from a circular open-air dance arbor. The scene recalled a friend's daughter, increasingly excited as she approached the Santa Ana Pueblo plaza during the winter fiesta, and yelling back, "Mama, Mama, I can smell the drums."

Forty or fifty dancers wove around a central altar built of concrete blocks and plastered over with fresh adobe mud to resemble a miniature, Aztec-style stepped pyramid. Its tiers sprouted burning candles, bundles of feathers, figurines, burning incense—all topped by a fragile sapling with a few leaves sticking into the air. One arbor facing the dance ground sheltered long-haired elders from a range of Mexican Indian tribal groups— Cochimi, Cucupa, Yaqui, Pai-Ipai and Kilihua. Whenever the dancers passed by them, a few peeled off to bend down, exchange handshakes, chuckle together and pat backs. Everyone seemed to know everyone else. Outside the arena, other men and women, swathed in towels and blankets, were coming and going from dome-shaped, tarp-covered sweat lodges; near the parked vehicles vendors sold Huichol and Tarahumara crafts and serapes.

The gathering resembled no powwow in my experience: Chicano "Aztec" dancers in sequined breechcloths, armbands and breastplates, with tall pheasant feathers bouncing atop elaborate headdresses; Plains Indian-style war dancers in hair roaches, anklet bells and feather bustles; mustached men in homemade turkey-feather bonnets and armor-hard rawhide ponchos reminiscent of the Indo-Hispanic "Comanche Dance" regalia of New Mexican folk dramas; Asian-looking and Indian-looking folks of all ages.

With each new "round," out came a different drum—the sharp tones of Aztec hollowed-log *huehuetls,* the booming dance-band drums used by American powwow singers, the insistent beats of handheld tom-toms. Some dances saw serpentine lines of dancers mimicking their leader's song and movements, much like southeastern "stomp dances." Others seemed free-form improvisations, like cavorting Northern Plains war dancers. No orthodoxy prevailed—women in T-shirts, long skirts and tennis shoes bounced around with babes in arms alongside old men holding gourd rattles and revolving in place as if in trance. I sensed the easier familiarity with body movement of Mexicans for whom dancing at birthdays, name days, family reunions, national and religious holidays is commonplace.

One Aztec-attired dancer seemed a master of ceremonies, allowing for prayers at intervals, striding about and orating in Spanish, maintaining the flow of dance rounds, blowing a giant conch-shell trumpet. During the afternoon break, I joined the line around his orange nylon tent for a private consultation. Sweat poured down his chest, and he gulped at a plastic water jug. He hailed from Morelia; as a teenager he'd joined the Grupo de la Montaña dance troupe. Occasionally he visited Los Angeles, but mostly served indigenous gatherings south of the border.

Others were eager for his time, so I handed him a book of mine and rose to leave. Pleased, he flipped through it. Reaching into his embroidered kit bag he extended a hawk feather wrapped in colored cloth at the quill. Regretfully I told him that the border guards would recognize an endangered species, we *blancos* weren't allowed to even handle these feathers. He laughed and pressed it against my chest, *"El gavilán no respeta las fronteras,"* he said. (The hawk knows no borders.)

For a newcomer to Los Angeles in the late 1990s, the presence of old Indian places in my vicinity, sacred or secular, came as a surprise. Already working on this book, I almost felt as if my subject was stalking me. My introduction to the Los Angeles expression of what scholar Brian Swann has termed the "shadow geography" that underlies many urban veneers came from a UCLA graduate student named Cindi Alvitre. Swann used the phrase to evoke the traces of old Indian lifeways within my old Lower East Side neighborhood in New York. Now I learned of similar shadows alongside Lincoln Boulevard, only blocks from my new apartment.

Cindi's background was not uncommon for a Southern California woman of native descent. When she was a girl in Orange County, her mother, a Tarascan Indian, called herself Mexican-American. Her father, a Gabrielino Indian with ancestors from both mainland and island Indian lineages, declared he was Mission Indian. From girlhood on, Cindi self-identified as "Native," although she eventually joined those who recouped their original name. Today she is a forty-nine-year-old grandmother; former chair of the Los Angeles Tongva-Gabrielino tribal council; a founding member of the tribe's Tiat, or plank-boat society; and a graduate student in cultural studies at UCLA. Today she also calls herself Tongva-Gabrielino and has reconnected to her ancestral home place, Catalina Island.

Her father was difficult, tough and inspiring. He was a construction worker, abalone diver, part-time crooner and U.S. Marine for twelve years, and his changing jobs kept the family on the move, shifting around Spanish-speaking neighborhoods in Santa Ana, Huntington Beach or Garden Grove. "In the old days they were known as *colonias*," says Cindi, "now I guess they'd be called barrios. But no matter where we lived, Dad made it a point that we always understood that, as Indians from here, we were always *home*, and that every place had a story."

He was ahead of his time. For decades Southern Californians with native blood preferred to pass as Mexican-American in order to avoid the stereotypical associations that were especially virulent in the Los Angeles basin after 1850—lazy, drunken digger Indians. Family lore identified her paternal great-grandmother as a Pimuvit, meaning a native of Pimu, or Santa Catalina Island. Forcibly removed in the 1820s, she was taken to San Juan Capistrano Mission and bore her father's father in Anaheim. "My father loved the outdoors; the ocean was dear to his heart." Cindi remembers their hangouts at the old Dana Point jetty and the stories he told that instilled caution, such as not looking at low-lying shooting stars; the story of Taqusch, who devoured women; and the dangers of poisonous "frog magic," which had caused her own great-great-aunt to go blind.

Wedged between Chumash and Luiseno territory, the beaches and three river basins that constitute today's greater Los Angeles cover perhaps fifteen hundred square miles. Before 1750, they were once home to 40 or 50 Tongva-Gabrielino Indian villages, each containing some 50 to 150 members. Organized into extended family lineages, they shared a common language, religious beliefs and eventually their forced consolidation at either the Capistrano or the San Gabriel Catholic Mission compounds. Originally built in 1771 close to the San Gabriel River, in what is today's Whittier Narrows, San Gabriel was soon relocated more safely above the river's flood level.

After the missions were secularized in 1834–36 and Americans turned

Spanish ranches in the basin into California's first wineries, a "day without an Indian" in the 1850s and 1860s might resemble a "day without a Mexican" 150 years later. Over time, Los Angeles forgot its original debt to Indian sweat and muscle. Back then it jailed Indians by the hundreds for vagrancy or drunkenness on Friday, and put them on chain gangs or auctioned them off the following Monday for four months of indentured field work. Paid in cheap liquor when their "sentence" was worked off, many Indians remained in this vicious cycle. Until the Indentured Servitude Act, which had legalized this servitude, was repealed in 1863, forced Indian labor maintained the area's vineyards, fed and bred its cattle herds, built the city center's first homes and streets and cleaned private residences.

Unlike the spread-out hamlets of the surviving Kumeyaay Indian groups inland, a number of which remained temporarily out of harm's way, early Los Angeles had little room for local Gabrielinos once this founding period was past. Following the familiar Mission Indian experience of disease, conversion, rebellion, secularization and poverty, many of them willingly lost identity as they intermarried into the Spanish-speaking barrios of surrounding counties or submerged themselves with the Basques, Italians and other disenfranchised of downtown's infamous "Nigger Alley." Not for another century would their mixed-blood descendants reclaim some semblance of their indigenous identity.

The city's Indians went underground, but the Los Angeles Basin retained what Swann calls "subliminal imprints" of their presence. Place-names echoed those who first settled here—Malibu, Cahuenga, Sespe, Topanga. Near my UCLA office was a little pool called Indian Springs, I was informed by my Mexican neighbor shortly after I moved in. Why the name? He didn't know, except that his father, a street peddler, always made sure his rounds passed there because the waters were sweet. But out of these drainage slopes, sunken alleys and shell middens, the "shadow geography" of the older, native Los Angeles in my neighborhood was about to rise up.

An independent-minded teenager, Cindi had married out of high school, moved to Alaska with her native Inupiat husband, had borne two daughters and learned to catch and smoke fish and knit heavy sweaters from her mother-in-law. Returning to Los Angeles as a single mom, she found her-

self in the thick of a native resurgence. "It was the midseventies, the cusp
of so much. The Capistrano tribal council was formed around that time;
the state's Native American Heritage Commission was got going. People
were talking about new environmental laws protecting sacred places.
There were protests over development and graveyards."

Before leaving La Quinta High School, Cindi had organized an Indian
club; her activist impulses resurfaced in the mid-1970s as she supported
the organization of the Capistrano Tribal Council. In that decade, protection for burial grounds, what writer Dolan H. Eargle, Jr., calls "the most
sacred places in Indian country . . . where the remains of those passed on
lie," became a rallying issue. Land developers working on or near old
Tongva-Gabrielino Indian sites kept finding Indian bones. One of Cindi's
first protests, in 1978, concerned a housing project around nine old Indian
sites in the vicinity of Turtle Rock, in Irvine County's San Joaquin Hills.
Then came the Prado Dam project, in the Anaheim Hills, which threatened to drown a number of old village locations and, despite Indian out-
cry, did. Whether they were facing construction of new racetracks, penal
institutions or freeways, Los Angeles Indians, now forming into a handful
of activist groups, were refusing to give up their pasts or their ancestors
without a fight.

By the late 1980s, the designation Tongva-Gabrielino, not Mission Indian, was heard more often, and site by embattled site, Southern California
was acknowledging its native heritage. My neighbor's old "Indian Springs,"
for instance, was soon formally named Kuruvungna Spring; today one can
visit it at Westwood's University High School by appointment only. Also
resurrected was the powerful twenty-two-acre village of *Puvungna,* on the
California State University at Long Beach campus. Since the early nineteenth century, this site had been identified as the Tongva-Gabrielino ritual
capital, where both their creator-god (*Chinigchinix*) and their first chief
(*Wewyoot,* who became the moon) were born. But it took an extended occupation by an eighty-four-year-old part-Indian woman in 1993 to get
campus officials to turn down a proposed strip mall on the land.

Throughout Tongva-Gabrielino country were other villages and burial
grounds. Too often Cindi's friends were not alerted to plans like those at
Long Beach, so they could not publicize their opposition. In the early 1990s,

excavations for a new Los Angeles Metropolitan Water District headquarters in downtown Los Angeles, across from the Olvera Street tourist zone, turned up twenty-three graves and goods intended to sustain the dead in the afterlife, probably associated with the major Tongva-Gabrielino village of Yangna. Flouting legal requirements, the requisite archaeological reports were never released to the general public, much less to possible native descendants.

When I moved to Los Angeles, the basin's last chunk of undeveloped real estate was the thousand or more acres surrounding the mouth of Ballona Creek, an area the Gabrielino knew as *Pwinukipar,* or "Full of Water." Located just south of Marina del Rey, this delta of beaches, lagoons and brackish marshes was now called the Ballona Wetlands. Once the property and airplane hangar of legendary Howard Hughes, its proposed future heated up in the 1980s in a struggle between developers and environmentalists. For drivers taking Lincoln Boulevard to the Los Angeles Airport, the open stretch offered fresh air and great views. As Marina del Rey retreated in one's rearview mirror it was possible to gaze over the cocklebur and pickleweed prairie and take in a sunset at the edge of the continent. Then the road curved uphill, slipping between Loyola Marymount College, which hugged the heights to the left and the softly undeveloped Westchester Bluffs to the right, before a straight shot to one's flight.

Few knew that this passage also cut through the Tongva-Gabrielino Indian past. Tussling over the wetlands' fate intensified during the 1990s. But the first time Indians learned what they might lose on the natural cliffs of El Segundo Sand Hills, which rise about 170 feet above the wetlands, came in June 2003. As they worked their way across 44 acres of prime overlook, preparing for construction of a gated community that would contain 114 million-dollar luxury homes, the bulldozers hit bones and grading momentarily halted. For their part, archaeologists were not particularly surprised; on some maps the mouth of Ballona Creek was identified as the general location for *Saangna,* a major Tongva-Gabrielino village.

Using her personal familiarity with regional archaeologists and easier access as a tribal representative, Cindi got me clearance to visit the high ground, roughly the size of a football field, a few weeks later. By then, hard-hat-wearing monitors of Tongva-Gabrielino descent and one native person designated as the MLD—an individual whose genealogy made her or him a Most Likely Descendant of the location's traditional occupants—were overseeing the archaeology.

The bulldozers had resumed operation, peeling up tons of earth to level the homesites but scrupulously steering around the rising pinnacles of earth where "cultural remains" had been found. Latticing the little summits were rectangular grids of stakes and strings where archaeologists troweled, brushed and recorded the household items belonging to Indians who had lived more than two thousand years ago. Exposed to the growls of machines and dusty winds tearing across the heights were softly curved grinding stones and pounding pestles used by women, chipped-edge stone tools wielded by both sexes, perforated shell beads worn around human necks, whale bones and baked hearths from old fires that had warmed those early Angelenos and their own fragile-looking excavated skulls and skeletons.

Within a week or two, the supervising archaeologist informed me, work would wrap up there. Next on his schedule was the digging of test trenches down below, at the southern edge of the Playa Vista Development acreage whose fate had caused such furor during past decades. That was mostly resolved: Steven Spielberg's proposal for a filmmaking complex was withdrawn, Playa Vista developers won their building permits and environmental protesters were mollified that, west of Lincoln Boulevard at least, a reclaimed stretch of wetlands would reach the sea. Already herons speared fish in recently planted reeds below the reformed Westchester Bluffs. Pairs of mallard ducks paddled within easy sight of a bird-viewing walkway that was bordered by fresh, rural-style, split-rail fencing. Signs educated visitors about native plants and animals, and over the following months the reconstructed ecology was beginning to look museum perfect.

As for that last unprobed patch of Ballona Creek bed just below Loyola Marymount's sleek classrooms, the archaeologist thought it was likely to hold "interesting material." By now construction was winding up on the surrounding condominiums, town houses and corporate buildings that were slated to house some thirteen thousand new residents. All that re-

mained on Playa Vista developer Steve Soboroff's to-do list was an environmental makeover for this corner. Once the mandated archaeological
reconnaisance was done, his master plan for transforming a series of stag-
nant pools and drainage sinks, all that remained after years of mangling
the old Ballona Creek bed, would produce what Soboroff called a "ripar-
ian corridor." Also envisaged was a memorial, including circular symbols
and statuary to be determined, devoted to the region's Indian history.

But in late winter 2004 the appearance of more Indian bones put a
crimp in their plans. As increasing numbers of skeletons rose out of the
ground, e-mails throughout the Southwest's archaeological network lured
dozens of graduate students and part-time excavators for lucrative con-
tract work; soon more than a hundred were hunkered over lumps in the
ground in the shade of big green tents. And week by week the dead body
count grew as well: forty-five, more than a hundred, over two hundred,
with the tally ending at four hundred before lawsuits and gag orders forbade archaeologists and developers from talking about what they were
turning up and quickly packing out of sight.

Reviews of early documents suggested to some archaeologists that the
sites I'd visited up on Westchester Bluffs—by now fully documented and
gone from the face of the earth—were possibly associated with a different
old Tongva port village by the name of *Guaspita*. For this community
Cindi Alviatre might have felt special affinity, since it was said to enjoy
close ties with—and possibly be populated by—Catalina Island (Pimu-
gunga) residents, people like her own father's ancestors. Other archaeologists preferred to tie the new graves to the *Saangna site*.

But from whichever village these forebears hailed, many of their descendants were up in arms about this "scrape and rape" approach to their
past. They had news clippings of Chinese graveyards being preserved
along the breakwater near downtown Victoria, British Columbia, of Jewish cemeteries being respected and retained in downtown Detroit, and of
African Americans and Indians from the nineteenth century allowed to
rest in peace in Flushing, Queens, New York. Why not here?

Years before David L. Belardes, a Juaneno Indian chief who lived in
the same region, had observed the pattern: "The [developers] just want to

fill every nook and cranny. They don't see that there's a value in leaving the land as the Creator meant it to be." And Tongva-Gabrielino writer Gloria Arrellanes now put her plea into poetry:

> I know this much—that you know and understand what is sacred and should not be disturbed because you say, "You cannot move the *Titanic* . . . don't disturb those that are in their watery grave."
>
> Don't disturb their graves . . .
>
> I also know this much—that you know and understand what hallowed ground is because you say, "Where the Twin Towers once stood is hallowed ground . . . it must be respected."
>
> . . . I know and understand this . . . don't disturb the burials . . . leave them undisturbed.
>
> You must understand this.

Once again Cindi arranged my access to the site. When we visited the archaeological tents at Playa Vista in early May the crews were shutting down for the day. The location of rib cages, skulls, basketry remains, ceremonial shells, beads, grinding stones, deer-bone whistles, waterproofed basketry canteens and other personal goods were identified with little plastic flags—again I experienced that sense of trespass and a sinking heart I'd felt as a boy when I saw arrowheads and pipes of old Pautuxant Indian villagers rising out of a freshly cut tobacco field near the Chesapeake Bay.

Each bone was carefully brushed clean, its surrounding dirt sifted and saved. Every burial was laid in its separate cardboard banker's box, which was labeled and stacked with others in metal shipping containers. As we edged around the labyrinth of marked stakes and string-bordered pits, the workers draped torn pieces of cloth over little wire frames above each grave, as if bedding them down for the night. By the time we left, the place looked like a miniature refugee camp.

As the numbers mounted, a Playa Vista lawyer was forced to remind newspaper reporters bluntly that his clients were not legally bound to consider anyone's wishes. Like most of these Southern California remnants, the Tongva were not among the 562 federally recognized Indian tribes.

Eventually, the Playa Vista excavations produced more than five hundred Indian bodies, which had been interred, according to rumors, in broken succession for a period of up to seven thousand years. If so, the site was one of the largest and oldest graveyards in California, if not the country.

By my last drive-by, the dig was over. The shipping containers had been relocated out of sight, to a temporary lab where osteologists had years of work cut out for them. Earthmovers were grading the environmental make-over of Ballona Creek. Its cosmetics had been roughed out—a perfect *S* shape with sheer sloping banks that only awaited implants of new sod and groomed pathways that would lead to the restored wetlands and also to the promised shrine which would honor the unearthed, boxed and dis-placed Indians who had once lived here. And thus, as the Choctaw Indian author Okah Tubbee wrote of his people's forced removal, "The burial ground of the Indian family became the garden spot of the white man."

CHAPTER FIFTEEN

WHERE MOUNTAINS CONGREGATE

Central California

In the early 1870s, a journalist-adventurer named Stephen Powers, who had recently crossed the United States on foot, took two summers to visit California Indian settlements. Backpacking from Yokuts country in the south to Yurok villages in the north, the thirty-one-year-old turned out eighteen articles, mostly for the *Overland Monthly*. Somewhat tainted by the racial prejudices of his day, his reports nonetheless provided invaluable glimpses into a range of little-known Indian communities that, during these years after the Gold Rush had peaked, seemed at death's door.

Powers walked the landscape we call Central California and then some. This mosaic of oceanfront, river valley, coastal and inland mountain ranges with broad valleys in between begins around present-day San Luis Obispo, at the northern boundary of Chumash Indian territory, and extends some over three hundred miles north, to around the Mendocino County line, or the northern end of Pomo Indian country.

During the previous century, these habitats underwent great change, but it was not over yet. Suppressing the controlled burning every fall by Indians of meadows and hillsides in order to enhance growth, Spanish ranchers transformed vast stretches of sage chaparral and native rye into grassy pastures covered with imported strains of broom, mustard and thistle for their multiplying herds of cattle, horses and sheep. Then Anglo-Americans harvested thousands of acres of pine forest for building construction, railroad ties and shoring timbers for mine tunnels. Oak groves were leveled for firewood and tannin (for processing leather), with hogs let loose on their acorns. As commercial mining replaced placer panning, hillsides were stripped of vegetation, allowing for the contamination of watersheds by runoff. In the decade of Powers's visits, hydrolic mining (shooting water through high-powered hoses to wash away the slopes) and pounding slurry to release gold particles sent tons of poisonous mercury into the streams.

Powers was particularly impressed by the personal affection and detailed familiarity that bound these Indians to their besieged surroundings. "The boundaries of all tribes," he noted, "are marked with the greatest precision, being defined by certain creeks, canyons, boulders, conspicuous trees, springs, etc., each of which objects has its own individual name." With their children, "they rehearse all these boulders, etc., describing each minutely and by name, with its surroundings." Then they tested the youngsters for what they'd learned, walking them around the hills to see if they could match the places with the verbal descriptions they'd memorized. Those who passed were more aware of their geography, Powers believed, "than any topographical engineer." A half century later, the life story of a western Mono Indian woman just north of the San Joaquin River epitomized this parochial wisdom: many of her ninety-five years were spent shifting residence—twenty-three times within a thirty-square-mile area whose plant and water and spiritual resources she knew as her own backyard.

One man who appreciated Powers's early picture of California Indians' ecology was University of California archaeologist and anthropologist Robert F. Heizer. At Berkeley he enthralled students with re-creations of native existence on the eve of white contact. Before Sir Francis Drake's brief visit in 1579 among the Miwok of Marin County, he told them, California "held between 500 and 600 . . . independent and separate definable groups," making it the most linguistically and ethnically diverse area in the world. "Living out the span of existence from birth to death within an area bounded by a horizon lying not more than 10 or 15 miles from one's village," he said of Central California Indians in particular, "and not having talked to more than 100 different persons in a whole life, must have made one's world small, familiar, safe and secure."

And these little worlds were everywhere. Along the Feather River, not far from today's state capital of Sacramento, one would have come across a different Maidu village community, each containing a few hundred souls, about every five miles. They knew one another, intermarried and conversed in a common tongue. But on a three-day hike between the present-day cities of Berkeley and Ukiah, Heizer told his students, an outsider such as Powers might have encountered speakers of Ohlone, Bay Miwok, Plains Miwok, Patwin, two different dialects of Cahuilla, three of Wappo, twenty-seven (mostly mutually unintelligible) of Pomo, two of Yukean, eventually reaching Indians who spoke a dialect known only to us as *To-chil'-pe ke'-ah-hahng*. And if the visitor headed back down the San Joaquin Valley, he might have contacted forty to fifty communities who spoke various dialects of Yokuts.

To make sense of this array of minicultures communicating bi- or trilingually in local dialects and exploiting their microhabitats, Heizer's teacher, Alfred Kroeber, sought an alternative to the overreaching word "tribe." A relic from Spanish years, *rancherías* seemed antiquated, nor did "village community" convey their islandlike independence within an ecological niche. He came up with "tribelet," which in the long run proved too cute to catch on. As to the proprietary feelings of these cultural entities toward their homelands, however, the master parted company with both Powers and Heizer. For Kroeber, the natives of California "did not think, like modern civilized man, of his people owning an area circumscribed by a definite line." These Indians grouped themselves by watersheds, with the influence of one thinning out where springs and streams began draining into another.

But Heizer disagreed, believing that the concept of "territory" for California natives was more akin to modern notions. Groups rather than individuals held ownership rights. "The idea that a certain, definable, extent of territory was owned and that the plants, minerals and the like attached to that land were also owned by the claimants," Heizer argued, "is supported by an abundance of statements made by Indians to that effect." For backstory on their disagreement, one of Heizer's students, Dean MacCannell, reminds us that in the 1950s and 1960s his teacher served as an expert witness on behalf of California Indian land claims cases, whereas Kroeber initially worried that anthropologists taking up activist causes would weaken their standards of scientific objectivity.

How their opinions might have changed two decades later, when the focus of court cases concerning Indian lands expanded from defining territories once occupied by humans to protecting those still inhabited by their spirits, is anybody's guess. But to illustrate how sites of a spiritual nature reflected the cultural diversity which captured the imaginations of Powers, Kroeber and Heizer, this chapter visits five mountains of the California Indian heartland.

A Center of Sorts—Mount Diablo

In the center of Contra Costa County, a 3,849-foot mountain swells out of an 18,000-acre state park. On the rare days that fog lifts from the viewing stands atop Mount Diablo, one can see twenty of the state's fifty-eight counties, four mountain ranges and high points two hundred miles away. It is also a prime vantage point for identifying peaks that are prominent in the mythology and religious life of Central California Indians.

But Diablo's summit feels too quickly achieved. Within easy driving distance of San Francisco, San Jose or Silicon Valley, one glides through the well-heeled enclaves of Walnut Creek and Concord and up tight switchbacks to brake at the wind-thrashed 1930s, WPA-style sandstone blockhouse at the crest. Despite the encroaching suburbia, some wildness peeks through. The park preserves sixteen rare or endangered plant and animal species, including the Alameda whip snake and the Diablo globe lily. Around one curve, my car was barred by the heftiest coyote I've ever seen, its needle nose drawing a bead on my grill.

For Indian communities between Mount Lassen, about 180 miles to the north, and Monterey, about the same distance down the coast, the mountain figured in genesis narratives. In the misty era before human existence, say the Bay Miwok, the land lay under water. Only Coyote was left alive, viewing the world from the promontory initially named by the Spanish Cerro de los Bolbones, after a local Miwok subgroup they knew as the Volvons. On the mountain's northern flank, said the Plains Miwok, Condor man once lived, roosting on a rock that was also his wife. After she bore their son, Prairie Falcon man, the boy and his grandfather, Coyote man, created the first people and gave them "everything everywhere so they can live."

On the crest of Diablo, added the Northern Sierra Miwok, a Mouse person named Too-le-loo took the fire he had stolen from the valley to create the sun. Fragments of other now largely forgotten narratives from the Ohlone, Nisenan and Wappo describe Diablo as the place where dogs came from, where oversized snakes hid out and where spirits danced and whistled in the nearby Indian burial grounds. Known as *Tuyshtak* to the Ohlone, *Oj.ompil.e* to the northern Miwok, *Supemenu* to the Southern Miwok, and *Sukku Jaman* to the Nisenan, here at Mount Diablo the Wintu talked to their spirits, the Pomo held ceremonies and the Miwok trekked in for multitribal, weeklong festivals that were held every fall.

Archaeologists believe Indians lived around Mount Diablo well before the time of Christ. By the Spanish arrival, in 1805, six different villages existed around its base. One, about seven miles north, where Buchanan Field stands today, came to the attention of Spanish soldiers as they were rounding up potential converts for the San Jose Mission. But under cover of night, the Indians slipped through a stand of willows and crossed the Carquinez Straits to safety.

Soldiers cursed their brushy escape route as *monte de Diablo*—literally "thicket of the devil." But within a few decades, suggests anthropologist Bev Ortiz, a former Diablo park historian who compiled Indian and Euro-American legends about the place, the designation was mistranslated as Devil Mountain and attached to the nearby heights. As tales often grow taller, other stories soon told of a Spanish run-in with Indians at the foot of Diablo, which featured "an unknown personage, decorated with the most extraordinary plumage" who appeared out of nowhere to rout the soldiers. Other narratives described this feathered spirit so precisely that some believe he was based on Spanish observations of a dancer enacting the feathered regalia of the Maidu Indian deity known as Kuksu.

Mount Diablo's name followed a familiar practice. Demonizing heathen places was long a Euro-Christian strategy in their spiritual conquest of the Americas. Before the expulsion of the Jesuits in 1767, the belief pervaded the Spanish colonies that American Indians were "consecrated to Satan"; in 1693, Cotton Mather had already written that the Devil "generally resembles an Indian." Places where Indians lived and worshipped were often likened to the Prince of Darkness and his underworld. Theologians of the Enlightenment may have put such rhetoric behind them, but it persisted in popular culture. And the practice intensified as whites went west. When Americans learned a lake in Minnesota was *wakan* to various Sioux peoples, meaning it contained spiritual power, they promptly called it Devil's Lake. The more a topography proved an obstacle in the path of progress, the more it seemed to acquire its Devil's Canyon, Hell's Half Acre or Dead Indian Creek.

As the Franciscan Felipe Arroyo, in charge of the San Juan Bautista mission, characterized local native beliefs in 1814, "When an Indian dies his soul would remain in their sacred places which the sorceress had for the purpose of asking pardon from the devil," after which the spirit wended its way to the western lands. The inability of contemporary American Indians to change designations such as Devil's Tower in Wyoming and Mount Diablo in California demonstrates the persistence of that tactic of conquest which scholars call "diabolism in New Spain."

North—Histum Yani, the Middle Mountain

Shards of myths and legends cling to other peaks in Diablo's orbit. About ninety miles north, a second, six-peaked "mountain island" lifts above the flatlands. Identified on the map as the Sutter or Marysville Buttes, the Maidu Indians esteemed the place as *Histum Yani,* or the "Middle Mountain."

As with the diverse settlements and dialect groups that are lumped as Miwok, the Maidu were no single nation. Occupying foothills and lowlands between the valley and the lower Sierras, their relatively self-sufficient, sovereign villages extended from Big Chico Creek down to the Yuba and Sacramento rivers. What partly united them was an understanding that certain rocks, glades, trees and springs were *ku'kini,* "places with power," and peopled by spirits.

For the Valley Maidu this cluster of extinct volcanoes lifting out of the Sacramento Valley was among the most potent. A compact assemblage of rocky spires, meadows, trees, caves and waterfalls, the buttes seem modeled by some pre-Cambrian bonsai master who cupped the Coast Range and the Sierra Nevada between his hands around 1.9 and 1.3 million years ago and squeezed magma through the valley's skin to spill hot rhyolite over the surface; then cooling temperatures, rainstorms and winds articulated the North and South Buttes, burnished the lower hills and attracted plants, animals, spirits and humans. Today the buttes are surrounded by rice fields, orchards, marshes and mysterious remnants of rock walls built by Chinese labor in the late nineteenth century.

Promoted by locals as America's smallest mountain range, the buttes are where the Maidu Indians say this earth began. Joining forces with his folksy cocreator, Coyote, the somber deity known as Earth Maker anchored a floating bird's nest in the water-covered world by means of four ropes braided from feathers. From dirt that his assistant, a mythic Turtle, brought up from the depths, Earth Maker then formed the world's topography on the nest. After creating the sun and moon, he and Turtle rested at the Middle Mountain. But then Earth Maker climbed up the butte's sacred North Peak, with its hollowed rock that one can reach by carved toe- and handholds, and pronounced, according to Maidu elder Lizzie Enos, "Now I will finish that for which the world was made. Now I shall give life to mankind, that he may use all that has been created." And after men, women and society were established, it was at the buttes that the Hesi, a central dance of the Maidu Kuksu religion, was instituted.

As humans were born at Middle Mountain, there they also bade farewell. Following death, and the proper burning of their property, the souls or "hearts" of the deceased retraced their lifetimes and relived their deeds. Only then were their spirits ready to enter a mysterious cavern in the buttes, eat food only palatable to spirits, replicate the experiences of the first man created by Earth Maker and Coyote and undergo a ritual washing before ascending to *Yo'ngkodo,* or the "Flower Land."

Only one word was needed for the Maidu spring season: *yo-meni,* or "flowers." Early Spaniards could hardly believe California's fields, "all abloom with different kinds of wildflowers of all colors," as Father Juan Crespi wrote in 1770, "all one mass of blossom, great quantities of white, yellow, red, purple and blue ones. . . ." Surely, believed the Maidu, no afterlife could improve on this, and hence it was known as the Flower World.

With their aromas, colors, seasonality and sexuality, the short, fragile but annually renewed life of flowers often evoke whatever more lasting and hopeful might lie beyond this earthly coil. And like migratory birds on their thousand-mile flyways or grizzly bears prowling the continental divide, such evocations can transcend human borders and cover lots of ground. Beginning in the highlands of southern Mexico, one can trace the attractions of flower imagery to Indians up into Central California.

With their floating gardens known as *chinampas,* the Aztecs cultivated those powers and associations near their ceremonial centers. Out in the countryside, the religious imaginations of Mexico's Indians put the seasonal miracle of blossoms in the thirsty, thorny desert to the service of myth and ritual. Magic mushroom-eating shamans of the southern Mexican Mazatec sang of a divine "flower world," as did the northern Mexican Yaqui when picturing the wilderness world of their pre-Catholic spirits.

In north-central California, Wintu women took their names from wildflowers. When Stephen Powers visited the Konkow Maidu at Round Valley, friends sneaked him into secret ceremonies held in their earth-roofed dance hall, where he recorded such lyrics as "My father formed me out of the sky, I sing among the mountain flowers, I sing among the flowering chamisa of the mountains." Before the Weda, or "Flower Dance," when the Maidu celebrated springtime, women went gathering. "Some women like poppies, and some women like different kinds of flowers," said Lizzie Enos, "they fix the flowers, put them on their heads, around their necks, over the shoulders, everyplace . . . they dressed in flowers." At the celebration's finale, the dancers tossed their garments of flowers and leaves into the river and jumped in after them.

Not far to the east of the Sutter Buttes, the discovery of gold on January 24, 1848, launched what one historian has called "the world's greatest stag party." With its epicenter near a Maidu camp at Coloma on the American River, this frenzied period crushed Indian lives and landscapes. Within three years an estimated hundred thousand rough-and-ready invaders staked claims to their hills and rivers. Initially, Indian miners outnumbered whites, but they were soon shunted aside; one state senator proposed other options, "Better to drive them at once into the ocean, or bury them in the land of their birth."

Thousands of Indians perished from starvation, disease and outright murder. Most Maidu remaining alive in 1863 were force-marched to the

Round Valley Reservation. By 1890, only a thousand Konkow and Nisenan Maidu were left alive, down from an estimated eight thousand before the "world rushed in." Meanwhile, the environment was ravaged, streams poisoned, tule marshes drained, wildfowl, elk and antelope slaughtered. For the thirty-five thousand square miles affected by the Gold Rush, the period between 1850 to 1865 witnessed, according to environmental historian Raymond Dasmann, the greatest destruction of wildlife for its period in the world.

Responding to the catastrophe, a loosely linked series of Nevada and California Indian prophets created their Ghost Dance—twenty years before the Plains Indian religious movement of the same name that climaxed with the Wounded Knee massacre. Desperately their followers prayed for apocalyptic release—this doomed world destroyed by fire or flood, a restored environment devoid of whites—and sang of their longing for the Flower World in a time when heaven seemed the only safe place.

> There above, there above
> On the roof
> Of the Earthlodge of the South
> Spirits dance
> And fall
> Flowers bend
> On their stems.
>
> We shall go
> Along the Flowery path
> Above we shall go
> Along the Milky Way we shall go
> Above we shall go.

West—Mount Tamalpais

Forty miles west of Mount Diablo, another suburban mountain looks over the Pacific Ocean. But the spiritual prominence that Mount Tamalpais has assumed for non-Indians eclipses any role it played in Coastal Miwok Indian life. In the spring of 1987, the date of August eighteenth was publicized by devotees of astrology and ancient Maya timekeeping as a magical moment when nine planets would form two equilateral triangles in the night sky. Around the world, members of alternative faiths scheduled "heal the earth" festivals for that day. In Marin County, veterans of 1960s "happenings" gravitated toward their old stomping grounds—the 6,200 acres of Mount Tamalpais State Park and its 2,751-foot mountain. "Every place is a sacred site, in a sense," said a local San Rafael organizer, but none were as suitable as "Tam" for an international music festival to celebrate this Harmonic Convergence.

Because Mount Tam is relatively unencumbered by remembered usage or present importance to Miwok Indians, few outsiders take note of its native past. Among those who try are dance innovator Anna Halprin, who cited that ancestry during the World Peace Dance Ritual, which she created on the mountain in 1988, and author Etel Adnan, whose book mentions "the Indian goddess," which Tam "used to be," and "the Indian . . . everywhere in the fog, totally a spirit" before he turns to the mountains of Egyptian and Buddhist traditions.

Yet there may be darker reasons for leaving Tam to its secrets. Fragments of Indian commentary gathered by anthropologist Bev Ortiz suggest a shadow side to the mountain's personality. From one Miwok leader she heard rumors of its being a "poison" place, where malevolent shamans sought power to harm rather than cure. When one reviews the written record on California Indian spirituality there is no avoiding the fact that many prayers and rituals were preoccupied with deflecting or defending against the worst that unpredictable fate or intentional evil can bring—and both might erupt from landscape.

For in the native view, the Sacred is rarely a stable, unitary or altogether benign category. The positive or negative powers of some landscapes and sites can be active or dormant, depending on time of year or receptivity of the petitioner. Superhuman energies can empower or destroy, as the contradictory connotations of the Latin root for "sacred" suggest, referring either to a "mystical aura of positive grace" or to a "sinister devotion" to infernal spirits, as anthropologist Raymond Firth puts it. Within the Latin word *daemon* exists a similar ambiguity: depending on the context it can mean "attendant power" or "evil spirit." Even the word "territory" can embody this ambivalence, as some suggest it derives from *territo + rium*, signifying "a place from which people are warned off." The extraordinary forces that inhabit or are manifested by particular locations, clouds, trees or rocks, or are the possession of animals and insects can work for or against humans; some are definitely better known for wreaking havoc than for bestowing blessings. And with an even broader range of such entities or their avatars, one is still never entirely sure. In the same way that we admire certain individuals for their "demonic" energy, we may still keep them at arm's length.

Throughout California were locations that Indian youngsters were warned against because of being "haunted" and "poisonous," in much the same way that ancient Greeks passed on knowledge of "sick" places that were infested by the *keres*, invisible spirits of death. Yet precisely to such locations were attracted would-be sorcerers, in hopes of gaining those skills and secrets for doing wrong. They included places such as *A-Kah* to the Yurok, a granite dome in the northern Siskiyou Mountains, the "center of the dark side of the world, where," says anthropologist Tim Buckley, "'bad doctors' get the strongest of their revolting powers." Along the Mendocino coast, the Pomo shamans known as Bear Doctors stored their death-dealing regalia in hollow trees, which everyone else regarded as dangerous and off-limits. Neighbors to the Miwok, the Wintu talked of "bad places," which were inhabited by half-coyote, half-wolf spirits, whom one dare not disturb by loud or offensive noises; and the Tongva-Gabrielino of Southern California remember the story behind Frog Place, where a mythic amphibian outmaneuvered Coyote with magic forces that still reside there today.

Across the bay from Mount Tamalpais lived the linguist-ethnographer who spent much of his career delving into such dark venues. Jaime de Angulo wrote ethnographic and fictional work that often contrasted native and white ideas of power. In the preface to what Ezra Pound deemed his best novella, called *The Lariat*, de Angulo warned his readers

> Beware, white man, of playing
> with magic of the primitive. It
> May be strong medicine. It may

kill you. Ye, sons and daughters,
foster children of the cities, if ye
would go in the wilderness in
search of your Mother, be careful
& circumspect, lest she lure you
into her secret places, whence ye
may not come back.

Place Like a Gaping Mouth—Breaking Through Landscape

About 135 miles east of Mount Diablo lifts the great wall of the High Sierras. Sunken in its midst is a sheer-sided, well-watered gorge that extends for about seven miles, which was known to the Southern Sierra Miwok Indian residents as *Awahni,* or "Place Like a Gaping Mouth." By the time Stephen Powers hiked through it in 1871, the surviving residents were lying low. Twenty years earlier the first military expedition sent to punish these Indians for assaulting whites had entered from the west. At Inspiration Point, the Mariposa Battalion became only the second group of outsiders to gaze upon one of the world's unforgettable vistas—Yosemite Valley.

In this stronghold, Indians hunted and foraged four thousand years ago; around 100 B.C. they established settlements along the valley's Merced River. It's unclear when direct ancestors of the Miwok moved in to hollow out the bedrock mortars, grind the clamshell beads and work the soapstone by which archaeologists distinguish their remains today. One scholar has tallied some thirty-seven of their permanent villages, summer settlements and seasonal campsites in the valley. By 1898 only six Sierra Miwok communities were left, along with forty-seven outlying settlements, all within a stretch of twenty-three miles.

Sustaining their families was the valley's abundant stock of trout, quail, grouse, deer, bear, smaller mammals, acorns, manzanita berries and "256 species of plants found in seven different plant communities," which ethnobotanist Kat Anderson says the Miwok had named and used for food, basketry and medicine. Every fall they groomed Yosemite by setting it afire to clear underbrush, resupply mature oaks with sunlight and nutrients, attract deer to head-level browse and create what some have compared to a

European game park. At the same time, they blazed Yosemite's first trade routes—west through Nevada Falls and Indian Canyon to Mono country, and also across the Wawona-Fresno Flats to the eastern foothills.

As a guide, Stephen Powers had Old Jim, a Miwok whom local whites complained was unreliable but whom Powers found well informed, even wise. Half Dome the Indian called *To-ke-ye,* the Merced was *Wa-kal'-la,* west of El Capitan loomed the mountain called *Kai-al'-a-wa,* Bridal Veil Falls was *Po-ho-no,* and so on. The stories that Old Jim and later Indians told scholars about Yosemite opened with their Genesis. That was when cannibal giants like U-wu-lin and Yel-lo-kin preyed on the First People; saviors like Fly and Eagle fought them off; Coyote created Yosemite's trees, streams and rocks; while Evening Star, Mountain Lion, Raven, Skunk and Gray Fox acquired the characteristics by which we recognize them today.

The next chapter of Miwok origin stories put people in the picture. Coyote sent Frog under the waters that covered the land to bring up handfuls of sand, and then food plants, men and women, and the sun for light and warmth. But Meadowlark persuaded him to let people die so the earth would not have to support too many of them.

A web of kinship bound the Miwok to this habitat. All creatures, places and planets were classified under either Earth (*tunuka*) or Water (*kikua*) categories. When talking about any of them, it was critical to identify to which "side" they belonged. Each tribal member, too, was classified this way. The Miwok learned who belonged to which by deciphering their personal names, which was critical to find out since one always married into the opposite side, or moiety.

Their geography reflected this division. North of the Merced River was the Land side, commonly called the Grizzly Bear Side; south lay the Water Side. That it was also known as the Coyote Side sounds counterintuitive, since they are land travelers. But the tie-in becomes clearer when one learns that Miwok mythology claims that Coyote himself originated from the "ocean beyond the sea." All these symbolic linkages connected humans to places and animals through sympathetic bonds of story and kinship.

After hearing how the Miwok had acculturated their valley, Powers was dismayed that Yosemite's takeover by whites included slapping "melodramatic and dime-novel" titles on its waterfalls and cliffs: Virgin Tears, Cataract of Diamonds, Goddess of the Valley. The valley's major booster, John Muir, hailed its natural "temples" and "cathedrals," and so one was dubbed. Old Jim would mutter of this meddling: "White man too much lie."

As with many of his environmental heirs, living Indians disappointed Muir. After coming into the Yosemite Valley in 1868, he was more interested in publicizing its emotional impact on him than in asking about its loss to Yosemite's native inhabitants. Muir might have sounded like a Taos Pueblo elder when he said of the Hetch Hetchy Valley that "no holier temple has ever been consecrated by the heart of man" and praised the "spiritual nature" of his "holy Yosemite," but he found the Miwok themselves "dirty," "deadly" and "squirrelish."

One wishes that Muir had engaged the Miwok personally, the way Stephen Powers did, or the way British playwright David Hare sought native perspectives when he visited Israel some years ago. As I read Hare's accounts in his 1998 theatrical monologue *Via Dolorosa,* I could not help projecting what Hare heard from one politician upon the sentiments of silenced American Indians like the Miwok. Surely Old Jim and his people felt the same sort of "mineral reaction" to place that Hare was told about (and which he heard about from Palestinians as well). Surely to them, too, "the emotion of these places was the very history . . . this is us," as the man added. As with the Miwok, a great deal of what had happened in Israeli past had also transpired within twenty-five miles of their conversation. Like the Israelis (and the Palestinians), the Miwok could identify the rocks where sacred figures fought against demons and oppressors and places where culture heroes taught them how to live properly and unseen spirits could still be contacted. "We're crippled without it," the Israeli told Hare, and his words could have come out of Miwok mouths, but Muir never elicited them.

And lest this comparison seem far-fetched, two years before Muir died in 1914 he could have read similar sentiments by another bearded white man who walked all over north-central California in the late nineteenth century and did talk with Indians: "We who trace our origin back to the monkey . . . or who believe in and search far and wide for the Garden of

Eden," wrote the wife of the intrepid folklorist-adventurer Jeremiah Curtin, after he had spent a season with the Modoc Indians, "cannot revere a country which is ours simply by chance of birth as the Indian reveres the country where his tribe originated. We cannot estimate the love an Indian has for his country. His holy places are not in far-off Palestine; they are before his eyes in his own birthplace, where every river, hill and mountain has a story connected with it, an account of its origin."

On the heels of Yosemite's territorial conquest came its aesthetic usurpation. Whether in the form of paintings or photographs, most of the monumental representations that opened Yosemite to railroads and tourism erased Indians from their scenes. When an 1886 view of the valley by Albert Bierstadt recently came up for auction, a Sotheby's expert observed, "It's very peaceful, as though it was meant to be light after a tragedy." Refusing to accept a reservation near Fresno, the resident chief of the Yosemite Miwok, named Tenaya, lived that tragedy. Soldiers hounded his people out of their homes, his son was lost in battle, and in 1853 he was killed by neighboring Mono Indians, but not before uttering a famous curse, recalled by Mariposa Expedition chronicler Lafayette Bunnell twenty years after he heard it. "Yes, American," said Tenaya, "my spirit will make trouble for you and your people . . . I will not leave my home but be with the spirits among the waterfalls, in the rivers and in the winds . . . you will fear the spirit of the old chief, and grow cold. . . ."

My last visit to Yosemite was in midfall, cottonwoods and aspens glowing yellow amid patches of early snow. Every road shoulder in what author Rebecca Solnit calls a "suburb without walls" was crammed with visitors who behaved as if they'd stepped behind the communion rail or onto a stage with a painted dropcloth. One penetrates such places by degrees, delving as deeply as time, discipline, focus and desire permit, experiencing them, in succession, as panamora, landscape, environment, habitat and spirited presence. Most visitors here stop at scenery where, as Solnit adds, nothing is supposed to happen. Venturing into these meadows felt like smudging a wet oil painting. The only human beings making "contact" were the specks everyone was pointing to halfway up the granite face of El Capitan—climbers taking four days to reach the crest.

The park fosters its prominence as nationalistic scenery. Toward dusk I visited the Indian museum, a vest-pocket installation that sacrifices archaeological and cultural background for introducing outsiders to Miwok families and basket makers who lived here last. But a special gallery show, "Experience Your America," featured sweeping photographs of other national parks, all in honeyed light, mostly devoid of people. The show upheld the Yosemite tradition of distancing spectators from spectacle that began in the 1850s with Thomas Ayres's drawings and Charles Weed's photographs, and continued through painters Albert Bierstadt and photographers Carleton E. Watkins and Ansel Adams. The viewer was stuck in a landscape looking at landscapes, twice removed from any environment, much less a habitat.

Adjoining the museum stands a reconstructed Miwok Indian village of the 1870s, which I caught just before closing time. Behind me Half Dome throbbed with sunset orange, as if from a furnace within the rock. Walking past the exhibit of the semisubterranean *hangi,* or ceremonial roundhouse, I was surprised to find that the building had come alive; a fire was burning inside. Out walked a stout, bushy-haired man, blinking from the smoke. Then I noticed other figures milling about, as if wordlessly taking over the place. Women with ribbon-bordered skirts and folding tables with Tupperware bowls stood near the *capy,* or sweathouse. Young men with glossy braids down their backs sat on benches. An older man leaned on a cane near an open fire beside the *chinnimi 'uuchu,* or shake-roof-period cabin. A Bear Dance was gearing up, the stout man told me. He was Miwok; his mother was born there before the Indian compound had been razed in 1969. "Now we gotta ask permission to even have this," he said, grimacing; "twice a year about we come here for this." He didn't invite me to stay.

The temperature was dropping. The rock climbers up on El Capitan were cocooned in their slings. The museum lights went dark; door locks clicked shut. Tourists bundled kids back to parking lots. The fire outlined Indians still arriving to celebrate the hibernation of the bears and the onset of winter. The one time I'd almost broken through this landscape, I wasn't wanted around.

South—The Cave of Hands

One way to preoccupy oneself hiking up Pico Blanco in Monterey County is to imagine the Great Flood nipping at Coyote's heels. That's how the local Costanoan Indians recalled this 1,145-foot mountain in their account of the world's beginning. First the water swallows the creeks and redwoods in the lower canyons, then it covers manzanitas, madrones and poison oak. Finally, Coyote is panting and all alone, gazing from this landmark of chalky limestone upon a world of waves.

Underwater is an island to the west where the dead live forever. On the ocean floor are landmarks that a later culture will identify as Point Sur, Molera Park, Bixby Creek. Gone are Coyote's cool lairs, sunning spots, thirst-quenching springs and tasty mice. The limestone hump beams in the sunlight. From a feather on the waves is born his friend Eagle. The waters start to subside; the trees and hillsides shake themselves. Coyote and Eagle walk down to a freshly rinsed landscape, where Eagle directs him to create human beings.

Coyote grabs the first good-looking woman for himself. But Humming Bird goes after him. Coyote paws and twists, but not fast enough. He is stabbed and dies, but of course Coyote always comes back to life. His people need him—to remind them about the wages of too much eating, screwing, lazing around and, in dire times, to save them again and again.

One descends from the exposed heights of Pico Blanco into its claustrophobic opposite, the Church Creek drainage. Fifteen miles into the Santa Lucia Mountains, narrow ravines and thick underbrush press from all sides, and one can see only twenty feet ahead. When I took this walk about twenty-five years ago, my destination was a sandstone vault where Indians sought shelter long ago. The visit was inspired by a Robinson Jeffers poem called "Hands," about hundreds of skeletallike appendages, daubed in white, which covered its walls. To Jeffers they had a message. "Look: we also were human," they were telling us. "We had hands, not paws. All hail you people with the cleverer hands, our supplanters in the beautiful country; enjoy her a season, her beauty and come down and be supplanted; for you also are human." It's a rare moment in his poetry when Jeffers isn't praising himself for standing alone against the elements, but here he let the hands know better.

Somewhere in the decade after his arrival in Carmel in 1914, Jeffers first saw the Cave of Hands. But the place had been visited well before that. Early padres at the Carmel and San Antonio missions heard rumors of painted caves in the mountains, and of the *ritos diabólicos* performed in them. The wealthy and curious were escorted there in the 1840s. As late as the 1880s ranchers noticed Indians still visiting the cave. In the 1960s, I heard about it from drug-addled backpackers who had vague memories of disembodied hands in the beams of their flashlights.

The site came to scholarly attention in 1929. Some years later an eight-foot trench in the southeastern end of the overhang yielded a deer bone and charcoal for the carbon-14 dating of 3,190 years ago. Of the thirty-six items on the archaeological site record form, I'd noticed no blank space specifically for "current use," spiritual or otherwise. Access today only came through archaeologists with trusting ties to the current landowners. They would take me in.

Autumn has a light touch in California. The air was cool and soft. Among the spires of awl-thin Santa Lucia fir surfaced the rusty yellows of valley oaks and sycamores. Overhead was a blue sky with filaments of cloud sprayed in a fan pattern. Soon we were ascending the southern incline of a tidy, beautiful canyon. Up ahead stood a formation of naked sandstone tipped back against the canyon wall and a large oak that shrouded the cave mouth.

About 100 yards to its southeast, the archaeologists pointed out a second stone monolith, with pronounced vertical lines grooved by wind and rain, jutting straight up—like a hand. No visitors had ever told me about it. Bedrock mortars had been counted around its base, but no archaeologists except these had noted its proximity to the paintings. No one had ever studied its four fingers, its double thumb. No one seems to have "seen" it. But there it stood—150 feet of solid hand.

Beneath the cave's twenty-foot ceiling, I moved among the three panels as if in a spell. Under the sooty walls there were more than 250 hands made by some mixed technique of tracing and filling in and resembling a huge light box of X-ray negatives. Fingers slightly outstretched, the hands tipped this way and that; about them were other signs: gridirons, pelts, hatchings as well as lovers' hearts, personal initials and KILROY WAS HERE that had been carved by vandals over the last half century.

They allowed me to stare and stare. I wondered if they were greeting me or pushing me away, the way I'd seen Indians block cameras with their hands in historical photos. I asked myself if they were communications from women or men or both. I thought about the contrast between sites of world religions like Hinduism, Buddhism and Islam, which so often enshrine depressions where gods or founder figures left footprints stamped into rock so that we would not underestimate the institutional power they can put on our necks, whereas the art of smaller-scale religious systems so often leaves us with these gentler points of contact across the centuries.

Working my way beneath the shadows of bay laurel, the rock seemed at the mercy of some inner turbulence. Where bullets or pockmarks had started the action, wind and rain were carving out buoy-sized bowls, the residue drizzling onto the floor, while nearby boils stuck out as harder rock withstood the erosion. Water seepage brought migrating minerals to stain the surface; lichen clung to the mottled patina. One hollowed dome was perforated by natural windows through which I saw branches and sky.

Late afternoon swept in quickly. As we were preparing to leave I found myself walking back and forth under the panels, as if incapable of saying good-bye. Each time I glanced at the hands they seemed more alive, glad to have us going, the place back to themselves. Driving out I caught a glimpse of the giant hand that seemed to be saluting the sky.

CHAPTER SIXTEEN

MOURNING AND RENEWAL

Northern California

Championing the sacred places of other people can touch a nerve. "Every time a white person talks about Indians," said an Indian academic at the University of British Columbia, "I get knots in my stomach." Those knots tighten only when the conversation turns to spirituality because many Indians feel they've been stripped of so much else. "Religion is for people who are afraid of hell," said a Lakota tribesman in a recent documentary; "spirituality is for people who've been there." Whether retained, recovered or reinvented, Indian prayers and rituals related to place have come through centuries of repression and intolerance; cunning and patience have kept them alive. They're not about to share them just yet.

Indians also resent outsiders mimicking their lifeways. They roll their eyes at young whites camping in "tribes" during weekend raves and street-corner longhairs who peddle "Indian"-style jewelry, "dream wheels" and sage sticks. They distrust white "shaman" poets who assume the poetic voices of humorously irreverent Coyote tricksters. They dislike "plastic medicine men" who advertise "vision-quest" workshops in glossy magazines about shamanism and scorn wannabes who claim to have been Indians in former lives. Many distrust the "cultural industry," which, in the words of a Canadian Indian writer, "is stealing—unconsciously, perhaps, but with the same devastating results—native stories as surely as the missionaries stole our religion, and the politicians stole our land and the residential schools stole our language . . . (It) amount(s) to cultural theft, theft of voice."

That thievery goes way back. The usurpation of American Indian lands was accompanied by an assault on their religious and emotional ties to place. After 1776, an arsenal of tools enabled the takeover of native homelands, from guns to treaties to presidential orders and judicial decisions. When early Puritans demonized their beliefs, or Catholic inquisitors attempted to uproot paganism in Mexico and Peru, the fight was in the open. This was an Armageddon between religious entities, angels versus demons, and between the landscapes that gave them refuge. But when the United States took over, the struggle for territory turned secular.

The Christian denominations that moved into the American West founded their separate kingdoms of God. But they shared a sense of property value, they placed the same premium on rugged individualism and they rarely objected to the new nation's commitment to exploit natural resources. One heard nothing of native holy lands. "What is the history of the American west?" author Wallace Stegner was once asked. Not culture wars or crusades between religious creeds. "One big real estate deal," he replied. And novelist Kurt Vonnegut, Jr., agreed: imagining how he would explain the country to visitors from another planet, "I wouldn't call Americans Americans. I would give them a name that told a lot about them immediately: I would call them Realtors."

Blazing the trails for these Realtors were explorers, missionaries, treaty makers, soldiers, ranchers, farmers and storekeepers. But even before the first Religious Crimes Code was imposed by the U.S. Indian Bureau against native rituals on Indian reservations in the 1880s, and a second wave of government suppression against ceremonies and dancing was aimed against the Southwestern Pueblos in the 1920s, most sacred places that stood in the Realtors' way were no longer in Indian hands. Of some 2 billion acres held by Indians in 1776, after the era of treaty making ended in 1868, about 140 million Indian-owned acres were left. And once the General Allotment Act of 1887 further chopped up Indian country, fewer than 50 million acres remained. During the twentieth century, dozens of land appropriations for mines, dams, military proving grounds, parks and wilderness areas took most of the rest.

Subtler kinds of cultural assault also undermined the survival of American Indian geographies and their spirits. For openers, their very existence was denied altogether. During his tour of Canada in 1916, the British poet Rupert Brooke detected the "unexplained fragrance" of old Indian place-names in the air. But to any mysteries left in their environments he turned a blind eye. "The maple and the birch conceal no dryads," he wrote, "and Pan has never been heard from amongst these reed-beds." After visiting Alberta—not far from Kootenai Falls and Priest Rapids, where Indian fishermen were still praying to the spirits that provide fish—Brooke added, "Look as long as you like upon a cataract of the New World, you shall not see a white arm in the foam. A godless place." And years later, author Richard L. Rubenstein agreed: "It is not likely that sacred places will be found in the foreseeable future on the North America continent save perhaps in French-Catholic Quebec."

Creative writers also "disappeared" the American Indian past and its mysteries. "No trolls," says an amusingly inept woodsman in a short story by Mark Halpern, during a scene set in the California Sierras—not far from where Washoe Indian stories describe their encounters with giants and Little People. "I was born American," he says, "and that cuts out trolls." The same went for Cherokee country, according to novelist William Humphrey, where the Little People "were departed now, powerless any longer to cheer or scare, dispelled by missionaries. Exorcised. Explained away. Scorned away. Now a tree was just a tree, a rock just a rock, and now when you went for a solitary walk in the woods you only had yourself to converse with."

Some would not allow the New World any room for ancestral shades or for the possibility of being haunted by them. As Rupert Brooke declared, "[In North America] the dead do not return." Whereas in his own country there were "more places for ghosts than people," observed Chinese anthropologist Fei Xiaotong after a trip around the States in 1943. He felt sorry that the restlessness of Americans left them "unable to form permanent ties with places" and hence "in a world without ghosts." Attaching that same sentiment to the West Coast, novelist Pico Iyer commented that his native "India had one thing that California lacked . . . native ghosts."

Others still hear something rustling in the treetops. They may not conjure these presences as horrifically as Stephen King's stories about retribution from disrupted Indian graves, but they still sense that historical misdeeds have tuned onetime ghosts into angry ghosts. "There is a *daimon* that dwells in places," D. H. Lawrence once wrote, and, quoting him, landscape historian Vincent Scully adds that this same spirit moves through

Americans "like a vengeful ghost, giving them their dreams." Former U.S. poet laureate Robert Hass writes of "the other California" whose "bitter absent ghosts dance to a stillness in the air./The Klamaths were routed and they disappeared." Yet D. H. Lawrence's fellow bohemian, the writer-linguist Jaime de Angulo, who talked with Klamath survivors, felt their spirits were still around. "In America the soil is teeming with the ghosts of Indians," he believed, and "Americans will never find spiritual stability until they learn to recognize the Indians as their spiritual ancestors."

A second cultural assault conceded the existence of American Indian spirits of place, but tore them out of context and trivialized them.

My introduction to the sentimentalizing of Indian stories about place came when I received a book entitled *Indian Legends of American Scenes* for my twelfth birthday. State by state, it offered forty-seven romanticized, rewritten tribal stories of famous tourist spots or natural landmarks. The collection hovered somewhere between the old polarized attitudes toward Indians, in which their feelings for a spirited landscape were alternately deplored or adored. "Lo, the poor Indian," wrote Alexander Pope, on the one hand, "whose untutored mind sees Beasts in the clouds, or hears them in the wind," while on the other hand, Kenneth Rexroth would wax that "our memory of the Indian connects us with the soil and the waters and the nonhuman life about us. They take for us the place of nymphs and satyrs and dryads—the spirits of the places."

When popular authors revised the Indian stories they dug out of academic collections of tribal folklore, they usually had little patience or training for fleshing out their cultural or religious contexts. It was easier to recast them in the mold of retold Greek myths, Aesop's fables or fairy tales by the Brothers Grimm. Obscure elements were dropped, meanings were twisted or reversed, references to bothersome symbols, rituals or social practices were often cut.

My new book was better than most. Of the origins of Mount Shasta in Northern California, it said that a creator being named Chareya poured rocks, earth and snow through a hole in the sky into darkness below. That gave him a foothold, so when he stepped upon the earth he could add trees, plants, flowers, animals and the sun to light and color them all. So pleased was he that he hollowed out that original mound and lived within it. No tribal attribution was given, no storyteller or original setting identified, no sense of when the story was told or why.

The abridgment came from a lengthy Modoc Indian narrative, which the anthologizer cribbed from a rewritten Indian story by the celebrated nineteenth-century spinner of California tall tales Joaquin Miller. Its general outline was not entirely bogus, even if the ramifications of a God not living in some heaven but still existing among his people—within, in fact, that very mountain right over there—were lost on most readers.

Named for a local Indian tribe, Mount Shasta was actually a key fixture in the mythologies and religious practices of half a dozen separate Indian cultures in the region. The Wintu people said Mole was really the one who began the mountain. The Achumawi had it as the place where Owl first looked for fire. The Karuk said it was where the first animals made their obsidian arrowheads to shoot at human beings. All sought power and succour at Shasta's springs and meadows.

The cultural history of Mount Shasta illustrates a third assault on Indian sacred geographies, which has intensified in recent decades.

A double-peaked mountain, and at 4,162 feet the country's second highest volcano, Shasta sits at the intersection of the Cascade, Sierra Nevada and Klamath mountain ranges. Visible for hundreds of miles, below its snow-covered slopes falls a wide skirt of aspen groves and alpine meadows fed by cold and hot springs. A generation after the Gold Rush, a writer named Frederick S. Oliver came to California and discovered Tibetan Buddhism. His 1894 novel, *A Dweller on Two Planets,* described Tibetan sages living there.

Occultists of Oliver's day believed in a "lost" continent known as Lemuria, or Mu. On this fugitive landmass were denizens who had evolved in isolation. As to where they lived today, in 1932 an amateur astronomer named Edgar Larkin told a *Los Angeles Star* reporter that he spotted Lemurians on Mount Shasta through his telescope. They were tall, with short-cropped hair and spotless white robes. Some said they were pre-Atlantis peoples, probably fourteen thousand years old, forerunners of today's American Indians. Then local residents reported them entering a grocery store in the town of Weed and paying for supplies with gold nuggets.

Soon the Tibetan Lemurians were joined by another race, the Yaktay-vians, who lived in Mount Shasta's gold-encrusted caverns and clanged bells to keep humans at arm's length. Later, Shasta's meadows were said to be landing pads where aliens refueled their UFOs. After that hikers re-ported running into the Gray Aliens, meeting a mysterious figure named Phylos (who had "dictated" Oliver's book) and sighting Big Foot. Mount Shasta got even more crowded as members of the Great White Brother-hood, the I Am movement, and other New Age groups decreed it to be one of the planet's nine sacred centers. By 1970, the mountain had become what writer Brad Olson calls the Epcot Center of "earth chakras," "power spots" and "vortex areas," which could heal the planet much like acupunc-ture points on the human body.

One aspect of Mount Shasta's new sphere of influence differed from other New Age destinations like Mount Tamalpais near San Francisco or Sedona in central Arizona. A number of Indian groups still told stories about the mountain and practiced rituals associated with it. Although its earlier residents, the Modoc, were scattered or had been shipped on prison trains to Oklahoma after the Lava Bed wars of 1872–73, Mount Shasta remained prominent in traditions of the Karuk, Yurok, Shasta, Hupa, Yana, Pit River and Wiyot.

Especially tenacious were ties between the peak and a small band of Wintu Indians led by a shaman named Florence Jones. Of the nine branches of the northern Wintun people, hers were the Winemem, the Middle Water group, who dwell along the McCloud River, which received its water from Shasta's snowmelt before passing it down to the Upper Sacramento River. To this community, Shasta was *Bulyum Puyuik,* the Great Mountain.

Jones's great-grandfather *Dol-le-ken-til-le-meh* was among the three hundred Wintu once invited by white emissaries to a feast. Noticing that whenever an Indian relieved himself in the woods the man never re-turned, her ancestor managed to evade the guard who came to kill him. Their trap exposed, the soldiers and volunteers wiped out the remaining forty-five warriors at the table. Just as that ancestor led ceremonies at sacred places, so did Florence's grandmother Judy, a noted medicine woman, and also her mother, the healer named Jennie Curl, who once lectured the ethnographer Dorothy Lee how evil times could force the world itself to rebel, the earth to be destroyed, floods to come, and trees and land to be reborn. As a child, Florence internalized these apocalyptic warnings, and now she prepared to deliver them anew.

Between 1850 and 1900, her Wintu group went through a living hell. At white contact, they numbered more than fourteen thousand. By 1908, the year of Florence's birth, disease, dislocation, hunger and mass killings by gold miners, ranchers and military irregulars had cut them down to fewer than four hundred souls. Her own village, near present-day Baird, California, had fallen in the path of this holocaust; then it was finally obliterated fifty years later by flooding behind Shasta Dam.

Two of Florence's favored sites were the doctors' training ground called Dekkas Rock, near her birthplace on the McCloud River, and Panther Meadows, a peaceful, off-road area on Mount Shasta's southern flank, which is carpeted with wildflowers and grasses and stands at 7,500 feet, just under the snow line. Here is where Florence was taken for her shamanic training, for which she'd been groomed since childhood. "Like going to college," she remembers, "and being a medical doctor or lawyer. There's lots of no-no's and lots of things I had to go through. All the sacred places, sacred springs, and sacred mountains."

Her designated successor, a Wintu woman named Caleen Sisk-Franco, gave filmmaker Toby McCloud a picture of Florence's special spring. "We call it *sauwel mem*," she said, "*Sauwel* means a place that has sacredness about it, like it's the beginning of something, or it's the life form of something. And *mem* is water. So, this is the life-giving water and it runs all the way through our land. The *winnemem* is the middle river (McCloud River), which comes from this spring. So, all this water from this *sauwel mem* gives life to everything downriver, down through the valley, all the way through Sacramento. It all comes from this life-giving force. When you recognize that, its kind of like your mother. That's your life-giver that brought you into this world. Without this spring, nothing else would be."

•   •   •

The mystical allure of Mount Shasta for non-Indians blossomed with the Harmonic Convergence celebrations of 1987. After New Age guidebooks spread the word, pale-bodied pilgrims were prancing across Panther Meadows in the nude, beating tom-toms, painting daisies on its rocks and leaving crystals and letting their dogs bathe in Florence's spring. Shasta's popularity among skiers and sliders also increased. Local promoters petitioned the Forest Service for permits to open two thousand acres surrounding Panther Meadows for downhill runs, seven new lifts and three lodges—a $21 million ski resort that could accommodate five thousand skiers per day on Shasta's slopes.

Wintu protests against these violations involved face-to-face confrontations with U.S. Forest Service officials; during one of them, Florence got so aroused she threw a finger back behind her head toward Shasta and warned: "Do you want to see it come down? Do you want that?" Her threat was foretold by an earlier Wintu medicine woman named Kate Luckie, when she informed anthropologist Cora Du Bois in 1925:

> People talk a lot about the world ending. Maybe this child (pointing to her eldest) will see something, but this world will stay as long as Indians live. When the Indians all die, then God will let the water come down from the north. Everyone will drown. That is because the white people never cared for land or deer or bear. When we kill meat, we eat it all up. When we dig roots, we make little holes. When we build houses, we don't ruin things. We shake down acorns and pine nuts. We don't chop down the trees. We use only dead wood. But the white people plow up the ground, pull up the trees, kill everything. The tree says, "Don't. I am sore. Don't hurt me." But they chop it down and cut it up. The spirit of the land hates them. The Indians never hurt anything, but the white people destroy all. They blast rocks and scatter them on the earth. The rock says, "Don't! You are hurting me." But the white people pay no attention. When the Indians use rocks, they take little round ones for their cooking. The white people dig deep tunnels. They make roads. They dig as much as they wish. They don't care how much the ground cries out. How

can the spirit of the earth like the white man? That is why God upset the world—because it is sore all over. Everywhere the white man has touched it, it is sore. It looks sick. So it gets even by killing him when he blasts. But eventually the water will come.

In 1988, the groundswell of support for the Wintu caused Forest Service supervisor Sharon Heywood to turn down the resort proposal.

A fourth insult to Indian sacred geographies is half-baked imitation. Some advocates for "deep" wilderness experiences that integrate women into land-based mysticism or restore grasslands and old forests have sought the gravity of ritual obligation and the mystery of symbolic manipulation. For an indigenous seal of authenticity or tips on how such rituals work, a few have enlisted American Indian examples for this task. Their new ceremonies have borrowed from the *Hako,* a Pawnee pipe ceremony for allying social groups; the *Kinaalda,* a Navajo puberty ceremony for young girls; and the *Hunka,* a Lakota rite of honoring and adopting.

A certain timidity accompanies these knockoffs, an uncertainty about how deeply their designers truly want the symbols to *work,* or the degree to which they believe they truly possess the power to turn back the clock. Indians say this is what comes from treating their traditions as if they were cruising through a spiritual supermarket. By contrast, the actual Indian rites that whites are emulating are often strikingly assertive. Their practitioners believe they can truly heal the sick. There is nothing hesitant about them. Some of them even claim the ability to "repair" or "fix" the world.

To appreciate one corner of Native America where this task is taken seriously, I recently went to northwestern California. Of the seven or more native groups who still live between the Pacific Ocean and the Siskiyou Mountains, with the Rogue River its northern boundary and Humboldt Bay the southern, the Hupa, the Yurok and the Karuk are best known.

To orient myself geographically in their river-and-mountain stronghold I left my compass at home. Here five directions take over—*upstream, downstream, uphill, downhill,* and *through.* Entering on Route 96, the bends and shallows of the Trinity River led me into the million-acre Six

Rivers National Forest, which stretches from Mendocino County to the Oregon border. A sequence of streams races through deep gorges and around cobblestone bars and sandy spits, the road cuts through sheer canyons, past river terraces edged with fruit trees and narrow sandbars, and finally reaches family compounds, trailer homes, a small grocery store, the Hupa motel-casino-museum complex and Laurel's Café.

Only Indians are permitted to net steelhead trout and Chinook salmon in these waters. Fish remains their mainstay, as I was reminded by a hand-drawn billboard depicting a salmon over the slogan "Dying for Water." It reflected local outrage over Klamath Falls dam managers diverting water for upstream farmers while leaving these lower river fishermen wading through dead, stinking fish that were prevented from swimming upstream to spawn.

In olden days, to reach deer, elk, mushrooms and timber and to acquire healing gifts and shaman's powers at the sacred places, one headed straight uphill. And then Indians would "drift" straight down in the daredevil fashion once taught to Yurok youth, keeping their balance as they half hurtled, half bounced on the springy manzanita scrub, twisting and braking to keep from cracking their skulls on river rocks below.

Soon I left behind the twelve-mile-by-twelve-mile "box" of the Hupa valley and negotiated the curvy road through the forty-seven-mile-long, two-mile-wide Yurok Reservation. Over the Weitchpec Bridge, I looked down at the Trinity River crashing into the Klamath. At a nearby fork I could turn left toward the legendary Yurok town of Pecwan or head right into the Karuk or upriver country. Never blessed with their own reservation, the Karuk have nonetheless posted signs at their own spiritual trails, ceremonial grounds and brush-dance pits at the hamlets of Orleans and Soames Bar.

Even though these tribes have lived here for nearly four thousand years, they don't believe they were here first. Whether they are called *Woge*, in the Algonquian-derived language of the Yurok, *Ikxareeyav* in the Hokan-related language of the Karuk, or *Kixunai* (or Immortals) to the Athapaskan-speaking Hupa, this race of supernatural spirit beings, who lived in what some call the "Beforetime," were their forerunners.

Their mystical creativity and mythic exploits established the river towns and the sacred High Country, where shamans learned their magic. Before departing for their heaven, some Immortals transformed into celestial bodies, rivers, trees, healing plants, frogs and the famous High Country places like Peak 8, Fish Lake, Little Medicine Mountain and Elk Valley. "Who did the old Indians say was God?" the Karuk writer Julian Lang once asked his grandmother. "Why, the Earth!" she replied. "Ever'thin. The rocks, the leaves, the mountains."

From the Immortals came the sacred stories and sacred trail system, whose tendrils were considered "alive" in their own right, especially the *Thkla-Mah,* or Ladder Path, by which shamans-in-training, or "ridge-walkers," reached the southern Siskiyou Mountain meditation places, the trail cairns, medicinal herbs and mythologically important sites. As Yurok activist Chris Peters characterized this culturally sensitive, twenty-five-square-mile highland, which Forest Service maps identify as the Blue Creek Planning Unit, "There are a number of prayer seats along the river. [But] the more important ones are in the high country areas—the Burl's Peak and the Doctor Rock–Chimney Rock areas. These are where high mountain medicine people go for fasting and praying. They make the connection that unites them as individuals with all of creation and with all of their spiritual needs."

Following the Gold Rush, the region was left untouched until the 1930s, when the Civilian Conservation Corps cut trails that soon widened into lumber roads, and it was not long before the Indian prayer sites had become garbage-strewn campgrounds. In the early 1960s, the government's multiple-use policy further opened the sanctuary. Projecting over an eighty-year period, the U.S. Forest Service planned a 2020 harvest of white cedar and Douglas fir at a total of more than 730 million board feet. To truck out the logs and avoid a circuitous route that would nearly double the drive, it planned to pave the last 6.2-mile gravel segment of a 75-mile road between Gasquet and Orleans—the infamous GO Road.

Indians complained that this unfinished Chimney Rock Section wound through a concentration of their sacred places. In the 1970s, as Indian traditionalists complained about timber companies taking over, I visited Six Rivers and saw the naked, blackened slopes from burned logging trim; the ash and dirt flushing downhill; the skies dark with smoke; and I heard Indian concerns about air pollution and worries that aerial spraying of the pesticide 2,4,5-T was coming dangerously close to their riverside homes.

Tribal elders added their voices against the GO Road. Renowned Yurok elder Calvin Rube recalled how, as an aspiring healer, he "was pulled to the mountain . . . for ten nights of fasting during the hottest part of the summer." If regular doctors wrote off his patients, "You can take them here," said Rube, "and in three days they're up and moving around. To pray to the real Creator—that's what Doctor Rock is all about." And from the Karuk perspective, elder Charlie Thom highlighted the essential connection between rituals performed by specialists by themselves in the High Country and the collective ceremonies that took place along the Klamath River. "They're putting through the GO Road. . . . That road goes right past Chimney Rock, Doctor Rock, Little Medicine Mountain, Flint Valley. Those are places where we can shoot medicine right down into the Brush Dance hole . . . just like radar."

To make their case, Six Rivers Forest Service personnel fell back on their multiple-use obligations: lumberjacks and backpackers deserved as much consideration as Indian seekers of medicine. Out of respect, however, they would reroute the road farther downslope, and they believed its effect "on archaeological sites would be indirect in nature." Their cultural studies proved contradictory: one found little evidence of Indians' using the heights, with the Yurok having "no further legitimate needs" there; a second concluded that the High Country was central to World Renewal ceremonies, constituted the heart of their belief system, and that "intrusions on the sanctity of the Blue Creek high country are . . . potentially destructive of the very core of Northwest [Indian] religious beliefs and practices."

That quote from a decision released by U.S. District Court Judge Stanley A. Weigel on May 24, 1983, was practically lifted from the second report. To me, Weigel had confided how profoundly moved he'd been by the dignified demeanor and unquestionable sincerity of Indian witnesses whom even he regarded as classic sages. But his wasn't the last word.

Forest Service appeals pushed the case up the judicial ladder until, for the second time, in 1987, it landed at the nation's court of last resort. No matter that the California Wilderness Act of 1984, which banned logging in the Blue Lake plot, had effectively halted the road extension. A precedent was at stake, whose effect, if Indians won, would ripple across the United States and could even cause revisiting the Tellico, San Francisco Peaks and Bear Butte decisions.

For protection of sacred landscapes on public lands the U.S. Supreme Court decision, handed down on April 19, 1988, was a major defeat, and a near-fatal blow to the ten-year-old American Indian Religious Freedom Act. Adopting what many newspaper editorials agreed was "so narrow a view of the First Amendment's guarantee of free exercise of religion that it also troubles the mainstream religious leaders who backed the Indians," Justice Sandra Day O'Connor wrote for the majority in the 5 to 3 ruling. Even though the invasion by hard hats, screaming chain saws and rumbling twenty-six-ton logging trucks "could have devastating effects on traditional Indian religious practices," she said, the First Amendment was inapplicable because Indians retained their freedom of religion—nobody forced them into practices that were inconsistent with their beliefs.

Aware that the Indians could not pack up these outdoor "churches" and move them to another site, dissenting Justice William Brennan characterized the ruling as "cruelly surreal" in that the religious freedom it promised these California Indians "amounts to nothing more than the right to believe that their religion will be destroyed." The decision left a bitter taste in Indian mouths. Successive federal and state laws in 1991 and 2001 tightened protection of Indian sacred places on federal lands. Yet the GO Road decision remains a potential threat to landscape spirits and the hopes of native peoples to transact with them.

When I visited the Hupa "center of the world" in 2004, it was for the climax of their ten-day Jump Dance, which is held every two years in late September. Cars spiraling dust down an unpaved lane bordered by blackberry bushes indicated that I was nearing the ceremonial grounds, the legendary village site of *Takmildin*. There was a cluster of portable toilets, a parking area along a shelf overlooking the Trinity River and onlookers standing around a barrier made from upright wooden planks.

From this turnoff, to the Yurok tribe's Pecwan village, and then to the Karuk's Katimin or "Upper Falls" village at Soames Bar, the valley road touched a number of "world center" places—each a precinct for holding World Renewal ceremonies. Alfred Kroeber was struck by the way these tribes anchored themselves to place, and emphasized "fixing" their worlds through such rituals. "It is the *locality* that has ceremonial preeminent sanctity," he noted, "something strangely old world and un-American in the Yurok attitude, a reminiscence of high places and fanes and hallowed groves."

That we exist on an unstable planet, particularly in Northern California, was never news to these Indians. Well before the white invasion, they experienced eruptions, famines, exploding stars, earthquakes, floods, eclipses and other calamities. What made the world turn upside down was people behaving badly. The Immortals knew humans couldn't stop their polluting ways. Without some sort of special effort, human weakness and moral entropy would eventually take us all down. The coming of whites only confirmed that knowledge by showing how bad it could get. In this corner of the state, a second epicenter of the California Gold Rush, it got very bad.

So every couple years, shortly before the fall acorn harvest and the first salmon run, the Yurok and Karuk and Hupa, each in their distinctive style, put things back on track. Since time immemorial, for ten straight days the Hupa have held what whites have called the Jump Dance. An artful display of deeply felt song, dance, prayer and oratory, it called for considerable endurance. From midmorning to night—and then again after meals served from open fires in family "tables" or open-air camps—teams of male dancers, one from the downriver community, the second from the upriver community, took turns dancing in a shallow pit.

I walked across the recently mowed grass, past an old-style wooden house with a gable roof of overlapping cedar planks. The small crowd of seventy or so was silent, motionless, concentrated. Except for a slight haze from a forest fire, which was drawing Hupa hot-shot crews, the sky was blue and cloudless, the mid-September sun still hot. A little farther on two more plank houses were shaded by thick old pepper trees, the shallower building a recently built incarnation of the old-style men's sweathouse.

Some of the thirteen dancers stared directly at us; some squinted just over our heads with entranced expressions. Behind them stretched a thirty-foot-tall screen of hand-split cedar planks. They sang in what music scholars know as the famous polyphony of northwestern California—two soloists alternating in plaintive descending melodies, slightly warbling in a sort of emotive trailing off—in order to evoke sobbing—which was underlain, almost comforted, by the basso chorus of their fellow dancers,

No powwow, no CD of Indian music, no picture book on Indian dance had prepared me for this—here was an altogether original blend of action, intention and mood. At every second beat the line of dancers facing us tromped down in unison with one foot, holding a split second so as to kick up little puffs of dust in their shallow dance trough. On three rock "seats," sunk in the ground side by side between back screen and pit, the dance leader, the Center Man, squatted briefly between dances, flanked by his two soloists. Their posture was reminiscent of an old photo I'd seen in the Smithsonian Institution archives: "Karuk sitting on sacred rock to fix the world" was written on its back.

Every dancer gripped a tubular basket, his medicine bag. Across their foreheads rippled "headrolls," wide bands bright with some sixty red woodpecker breasts, topped by lone eagle plumes. Around their necks clattered shell necklaces. Most had black stripes on cheekbones, some on chins. Instead of belts, their free hands gripped the loose ends of deer-skin kilts.

The Center Man's movements were energetic, theatrical. With each beat he alternated posture, looking first here, then there, each time bending, stooping deeply, ducking his head like a bantam woodpecker. The more restrained, somber chorus swung their baskets in sweeping arcs, up and down with each beat.

Atop the southern end of the wooden fence behind them lifted the Christmassy tip of a tiny Douglas fir. Its slender branches had been trimmed to form a spiral from base to point, creating a trail down which the Immortals were said to descend from heaven so they could dance *behind* the men in front of them. They were not only present to witness these humans "fixing" the world, they actually took part.

Between us and the dancers smoldered a wispy fire, attended by a fire keeper or dance team guide, ever alert to fix a loose headdress, pick up a dropped item, poke the embers and sprinkle bits of aromatic angelica root. The crowd became participants, standing reverentially in the sun, shooshing noisy kids as if in church, a number of women looking regal in traditional basketry hats, a few babies in old-style hand-woven cradles— their attention bolstering the dancers' mission.

As the dancing went past nightfall, the fire tender whipped the coals into a full blaze. Now the presence of the Immortals was felt in the distorted, oversized shadows of the dancers projected against the screen of gleaming wood. Heat from the bonfire caused sweat to shine on torsos. In the middle of each dance round, they laid folded kilts and ceremonial baskets on the ground, gripped one anothers' hands and all together jumped in place.

The earth, she actually liked it, someone explained to me later that night, when we were sitting in folding chairs beside the river's muffled rush. On our knees we balanced paper plates of potato salad, fry bread, gravy and venison and wooden bowls of gelatinous acorn soup, into which we dipped flank-smoked salmon and eel. The dancers had pounded the earth to offer her "reassurance," he added, sending their message of support. The Immortals "from the sky" had joined them, as the shadows suggested, happy to be back with their people, with their two years of nostalgia for this land they had left, known as *natinix*, or "where the trails and journeys lead back," temporarily assuaged.

On the following and final day, the smoke from the growing Del Loma Fire hung low along the valley. Low-flying helicopters periodically drowned out the singing. During the afternoon, the determination of the dancers and singers hardened. Where columns of Pueblo Indian dancers shuffled and sprang, these bare feet stomped; the regular pounding set up vibrations we bystanders could almost feel.

If ever dancers were sending a message, it was here and now. At the same time, there were moments beginning a segment of the dance when, holding hands and facing us, they reprised that leap into the air, as if counteracting the downward pounding, as if, like during certain shamanic performances, they were hurling themselves into that realm of the spirits. Only the Center Man's vigorous dipping down alleviated the gravity— one or the other leg touching the ground in exhausting knee bends, his imperious expression for a moment in the crouch, wearing that almost-confrontational gaze of Maori and South Indian dancers, eyes full of pride, even defiance.

Now, it was said, the "regalia" came to life and danced as well. The red-feathered headrolls with their swaying buckskin side flaps, the shaking of thick shell necklaces, the rising and falling of the uterine-shaped medicine baskets. Flanking the Center Man, the two soloists shut tight their eyes as they took turns pealing their arias with a throat-catching mournfulness that seemed to transfix observers with empathy for the effort being made on their behalf—creating an intense symbiosis between viewers and performers that reminded me of the support lent to Plain Indians Sun Dancers in their hardest hours. Meanwhile, the wings of this chorus line, five or six men to each side, eyes trained on the ridge line across the river as if on another world, boomed their accompaniment and swooped their medicine baskets as if to illustrate the purpose of upward yearning.

Toward dusk came the culmination. Up- and downriver dance groups joined forces, and after ten days of separateness, now faced one another across the fire. In celebration of the unity that humans find so difficult to achieve, the dancing and singing compounded in earnestness and joy. They were not together long, but for that moment, we all bore witness. In Hupa country, at least, the world was enjoined—which for this interval was a microcosm of everywhere.

And here they slowly retreated to their separate domains across the spread-out camp, the downstream Center Man making sure to stomp on another sacred rock. Yet the singers and dancers seemed to cling to their respective brotherhoods, as if reluctant to dissipate the purpose, devotion and proximity to their ancestors and the mood that now was thick in the air. Close and almost shoulder high was the Big Dipper, but the moon never showed his face. In fact, I later learned, the whole affair had been scheduled so he could actually join us, dancing along with the rest of the Immortals. All of the dancers jumped in place one last time, held hands and lingered as if to help their ancestors feel at home for as long as possible.

Then, with a collective shout to the skies, it was over.

Coming down off all this, an interval of total silence, like an indrawn breath, slowly broke into little bursts of talk and laughter, a request for a cigarette, cars catching ignition and turning on their beams, the chugging of water from plastic jugs, kids wrapping arms around their dads' naked legs, repacking family heirlooms from the heads, necks, hands that had brought them to life, dancers trailing back to pickups to change clothes, heading for the cook shelters and the honor of being served first at the long tables, reliving the best singing parts or gossiping about what was different from other times, the cooking camps becoming pools of light from wood fires and Coleman lanterns, the reassuring tinkle of dishes and pots, the squeals from children and murmurings of parents and older folks kicking back beneath the emerging stars.

Explanations were unnecessary. This was by Hupa for Hupa in Hupa country. We handful of strangers were treated with a light, confident hospitality, but for the most part we were invisible.

However, there had been a moment earlier in the day when the ceremonial leader allowed himself a few remarks to everyone in English, a halting summary of these ten days of telling the earth how badly everyone wanted it to stay alive and well. First he looked around, got everybody's attention and geared himself up. "We keep doing this," he said. "We don't let up. Somebody may criticize, talk whether we doing it right." He scowled a little, dribbling more angelica root into the flames.

He looked around the crowd as if daring someone to do just that. "But we keeping it on. And I'm glad we came together to do this. Look at us," he said, turning to the dancers. "Thank you, dancers, thank you, thanks, for working this, working hard, doing it." Turning to the rest of us, he added, "Thank you too, for being here, sticking around for this with us."

The fire crackled, he tossed in more root bits. We watched and waited. The smoke spun with an odor like burning celery. "We praying for the sick, against bad things. We doing this, keeping it."

Then he reminded us how to behave on rare occasions like this, when people came together in accordance with the ancestors' wishes, and welcomed them back, and worked with concentration and energy to renew the fish, trees, mountains, rivers and other fellow creatures, and danced and prayed to restore health and peace and equilibrium to the world. He said the last thing I expected to hear:

"Put a smile on your face."

Acknowledgments

Thanks to Gretchen M. Bataille for whom I first presented this subject (Iowa State University, 1978), to Robert M. Lewis for my "America as Holy Land" (*North Dakota Quarterly,* vol. 48, no. 4, Autumn, 1980), to the late Joseph Epes Brown and Sam Gill for my seminars on sacred geography (University of Montana, spring, 1983; University of Colorado, summer, 1984), to Tim Buckley for commissioning my "Speaking of Practicable Things" for "Religion and Realpolitik: American Indian Sacred Lands," special issue of *ARC (Anthropology Resource Center) Newsletter* 5(4), 1981, and to Ines M. Talamantez for my "Unto These Mountains: Toward the Study of Sacred Geography," *New Scholar* 10(1–2), 1986. For assistance, encouragement, wisdom I thank Gerard Baker, Malcolm Margolin, Frederick Hoxie, Sam Deloria, Sam Gill, Suzan Harjo, Toby McLeod, Edmund Carpenter, Patricia Cummings, William Simmons, Jay Miller, Alfonso Ortiz, Larry Loendorf, David Ruppert and Tom Thiessen. Raymond Fogelson always supported this work. Specific debts are cited below, but special gratitude to Dave Whitley, Bert Snyder, Don Cosentino and Linda Feldman for critiquing the manuscript, Laurie Miller for technical help, Ken Wade for bibliographic assistance, and Susan Bergholz and Michael Millman for patience and loyalty.

Sources

These narratives draw on tribal profiles by scholars, writings and oral histories by native spokespersons, personal experiences and interviews, archival and journalistic sources. Materials consulted and quoted are provided chapter by chapter below. Given the wide range of tribes, cultures, languages and types of research data represented in this book, it has been impossible for me to standardize their orthographies. I have had no alternative but to rely on the English-language approximations for native words and names that I have found in these sources.

INTRODUCTION

x *Certainly one of the results:* Kenneth MacLeish, "The Top End of Down Under," *National Geographic,* 143(2), 1973, p. 172.

xi *After that experience:* For typologies and overviews of American Indian sacred places (and human remains and religious objects), I have borrowed from "Protection of American Indian Sacred Geography," Deward E. Walker, Jr., in *Handbook of American Indian Religious Freedom,* Christopher Vecsey, ed. (New York: Crossroad, 1991); Andrew Guilford, *Sacred Objects and Sacred Places: Preserving Tribal Traditions* (Boulder, CO: University Press of Colorado, 2000); *Sacred Sites, Sacred Places,* David L. Carmichael et al. eds. (London: Routledge, 1994); *Stars Above, Earth Below: American Indians and Nature,* Marsha C. Bol, ed. (Niwot, CO: Robert Rinehart Publisher, 1998); *Earth and Sky: Visions of the Cosmos in Native American Folklore,* Ray A. Williamson and Claire R. Farrer, eds. (Albuquerque: University of New Mexico Press, 1992); *Sacred Lands of Indian America,* Jake Page, ed. (New York: Harry N. Abrams, 2001); Christopher McLeod's film *In the Light of Reverence* (Bullfrog Films, 2002); Peter Matthiessen, *Indian Country* (New York: Viking, 1984); and essays by Vine Deloria, Jr., in *For This Land: Writings on Religion and Native America* (New York: Routledge, 1999) and *Spirit and Reason: The Vine Deloria, Jr., Reader* (Golden, CO: Fulcrum Pub., 1999).

xvi *At long last, in late 1977:* On this legislation: American Indian Religious Freedom Act Report P.L. 95–341, U.S. Department of the Interior, Washington, D.C., August 1979; for criticism of the report's simplistic and misleading distinction between "commemorative" (non-Indian, "world," creed-based and usually begun by a founding figure) religions and "continuing" (Indian, lacking written doctrines, emphasizing rituals and periodic "recreations" of the world) religions: David M. White, "Native American Religious Issues ... Are Also Land Issues," *Wassaja,* 13 (3), 1980.

CHAPTER ONE: Worlds in an Island—*Penobscot*

4   *At one time, this stretch:* On Indian Island place-names: Fanny Hardy Eckstorm, *Indian Place-Names of the Penobscot Valley and Maine Coast* (Orono, ME: University of Maine, 1974), pp. 35–36.

4   *"A number of travelers":* Fodor Shell Travel Guide USA (New York: David McKay, Inc., 1966), p. 381.

4   *For three months:* My sojourns were June–July, October 1972, with thanks to Merry Ring, Millie Howe and Ted Mitchell. The previous year Peter Anastas lived there. His *Glooskap's Children: Encounters with the Penobscot Indians of Maine* (Boston: Beacon Press, 1973) deepened my understanding of the island, as did Frank G. Speck's *Penobscot Man: The Life History of a Forest Tribe in Maine* (New York: Octagon Books, 1940, reprint 1970) and Bunny McBride's *Women of the Dawn* (Lincoln, NB: University of Nebraska Press, 1999).

5   *But former generations:* See Bruce J. Bourque, *Twelve Thousand Years: American Indians in Maine* (Lincoln, NB: University of Nebraska Press, 2001).

6   *The hundred-year-old house:* Mary P. Sherwood, *Joseph Polis: Thoreau's Indian Guide* (Berwick, Ontario: Stormont Press, 1970).

6   *In the late sixteenth century:* On Glooskap's life and narratives: Joseph Nicolar, *Life and Traditions of the Red Man* (Bangor, ME: C. H. Glass, 1893); Frank G. Speck, "Penobscot Tales and Religious Beliefs," *Journal of American Folklore* 48(187) 1935, and "Penobscot Transformer Tales," *International Journal of Linguistics* 1(3) 1918. As anthropologist Claude Lévi-Strauss writes, "... the Penobscot of Maine exemplify a general tendency on the part of the northern Algonkin to interpret all the physiographic aspects of the tribal territory in terms of the peregrinations of the civilizing hero Gluskabe and other mythical personages or incidents." Claude Lévi-Strauss, *The Savage Mind* (Chicago: University of Chicago Press, 1970), p. 166.

8   *This mythic landscape also featured:* On the Penobscot and Mount Katahdin: John C. Warren, "Pomola, the Spirit of Mt. Katahdin," *New England Magazine* 52, 1915; Fannie H. Eckstorm, "The Katahdin Legends," *Appalachia* 16, December 1924; Nicholas M. Smith, "The Three Faces of Khatahdin," papers of the 22nd Algonquian Conference, Ottawa: Carleton University, 1991; Alvin H. Morrison, "The Spirit of the Law Versus the Storm Spirit: A Wabanaki Curse," papers of the 13th Algonquian Conference, Ottawa: Carleton University, 1982; Fannie H. Eckstorm Papers, Bangor Public Library, Bangor, Maine.

9   *And in the dead of winter:* Stories about Old John Neptune and by Clara Neptune are from Fannie H. Eckstorm Papers and her wonderful *Old John Neptune and Other Maine Shamans* (Portland, ME: Southworth-Anthoensen Press, 1945).

10   *One celebrity trespasser:* Mary P. Sherwood, *Thoreau's Penobscot Indians* (Berwick, Ontario: Stormont Press, 1970).

10   *Amid its swirling mists:* W. D. Wetherell, "Far from Andes or Alps, Celebrating Small Peaks," *New York Times,* June 6, 1999, p. 35; one is reminded of D. H.

Lawrence's belief that "this effort into sheer naked contact [specifically with a mountain], without an intermediary or mediator, is the root meaning of religion," *Phoenix: The Posthumous Papers of D. H. Lawrence* (New York: Penguin Books, 1985), p. 147.

11 *Thoreau yanked his readers:* Henry D. Thoreau, *The Maine Woods* (Princeton: Princeton University Press, 1972), p. 71; also references in *The Indians of Thoreau: Selections from the Indian Notebooks,* Richard F. Fleck, ed. (Albuquerque: Hummingbird Press, 1974).

13 *Eventually I became friends:* Interviews with Senabeh, July/October 1972; other sources: Pamela Wood's "Medicine Man of the Penobscots," *SALT* 4(4), 1979 and "Go Back Home, Senabeh," *SALT* 5(1), 1979; Lee-Ann Konrad and Christine Nichols, *Artists of the Dawn* (Northeast Folklore Society, 1987).

14 *"Stamp on ground":* Fannie H. Eckstorm Papers, "The Name of Neptune," n.d.

14 *"The land! Don't you":* William Carlos Williams, *In the American Grain* (New York: New Directions, 1956), p. 74.

15 *"I don't know that I like":* "Voice in the Wilderness, Interview with Gary Snyder," *San Francisco Review of Books,* Summer 1989, p. 53.

16 *What clay is to the Pueblo:* On Maine Indian wood arts, Fannie H. Eckstorm, *The Handicrafts of the Modern Indians of Maine,* Bull. III (Bar Harbor, ME: Abbe Museum, 1932).

17 *Versions of the same story:* Historian Fannie H. Eckstorm once chided Frank Speck for getting his Penobscot Little People mixed up: "Dr. Speck has not mastered our Indian mythology. He confuses the *Mikumwes* (corresponding somewhat to our Robin Goodfellow) with the Indian *Waganagameswak,* or little rock fairies, and calls both 'water nymphs!' Whoever his informant may have been, he must have had in mind the *Alambaguenosisak,* 'under-still-water-little-folks,' the true water fairies; but what Doctor Speck had in *his* mind is something still different, the *Nodumkenowet,* or merman. . . ." Fannie H. Eckstorm, review of F. G. Speck's *"Penobscot Man," New England Quarterly* 13(4), 1940, p. 744.

18 *"A sacred spot never presents":* Lucien Levy-Bruhl, *L'Expérience Mystique et les symboles chez les primitifs* (Paris, 1938), p. 183.

18 *And finally it was a separate:* John Fowles, *Islands* (Boston: Little, Brown, 1978), p. 17.

19 *"Land means Penobscot reverence":* *Maine Indian Newsletter* 5(1), January 1972, p. 6.

CHAPTER TWO: Naming the Spirits—*Ojibwa*

20 *A designation by:* Ernest S. Burch, Jr., "The Nonempirical Environment of the Arctic Alaskan Eskimo," *Southwestern Journal of Anthropology* 27, 1971.

20 *A scholar who followed:* Career of A. Irving Hallowell in Melford Spiro's obituary, *American Anthropologist* 78(3), 1976, Hallowell's own "On Being an Anthropologist," in *Crossing Cultural Boundaries,* S. T. Kimball and J. B. Watson, eds. (San Francisco: Chandler Publishing), pp. 51–62.

21 *A latecomer to anthropology:* Hallowell's summary of this work is *The Ojibwa of Berens River, Manitoba: Ethnography into History,* Jennifer S. H. Brown,

ed. (Fort Worth, TX: Harcourt Brace Jovanovich, 1992). More on Ojibwa in Jack H. Steinbring, "Saulteaux of Lake Winnipeg," *Handbook of North American Indians;* another, if geographically distant, classic on the environmental knowledge of a boreal forest Indian people is Richard K. Nelson, *Make Prayers to the Raven: A Kuyokan View of the Northern Forest* (Chicago: University of Chicago Press, 1983).

21 *Hallowell exchanged looks:* On Chief Berens: Jennifer S. H. Brown, "A Place in Your Mind for Them All," in *Being and Becoming Indian,* James Clifton, ed. (Chicago: Dorsey Press, 1989), pp. 204–25; "A. I. Hallowell and William Berens Revisited," *Papers of the 18th Algonquian Conference,* William Cowan, ed. (Ottawa: Carleton University, 1987); "Fields of Dreams: Revisiting A. I. Hallowell and the Berens River Ojibwa," in *Perspectives on Native North America: Cultures, Histories, and Representations,* Sergei A. Kan and Pauline Turner Strong, eds. (Lincoln, NB: University of Nebraska Press, forthcoming).

22 *The more than thirty:* J. Peter Denny and Jose Mailhot, "The Semantics of Certain Abstract Elements in the Algonquian Verb," *International Journal of American Linguistics* 42(2), 1976.

22 *Each had its proper name:* A. Irving Hallowell, "Cultural Factors in Spatial Orientation," *Culture and Experience* (Philadelphia: University of Pennsylvania Press, 1955).

23 *One described him with his head:* The nineteenth-century ethnographer Henry R. Schoolcraft, traveling with Ojibwa, was also shown locations associated with their mythic trickster: " 'There,' said one Indian, indicating some green stone boulders, 'are pieces of the rock broken off in Manabozho's combat with his father.' 'This is the duck,' said another man, referencing a story about the sources of the Mississippi, 'that Manabozho kicked,' while a third Indian added, 'Under that island Manabozho lost a beaver.' " Henry R. Schoolcraft, *The Myth of Hiawatha and Other Oral Legends* (Philadelphia: J. B. Lippincott & Co., 1856), p. 20.

23 *The farther Hallowell got:* A. Irving Hallowell, "Temporal Orientation in Western Civilization and in a Pre-Literate Society," *American Anthropologist* 39, 1937.

24 *Up in Canada, Willie Berens:* For Hallowell's summary on the Ojibwa "behavioral environment": "Ojibwa Ontology, Behavior, and World View," in *Culture in History: Essays in Honor of Paul Radin,* Stanley Diamond, ed. (New York: Columbia University Press, 1960).

25 *For now, however, he was entranced:* Hallowell, *The Ojibwa of Berens River, Manitoba: Ethnography into History,* 1992, pp. 9–10.

26 *Central to Ojibwa metaphysics:* Described in Christopher Vecsey, *Traditional Ojibwa Religion and Its Historical Changes* (Philadelphia: American Philosophical Society, 1983).

26 *Into Hallowell's head:* On Speck: *The Life and Times of Frank G. Speck,* Robert Blankenship, ed. (Philadelphia: University of Pennsylvania Publications in Anthropology 4, 1991), and Loren Eisley's reminiscence, Chapter 9 in *All the Strange Hours: The Excavation of a Life* (New York: Charles Scribner's Sons, 1975).

27 *Some residents of Lake Pikangikum:* Thanks to Jennifer S. H. Brown for Hallowell's unpublished "Rocks and Stones" (eight pages), from the A. Irving Hallowell Papers, Philadelphia: American Philosophical Society, [c. 1936]. Quote on Husserl is from Evan M. Zuesse, *Ritual Cosmos: The Sanctification of Life in African Religions* (Athens, OH: Ohio University Press, 1979), p. 240.

30 *In their private libraries:* Agehananda Bharati, "Anthropological Approaches to the Study of Religion: Ritual and Belief Systems," *Biennial Review of Anthropology, 1971,* Bernard J. Siegal, ed. (Stanford: Stanford University Press, 1972), p. 233.

30 *What ultimately won out:* On the concept: Nurit Bird-David, "'Animism' Revisited: Personhood, Environment and Relational Epistemology," *Current Anthropology* 40, Supplement, 1999.

32 *Of Ojibwa beliefs about the universe:* A. Irving Hallowell, "Some Empirical Aspects of Northern Saulteaux Religion," *American Anthropologist* 36, 1934, p. 391.

32 *Ojibwa thinking process:* In Hallowell, "Rocks and Stones," p. 1.

32 *By 1942 he was ready to jettison:* A. Irving Hallowell, "The Role of Conjuring in Saulteaux Society, in *Publications of the Philadelphia Anthropological Society,* vol. 2 (Philadelphia: University of Pennsylvania Press, 1942), p. 7.

34 *In some areas: New York Times,* October 12, 1990, p. A1. See also: J. Baird Callicott and Michael P. Nelson, *American Indian Environmental Ethics: An Ojibway Case Study,* Upper Saddle River, NJ: Pearson Prentice Hall, 2004.

CHAPTER THREE: Hills of Hidden Meaning—*Choctaw*

35 *One Saturday:* The Mendota Mental Health Institute effigy mound photographic project was supervised by Dr. James B. Stoltman, professor emeritus, Department of Anthropology, University of Wisconsin Madison, in late April 1993.

36 *The mounds our students:* On effigy mounds: Robert A. Birmingham and Leslie E. Eisenberg, *Indian Mounds of Wisconsin* (Madison, WI: University of Wisconsin Press, 2000), Chapter 5; "The Woodland Tradition," Katherine P. Stevenson et al., *The Wisconsin Archeologist* 78(1–2), 1997, Chapter 7; William M. Hurley, "The Late Woodland Stage: Effigy Mound Culture," *The Wisconsin Archeologist* 67 (3–4); materials in *The Society,* the journal of the Ancient Earthworks Society (Madison, WI), 1987.

37 *Did they represent protective:* Frances Densmore, "A Winnebago Explanation of Effigy Mounds," *American Anthropologist* 30, 1928; Paul Radin, *The Winnebago Tribe,* 37th annual report, Bureau of American Ethnology (Washington, D.C.: Smithsonian Institution, 1923); Jay Miller paraphrasing archaeologist Jerald Milanich in "Instilling the Earth: Explaining Mounds," *American Indian Culture and Research Journal* 25(3), 2001, p. 161. In Miller's own theory, for American Indian peoples, mounds "apply weight to hold, stabilize, calm and still" a volatile, unsteady and unpredictable natural world, both in the heavens and under one's feet (pp. 172–73).

38 *More likely, according to:* For mounds overview and current theories: Roger G. Kennedy, *Hidden Cities: The Discovery and Loss of Ancient North American Civilization* (New York: Penguin Books, 1996).

39 *More grounded, however:* Bradley T. Lepper, "Tracking Ohio's Great Hopewell Road," *Archaeology,* November–December 1995, and "The Newark Earthworks and the Geometric Enclosures of the Scioto Valley: Connections and Conjectures," in P. J. Pacheco, *A View from the Core: A Synthesis of Ohio Hopewell Archaeology* (Columbus, OH: Ohio Archaeological Council, 1996); Warren R. De Boer, "Ceremonial Centres from the Cayapas (Esmeraldas, Ecuador) to Chillicothe (Ohio, USA)," *Cambridge Archaeological Journal* 7(2), 1997.

41 *Settlements that reflect:* Lynne Goldstein, "The Implications of Aztalan's Location," *New Perspectives on Cahokia: Views from the Periphery,* James B. Stoltman, ed. (Madison, WI: Prehistory Press, 1991); William M. Hurley, "Aztalan Revisited," *The Wisconsin Archeologist* 58(4) 1978.

42 *Comparisons may be odious:* On Cahokia: Rinita A. Dalan et al., *Envisioning Cahokia: A Landscape Perspective* (DeKalb, IL: Northern Illinois University Press, 2003); Claudia G. Mink, *Cahokia: City of the Sun* (Collinsville, IL: Cahokia Mounds Museum Society, 1992); for linkage to native astronomy, P. Clay Sherrod and Martha Ann Rollingson, *Surveyors of the Ancient Mississippi Valley: Modules and Alignments in Prehistoric Mound Sites* (Fayetteville, AR: Arkansas Archeological Survey, Research Series 28, 1987); Vernon James Knight, Jr., "Symbolism of Mississippian Mounds," *Powhatan's Mantle: Indians in the Colonial Southeast,* Peter H. Wood, Gregory A. Waselkov, and M. Thomas Hatley, eds. (Lincoln, NB: University of Nebraska Press, 1989).

43 *But at least one pocket:* On the Natchez: John R. Swanton, "Early Accounts of the Natchez," *The North American Indians: A Sourcebook,* Roger C. Owen et al., eds. (New York: Macmillan, 1967); Mary Ann Wells, "The Lament of the Tattooed Serpent," *Native Land: Mississippi 1540–1798* (Jackson, MS: University Press of Mississippi, 1994); John Swanton, "Sun Worship in the Southeast," *American Anthropologist* 30, 1928; Robert S. Neitzel, *The Grand Village of the Natchez Revisited,* Archaeological Reports 12 (Jackson, MS: Mississippi Department of Archives and History, 1983).

47 *No American Indians construct:* Thanks to Kenneth H. Carleton, tribal archaeologist for the Mississippi band of Choctaw Indians, for showing me both Nanih Waiyas in March 1991, and his articles "Where Did the Choctaw Come From?: An Examination of Pottery in the Areas Adjacent to the Choctaw Homeland," in *Perspectives on the Southeast: Linguistics, Archaeology, and Ethnohistory,* Patricia B. Kwachka, ed. (Athens, GA: University of Georgia Press, 1994), and "Mother Mound," in *Ancient Architects of the Mississippi,* special issue of *Common Ground* (Washington, D.C.: National Park Service Archeology and Ethnography Program, Spring 1996). Best synthesis of Choctaw history: Patricia Galloway, *Choctaw Genesis 1500–1700* (Lincoln, NB: University of Nebraska Press, 1995). On the Nanih Waiya mound and cave: William Brescia, "Choctaw Oral Tradition Relating to Tribal Origin," in *The Choctaw Before Removal,* Carolyn Keller, ed. (Jackson, MS: University Press of Mississippi, 1985), which excerpts from Harry S. Halbert, "Nanih Waiya, the Sacred Mound of the Choctaws," *Mississippi Historical Society* 2, 1899, and "A Choctaw Migration Legend," *American Antiquarian and Oriental Journal* 16, 1894, Gideon Lincecum, "Choctaw Traditions about Their Settlement in Mississippi and the Origin of Their Mounds," *Publication of the Mississippi Historical Society* 8, 1904, and David L. Bushnell, Jr., "Myths of the Louisiana Choctaw," *American Anthropologist* 12, 1910.

48 *The next day, reports this version:* C. Worsham, *Chahta Hapia Hoke: We Are Choctaw* (Philadelphia: Mississippi Band of Choctaw Indians, 1981), p. 6.

49 *Their narrative follows:* David. I. Bushnell, *The Choctaw of Bayou Lacomb, St. Tammany Parish, Louisiana,* Bureau of American Ethnology, bull. 48 (Washington, D.C.: Smithsonian Institution, 1909), p. 526.

49 *One way to untangle:* The dichotomy between sacred sites consecrated by human ritual and those by superhuman agency is reflected in the contrast between

migration and creation stories and occurs beyond North America. In Africa the religious geographer Erich Isaac similarly distinguishes between places associated with "covenant"-oriented and "creation"-oriented religions ("The Act and the Covenant," *Landscape,* winter, 1961–62), while cultural geographer Paul Fickler juxtaposes "historical-religious holiness,"of the sort surrounding the personalities and locales of "founder faiths" with their saints and sects, and "nature-magic" sacredness, as a property of natural places or special objects ("Fundamental Questions in the Geography of Religions," *Readings in Cultural Geography,* Philip L. Wagner and Mary W. Mikesell, eds. (Chicago: University of Chicago Press, 1962).

50 *For the Choctaw of historical times:* Charles Roberts, "A Choctaw Odyssey: The Life of Lesa Philip Roberts," *American Indian Quarterly,* Summer 1990, p. 262.

50 *A glimpse of the emotional toll:* W.E.S. Folsom-Dickerson, *The White Path* (San Antonio, TX: Naylor Co., 1965), pp. 26–27.

51 *The orifice seemed to incarnate:* On these caves: *In the Maw of the Earth Monster: Mesoamerican Ritual Cave Use,* James E. Brady and Keith M. Prufer, eds. (Austin: University of Texas, 2005); Richard F. Townsend, "The Renewal of Nature at the Temple of Tlaloc," *The Ancient Americas: Art from Sacred Lansdcapes* (Chicago: Art Institute of Chicago, 1993).

CHAPTER FOUR: **Between River and Fire—***Cherokee*

52 *Sacred places of the old-time Cherokee:* On Cherokee history, religious geography, and folkore: James Mooney, *Myths of the Cherokee,* 19th annual report, Bureau of American Ethnology (Washington, D.C.: Smithsonian Institution, 1900), in which Mooney notes, "As with other tribes and countries, almost every prominent rock and mountain, every deep bend in the river, in the old Cherokee country had its accompanying legend. It may be a little story that can be told in a paragraph, to account for some natural feature, or it may be a chapter of a myth that has its sequel in a mountain a hundred miles away. As is usual when a people has lived for a long time in the same country, nearly every important myth is localized, thus assuming a more definite character" (p. 231). Also *Living Stories of the Cherokee,* Barbara R. Duncan, ed. (Chapel Hill, NC: University of North Carolina Press, 1998); Barbara L. Reimensnyder, "Cherokee Sacred Sites in the Appalachians," in *Cultural Heritage Conservation in the American South,* Benita J. Howell, ed. (Athens, GA: University of Georgia Press, 1990); Douglas A. Rossman, *Where Legends Live: A Pictorial Guide to Cherokee Mythic Places* (Cherokee, NC: Cherokee Publications, 1988).

53 *The homeland of the Overhill Cherokee:* For Little Tennessee Valley history: Alberta and Carson Brewer, *Valley So Wild: A Folk History* (Knoxville, TN: East Tennessee Historical Society, 1975).

53 *This river was born: The Great Smokies and the Blue Ridge: The Story of the Southern Appalachians,* Roderick Peattie, ed. (New York: Vanguard Press, 1943).

53 *For at least nine thousand years:* For archaeological background on the Little Tennessee River basin and Tellico salvage archaeology thanks to Jefferson Chapman for interviews in February 1994 and for his *Tellico Archaeology* (Knoxville, TN: Tennessee Valley Authority, 1985); William Bruce Wheeler and Michael J. Mcdonald, *TVA and the Tellico Dam, 1936–1979: A Bureaucratic Crisis in Post-Industrial America* (Knoxville, TN: University of Tennessee Press, 1986).

54 *According to Cherokee tradition:* Charles Hudson, "Cherokee Concept of Natural Balance," *Indian Historian* 3, 1970.

55 *Also in the landscape:* Quoted in Raymond D. Fogelson, "The Conjuror in Eastern Cherokee Society," *Journal of Cherokee Studies* 2(2), 1980, p. 77.

56 *"I've been in Hell":* Quoted in *WPA Guide to Tennessee* (Knoxville, TN: University of Tennessee Press, 1986), p. 354.

56 *But to naturalist William Bartram:* Quoted in Jefferson Chapman, Hazel R. Delcourt and Paul A. Delcourt, "Strawberry Fields, Almost Forever: Generations of Prehistoric Native Americans Transformed the Landscape of Eastern Tennessee," *Natural History* 9, 1989, p. 31, from William Bartram, "Observations on the Creek and Cherokee Indians," *Transactions of the American Ethnological Society* 3, 1853.

57 *Yet the early British trader:* Quoted in *Valley So Wild*, p. 14.

57 *The Little Tennessee:* From James Mooney, "The Cherokee River Cult," *Journal of American Folk-Lore* 12(48), 1900, and analysis in Alan Edwin Kilpatrick, "Going to the Water: A Structural Analysis of Cherokee Purification Rituals," *American Indian Culture and Research Journal* 15(4), 1991.

58 *As for the* loca sacra *category:* On Chota's history thanks to Sara Gwenyth Parker and her "The Transformation of Cherokee Appalachia," Ph.D. dissertation, Ethnic Studies, U.C. Berkeley, 1991; Ronald Wright, *Stolen Continents: The "New World" Through Indian Eyes* (Boston: Houghton Mifflin Co., 1992); Duane Champagne, "Symbolic Structure and Political Change in Cherokee Society," *Journal of Cherokee Studies* 8(2), 1983.

59 *To the Cherokee, their ritual fires:* Will West Long, quoted in John Witthoft, "Cherokee Beliefs Concerning Death," *Journal of Cherokee Studies* 8(2), 1983, p. 72.

63 *Many became Christians:* Catherine L. Albanese, "Exploring Regional Religion: A Case Study of the Eastern Cherokee," *History of Religions* 23(3), 1984.

63 *They often arrived in Model Ts:* Aggie Ross Lossiah, "The Story of My Life as Far Back as I Can Remember," Joan Greene, ed., *Journal of Cherokee Studies,* 9(2), 1984, p. 89.

64 *Another old Indian who visited:* Quoted in *Valley So Wild*, p. 347.

64 *"If the water covers Chota":* Quoted in Harold Stambor, "Manifest Destiny and American Indian Religious Freedom, *Sequoyah, Badoni,* and the Drowned Gods," *American Indian Law Review,* 10, 1982, p. 63.

64 *Another elder remembered:* "Forgotten People of the Tellico Dam Fight," *New York Times*, November 11, 1979, p. 29.

65 *"The lake resulting from the dam":* William O. Douglas, "This Valley Waits to Die," *True,* 50, May 1969, pp. 42, 95.

65 *Near the site of Chota:* James C. Kelly, "Oconostota," *Journal of Cherokee Studies,* 3(4), 1979.

66 *Biologists alerted them:* Arlene Fradkin, *Cherokee Folk Zoology: The Animal World of a Native American People, 1700–1838* (New York: Garland Publishing Co., 1990), p. 131.

67 *With environmentalists peeling off:* An exception was author-naturalist Peter Matthiessen, whose powerful writings against the dam and for Cherokee religious rights included "This River Is Waiting to Die," *Sports Afield* 167, 1972; "The Price of Tellico," *Newsweek,* December 17, 1979; "How to Kill a Valley," *New York Review of Books,* 27(1), 1980.

69 *As I paid my respects:* John P. Brown, *Old Frontiers* (Kingsport, TN: Southern Publishers, 1939), p. 130.

CHAPTER FIVE: A Tale of Three Lakes—*Taos/Zuni*

73 *Since outsiders are not allowed:* James Cordova, "Blue Lake," in *New America: A Review* 2(3) (Albuquerque: University of New Mexico Publications Board, 1976), p. 14.

73 *For six thousand feet:* On the Taos Blue Lake story, the definitive chronicle remains R. C. Gordon-McCutchan, *The Taos Indians and the Battle for Blue Lake* (Santa Fe, NM: Red Crane Books, 1991); on the pueblo itself: John J. Bodine, "Taos Pueblo," Vol. 9, *Handbook of North American Indians* (Washington, D.C.: Smithsonian Institution, 1979); Merton L. Miller, *Preliminary Study of the Pueblo of Taos* (Chicago: University of Chicago Press, 1898).

74 *Mabel gained respect:* Mabel Dodge Lujan, *Winter in Taos* (New York: Harcourt, Brace & Co., 1935), pp. 203–4.

75 *The August trek:* John J. Bodine, "The Taos Blue Lake Ceremony," *American Indian Quarterly,* Spring 1988; "The Blue Lake Ceremonies: A Glimpse of Indian Religion," *American Indian Life,* bull. 13, October 1928; Frank Waters, "Pilgrimage to Blue Lake," Pt. II, Chapter 9, in *Masked Gods: Navaho and Pueblo Ceremonialism* (New York: Ballantine, 1950).

75 *Of pilgrimage there is:* On pilgrimages: Victor Turner, "Pilgrimages as Social Processes," Chapter 5, *Dramas, Fields, and Metaphors: Symbolic Action in Human Society* (Ithaca, NY: Cornell University Press, 1974).

76 There *is where Coyote did it:* M. Jane Young, *Signs from the Ancestors: Zuni Cultural Symbolism and Perceptions of Rock Art* (Albuquerque: University of New Mexico Press, 1988), p. 151.

77 *Reaching its shores:* Quoted in Bodine, *The Taos Blue Lake Ceremony,* 1988, p. 96.

77 *As one man illustrated:* Alfonso Ortiz, *The Tewa World* (Chicago: University of Chicago Press, 1969), p. 24. Pueblo cosmological principles and religious practices are summarized in Elsie Clews Parsons, *Pueblo Indian Religion,* 2 vols. (Chicago: University of Chicago Press, 1939); Kurt F. Anschuetz, "A Healing Place: Rio Grande Cultural Landscapes and the Petroglyph National Monument," *"That Place People Talk About": The Petroglyph National Monument Ethnographic Landscape Report,* by Kurt F. Anschuetz et al., Albuquerque: National Park Service, Petroglyph National Monument, 2002.

78 *Sometimes Pueblo cosmology is:* These concepts are illustrated in Rina Swentzell, "Pueblo Space, Form, and Mythology," *Pueblo Style and Regional Architecture,* Nicholas C. Markovich, Wolfgang F. E. Preiser, Fred C. Sturm, eds. (New York: Van Nostrand Reinhold, 1990).

78 *At Taos they do this:* On equinoctial races at Taos: Peter Nabokov, "Running, Power, and Secrecy at Taos,"*American West,* September/October 1982.

78 *"We are the people who live":* Quoted in Miguel Serrano, *C. G. Jung & Hermann Hesse: A Record of Two Friendships* (New York: Schocken Books, 1966), p. 87. Of this encounter with Antonio Mirabal (Mountain Lake), Jung told Jaime de Angulo, "I had the extraordinary sensation that I was talking to an Egyptian priest of

the fifteenth century before Christ." Gui de Angulo, *Jaime in Taos: The Taos Papers of Jaime de Angulo* (San Francisco: City Lights, 1985), p. 87.

78 *By the time Jung heard:* On the Blue Lake struggle: John J. Bodine, "Blue Lake: Struggle for Indian Rights," *American Indian Law Review* 1(1), 1973; "Taos Blue Lake Controversy," *Journal of Ethnic Studies* 6(1), 1978.

78 *"We have no buildings there":* Quoted in "Taos Seeks Justice," *Indian Affairs,* newslettter of the Association on American Indian Affairs, Inc., No. 63, 1966, p. 1.

78 *The Taos campaign to convey:* Background in Lawrence C. Kelly, "The Religious Freedom Issue," *The Assault on Assimilation: John Collier and the Origins of Indian Policy Reform* (Albuquerque: University of New Mexico Press, 1983).

79 *"Now may I ask a question":* Quoted in John T. Whatley, "The Saga of Taos Blue Lake," *Indian Historian* 21(3), 1969, p. 23.

79 *By 1960, one could hear:* Quoted in Gordon-McCutchan, *The Taos Indians and the Battle for Blue Lake,* 1991, p. 62.

80 *Six years later, however:* Ibid., p. 93.

80 *When a sympathetic priest:* From R. C. Gordon-McCutchan's interview with the Reverend Dean Kelly, November 29, 1989. Quoted in ibid., pp. 118–19.

80 *Aware that evoking:* Of watersheds, poet Gary Snyder says, "Symbolically and literally they're the mandalas of our lives. They provide the very idea of the watershed's social enlargement, and quietly present an entry into the spiritual realm that nobody has to think of, or recognize, as spiritual." Trevor Carolan, "The Wild Mind of Gary Snyder," *Shamabala Sun,* May 1996, p. 24.

80 *In the opinion of Taos historian:* Ibid., p. 119.

80 *Inspired by the Taos cause:* From R. C. Gordon-McCutchan's interview with Suzie Poole, quoted in ibid., pp. 177–79.

81 *What was preoccupying the group:* On the Zuni leg of the Coronado expedition: J. Wesley Huff, "A Coronado Episode," *New Mexico Historical Review* 26(2), 1951; Edmund J. Ladd, "Zuni on the Day the Men in Metal Arrived," *The Coronado Expedition to Tierra Nueva: The 1540–1542 Route Across the Southwest,* Richard Flint and Shirley Cushing Flint, eds. (Niwot, CO: University Press of Colorado, 1997); Frederick W. Hodge, *History of Hawikuh* (Los Angeles: The Southwest Museum, 1937); Henry E. Bolton, *Coronado: Knight of Pueblos and Plains* (New York: Whittlesey House, 1949); *The Journey of Coronado, 1540–1542,* George Parker Winship, tr. and ed. (Golden, CO: Fulcrum Pub., 1990).

83 *When tribal consultants:* T. J. Ferguson and E. Richard Hart, *A Zuni Atlas* (Norman, OK: University of Oklahoma Press, 1985), p. 51.

84 *And Zuni elders add:* Quoted in E. Richard Hart, Zuni and the Grand Canyon: A Glen Canyon Environmental Report (Seattle, WA: Institute of the North American West, 1995), p. 3.

84 *"All matter [to the Zuni]":* Ruth L. Bunzel, "Introduction to Zuni Ceremonialism," in *Zuni Ceremonialism* (Albuquerque: University of New Mexico Press, 1932, 1992), p. 483.

85 *But they were unaware:* On Zuni heaven: E. Richard Hart, "Protection of Kolhu/wala:wa ('Zuni Heaven'): Litigation and Legislation," *Zuni and the Courts: A Struggle for Sovereign Land Rights,* E. Richard Hart, ed. (Lawrence, KS: University Press of Kansas, 1995); Barton Wright and Duane Dishta, *Kachinas of the Zuni*

(Flagstaff, AZ: Northland Press, 1985); Will Roscoe, *The Zuni Man-Woman* (Albuquerque: University of New Mexico Press, 1991); "Spirit World of the Zunis," *The Zunis: Self-Portrayals* (Albuquerque: University of New Mexico Press, 1972); Douglas Preston, *Cities of Gold: A Journey Across the American Southwest,* Chapter 19 (Albuquerque: University of New Mexico Press, 1992), pp. 266–75; *Cushing at Zuni: The Correspondence and Journals of Frank Hamilton Cushing, 1879–1884,* Jesse Green, ed. (Albuquerque: University of New Mexico Press, 1990).

86 *Getting the right to:* Hank Mershorer, "The Sacred Trail to Zuni Heaven: A Study in the Law of Prescriptive Easements," *Zuni and the Courts: A Struggle for Sovereign Land Rights,* E. Richard Hart, ed. (Lawrence, KS: University Press of Kansas, 1995).

87 *The future for a third sacred lake:* On Zuni salt lake: Nat Stone, "The Spirit of Zuni Salt Lake," *Preservation,* 56(3), 2004, p. 45; Barbara Tedlock, "Old Lady Salt," *The Beautiful and the Dangerous: Encounters with the Zuni Indians* (New York: Viking, 1992); E. Richard Hart and T. J. Ferguson, *The Fence Lake Mine Project* (Salt Lake City: Institute of the North American West, 1993).

87 *As the Zuni tell it:* The Zuni People, "Story of Salt Lake," *The Zunis: Self-Portrayals* (Albuquerque: University of New Mexico Press, 1972), pp. 205–6.

90 *"We do this not only for":* Jung recalled this conversation variously; I combine Serrano, *C. G. Jung & Hermann Hesse: A Record of Two Friendships,*1966, pp. 87–88, with Carl Jung, *Memories, Dreams, Reflections* (New York: Pantheon, 1962), p. 252.

CHAPTER SIX: **Place as Personal—***Navajo/Apache*

91 *Understanding Navajo Indian history:* Of Navajo perspectives on their origins, writes historian Peter Iverson, "Navajo history does not start in Alaska or northwestern Canada. . . . It begins with Changing Woman, with the Hero Twins, with monsters, and with blue horses. It begins with the sacred mountains." *Dine: A History of the Navajos* (Albuquerque: University of New Mexico Press, 2002), p. 5.

91 *In laying claim:* In place of Anasazi, meaning "enemy ancestors," today's preferred term for the builders of the Mesa Verde and Chaco Canyon ruins is "ancestral Pueblo."

91 *One strategy that the Navajo:* Editha Watson introduced me to Richard Van Valkenburg's tallies of Navajo sacred places for the U.S. Indian Service from the 1930s, then gave me her compilation, *Navajo Sacred Places* (Window Rock, AZ: Navajo Tribal Museum, 1964). Cultural geographer Stephen C. Jett shared findings on Navajo places, including especially his work in Canyon de Chelley. Other inventories include Alan Wilson, with Gene Dennison, *Navajo Place Names: An Observer's Guide* (Guilford, CT: Jeffrey Norton Publishers, 1995); Laurence D. Linford, *Navajo Places: History, Legend, Landscape* (Salt Lake City: University of Utah Press, 2000). For collaborations between Klara B. Kelley and Navajos listing/interpreting *dahodiyini* locations (associated with old narratives, historical events and ceremonial/traditional activities) see Klara B. Kelley and Harris Francis, "Places Important to Navajo People," *American Indian Quarterly* 17(2), 1993; Klara B. Kelley and Harry Francis, *Navajo Sacred Places* (Bloomington, IN: Indiana University Press, 1994); Klara B. Kelley, Alexa Roberts and Richard M. Begay, *Bit'iis Nineezi (The*

River of Neverending Life, Navajo History and Cultural Resources of the Grand Canyon and the Colorado River (Window Rock, AZ: Navajo Nation Preservation Dept., 1995).

92 *When Pueblo Indian friends: Finding the Center: Narrative Poetry of the Zuni Indians,* Dennis Tedlock, ed. and tr. (Lincoln, NB: University of Nebraska Press, 1972), p. 297.

93 *Each peak also had:* Karl W. Luckert, personal communication to me, June 10, 1981.

94 *Wearing hard-soled moccasins:* Karl W. Luckert, *The Navajo Hunter Tradition* (Tucson: University of Arizona Press, 1975), p. 195.

94 *Because of these origins:* W. W. Hill, *The Agricultural and Hunting Methods of the Navaho Indians* (New Haven: Yale University Press, 1938), p. 53.

95 *But a dozen or so Navajo:* Navajo history of Rainbow Bridge from Karl W. Luckert, *Navajo Mountain and Rainbow Bridge Religion* (Flagstaff, AZ: Museum of Northern Arizona, 1977).

96 *"Time and again": Navajo Stories of the Long Walk Period,* Ruth Roessel, ed. (Tsaile, AZ: Navajo Community College Press, 1973), p. xi.

97 *"After we get back":* Quoted in *Navajo: A Century of Progress, 1868–1968,* Martin A. Link, ed. (Window Rock, AZ: The Navajo Tribe, 1968), p. 68.

97 *"When we saw the top":* U.S. Congress, 49th First Session, House of Representatives, Executive Document No. 263, p. 15.

97 *"Outside my own country":* Quoted in Robert S. McPherson, *Sacred Land, Sacred View: Navajo Perceptions of the Four Corners Region* (Salt Lake City: Brigham Young University, 1992), p. 2.

98 *And a hundred years later:* Quoted in Joseph Campbell, *Myths to Live By* (New York: Bantam, 1984), pp. 221–22.

98 *Explained a Navajo woman:* Emily Benedek, *Beyond the Four Corners of the World: A Navajo Woman's Journey* (New York: Alfred A. Knopf, 1995), p. 6.

98 *But this Navajo version:* Stewart Aitchison, *Red Rock—Sacred Mountain* (Stillwater, MN: Voyageur Press, 1992), p. 35. Writes geographer J. M. Powell of this relationship, "And those [American Indian] traditions were built upon a sense of territoriality which was frequently place-specific and rich in definitions of sacred grounds; it was also abundantly expressive of a reverent I-Thou relationship with nature which was, in practice, a far better guarantor of ecological integrities than anything in the contemporary repertoire of the white settler [which, Powell adds later, does not mean that Indians did not transform their environments]." *Mirrors of the New World: Images and Image-Makers in the Settlement Process* (Hamden, CT: Archon Books, 1977), p. 87.

99 *Petroleum came next:* On Navajo oil: Kathleen P. Chamberlain, *Under Sacred Ground: A History of Navajo Oil* (Albuquerque: University of New Mexico Press, 2000).

99 *Outsiders were now:* Quoted in Robert S. McPherson, *Navajo Land, Navajo Culture: The Utah Experience in the Twentieth Century* (Norman, OK: University of Oklahoma Press, 2001), p. 187.

99 *"Bulldozers tore up the land":* Ibid.

99 *Klara Kelley and Harris Francis reported: Navajo Sacred Places,* Kelley and Francis, p. 163.

100 *More promising to tribal coffers:* On Navajo coal: Philip Reno, *Mother Earth, Father Sky: Navajo Resources and Economic Development* (Albuquerque: University of New Mexico Press, 1981).

100 *This intractable problem began:* On the Joint Use Area conflict and the struggle over Big Mountain: David M. Brugge, *The Navajo-Hopi Land Dispute: An American Tragedy* (Albuquerque: University of New Mexico Press, 1994); Catherine Feher-Elston, *Children of Sacred Ground: America's Last Indian War* (Phoenix: Northland Publishing, 1988); Anita Parlow, *Cry, Sacred Ground: Big Mountain U.S.A.* (Washington, D.C.: Christic Institute, 1988).

103 *"Holy children of":* Quoted in Luckert, *Navajo Mountain and Rainbow Bridge Religion,* 1977, pp. 86–99.

104 *Uranium was the next mixed blessing:* On Navajo uranium: "Navajo Miners Battle a Deadly Legacy of Yellow Dust," *New York Times,* May 13, 2003, p. D5.

106 *So in his effort to decontaminate:* Peter H. Eichstaedt, *If You Poison Us: Uranium and Native Americans* (Santa Fe: Red Crane Books, 1994). On central concept of *Hozho:* Gary Witherspoon, *Language and Art in the Navajo Universe* (Ann Arbor: University of Michigan Press, 1977).

106 *An overview of Athapaskan-speaking:* Originally published in 1984, 1988, 1993 and 1995, anthropological linguist Keith Basso's four essays on Apache place-names were resequenced for his prizewinning *Wisdom Sits in Places: Landscape and Language Among the Western Apache* (Albuquerque: University of New Mexico Press, 1996). Informing his readers that Western Apaches have three terms for marking kinds of "sacredness" and no term for "nature," Basso questions the utility of general words like "sacred" or "holy." He argues that they are incapable of communicating the regionally diverse, linguistically subtle and metaphysically sophisticated nature of native systems of thought and urges their avoidance altogether (p. 156).

108 *One incident, included in his earliest essay:* Basso, *Wisdom Sits in Places,* pp. 56–57.

109 *One of Basso's teachers:* Ibid., p. 59.

110 *Another of Basso's mentors:* Ibid., p. 127.

CHAPTER SEVEN: **Christ in the Flower World—***Yaqui*

111 *"These two facets":* Michael J. Sallnow, *Pilgrims of the Andes: Regional Cults in Cusco* (Washington, D.C.: Smithsonian Institution Press, 1987), p. 269. On *huacas: The Huarochiri Manuscript: A Testament of Ancient and Colonial Andea Religion,* Frank Salomon and George L. Urioste, eds. and trs. (Austin: University of Texas, 1991), in which they are defined as "any material thing that manifested the superhuman: a mountain peak, a spring, a union of springs, a rock outcrop, an ancient ruin, a twinned cob of maize, a tree split by lightning" (p. 17).

111 *An anthropologist:* Edward H. Spicer's writings on Yaquis include *Pasqua: A Yaqui Village in Arizona* (Tucson: University of Arizona Press, 1940, 1984); *Potam: A Yaqui Village in Sonora* (Menasha, WI: American Anthropological Assn., 1954); "The Yaqui Town," *The Yaquis: A Cultural History* (Tucson: University of Arizona Press, 1980); *Cycles of Conquest* (Tucson: University of Arizona Press, 1962).

112 *To glimpse this twist:* Thanks to Kirstin C. Erickson and her adoptive Yaqui

family for my November 1997 visit and for her "Ethnic Places, Gendered Spaces: The Expressive Constitution of Yaqui Identities" (Ph.D. dissertation, University of Wisconsin-Madison, Anthropology, 2000).

112 *Behind us Kirstin indicated:* Material from Ruth W. Giddings, *Yaqui Myths and Legends* (Tucson: University of Arizona Press, 1959, 1993); Muriel Thayer Painter, *With Good Heart: Yaqui Beliefs and Ceremonies in Pascua Village* (Tucson: University of Arizona Press, 1986); Kathleen M. Sands, "The Singing Tree: Dynamics of a Yaqui Myth," *American Quarterly* 35(4), 1983; Mini K. Valenzuela, *Yoeme: Lore of the Arizona Yaqui People* (Tucson: University of Arizona Press, 1977); Kirstin C. Erickson, "'They Will Come from the Other Side of the Sea': Prophecy, Ethnogenesis, and Agency in Yaqui Narrative," *Journal of American Folklore* 116(462), 2003, p. 471.

114 *You are an enchanted flower:* From a landmark study: Larry Evers and Felipe S. Molina, *Yaqui Deer Songs/Maso Bwikan: A Native American Poetry* (Tucson: University of Arizona Press, 1987), p. 44.

115 *The episode's influence:* Nicholas Bromell, "Family Secrets," *Harper's Magazine,* July 1992, p. 68.

115 *"The sorcery in Don Juan":* Oscar Ichazo on Carlos Castaneda, *New Age Journal,* June 1976.

116 *Twenty years before Carlos Castaneda:* On Spicer and Juan Valenzuela: Larry Evers and Felipe S. Molina, "The Holy Dividing Line: Inscription and Resistance in Yaqui Culture," *Journal of the Southwest,* vol. 34, no. 1, Spring, 1992, pp. 15–17; Rosamond B. Spicer, "A Full Life Well Lived: A Brief Account of the Life of Edward H. Spicer," *Journal of the Southwest* 32(1), 1990.

120 *"We feel sorry":* Quoted in Evers and Molina, "The Holy Dividing Line," p. 39.

120 *"They are hurting":* Quoted in ibid., p. 9.

121 *Under a series of hero martyrs:* Kirstin C. Erickson, "Moving Stories: Displacement and Return in the Narrative Production of Yaqui Identity," *Anthropology and Humanism* 28(2), 2003; Evelyn Hu-DeHart, *Yaqui Resistance and Survival: The Struggle for Land and Autonomy, 1821–1910* (Madison, WI: University of Wisconsin Press, 1984).

123 *Then is when and where:* Richard Schechner, "Waehma: Space, Time, Identity, and Theatre at New Pascua, Arizona," in *The Future of Ritual: Writing on Culture and Performance* (London: Routledge, 1993), p. 98.

124 *Only a stone's throw:* Quoted in Evers and Molina, "The Holy Dividing Line," pp. 15–17.

127 *"Coyote Dancers are here":* On the role, music and verses of this Yaqui Bow Leaders' Society: Larry Evers and Felipe S. Molina, *Wo'i Bwikam: Coyote Songs* (Tucson: Chax Press, 1990).

CHAPTER EIGHT: **Draining the Sacred Places—*Hopi***

129 *Walking closer, one realizes:* On Hopi prayer sticks and shrines: Barton Wright, "Ritual Objects," Chapter 4, *Hopi Material Culture* (Flagstaff, AZ: Northland Press, 1969); J. Walter Fewkes, "Hopi Shrines Near the East Mesa, Arizona," *American Anthropologist* 8, 1906.

129 *A sensitivity to wind:* James K. McNeley, *Holy Wind in Navajo Philosophy* (Tucson: University of Arizona Press, 1981).

130 *"You ask why":* Quoted in Peter Nabokov, "Hopis and the Love Generation," *Native American Testimony* (New York: Viking, 1999), pp. 392–93.

131 *Or as territorial historian:* Quoted in Charles Bowden, "Mountain Lying Down: Rediscovering the Kaibab Plateau," *Arizona Highways* 67(8), 1991, p. 26.

131 *One body of narratives:* Ekkehart Malotki and Michael Lomatuway'ma, *Maasaw: Profile of a Hopi God* (Lincoln, NB: University of Nebraska Press, 1987).

131 *To the early ethnographer:* Alexander M. Stephen, "Hopi Tales," *Journal of American Folklore*, 42, 1929, p. 55.

132 *Those footsteps defined Hopitutskwa:* Peter M. Whiteley, "Hopitutskwa: An Historical and Cultural Interpretation of the Hopi Traditional Land Claim," expert witness report presented to the court in *Masayesva vs. Zah vs. James* (unpublished, 1989, ninety-four pages); Louis A. Hieb, "Social Memory and Cultural Narrative: The Hopi Construction of a Moral Community," *Journal of the Southwest*, Vol. 44, No. 1, Spring, 2002.

132 *Wherever they halted:* On springs: Peter M. Whiteley, "Paavahu and Paanaqawu: The Wellsprings of Life and the Slurry of Death," *Cultural Survival Quarterly* 19(4), 1996; Walter Hough, "Sacred Springs of the Southwest," *Records of the Past*, 5, 1906.

133 *The process by which the clans:* Hartman Lomawaima, "Hopification, a Strategy for Cultural Preservation," Chapter 5, *Columbian Consequences,* Vol. 1, David Hurst Thomas, ed. (Washington, D.C.: Smithsonian Institution Press, 1989).

133 *They do this:* Armin Geertz, "A Reed Pierced the Sky: Hopi Indian Cosmography on Third Mesa, Arizona," *Numen*, 31, 1984, p. 230.

133 *Were it not for the Joint Use Area:* On the JUA: David M. Brugge, *The Navajo-Hopi Land Dispute: An American Tragedy* (Albuquerque: University of New Mexico Press, 1994).

134 *"The elders say that the shrines":* Quoted in Jake and Susanne Page, "Inside the Sacred Hopi Homeland," *National Geographic* 162(5), 1982, p. 626; the five-day boundary shrine pilgrimage also described in *Qua'toqti* "The Eagle's Cry," *New Oraibi,* October 19, 1978.

135 *The Hopi priests:* Research on Hopi habitats by Hopis, with anthropologist T. J. Ferguson: overview in Leigh Jenkins, Kurt E. Dongoske, and T. J. Ferguson, "Managing Hopi Sacred Sites to Protect Religious Freedom," *Cultural Survival Quarterly* 19(4), 1996, detailed in *Managi Ongtupqa Niqw Pisisvayu (Salt Canyon and the Colorado River): The Hopi People and the Grand Canyon* (Kykotsmovi, AZ: Hopi Cultural Preservation Office, 1998).

135 *The final stop:* On Woodruff Butte: thanks to Christopher McLeod for background research, interview transcripts for film, "In the Light of Reverence" (2002); Peter M. Whiteley, "The End of Anthropology at Hopi," *Journal of the Southwest* 35(2), 1993; Kurt E. Dongoske, Michael Yeats, and T. J. Ferguson, "Religious Freedom, Is It Truly Guaranteed for All Americans? A Hopi Case Study," paper, American Anthropological Association, November 24, 1996.

136 *Though not a Hopi:* On Hopi ties to San Francisco Peaks: John J. Feeney, Jr., "The Sacred Mountain of the Navajo and Hopi Indians: Recreational Expansion

and Religious Freedom on the San Francisco Peaks," unpublished report for Dr. and Mrs. Richard F. Wilson, submitted to U.S. Forest Service, Department of Agriculture, January 22, 1979; Christopher McLeod, "Healing the Sacred Sites," Sacred Land Film Project, La Honda, CA, 2000 annual report; *Save the Peaks Coalition* newsletter (Flagstaff, AZ), September 12, 2004.

137 *It was as if the new landscapes:* In this attitude Catholicism, as described in Fernando Cervantes, *The Devil in the New World: The Impact of Diabolism in New Spain* (New Haven: Yale University Press, 1994), and Protestantism found common ground. As Thomas Merton describes Christian demonization of Indian places: "The Puritans inherited a half-conscious bias against the realm of nature. . . . They hated it as a *person,* an extension of the Evil One, the Enemy opposed to the spread of the Kingdom of God. And the wild Indian who dwelt in the wilderness was also associated with evil" ("The Wild Places," *The Center Magazine* 1, 1969, pp. 40–44.

137 *During an archaeological dig:* Thanks to Charles E. Adams for sharing this experience; also for *Homol'ovi II: Archaeology of an Ancestral Hopi Village, Arizona,* Charles E. Adams and Kelley Hayes, eds. (Tucson: University of Arizona Press, 1991).

140 *And five years later:* Quoted in *Wilson v. Block, The Federal Reporter,* 2nd Series, U.S. Court of Appeals, 1983, pp. 740–41.

140 *In a painting by the Navajo artist:* Leland Wyman, *The Sacred Mountains of the Navajo in Four Paintings by Harrison Begay* (Flagstaff, AZ: Northland Press, 1967), fig. 4.

140 *Six years before they joined forces:* Quoted in Patrick Graham, et al., *San Francisco Peaks, a Plea to Protect* (Window Rock, AZ: Plateau Sciences Society, Navajo Tribal Museum, 1972).

141 *In testimony against the development:* Quoted in Aitchison, *Red Rock, Sacred Mountain,* p. 35.

141 *In what resembled:* Quoted in ibid., p. 116.

141 *To Emory Sekaquaptewa:* Quoted in John P. Duncklee, "Man-Land Relationships on the San Francisco Peaks" (unpublished ecological paper, n.d., deposited in Flagstaff's Museum of Northern Arizona Library), p. 75.

145 *The disappearance of any of them:* Whiteley, "Paavahu and Paahaqawu: The Wellsprings of Life and the Slurry of Death," p. 42.

CHAPTER NINE: A Geology of Power—*Plateau*

149 *"I was just endlessly":* Quoted in *New York Times,* April 3, 1999, p. A17.

149 *One American Indian region:* On Plateau Indian cultures: *Plateau.* Vol. 12, Deward E. Walker, Jr., ed., *Handbook of North American Indians* (Washington, D.C.: Smithsonian Institution Press, 1998); Verne F. Ray, *Cultural Relations in the Plateau of Northwestern America,* Vol. 3 (Los Angeles: Publications of the F. W. Hodge Anniversary Publications Fund, 1939); James A. Teit, *The Salishan Tribes of the Western Plateau,* Annual Report No. 45 (Washington, D.C.: Bureau of American Ethnology, 1928).

150 *To Indians, those geological:* Among Plateau folklore collections pertaining to environmental change: Ella E. Clark, *Indian Legends from the Northern Rockies* (Norman, OK: University of Oklahoma Press, 1966); *Folk-Tales of Salish and Sa-*

haptin Tribes, James Teit and Franz Boas, eds. (Lancaster, PA: Memoirs of the American Folklore Society, No. 11, 1917); Rodney Frey, *Stories That Make the World: Oral Literature of the Indian Peoples of the Inland Northwest as Told by Lawrence Aripa, Tom Yellowtail and Other Elders* (Norman, OK: University of Oklahoma Press, 1995); Rodney Frey and Dell Hymes, "Mythology," in *Plateau,* Vol. 12, op. cit., Deward E. Walker, ed.

150 *"Perhaps nowhere in America":* Verne F. Ray, "The Bluejay Character in the Plateau Spirit Dance," *American Anthropologist,* 39, 1937, p. 593f.

151 *I was paying my respects:* Quotes from Carling Malouf and Thain White, "Recollections of Lasso Stasso," *Anthropology and Sociology Papers* #12 (Missoula, MT: University of Montana, 1952); on Columbia plateau sites: James D. Keyser, "Western Montana Rock Art: Images of Forgotten Dreams," *Montana: Magazine of Western History* 42(3), 1992.

152 *It has been argued:* This debate over whether hunting magic or vision questing came first is reflected in competing interpretations of Mohave Desert rock art, where sheep depictions are said to support the former while other pictographs are interpreted as mementos of the latter (Lawrence Biemiller, "Rock Star," in *UCLA Magazine,* Summer, 2001, p. 19).

152 *"Before the Black Robes came":* Quoted in Arthur L. Stone, *Following Old Trails* (Missoula, MT: Morton John Elrod, 1913), p. 94.

153 *Explained another Plateau Indian:* Quoted in Marius Barbeau, *Indian Days on the Western Prairies,* bull. 1663, Anthropology Series No. 46 (Ottawa: National Museum of Canada, 1960), p. 50.

154 *Wrote Father Urban Grassi:* Quoted in Sister Maria I. Raufer, *Black Robes and Indians of the Last Frontier* (Milwaukee: Bruce Publishing Co., 1966), p. 155.

154 *Across the sacred geographies:* Based on lifelong study of Plateau Indian religions in particular, Deward E. Walker, Jr., rejects the view of French sociologist Emile Durkheim that sacred places are always forbidden zones set aside from the profane and favors the more flexible argument of scholar Mircea Eliade "that the sacred can be accessed and experienced directly through ritual practice at appropriate times and geographical locations" ("Durkheim, Eliade, and Sacred Geography in Northwestern North America," in *Chin Hills to Chiloquin: Papers Honoring the Versatile Career of Theodore Stern,* Eugene, OR: Department of Anthropology, 1966, p. 67).

155 *All Plateau peoples:* On river-connected beliefs: Eugene S. Hunn, *Nch'i-Wana: "The Big River," Mid-Columbia Indians and Their Land* (Seattle: University of Washington Press, 1990); Kenneth D. Tollefson and Martin L. Abbott, "From Fish Weir to Waterfall," *American Indian Quarterly* 17(2), 1993.

155 *Just before the Columbia River:* On Priest Rapids: Robert E. Greengo, *Studies in Prehistory: Priest Rapids and Wanapum Reservoir Areas, Columbia River,* final report to the U.S. Department of Interior (Seattle, WA: University of Washington, 1982); *An Archaeological Survey of the Priest Rapids Reservoir: 1981,* Randall F. Schalk, ed. (Laboratory of Archaeology and History, Pullman, WA: Washington State University, 1982).

156 *Among local officials:* On Smohalla, his religion and influence: Robert H. Ruby and John A. Brown, *Dreamer-Prophets of the Columbia Plateau: Smohalla and Skolaskin* (Norman, OK: University of Oklahoma Press, 1989); Click Relander, *Drummers and Dreamers* (Caldwell, OH: Caxton Printers, 1956); Clifford E. Trafzer

and Margery Ann Beach, "Smohalla, the Washani, and Religion as a Factor in Northeastern Indian History," in *American Indian Prophets,* Clifford E. Trafzer, ed. (Sacramento, CA: Sierra Oaks Publishing Co., 1986).

156 *In the 1880s, a veteran:* Quotes from this interchange in E. L. Huggins, "Smohalla, the Prophet of Priest Rapids," *Overland Monthly,* February 1891, pp. 208–15.

159 *In July of 1884:* Quotes from this interchange in Junius W. MacMurray, "The 'Dreamers' of the Columbia River Valley in Washington Territory," *Transactions of the Albany Institute,* Vol. 11 (Albany, NY: Webster and Skinners, 1887), pp. 241–48.

160 *Then MacMurray heard:* Ibid., p. 248.

160 *Under the name of the Washani Faith:* On the Plateau Indian religion known as Washani, Washat, or Seven Drums, see Deward E. Walker, Jr., and Helen H. Schuster, "Religious Movements," *Plateau,* Vol. 12, *Handbook of North American Indians,* Deward E. Walker, Jr., ed. (Washington, D.C.: Smithsonian Institution, 1998).

163 *But scholars hired by Northern Lights:* Initial Decision, U.S. Federal Energy Regulatory Commission, Northern Lights, Inc., Project No. 2752-000, April 23, 1982, pp. 90–91; Olga W. Johnson, *Flathead and Kootenay: The Rivers, the Tribes and the Region's Traders* (Glendale, CA: Arthur H. Clark Co., 1969).

163 *Skeptics suggested:* Other Indian groups involved in land disputes have been similarly challenged about whether they were opportunistically transforming local sites into spiritually pivotal locations, such as the Penobscot of Maine about Mount Katahdin (Alvin H. Morrison, "The Spirit of the Law Versus the Storm Spirit: A Wabanaki Case," Papers of the Thirteenth Algonquian Conference, 1982); the Havasupai of Arizona about Grand Canyon (Carma Lee Smithson and Robert C. Euler, "Preface," *Havasupai Legends: Religion and Mythology of the Havasupai Indians of the Grand Canyon* [Salt Lake City: University of Utah Press, 1994, pp. x–xi]); and the Chumash of California about Point Conception (Brian Haley and Larry Wilcoxon, "Anthropology and the Making of Chumash Tradition," *Current Anthropology* 38(5), 1997).

163 *At first, the writings:* Emile Durkheim, *The Elementary Forms of the Religious Life* (New York: Collier Books, 1915, 1961), p. 52.

164 *Without benefit of fieldwork:* Thanks to David L. Carrasco for his unpublished affidavit on behalf of the Indian claims, "Sacred Space and Religious Vision in World Religions: A Context to Understand the Religious Claims of the Kootenai Indians," 1982, n.p.

164 *These analogies between:* Mircea Eliade, Chapter 1; *The Myth of Eternal Return* (Princeton, NJ: Princeton University Press, 1954); Ruth Benedict, *Patterns of Culture* (New York: World Publishing, 1963), Chapter 10. For critics: Guilford Dudley III, *Religion on Trial: Mircea and His Critics* (Philadelphia: Temple University Press, 1976); John A. Saliba, *Mircea Eliade: An Anthropological Evaluation* (Leiden, Germany: E. J. Brill, 1976); Sam. D. Gill, *Mother Earth: An American Story* (Chicago: University of Chicago Press, 1987).

167 *Without compelling evidence:* Initial Decision, U.S. Federal Energy Regulatory Commission, Northern Lights, Inc., Project 2752-000, April 23, 1982, p. 5.

CHAPTER TEN: **Priestly Skies, Shamanic Earth—***Pawnee*

169   *In 1962, a young urologist:* Thanks to Pahaku owners Lou and Geri Gilbert and caretaker Cherrie Beam-Clarke for visits and interviews between May 1996 and June 2001, and their privately commissioned ecological report: A. Tyrone Harrison, *Pahuk Bluff: An Important Historic-Natural Area in Saunders County, Nebraska*, December, 1984.

169   *Since at least the fourteenth century:* On the Pawnee: Douglas R. Parks, "Pawnee," in *Plains*, Vol. 13, Pt. 1, *Handbook of North American Indians*, Raymond J. DeMallie, ed. (Washington, D.C.: Smithsonian Institution Press, 2001); Gene Weltfish, *The Lost Universe* (Lincoln, NB: University of Nebraska Press, 1965, 1977); Alexander Lesser, *The Pawnee Ghost Dance Hand Game* (Lincoln, NB: University of Nebraska Press, 1933, 1996).

171   *Three years after the Gilberts:* Thanks to Douglas R. Parks for his unpublished Harry Mad Bear text, elicited in August 1966: "Pacha and the Doctors' Dance," which features the sacred site of Pahaku.

172   *In writings by Melvin Gilmore:* Melvin R. Gilmore, "Trip with White Eagle Determining Pawnee Sites, August 27–29, 1914" and "The Legend of Pahuk," mss. 1914 (Lincoln, NB: Nebraska Historical Society Collections); "The Holy Hill Pahok," in *Prairie Smoke* (St. Paul, MN: Minnesota Historical Society Press, 1987).

173   *From Pawnee friends:* Cited in Louise Pound, "Nebraska Cave Lore," *Nebraska History* Vol. 29, 1948, p. 302.

173   *Then Parks reviewed the work:* Waldo R. Wedel, "Native Astronomy and the Plains Caddoans," in *Native American Astronomy*, Anthony F. Aveni, ed. (Austin, TX: University of Texas Press, 1977).

174   *From the "red rascals":* Judith A. Boughter, *The Pawnee Nation: An Annotated Research Bibliography* (Lanham, MD: The Scarecrow Press, 2004), p. 45.

174   *From lance and arrow points:* On Pawnee archaeology: *The Cellars of Time* (Lincoln, NB: *NEBRASKAland* magazine, 72(1), 1994); Waldo R. Wedel, "Some Reflections on Plains Caddoan Origins," *Nebraska History* 60(2), 1979, pp. 272–93.

177   *Pawnee priests looked:* On Pawnee astronomy: Von Del Chamberlain, *When Stars Came Down to Earth: Cosmology of the Skidi Pawnee Indians of North America* Los Altos, CA: Ballena Press, 1982), and Douglas R. Parks's critique, "Interpreting Pawnee Star Lore: Science or Myth?," *American Indian Culture and Research Journal* 9(1), 1985.

178   *From Alice Fletcher's:* Alice C. Fletcher, *The Hako: A Pawnee Ceremony*, Bureau of American Ethnology, 22nd Annual Report, Pt. 2 (Washington, D.C.: Smithsonian Institution, 1904), pp. 77–78.

179   *Sixteen years after Doug Parks:* Account from a prizewinning essay by Douglas R. Parks and Waldo R. Wedel, "Pawnee Geography: Historical and Sacred," *Great Plains Quarterly* 5(3), 1985.

181   *"To make tourists":* W. E. Webb, *Buffalo Lands* (Philadelphia: George Maclean, 1874), pp. 398–401.

183   *But when white settlers:* The rapidity of ecological transformations in Pawnee country is covered by Richard White, "The Cultural Landscape of the Pawnees," *Great Plains Quarterly* 2, 1982, and Chapters 6–9, in his *Roots of Depen-*

dency: Subsistence, Environment, and Social Change Among the Choctaws, Pawnees, and Navajos (Lincoln, NB: University of Nebraska Press, 1983).

184 *In 1846 they were forced:* David J. Wishart, "The Dispossession of the Pawnee," *Annals of American Geographers* 69(3), 1979; Alexander Lesser, *The Pawnee Ghost Dance Hand Game* (Madison, WI: University of Wisconsin Press, 1933, 1978).

187 *Three years later:* T. W. Morgan to the Gilberts, July 18, 1994; Vic Wasserman, "Return of the Pawnee," *Nance County Journal*, Vol. 116, No. 24 (Fullerton, NB), June 15, 1994, p. 1.

CHAPTER ELEVEN: **Journeys to Promised Lands—*Hidatsa/Crow***

188 *The distinction is:* In the Diane Johnson review of Joan Didion's *Where I Was From, New York Times Book Review*, December 4, 2003, p. 4.

189 *The first major tribe:* On the Mandan: Alfred W. Bowers, *Mandan Social and Ceremonial Organization* (Moscow, ID: University of Idaho Press, [1950], 1991).

191 *Next to arrive in Mandan country:* On the Hidatsa: Alfred W. Bowers, *Hidatsa Social and Ceremonial Organization* (Lincoln, NB: University of Nebraska Press, 1965, 1992); W. Raymond Wood, *The Origins of the Hidatsa Indians: A Review of Ethnohistorical and Traditional Data* (Lincoln, NB: J & L Reprint Co., 1980, 1986).

191 *"We thought our fields sacred":* Buffalo Bird Woman, *Waheenee: An Indian Girl's Story: Told by Herself to Gilbert L. Wilson* (Lincoln, NB: University of Nebraska Press, Bison Books, 1921, 1981), p. 41; see also Gilbert L. Wilson, *Buffalo Bird Woman's Garden: Agriculture of the Hidatsa Indians* (St. Paul, MN: Minnesota Historical Society Press, 1917, 1987), p. 27, in which Buffalo Bird Woman says, "We cared for our corn in those days as we would care for a child; for we Indian people loved our gardens, just as a mother loves her children; and we thought that our growing corn liked to hear us sing, just as children like to hear their mother sing to them."

191 *One important Hidatsa deity:* Alan R. Woolworth, "Archeological Investigations at Site 32ME59 (Grandmother's Lodge)," *North Dakota History* 23(2), 1956.

192 *Of all these promontories:* On the Hidatsa's "Earthnaming" rite, last of the "buffalo-calling rituals" and the ceremony that consolidated the tribe's tribal territory: Bowers, op. cit., pp. 433–38.

193 *Around 1849, a white trader:* Leroy R. Hafen, *Broken Hand: The Life of Thomas Fitzpatrick: Mountain Man, Guide and Indian Agent* (Lincoln, NB: University of Nebraska Press, 1931, 1973), especially Chapters 14 and 15 on the 1851 Treaty Council; also Raymond J. DeMallie, "Touching the Pen: Plains Indian Treaty Councils in Ethnohistorical Perspective," in *Ethnicity on the Great Plains,* Frederick C. Luecke, ed. (Lincoln, NB: University of Nebraska Press, 1980). Thanks to Ray DeMallie for a complete transcript of the St. Louis *Missouri Republican* newspaper dispatches, October 6–November 30, 1851, on the Fort Laramie council.

193 *But a story:* From *Autobiography of Crow's Heart*, unpublished manuscript, courtesy of Alfred W. Bowers in July 1983, pp. 90–92, based upon interviews Bowers conducted with Crow's Heart in 1929–1931.

196 *One well-tailored group:* On the Crow: Frederick E. Hoxie, *Parading Through History: The Making of the Crow Nation in America, 1805–1935* (New York: Cambridge University Press, 1995).

196 *"the finest delegation of Indians"*: Quoted in Hafen, *Broken Hand,* p. 295.

197 *The origin story of the Crow tribe:* My synthesis of Crow origin/migration stories is in "Cultivating Themselves: The Inter-Play of Crow Indian Religion and History" (Ph.D. dissertation, anthropology, U.C.- Berkeley, 1988).

199 *Opening his account:* Quotes from Barney Old Coyote in "Crow," *Encyclopedia of North American Indians,* Frederick E. Hoxie, ed. (Boston: Houghton Mifflin Co., 1996), p. 146.

201 *During the last quarter century:* On Mandan, Hidatsa and Three Affiliated Tribes history: Edward M. Bruner, "Mandan," in *Perspectives in American Indian Culture Change* (Chicago: University of Chicago Press, 1961); the magnificent Minnesota Historical Society Museum in St. Paul, MN, exhibition and catalog: Carolyn Gilman and Mary Jane Schneider, *The Way to Independence: Memories of a Hidatsa Indian Family, 1840–1920* (St. Paul, MN: Minnesota Historical Society Press, 1987).

203 *A few years later:* Thanks to Stanley A. Ahler for allowing Wayne Olts and me to film excavations at the Flaming Arrow/Charred Body village on Turtle Creek in July 1983 and to interview Dr. Alfred Bowers during his on-site visit; work summarized in Stanley A. Ahler, Thomas D. Thiessen, Michael K. Trimble, *People of the Willows: The Prehistory and Early History of the Hidatsa Indians* (Grand Forks, ND: University of North Dakota Press, 1991).

203 *Next I wanted to see:* On "Medicine Hole Cave," also known as Singer Butte and home of the sacred speckled owl, see Alexis Duxbury, "Killdeer Mountains Legacy," *North Dakota Outdoors* 51(2), 1988.

204 *At the Bismarck museum:* This experience is in Timothy P. McCleary, "Quest for the Morning Star Stone," *North Dakota Quarterly* 67(3–4), 2000.

205 *Noticing this parallel:* Joe Medicine Crow, "Crow Creation Story," *Archaeology in Montana,* Special Issue: Symposium on Crow-Hidatsa Separation, #1, 1980, p. 67.

CHAPTER TWELVE: The Heart of Everything—*Lakota/Cheyenne/Kiowa*

207 *Geography texts describe:* General works on the Hills and associated historical and religious disputes include: "The Heart of Everything That Is," William Greider, *Rolling Stone,* May 7, 1987; Mario Gonzalez, "The Black Hills: The Sacred Land of the Lakota and Tsistsistas," *Cultural Survival Quarterly,* Winter, 1996; Tom Charging Eagle and Ron Zeilinger, *Black Hills: Sacred Hills* (Chamberlain, SD: Tipi Press, 1992); Edward Lazarus, *Black Hills, White Justice: The Sioux Nation Versus the United States, 1775 to the Present* (New York: HarperCollins, 1991); Francis White Lance, *Why the Black Hills Are Sacred* (Rapid City, SD: Ancestors Inc., 2004).

207 *Reaching for an adequate:* Patricia C. Albers's unpublished opus on the Wind Cave and the Black Hills: "The Home of the Bison: An Ethnographic and Ethnohistorical Study of Traditional Cultural Affiliations to Wind Cave National Park" (U.S. National Park Service and The Department of American Indian Studies, University of Minnesota, September 29, 2003), p. 441.

207 *Well before white explorers:* Ibid., pp. 14–15.

207 *And upward of thirteen thousand:* On geological and archaeological history of the Hills: Linea Sundstrom, *Storied Stone: Indian Rock Art in the Black Hills Country* (Norman, OK: University of Oklahoma Press, 2004).

207 *The density and variety:* Linea Sundstrom, "The Sacred Black Hills: An Eth-nohistorical Review," in *American Indians,* Nancy Shoemaker, ed. (Malden, MA: Blackwell Publishers Inc., 2001), pp. 189–90.

208 *But by July of 1874:* James Calhoun, *With Custer in '74: James Calhoun's Diary of the Black Hills Expedition,* Lawrence A. Frost, ed. (Provo, UT: Brigham Young University Press, 1979), p. 40.

210 *As much gold:* Donald Worster, "The Black Hills: Sacred or Profane?," *Under Western Skies: Nature and History in the American West* (New York: Oxford University Press, 1992), p. 107.

210 *Few places in America:* For background: Jesse Larner, *Mount Rushmore: An Icon Reconsidered* (New York: Thunder's Mouth Press/Nation Books, 2002). Expressing some Indian responses to this site is Lakota educator and author Elizabeth Cook-Lynn, through her poem "Mount Rushmore": "Owls hang in the night air/between the visages of Washington, Lincoln,/The Rough Rider, and Jefferson; and coyotes/mourn the theft of sacred ground./A cenotaph becomes the tourist temple/of the profane" (*Seek the House of Relatives* [Marvin, SD: The Blue Cloud Quarterly Press, 1983]). Cook-Lynn has also weighed in on the Crazy Horse Memorial: "Is the Crazy Horse Monument Art? Or Politics?" in *Anti-Indianism in Modern America: A Voice from Tatekeya's Earth* (Urbana, IL: University of Illinois Press, 2001). Even though Great Plains chronicler Mari Sandoz approved of such a memorial, she felt "Ziolkowski's conception is too Germanic, with the heavy-muscled, rounded chest figure, and the Germanic hair blowing back" (*Letters of Mari Sandoz,* Helen Winter Stauffer, ed. [Lincoln, NB: University of Nebraska Press, 1992], p. 160).

211 *In his 1992 overview:* Op. cit., p. 142.

211 *To Worster, the Sioux position:* Ibid., p. 150.

211 *Yet while he was:* Ibid., p. 153.

211 *For visual documentation:* Borrowing Bad Heart Bull's four hundred drawings for her academic thesis (published as Amos Bad Heart Bull and Helen H. Bliss, *A Pictographic History of the Western Sioux,* Lincoln, NB: University of Nebraska Press, 1995), Helen Bliss had them photographed before returning the old ledger book in 1940 to Bad Heart Bull's sister, Mrs. Dolly Pretty Cloud, with whom it was buried. Using concepts in Bad Heart Bull's map of Black Hills sacred sites (Bad Heart Bull and Bliss, p. 289) are Julian Rice, "Beyond the Race Track: *Paha Wakan Lakota,*" *North Dakota Quarterly,* Spring, 1985, and Ronald Goodman, *Lakota Star Knowledge: Studies in Lakota Stellar Theology* (Rosebud, SD: Sinte Gleska University, 1992). Other cartographic materials that may still turn up include paintings by artist Eagle Hawk, mentioned by Mari Sandoz as depicting He Dog and Crazy Horse guarding the Black Hills (*Letters of Mari Sandoz,* Helen Winter Stauffer, ed. [Lincoln, NB: University of Nebraska Press, 1992], pp. 236–37).

212 *That name derived:* Among Black Hills "Great Race" narratives are "To Feed My People: The Race Between the Buffalo and Man," told by Cheyenne Mary Little Bear Inkanish (*American Indian Mythology,* Alice Marriott and Carol K. Rachlin, eds. [New York: Thomas Y. Crowell, 1968]).

212 *As for the lack:* Bishop William H. Hare to the *New York Tribune,* July 30, 1880.

213 *Referring to the 1805–1834 period:* George E. Hyde, *Red Cloud's Folk: A History of the Oglala Sioux* (Norman, OK: University of Oklahoma Press, 1937), p. 42.

213 *Through this opening:* Luther Standing Bear, *My People the Sioux* (Boston: Houghton Mifflin, Co., 1928), p. 17.

214 *This was the mystical experience:* John Neihardt, *Black Elk Speaks* (Lincoln, NB: University of Nebraska Press [1932] 1961), p. 43.

214 *According to Indians:* These Lakota sites are enumerated in Linea Sundstrom, op. cit., pp. 166–79; but Sundstrom also discusses Black Hills places that have been spiritually meaningful for the Cheyenne, Arapaho, Kiowa, Kiowa-Apache, Arikara and Mandan.

215 *Best known of the Black Hills:* On Kiowa stories about the Tower, see N. Scott Momaday, *The Way to Rainy Mountain* (Albuquerque: University of New Mexico Press, 1969, pp. 8–9), and John Peabody Harrington, "Kiowa Memories of the Northland," in *So Live the Worlds of Men, Seventieth Anniversary Volume, Honoring Edgar Lee Hewitt,* D. D. Brand and F. E. Harvey, eds. (Albuquerque: University of New Mexico Press, 1939), pp. 162–76, in which the siblings escaping from the female bear become the Pleiades instead of the Big Dipper. A full Cheyenne version is Jeannette Howlingcrane's "Bear Tepee," in *Cheyenne Texts: An Introduction to Cheyenne Literature,* Wayne Leman, ed. (Greeley, CO: Museum of Anthropology, University of Northern Colorado, 1980), pp. 13–16.

217 *But after Indians protested:* Ralph L. Beals, "Ethnological Report: Devil's Tower National Monument," U.S. National Park Service, March 20, 1934, p. 1.

217 *Complaining about the climbing craze:* Quoted in Barry Tindall, "Aldo Leopold—A Philosophy and a Challenge," *Issues in Outdoor Recreation,* Clayne R. Jensen and Clark T. Thorstenson, eds. (Minneapolis, MN: Burgess Publishing Co., 1972), p. 5. Support for climbing the Tower is still widespread; as part of its campaign to "Do the American Classics," one national magazine urged readers to "rediscover the routes that inspired the pioneers of adventure: Climb Devils Tower" (*National Geographic Adventure,* April 2002, p. 77), while an environmental journal proudly dispatched its senior editor "to climb Devil's Tower, a fantastic fluted rock stump that looms over the sagebrush of northeastern Wyoming" (*Audubon,* December 2002, p. 122); neither piece hinted at Indian cultural concerns over the Tower.

218 *In the opinion of Dave Ruppert:* Personal communication to author, October 1996.

218 *To seal this "gift of the earth":* The central role of the Black Hills and Bear Butte, or *Nowah'wus* ("the hill where people are taught"), in the origin of the Cheyenne's Massaum, or "wonderful dance," the narrative of how the legendary Cheyenne leader Sweet Medicine received the Sacred Arrows and his establishment of the Tsistsistas nation, are in Karl H. Schlesier, *The Wolves of Heaven: Cheyenne Shamanism, Ceremonies, and Prehistoric Origins* (Norman, OK: University of Oklahoma Press, 1987), pp. 76–83, and Father Peter J. Powell, *Sweet Medicine: The Continuing Role of the Sacred Arrows, the Sun Dance, and the Sacred Buffalo Hat in Northern Cheyenne History,* 2. vols. (Norman, OK: University of Oklahoma Press, 1969), pp. 412–28.

218 *"For those who climb":* Peter J. Powell, "Power for New Days," in *The Plains Indians of the Twentieth Century,* Peter Iverson, ed. (Norman, OK: University of Oklahoma Press, 1985), p. 249.

219 *In the stories of Lakota: A Song from a Sacred Mountain,* Anita Parlow, ed. (Pine Ridge, SD: Oglala Lakota Rights Fund, 1983), p. 2.

219 *In February 1982:* Narratives and testimonies regarding Bear Butte's spiritual powers and legal disputes are collected in *A Song from a Sacred Mountain,* Anita Parlow, ed. Other Bear Butte accounts include Frank Fools Crow on his vision quests there since 1914, in *Fools Crow,* Thomas E. Mails, ed. (New York: Doubleday & Co., 1979); the fine summary "Bear Butte, South Dakota," in Andrew Guilford, *Sacred Objects and Sacred Places* (Boulder, CO: University Press of Colorado, 2000), pp. 144–48; "The Mysterious Butte," in Marie L. McLaughlin, *Myths and Legends of the Sioux* (Lincoln, NB: University of Nebraska Press, [1916] 1990), pp. 104–7; "Legends of Bear Butte," in James LaPointe, *Legends of the Lakota* (San Francisco: Indian Historian Press, 1976), pp. 111–13.

221 *This was around the time:* Patricia C. Albers, typescript of "Caves, Bison, Breath, and Winter: Synedoche and Synergism in Lakota Thought," paper presented at the Annual Conference of the Plains Anthropological Society, Billings, Montana, October 2004, p. 8.

221 *From her research:* Ibid., p. 2.

222 *"In being able":* Ibid., p. 9.

CHAPTER THIRTEEN: Singing the Origins—*Colorado River*

225 *Back then the West Coast:* Although tangential to my narrative, recent debate (summarized in Brian M. Fagan, "The Myth of the Garden of Eden: Later Societies of the West Coast," *Ancient North America* [London: Thames & Hudson, 2005]) juxtaposes the view of California's "environmental diversity and unparalleled riches" (as characterized in M. Kat Anderson, Michael G. Barbour and Valerie Whitworth, "A World of Balance and Piety: Land, Plants, Animals and Humans in a Pre-European California," in *Contested Eden: California Before the Gold Rush,* Ramon A. Gutierrez and Richard J. Orsi, eds. [Berkeley: University of California Press, 1998]) against research (summarized in *Prehistoric California: Archaeology and the Myth of Paradise,* L. Mark Raab and Terry L. Jones, eds. [Salt Lake City: University of Utah Press, 2004]) that challenges the image of California's stable, benign climate; argues for oscillating phases of aridity and scarcity; and maintains that acorn-based lifestyles were relatively late phenomena. Excellent on California Indian exploitation of natural resources: *Before the Wilderness: Environmental Management by Native Californians,* Thomas C. Blackburn and M. Kat Anderson, eds. (Menlo Park, CA: Ballena Press, 1993), and M. Kat Anderson, *Tending the Wild: Native American Knowledge and the Management of California's Natural Resources* (Berkeley: University of California Press, 2005).

226 *And California Indian history:* General works on California Indians include: Alfred L. Kroeber, *Handbook of the Indians of California,* bull. 78, Bureau of American Ethnology (Washington, D.C.: U.S. Government Printing Office, 1925); *California,* Vol. 8, *Handbook of North American Indians,* Robert F. Heizer, ed. (Washington, D.C.: Smithsonian Institution, 1978); *Surviving Through the Days: A California Indian Reader,* Herbert W. Luthin, ed. (Berkeley: University of California Press, 2002).

227 *As Alfred Kroeber:* Alfred L. Kroeber, "The Nature of Land-Holding Groups" (1954), for the California Indian Claims Case (Dockets 31–37), republished in *Aboriginal California: Three Studies in Culture History,* Robert F. Heizer, ed. (Berkeley: University of California Archaeological Research Facility, 1966), p. 119.

227   *A tally in 1980:* California Native American Heritage Commission, *Guide to Cultural Resource Preservation* (Sacramento, CA: Native American Heritage Commission, 1980).

227   *As the Haida:* George F. MacDonald, *Haida Monumental Art: Villages of the Queen Charlotte Islands* (Vancouver, Canada: University of British Columbia Press, 1983), p. 3.

228   *And from the Costanoan Indians:* Quoted in Kroeber, *Handbook,* 1925, p. 471.

228   *Tallest of America's Indians:* Jill Leslie Furst, *Mojave Pottery, Mojave People: The Dillingham Collection of Mojave Ceramics* (Santa Fe: School of American Research Press, 2001); Lorraine M. Sherer, *The Bitterness Road, the Mojave: 1604–1860* (Menlo Park, CA: Ballena Park, 1994); Jack D. Forbes, *Warriors of the Colorado: The Yumas of the Quechan Nation and Their Neighbors* (Norman, OK: University of Oklahoma, 1965).

229   *As anthropologist Howard Campbell:* In Robert Zingg, *Behind the Mexican Mountains,* Howard Campbell, John Peterson and David Carmichael, eds. (Austin, TX: University of Texas Press, 2001), p. 296.

230   *In 1900, the future dean:* Material from Alfred L. Kroeber field notebooks in Bancroft Library Archives, University of California-Berkeley.

232   *A drop of rain falling:* Alfred L. Kroeber, "The Mohave Account of Origins," *Journal of American Folklore* 19, 1926; John G. Bourke, "Notes on the Cosmogony and Theogony of the Mojave Indians of the Rio Colorado, Arizona," *Journal of American Folk-Lore* 2(6), 1889; John Peabody Harrington, "A Yuma Account of Origins," *Journal of American Folk-Lore* 21, 1908.

233   *Eight years his junior:* On Harrington: Victor Golla, "John P. Harrington and His Legacy," *Anthropological Linguistics,* Special Issue on J. P. Harrington, 33(4), 1991; Carobeth Laird, *Encounter with an Angry God: Recollections of My Life with John Peabody Harrington* (Banning, CA: Malki Museum Press, 1975).

233   *Exasperated by yet another example:* Quoted in John R. Johnson, Amy Miller, and Linda Agren, "The Papers of John P. Harrington at the Santa Barbara Museum of Natural History," *Anthropological Linguistics* 33(4), 1991, p. 373.

234   *The Mohave believed:* George Devereux, "Dream Learning and Individual Ritual Differences in Mohave Shamanism," *American Anthropologist* 59, 1952; Kenneth M. Stewart, "Mojave Indian Shamanism," *The Masterkey* 44, 1970, pp. 15–17.

234   *One of Kroeber's:* Quoted in Kroeber, *Handbook,* 1925, pp. 783–84.

235   *A second similarity:* On geographical references in Colorado River Indian song traditions: Philip M. Klasky, "An Extreme and Solemn Relationship" (master's thesis, Geography, San Francisco State University, 1977); Philip M. Klasky's "Storyscape Project," based on song-collecting work with Mohave tribal vice chairman and elder Llewellyn Barrachman, also reported in his "Song of the Land," *News from Native California* 12(1), Fall 1998, and "House of Night: The Mojave Creation Songs Return to the Keepers of the River," *News from Native California,* 13(1), Fall 1999.

235   *"What impressed Kroeber":* Donald Bahr, "Dream Songs," in *Handbook of Native American Literature,* Andrew Wiget, ed. (New York: Garland Publishing Co., 1996), p. 120. Also see *Spirit Mountain: An Anthology of Yuman Song and Story,* Leanne Hinton and L. Watahomigie, eds. (Tucson: Sun Tracks/University of Arizona Press, 1984).

236 *One reason Kroeber:* Alfred L. Kroeber, *A Mohave Historical Epic, Anthropological Records* 11(2) (Berkeley: University of California Press, 1951).

237 *If Bruce Chatwin:* On the remarkable life of Jaime de Angulo: Gui de Angulo, *The Old Coyote of Big Sur: The Life of Jaime de Angulo* (Berkeley: Stonegarden Press, 1995); Robert Brightman, "Jaime de Angulo and Alfred Kroeber: Bohemians and Bourgeois in Berkeley Anthropology," in *Significant Others: Interpersonal and Professional Commitments in Anthropology,* Richard Handler, ed. (Madison, WI: University of Wisconsin Press, 2004); Wendy Leeds-Hurwitz, *Rolling Around in Ditches with Shamans* (Lincoln, NB: University of Nebraska Press, 2004).

237 *In his memoir of hanging out with Pit River natives:* Jaime de Angulo, *Indians in Overalls,* included in *A Jaime de Angulo Reader,* Bob Callahan, ed. (Berkeley: Turtle Island, 1979), p. 208.

238 *Along with their creation stories:* Alfred L. Kroeber, *More Mohave Myths, Anthropological Records* 27 (Berkeley: University of California Press, 1972); Alfred L. Kroeber and G. B. Kroeber, *A Mohave War Reminisce, 1854–1880,* Publications in Anthropology Series 10 (Berkeley: University of California Press, 1973).

238 *And last, the Yuman ways:* Charles A. Lamb, "A Brief Description of the Cultural Significance of Intaglios and the Present Status of Preservation Efforts," Colorado River Indian Tribes Museum, unpublished manuscript, 1986; Lee Emerson, "A Quechan Man Speaks: Petroglyphs of Ancient Man," *Indian Historian* 4(1), 1971; Elaine Maryse Solari and Boma Johnson, "Appendix A. Intaglios: A Synthesis of Known Information and Recommendations for Management," *Hohokam and Patayan: Prehistory of Southwestern Arizona,* Randall McGuire and Michael B. Schiffer, eds. (San Diego: Academic Press, 1982); Boma Johnson, *Earth Figures of the Lower Colorado and Gila River Deserts: A Functional Analysis* (Yuma, AZ: Bureau of Land Management, 1985); Barry Lopez, "The Stone Horse," in *Crossing Open Ground* (New York: Charles Scribner's Sons, 1988), pp. 12, 16.

240 *All his wife, Theodora, could add:* Theodora Kroeber, *Alfred Kroeber: A Personal Configuration* (Berkeley: University of California Press, 1970), p. 220.

241 *"I have long pondered":* Kroeber, *More Mohave Myths,* 1972, p. xii.

242 *"To them Mastamho said":* Theodora Kroeber, "Literature of the First Americans," in *Look to the Mountaintop,* Charles Jones, ed. (San Jose, CA: Gousha Publications, 1972), p. 15.

242 *"The peaks reach":* Theodora Kroeber, op. cit., 221–20.

242 *"The Yumans have kept much":* Theodora Kroeber and Robert F. Heizer, *Almost Ancestors: The First Californians* (San Francisco: Sierra Club, 1968), p. 42.

243 *"Many ages ago":* Charles F. Thomas, Jr., "Ah-Ve-Koov-o-Tut, Ancient Home of the Mohave," *The Desert Magazine* 9(1), 1945, p. 17.

CHAPTER FOURTEEN: **Beyond the Goddess—*Southern California***

244 *In 1974, the phone rang:* Thanks to Charlotte McGowan for interview, September 2003.

245 *The homeland of the Indians:* On Kumeyaays: Florence C. Shipek, *Pushed into the Rocks: Southern California Indian Land Tenure, 1769–1986* (Lincoln, NB: University of Nebraska Press, 1987).

248 *"We went farther and farther":* Quoted in Florence C. Shipek ("as told to"), *The Autobiography of Delfina Cuero* (Morongo Indian Reservation, CA: Malki Museum Press, 1970), pp. 26, 67.

248 *One old Cupeño woman:* Quote from Mrs. Cela Apapas in Charles F. Lummis, "The Exiles of Cupa," *Out West* 16(5), 1902, p. 475.

249 *"He told us about":* From a Charlotte McGowan interview and her *Ceremonial Fertility Sites in Southern California,* San Diego Museum Papers No. 14 (San Diego: San Diego Museum of Man, 1982); also see David S. Whitley, "The Power of the Vulva," site 10, in *A Guide to Rock Art Sites in Southern California and Southern Nevada* (Missoula, MT: Mountain Press Pub. Co., 1996).

250 *And in striking contrast:* Quotes from girls' and boys' puberty ritual "sermons" in Kroeber, *Handbook,* 1925, pp. 684–85. While Kumeyaay ritual ground paintings represented "the special significance of their land base for their group identity" with attention to geographical realities, those of the neighboring Luiseno seemed to portray "a cosmological, not geographical world," according to Diana D. Wilson's "Report on Kumeyaay Cultural Affiliation," prepared for the University of California-Los Angeles NAGPRA Coordinating Committee (2002), p. 26.

250 *Straddling the invisible:* On Mount Kuchamaa (Mount Tecate), thanks to Dennis Gallegos for "Otay/Kuchamaa: Cultural Resource Background Study," prepared for USDI Bureau of Land Management, California Desert District (Carlsbad, CA: Gallegos and Associates, 2002), with its synthesis of 1979 environmental impact report on the mountain with information from anthropologist Florence Shipek; also, as told to Florence C. Shipek, *The Autobiography of Delfina Cuero* (Banning, CA: Malki Museum Press, 1970), p. 50; Leigh Fenly, "Kuchumaa: Mountain of Sacred Spirits," *San Diego Union,* July 25, 1982; Katherine Lobo, "Sacred Kuchumaa Mountain Holds Strange Mystical Power over Indians," *Tijuana Magazine,* April 1982.

251 *If a sacred mountain like Tecate:* On W. Y. Evans-Wentz: thanks to Ken Wade, and to Ken Winkler for his Evans-Wentz biography, *Pilgrim of the Clear Light* (Berkeley: Dawnfire Books, 1982); Donald S. Lopez, "Forward," in *The Tibetan Book of the Dead,* W. Y. Evans-Wentz, comp. and ed. (New York: Oxford University Press, 2000).

252 *But strong exception:* Florence C. Shipek review of W. Y. Evans-Wentz, *Cuchama and Sacred Mountains* (Chicago: Swallow Press/Ohio University Press, 1981) in *Journal of California and Great Basin Anthropology* 5(2), 1983; Shipek, "Kuuchamaa: The Kumeyaay Sacred Mountain," *Journal of California and Great Basin Anthropology* 7(1), 1985.

253 *To see Mount Tecate:* These Baja visits occurred in May 2003. To understand them I thank Michael Wilken-Robertson of the Instituto de Culturas Nativas de Baja California, Asociación Civil, for interviews in September 2004, and his edited volume *The U.S.-Mexican Border Environment: Tribal Environmental Issues of the Border Region* (San Diego: Southwest Center for Environmental Research/San Diego State University Press, 2004); on old native camps and sacred sites in the Rancho Viejo vicinity: William D. Hohenthal, Jr., *Tipai Ethnographic Notes: A Baja California Indian Community at Mid-Century* (Novato, CA: Ballena Press, 2001).

255 *Already working on this book:* Thanks to Brian Swann for an early look at his

introduction, *Algonquian Spirit* (Lincoln, NB: University of Nebraska Press, 2005). Special thanks to Cindi M. Alvitre for interviews in July 2004; for additional background on Gabrielino sites, thanks to Dr. Chester King, specialist in Southern California prehistory, to Wendy G. Teeter of UCLA's Fowler Museum for background on Playa Vista excavations and associated collections, to Carrie Martell for her master's thesis, "Sa'angna: Tonvga Perspectives on Development of the West Bluffs and Ballona Wetlands" (UCLA-American Indian Studies, 2004), to Rob Wood of California's Native American Heritage Commission for updates on Playa Vista burials, and to Jeffrey H. Altschul and Donn R. Grenda of Statistical Research Inc. for admission to the Westchester Bluffs and Playa Vista sites.

258 *In that decade:* Dolan H. Eargle, Jr., *Native American Guide: Weaving the Past and Present* (San Francisco: Trees Company Press, 2000), p. 49.

258 *By the late 1980s:* On Tongva-Gabrielino history and sites in the Los Angeles basin: William McCawley, *The First Angelinos: The Gabrielino Indians of Los Angeles* (Banning, CA: Malki Museum Press/Ballena Press, 1996). For additional information on toponyms: Leanne Hinton, "Native Californian Names on the Land," *Flutes of Fire: Essays on California Indian Languages* (Berkeley: Heyday Books, 1994), while an exemplary presentation of a Southern California tribal landscape is Lowell John Bean, Sylvia Brakke Vane, and Jackson Young, *The Cahuilla Landscape: The Santa Rosa and San Jacinto Mountains,* Anthropological Papers No. 37 (Menlo Park, CA: Ballena Press, 1991).

259 *When I moved to Los Angeles:* Background on the Ballona Creek wetlands: "At the Base of the Bluff: Archaeological Inventory and Evaluation Along Lower Centinela Creek, Marina del Rey," a report of the Playa Vista Archaeological and Historical Project, Jeffrey H. Altschul, Anne Q. Stoll, Donn R. Grenda and Richard Crolek-Torello, eds. (Tucson: Statistical Research Inc., 2003). And Jeffrey H. Altschul, Jeffrey A. Homberg and Richard S. Ciolek-Torrello, "Life in the Ballona: Archaeological Investigations at the Admiralty Site (CA-LAn-47) and the Channel Gateway Site (CA-LAn-1596-h)" (Tucson: Statistical Research, Inc., 1992).

261 *Years before David L. Belardes:* David L. Belardes, "The Ancestral Homeland and Archaeology," in *California Indians & Archaeology: A Special Report* (Berkeley: *News from Native California* 9[4], Summer 1996), p. 7.

262 *And Tongva-Gabrielino writer:* Gloria Arellanes, "What I Know," *News from Native California* 18(1), 2004, p. 14.

263 *And thus, as the Choctaw:* Okah Tubbee, *The Life of Okah Tubbe,* Daniel F. Littlefield, Jr., ed. (Lincoln, NB: University of Nebraska Press, 1988), p. 67.

CHAPTER FIFTEEN: **When Mountains Congregate—*Central California***

264 *In the early 1870s:* Stephen Powers, *Tribes of California* (Berkeley: University of California, 1877, 1976), pp. 109–10.

265 *"Living out the span":* Robert F. Heizer, "Natural Forces and World View," *California,* Vol. 8, Robert F. Heizer, ed., *Handbook of North American Indians* (Washington, D.C.: Smithsonian Institution, 1978), p. 649.

266 *"The idea that a certain, definable":* Quoted in Dean MacCannell, "Geography of the Unconscious: Robert F. Heizer Versus Alfred Kroeber on the Drawing of Indian Territorial Boundaries," *Cultural Geographies* 9, 2002, p. 6.

267 *In the center of Contra Costa County:* Bev Ortiz, "Mount Diablo as Myth and Reality: An Indian History Convoluted," *American Indian Quarterly* 13(4), 1989; "Mount Diablo State Park: General Plan," California Department of Parks and Recreation, November 1989.

268 *Mount Diablo's name:* Fernando Cervantes, *The Devil in the New World: The Impact of Diabolism in New Spain* (New Haven: Yale University Press, 1994). See also: James Brooke, "What's in a Name/An Affront, Say Some Tribes," *New York Times,* November 17, 1996, p. A28, in which Dr. Roger L. Payne, executive director of the U.S. Department of the Interior's U.S. Board of Geographic Names, explained, "Europeans tended to place 'Devil' on a feature of unusual nature, something that seemed to be created out of hellish forces."

269 *As the Franciscan Felipe Arroyo:* Quoted in *As the Padres Saw Them: California Indian Life and Customs as Reported by the Franciscan Missionaries, 1813–1815,* introduced and translated by Maynard Geiger, OFM (Santa Barbara, CA: Santa Barbara Mission Archive Library, 1976), p. 145.

269 *Shards of myths and legends:* On Sutter Buttes: Walt Anderson, *Inland Island: The Sutter Buttes* (Prescott, AZ: Natural Selection and the Middle Mountain Foundation, 2004); Louise Butts Hendrix, *Sutter Buttes: Land of Histum Yani* (Marysville, CA: Normart Printing Co., 1980); Peter Michael Jensen, "Notes on the Archaeology of the Sutter Buttes, Ca.," Papers on California and Great Basin Prehistory No. 2, Center for Archaeological Research at Davis, 1970; references in Roland B. Dixon, *The Northern Maidu* (New York, NY) American Museum of Natural History, bull. 27, 1905; Brian Bibby, *Deeper Than Gold* (Berkeley: Heyday Books, 2005); *The Maidu Indians Myths and Stories of Hanc'ibyjim,* William Shipley, ed. (Berkeley: Heyday Books, 1991).

270 *But then Earth Maker:* Quoted in Richard Simpson, *Ooti: A Maidu Legacy* (Milbrae, CA: Celestial Arts, 1977), p. 28.

270 *With their aromas:* Jane H. Hill, "The Flower World of Old Uto-Aztecan," *Journal of Anthropological Research* 48, 1992.

271 *Before the Weda, or "Flower Dance":* Quote from Lizzie Enos, in Simpson, *Ooti: A Maidu Legacy,* p. 46. Flower imagery and songs from Maidu in Powers, *Tribes of California,* pp. 307–9, from the Wintu in "Wintu Songs," *Anthropos* 30, 1935, pp. 383–94.

272 *For the thirty-five thousand square miles:* From Gary Snyder, "On Geography," an interview conducted by Richard Grossinger and David Wilk, November 9, 1971, p. 146.

272 *Forty miles west of Mount Diablo:* Thanks to ethnohistorian Beverly R. Ortiz for an interview, July 2003, regarding fragmentary Coast Miwok information on Tamalpais; also: Lincoln Fairley, *Mount Tamalpais: A History* (San Francisco: Scottwall Associates, 1987).

274 *In the preface:* In *A Jaime de Angulo Reader,* Bob Callahan, ed. (Berkeley: Turtle Island, 1979), p. 90.

276 *As a guide:* Powers, *Tribes of California,* pp. 361–68.

276 *A web of kinship:* On correspondences between Miwok social organization and Yosemite ecology: Edward W. Gifford, "Miwok Moieties," *University of California Publications in American Archaeology and Ethnology* 12(4), 1916; C. Hart Merriam, "Indian Village and Camp Sites in Yosemite Valley," *Sierra Club Bulletin,*

10, 1917. On Yosemite Indians: S. A. Barrett and E. W. Gifford, *Miwok Material Culture: Indian Life of the Yosemite Region* (Yosemite National Park: Yosemite Association, 1933, 1994).

277 *As with many of his environmentalist heirs:* Quoted in Richard F. Fleck, *Henry Thoreau and John Muir Among the Indians* (Hamden, CT: Archon Books, 1985), p. 50; best critical collection of Yosemite Indian stories and place-names: *Legends of the Yosemite Miwok,* Frank La Pena, Craig D. Bates and Steven P. Medley, compilers (Yosemite National Park: Yosemite Association, 1993).

277 *the same sort of "mineral reaction":* David Hare, *Via Dolorosa & When Shall We Live?* (London: Faber and Faber, Ltd., 1998), p. 23.

277 *And lest this comparison:* M. A. Curtin, introduction to Jeremiah Curtin, *Myths of the Modocs: Indian Legends of the Northwest* (New York: Benjamin Blom Inc., [1912], 1971), p. vi.

278 *When an 1886 view:* Quoted in *New York Times,* November 7, 2003, p. B26.

278 *"Yes, American," said Tenaya:* Lafayette Bunnell, *Discovery of the Yosemite in 1851* (Golden, CO: Outbooks, 1880, 1980), p. 132.

278 *Every road shoulder:* Rebecca Solnit is also good on Muir and the "disappeared" Yosemite Miwok: "Water, or Forgetting the Past: Yosemite National Park," Part II of her *Savage Dreams: A Journey into the Landscape Wars of the American West* (Berkeley: University of California Press, 1994).

279 *Adjoining the museum:* Credit for the Yosemite Indian Musem, outdoor exhibits, and research archive goes to curator Craig D. Bates, also author of the museum guide, *The Miwok in Yosemite* (Yosemite National Park: Yosemite Association, 1996).

280 *One way to preoccupy oneself:* From J. Alden Mason's "The Ethnology of the Salinan Indians," *University of California Publications in American Archaeology and Ethnology* 10, 1912, and "Language of the Salinan Indians," *University of California Publications in American Archaeology and Ethnology* 14, 1918; Pico Blanco (or "Pahch-kah-lah che-pil") is cited in the Rumsen Costanoan creation story: Alfred L. Kroeber, "Myths of South Central California," *University of California Publications in American Archaeology and Ethnology* 2, 1904.

280 *One descends from the exposed heights:* Abridged from my "Connection: The Cave of Hands," *Parabola* 6(1), 1981. This Church Creek rock shelter was pictured in Julian H. Steward's 1929 overview of California petroglyphs, identified as Site 4-Mnt-44 in Arnold R. Pilling's 1948 survey of Northern Monterey County's archaeology, and when I visited twenty-five years ago, was under study by archaeologists Gary S. Breschini and Trudy Haversat, whom I thank for taking me there. On archaeology of California "hand print" petroglyphs, see considerations of "topographic literacy" in Janet Lever, "In Touch with the Art," and Steve Freers, "The Hand Prints at CA-RIV-114: A Forensic and Anthropomorphic Study," both in *American Indian Rock Art,* Vol. 27 (Tucson: American Rock Art Research Association, 2001); also David Lewis-Williams and Jean Clottes on similar prints on another continent: "In the case of positive handprints, the inside of the hand was covered with paint and pressed against the wall. They might have had the same significance as hand stencils, that is, they established an intimate relationship between the participants and the hidden world of the spirits," *Les Chamanes de la Prehistoire: Trans et Magie dan les Grottes Ornees* (Paris: Edition du Seul, 1966), p. 95.

CHAPTER SIXTEEN: **Mourning and Renewal**—*Northern California*

283 *They distrust white "shaman" poets:* Geary Hobson, "The Rise of the White Shaman as a New Version of Cultural Imperialism," in *The Remembered Earth: Anthology of Contemporary Native American Literature* (Albuquerque: University of New Mexico Press, 1979).

283 *They dislike "plastic medicine men":* Alice B. Kehoe, "Primal Gaia: Primitivists and Plastic Medicine Men," *The Invented Indian: Cultural Fictions and Government Policies,* James A. Clifton, ed. (New Brunswick, NJ: Transaction Pub., 1990).

284 *And novelist Kurt Vonnegut, Jr.:* Kurt Vonnegut, Jr., *Wampeters, Foma and Granfalloons* (New York: Delacorte, 1974), p. 202.

284 *before the first Religious Crimes Code:* Background on Indian Bureau attempts to suppress Sun Dances and other religious and social practices in the historical review section of the American Indian Religious Freedom Act Report, P.L. 95-341, Washington, D.C., Federal Agencies Task Force, August 1979.

284 *During his tour of Canada: Rupert Brooke in Canada,* Sandra Martin and Roger Hall, eds. (Toronto: Peter Martin Assoc., 1978), pp. 120, 126.

285 *And years later:* Richard L. Rubenstein, *Morality and Eros* (New York: McGraw-Hill, 1970), p. 180.

285 *"No trolls":* Mark Helprin, "Jesse Honey, Mountain Guide," *The New Yorker,* February 28, 1983, p. 40.

285 *The same went:* William Humphrey, *No Resting Place* (New York: Delacorte/Seymour Lawrence, 1989), p. 41.

285 *Whereas in his own country:* Fei Xiaotong, "The Shallowness of Cultural Tradition," in *Land Without Ghosts,* R. David Arkush and Leo O. Lee, eds. (Berkeley: University of California Press, 1993), pp. 177–80.

285 *Attaching that same sentiment:* Pico Iyer, *Abandon: A Romance* (New York: Alfred A. Knopf, 2003), p. 122.

285 *"There is a* daimon *that dwells":* Vincent Scully, *American Architecture and Urbanism* (New York: Praeger Publishers, 1969), p. 14.

286 *Former U.S. Poet Laureate:* Quote from Robert Hass, "Palo Alto: The Marshes," *Red Buffalo: A Radical Journal of American Studies* (Summer, 1971), p. 47.

286 *Yet D. H. Lawrence's:* Quoted in Gui de Angulo, *Jaime in Taos: The Taos Papers of Jaime de Angulo* (San Francisco: City Light Books, 1985), p. 93.

286 *My introduction:* Marion E. Gridley, *Indian Legends of American Scenes* (Chicago: M. A. Donohue & Co., 1939).

286 *"Lo, the poor Indian":* Alexander Pope, *Essay on Man,* Epistle i, line 99, 1733–34.

286 *while on the other hand:* Kenneth Rexroth, *More Classics Revisited,* Bradford Morrow, ed. (New York: New Directions, 1989), p. 35.

287 *The abridgment came:* Joaquin Miller, *Life Among the Modocs: Unwritten History* (San Jose, CA: Urion Press, 1873, 1982).

287 *The cultural history of Mount Shasta:* From Michael Zanger, "Modern Myths and the Sacred Mountain," *Mt. Shasta: History, Legend & Lore* (Berkeley: Celestial Arts, 1992); Phylos the Thibetan [Frederick S. Oliver], *A Dweller on Two Planets* (Los Angeles: Poseid Pub. Co. [1894], 1920).

288 *Especially tenacious:* On Florence Jones and Mount Shasta: Peter H. Knudt-
son, "Flora Jones, Shaman of the Wintu," *Natural History* 84(5), 1975; Marco Mas-
carin, "To Meet a Mountain: The Traditional Teachings of Florence Jones," *Shaman's
Drum: A Journal of Experiential Shamanism,* No. 39, 1995; Bev Ortiz, "An Interview
with Florence Jones," *News from Native California* 9(3), 1996.

289 *Between 1850 and 1900:* On the Wintu, Alice R. Hoveman, *Journey to Justice:
The Wintu People and the Salmon* (Redding, CA: Turtle Bay Exploration Park,
2002).

289 *Her designated successor:* Quoted in *Teacher's Guide: In the Light of Reverence* (La Honda, CA: The Sacred Land Project, 2002), p. 41.

290 *Wintu protests:* Charles M. Miller, "The Battle for the Sacred Earth," *Winds
of Change* 14(3), 1999; Michelle Alvarez, "Mount Shasta: A Question of Power,"
News from Native California 8(3), 1994; Patricia Cummings, "Native Religions,
New-Agers, and the Forest Service," *Inner Voice,* September/October 1992.

290 *Her threat was foretold:* Quoted in Cora Du Bois, *Wintu Ethnography, University of California Publications in American Archaeology and Ethnology* 36(1),
1935, p. 75.

291 *To appreciate one corner:* On Yurok-Karuk, thanks to Thomas Buckley for
information and guidance; T. T. Waterman, "Yurok Geographical Concepts," from
*Yurok Geography, University of California Publications in American Archaeology and
Ethnology* 16 (Berkeley: University of California Press, 1920); Leanne Hinton, "Up-
river, Downriver: The Vocabulary of Direction," *Flutes of Fire: Essays on California
Indian Languages* (Berkeley: Heyday Books, 1994); Richard Keeling, "The Sacred
Landscape," *Cry for Luck: Sacred Song and Speech Among the Yurok, Hupa, and Karok
Indians of Northwestern California* (Berkeley: University of California Press, 1992);
Julian Lang, *Ararapikva: Creation Stories of the People,* Julian Lang, ed. and tr.
(Berkeley: Heyday Books, 1994).

293 *Following the Gold Rush:* Thomas Buckley, "The GO-Road," Chapter 6 in
Standing Ground: Yurok Indian Spirituality, 1850–1990 (Los Angeles: University of
California Press, 2002), which incorporates his important piece on the need for pro-
tecting total, ambient environments: "Sacred Sites as Commodities: Federal Defini-
tion of 'Cultural Resources'" (delivered to the American Anthropological Association,
Los Angeles, 1978); Peter Matthiessen, "Stop the GO Road," *Audubon* 82, 1979.

295 *When I visited the Hupa:* On Hupa, thanks to Lee Davis for advice, her dissertation, "On This Earth: Hupa Land Domains, Images and Ecology on 'Deddeh
Ninnisan'" (Department of Anthropology, University of California-Berkeley, 1988)
and for introducing me to ethnographer Pliny E. Goddard's *Life and Culture of the
Hupa, University of California Publications in American Archaeology and Ethnology*
1(1), (Berkeley: University of California Press, 1903), and *Hupa Texts, University of
California Publications in American Archaeology and Ethnology* 1(2), (Berkeley: University of California Press, 1904); and to Julian Lang for his writings and personal
advice before the 2003 Hupa Jump Dance.

296 *So every couple of years:* On the Jump Dance: Julian Lang, "The Basket and
World Renewal," *Parabola* 16(3), 1991; Tim Ames, "The Jump Dance Basket of
Northwestern California," *American Indian Art Magazine* 29(3), 2004; Thomas
Buckley, "World Renewal," *Parabola* 13(2) and "Renewal as Discourse and Dis-

course as Renewal in Native Northwestern California," in *Native Religions and Cultures of North America: Anthropology of the Sacred*, Lawrence E. Sullivan, ed. (New York: Continuum, 2000), and "Jump Dance," Chapter 11 in his *Standing Ground: Yurok Indian Spirituality, 1850–1990* (Los Angeles: University of California Press, 2002); Richard Keeling, "Rituals to Repair the World," in *Cry for Luck: Sacred Song and Speech Among the Yurok, Hupa, and Karok Indians of Northwestern California* (Berkeley: University of California Press, 1992).

Index